THE CLEOPATRAS

Lloyd Llewellyn-Jones

THE CLEOPATRAS

The Forgotten Queens of Egypt

BASIC BOOKS

New York

Basic Books
Hachette Book Group
1290 Avenue of the Americas, New York, NY 10104
www.basicbooks.com

Printed in the United States of America.

Originally published in 2024 by Wildfire in Great Britain
First U.S. Edition: May 2024

Published by Basic Books, an imprint of Hachette Book Group, Inc. The Basic Books name and logo is a registered trademark of the Hachette Book Group.

The Hachette Speakers Bureau provides a wide range of authors for speaking events. To find out more, go to hachettespeakersbureau.com or email HachetteSpeakers@hbgusa.com.

Basic books may be purchased in bulk for business, educational, or promotional use. For more information, please contact your local bookseller or the Hachette Book Group Special Markets Department at special.markets@hbgusa.com.

The publisher is not responsible for websites (or their content) that are not owned by the publisher.

Designed and typeset by EM&EN

Library of Congress Cataloging-in-Publication Data has been applied for.
[insert CIP data when available]

ISBNs: 9781541602922 (hardcover), 9781541602939 (ebook)

LSC-C

10 9 8 7 6 5 4 3 2 1

In Memory of Rafhat

A thousand of bread, a thousand of beer,
and a thousand of all the good offerings of the year,
my brother

'Eternity was in our lips and eyes'

– Cleopatra, in *Antony and Cleopatra*
by William Shakespeare

Contents

Illustrations

Naming the Ptolemies and Cleopatras

The Hellenistic Greeks did not use the ordinal numbering system that we always employ to distinguish various rulers of the same name (for instance, Cleopatra III and Cleopatra IV). They preferred to use epithets instead, although in modern scholarship, if an epithet was used by more than one ruler, its second occurrence might be so marked (for example, Ptolemy III Euergetes I and Ptolemy VIII Euergetes II).

Contemporary scholarship has assigned ordinal numbers to the Ptolemies and Cleopatras. Occasionally the Cleopatras are subject to several different numbering systems, especially the following queens:

Cleopatra Tryphaina: sometimes referred to as Cleopatra V

Cleopatra Selene: occasionally referred to as Cleopatra V or
    Cleopatra VI

Cleopatra V Berenice III: sometimes called Berenice III

Cleopatra VI Tryphaina: might be referred to as Cleopatra V

I have followed my own historical instincts in assigning ordinal numbers to the Cleopatras, but I have chiefly followed the system of the *Paully-Wissowa Real Encyclopädie*. The names of the Cleopatras are often found in classical sources, although many of the Cleopatras are also known from contemporary Egyptian documents too. In fact, the latter are the best sources we have to prove that some of the Cleopatras became senior rulers. Only one queen – Cleopatra VI Tryphaina – is known from contemporary Egyptian sources but does not appear in the classical accounts.

The Seleucids and the Cleopatras

Here is a convenient list of the intermarriages between the two dynastic lines:

Seleucid	Ptolemy
Cleopatra I Syra	wife of **Ptolemy V**
Alexander Balas	first husband of **Cleopatra Thea**, daughter of Ptolemy VI and Cleopatra II
Demetrius II	second husband of **Cleopatra Thea**, daughter of Ptolemy VI and Cleopatra II
Antiochus VII Sidetes	third husband of **Cleopatra Thea**, daughter of Ptolemy VI and Cleopatra II
Antiochus VIII (Grypus)	husband of **Cleopatra Tryphaina**, daughter of Ptolemy VIII and Cleopatra III
Antiochus IX Kyzikenos	second husband of **Cleopatra IV**, daughter of Ptolemy VIII and Cleopatra III
Antiochus VIII (Grypus)	third husband of **Cleopatra Selene**, daughter of Ptolemy VIII and Cleopatra III
Antiochus IX Kyzikenos	fourth husband of **Cleopatra Selene**, daughter of Ptolemy VIII and Cleopatra III
Antiochus X Eusebes	fifth husband of **Cleopatra Selene**, daughter of Ptolemy VIII and Cleopatra III
Seleucus Kybiosaktes	first husband of **Berenice IV**

PTOLEMIES AND SELEUCIDS
The Families of Cleopatra III and Cleopatra Thea

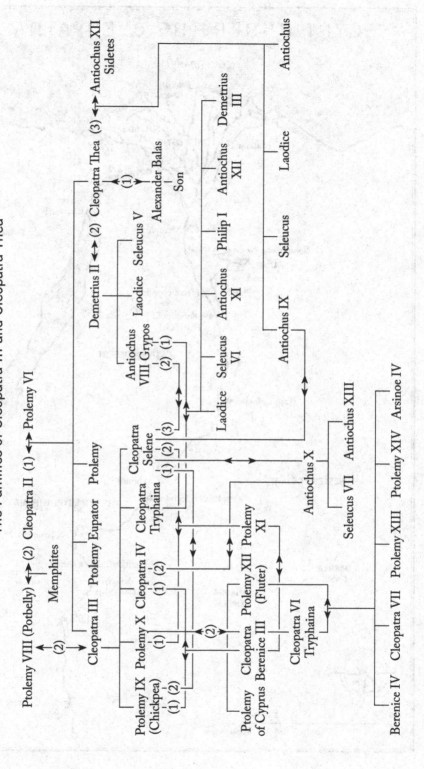

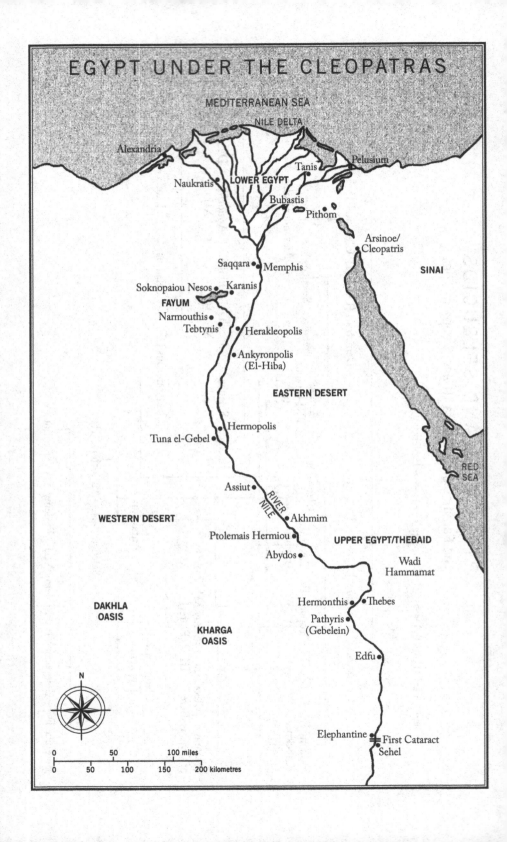

EGYPT UNDER THE CLEOPATRAS

MEDITERRANEAN SEA

NILE DELTA

Alexandria

Pelusium

Tanis

Naukratis

LOWER EGYPT

Bubastis

Pithom

Arsinoe/
Cleopatris

SINAI

Saqqara • Memphis

Soknopaiou Nesos • Karanis

FAYUM

Narmouthis •

Tebtynis •

Herakleopolis

Ankyronpolis
(El-Hiba)

EASTERN DESERT

Hermopolis

Tuna el-Gebel •

Assiut •

RIVER NILE

Akhmim

WESTERN DESERT

Ptolemais Hermiou •

UPPER EGYPT/THEBAID

Abydos •

Wadi
Hammamat

Hermonthis • Thebes

Pathyris
(Gebelein)

**DAKHLA
OASIS**

**KHARGA
OASIS**

Edfu •

N

Elephantine
Sehel

First Cataract

| 0 | 50 | 100 miles |
| 0 | 50 | 100 | 150 | 200 kilometres |

RED
SEA

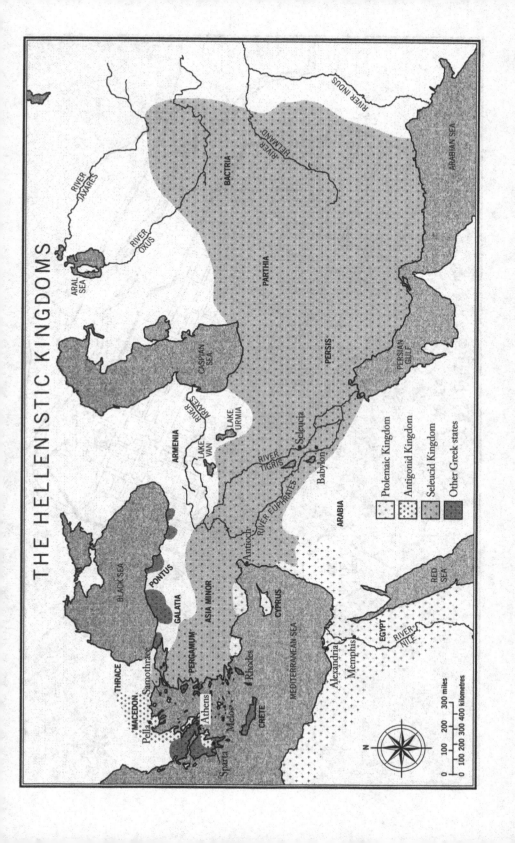

THE HELLENISTIC KINGDOMS

RIVER JAXARES

RIVER OXUS

ARAL SEA

BACTRIA

RIVER HELMAND

RIVER INDUS

ARABIAN SEA

PARTHIA

PERSIS

PERSIAN GULF

CASPIAN SEA

RIVER ARAXES

ARMENIA

LAKE URMIA

LAKE VAN

Seleucia

RIVER TIGRIS

Babylon

ARABIA

RIVER EUPHRATES

Ptolemaic Kingdom

Antigonid Kingdom

Seleucid Kingdom

Other Greek states

Antioch

BLACK SEA

PONTUS

GALATIA

ASIA MINOR

PERGAMUM

CYPRUS

RED SEA

EGYPT

RIVER NILE

THRACE

MACEDON

Samothrace

Pella

Athens

Melos

Sparta

Rhodes

MEDITERRANEAN SEA

CRETE

Alexandria

Memphis

N

0   100   200   300 miles

0   100 200 300 400 kilometres

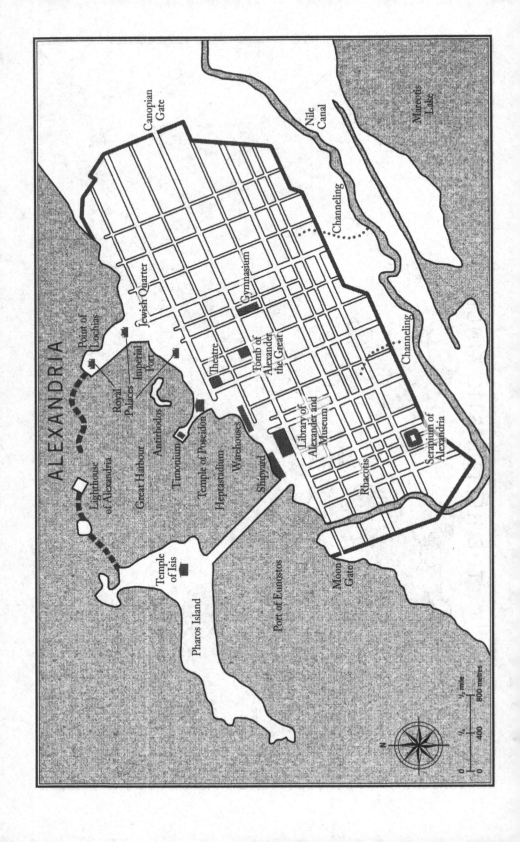

Introduction

Cleopatra was the queen of Egypt.
She lived way back in the early times.
And what a time she had . . .

– Mae West, *My Little Chickadee* (1940)

Mae West's succinct summation of the life of Cleopatra focuses, naturally, on the queen's infamy – something that Mae West knew all about (her co-star W.C. Fields, incidentally, once described West as 'a plumber's idea of Cleopatra'). The colourful set-pieces of Cleopatra's notorious life – unrolled in a carpet at the feet of Julius Caesar; sailing up the River Cydnus in her enormous love-boat on a mission to seduce Marc Antony; and, of course, her dramatic suicide by fatal snakebite – were stage-managed masterpieces created for lasting effect. 'What a time she had' indeed. The queen (like Mae West herself) was a brilliant self-publicist, one of history's brightest and best. Consequently, those enduring scenes from the life of Cleopatra are burned into our imaginations; we have replayed them over and over again to the point where Cleopatra inhabits an illusory, larger-than-life world which is, at one and the same time, antiquated and contemporary, peculiar yet desirable.

The queen was, of course, already a legend in her lifetime, but there are few historical figures whose long-lasting reception has been as heavily distorted as Cleopatra's. Her life and deeds were for a long time known to us only from accounts created by her enemies, the Romans. The greatest Roman poets degraded her by castigating her as a 'harmful virago' (Virgil) and a 'mad queen' (Horace). For her foes, the historical Cleopatra (*c.* 69–30 BCE) was a malicious temptress, treacherous and conspiratorial, foreign, incestuous, daring, lying, two-timing, sumptuous, luxurious, indecent, vain and greedy. She was the *regina meretrix*, as Propertius called her in a memorable moniker – 'queen of whores.' In Roman eyes she was the *fatale monstrum*, 'the ultimate monster.' Many of the slurs have stuck. We want Cleopatra to be a vamp.

Her storyline plays out like a great soap opera, a costume drama of epic proportions, and it is little wonder that through many centuries the Egyptian queen has become an incarnation of the mores and fancies of the age. Each and every generation has claimed, shaped, moulded and invented its own – singular – Cleopatra, one suited to the climate of the times. In recent decades alone, Cleopatra has been cast as a victim, a *femme fatale*, a heroine and a romantic. She has been claimed from history as a gay icon and as a feminist superstar. Cleopatra has appeared as a champion of the #MeToo movement and a powerful cultural idol for Black Lives Matter.

Ever since her asp-induced suicide, Cleopatra has been celebrated in the arts of the west: she appears in countless paintings – in oil on canvas, in watercolours on paper, and in graphic design posters; she has been celebrated on the stage by Shakespeare and Shaw and has had music composed for her by Handel (in his sublime *Giulio Cesare*), Massenet and Samuel Barber; authors from Chaucer and Rabelais to Gautier and Colleen McCullough have written her into novels, poems and essays, and Cleopatra has been used to advertise everything from soap to cigarettes. Of course, Cleopatra has been a very popular icon with moviemakers, and perhaps it is the cinematic image of the Queen of the Nile which dominates our perception of her.

Cleopatra has been so ornamented with superlatives and so loaded with adjectives reflecting what is seen as her exceptionalism and her dynamism that she almost disappears beneath their weight. She is the 'most famous queen of Egypt', she is the 'most exotically beautiful', she is Cleopatra 'the Great'. While we yearn for

Cleopatra to be the violet-eyed Elizabeth Taylor, shimmering in a variety of low-cut gold-lamé gowns, the historical woman behind the legend was radically different. No great beauty, yet a woman of some physical charm, high intellect and spellbinding charisma, Cleopatra was a consummate politician who put the safety and longevity of her royal house at the forefront of all her policies. She was the only one of the foreign Macedonian Ptolemaic rulers to have learned the Egyptian language (Greek was her mother tongue). A recent discovery of an administrative papyrus which records a tax exemption on the sale of imported wine to a Roman merchant called Publius Canidius, a good friend of Marc Antony, includes a word scribbled in Greek in Cleopatra's own hand: *ginesthoi*, she wrote, 'So be it.' The papyrus is hardly evidence for her devotion to bureaucratic detail but it does show that the queen was happy to grant lucrative favours to Antony's friends. Cleopatra's true talent lay in imperial politics which, more than any previous Ptolemaic ruler, she transformed into global politics. She was very receptive to the model of ancient pharaonic sovereignty and liked to link herself to Egypt's rich historical heritage – but she also dreamed of the expansion of Hellenism throughout the world, and she used the two most powerful Romans of the day, Julius Caesar and Marc Antony, to further her aspirations.

But Cleopatra – the Liz Taylor Cleopatra whom we *think* we know so well – was, in reality, the seventh (and final) Egyptian queen to bear the name. 'Cleopatra' had become the royal name *par excellence* amongst the queens of the Ptolemaic dynasty, the last ruling family of Egypt. The fact that there were six other Cleopatras largely goes unnoticed in popular culture and even in scholarship, mainly because the appearance of six other Cleopatras does not suit the standard narrative of the 'Cleopatra story', which is intent on making Cleopatra VII (which is how she should be referred to) into a singularly unique woman, progressively ahead of her time. Much of Cleopatra VII's success in popular contemporary understanding is built on the premise of her exceptionality and the notion that, in an ancient world of nameless, faceless and silent women, Cleopatra alone dared to take on the patriarchy, represented most strongly by Rome. It is a compelling narrative, but it is not quite true.

It would be wrong to strip Cleopatra VII of the cultural *kudos* she has acquired over time (the accolades were hard-won and worthy of respect), but to do justice to the *historical* queen Cleopatra VII, we must, at the very least, try to place her firmly into the context of her world. Cleopatra VII's dynamic quest for authority in a male-dominated world was not exclusively hers; it had been anticipated for a century and a half by a line of ancestral Cleopatras – the mother, grandmothers and great-grandmothers of Cleopatra VII. They had made a success of holding and maintaining regnal power on the throne, which made it possible for Cleopatra VII to sit at the helm of governance and rule Egypt in her own authority, without the need of a male superior. The fact of the matter is this: for all her extraordinary accomplishments (and they *are* extraordinary indeed), Cleopatra was the last vestige of a royal dynasty of other outstanding, capable and imposing Cleopatras who wielded absolute power and courted unrivalled authority. Cleopatra VII may well be the best known to us, but she can only be truly comprehended when she is encountered alongside the other women of her family. When taken as a collective, the seven Cleopatras set a new model for female power in antiquity. Together the Cleopatras created for themselves a space in which to exercise supreme power, and by masquerading as compliant wives, daughters and sisters, they dominated the political world of men, for they easily outstripped the Ptolemaic kings in vigour, finesse, ambition, rigour, vision and ability. The final century and a half of three millennia' worth of male rulership in Egypt was a golden age for royal women, a period when queens finally came into their own. This is the story of Cleopatra VII and the other great Cleopatras, the forgotten queens of Egypt.

*

This is the first book to bring together the lives of the seven Cleopatras, the powerful queens who dominated Egypt in the last centuries of its independence before it was swallowed up into the

Roman empire. It showcases an exceptional time in history – a period of more than a century and a half (192 BCE–30 BCE) – when a remarkable group of women, the Cleopatras, managed to overcome the limitations of the gender roles they had been assigned at birth. They challenged the various patriarchal norms and values which traditionally have silenced women (even queens) and relegated them to the bedroom and the birth-stool. In the royal patrilineal systems of antiquity, like that of the Ptolemaic dynasty, there was an inbuilt tension between women's high birth and the common subservience generally expected of women in their relationships with men. In other words, the gender norms expected of 'ordinary' (non-royal) women did not necessarily apply to queens and princesses. It is probable that as the Cleopatras became increasingly successful at amassing political power, the Ptolemaic family began to consider its women to be 'socially male', a concept which gave queens and princesses more freedom to operate in the political and socio-cultural spheres denied to other women.

Queens are very much in fashion these days and are receiving scholarly attention like never before. Why is this the case? The phenomenon of queenship tends to raise basic questions of female influence and power in what we perceive as naturally male areas of authority. In most places, and for much of human history, the political, social and cultural power of monarchy has been accorded to men, an offshoot of a patriarchal world view in which women were held to be the weaker, less capable sex. The natural order dictated that kings ruled over queens. But because queens were not 'born' but 'became', queenship was less fixed than kingship and was largely dependent on the individual personalities, temperament and family connections of the women who held the title. Some women, under certain circumstances, could overcome institutional obstacles and become the dominant partner on the throne, or occasionally the sole occupant of a throne. Queens interest us because they are anomalous. One might say that the most fascinating historical queens were liminal beings, outsiders to the norms of queenly behaviour. After all, when a queen acted as a good consort and supported her husband by doing her wifely duties – giving birth to offspring, rearing children and being chastely loyal her spouse – she was regarded as 'successful', a model of womanhood to be emulated by all women. Such queens are barely perceptible in the historical record. *But* if a queen over-stepped her allotted role and took power for herself – perhaps as the more efficient or competent partner in a marriage, or as a regent for an infant son, or, worse, simply from the desire to rule alone – then she was an aberration of her sex, abnormal, devious, dangerous; she was liminal. The Cleopatras we will encounter in this book were liminal figures all. They shattered the rules of what it meant to be a queen.

The Cleopatras were the power brokers of the Ptolemaic dynasty and they used the authority they accrued to reshape the gender norms of the society in which they operated. Consequently, every Cleopatra wielded progressively the same power-prerogatives of their masculine consorts. Utterly remarkable is the momentous change that occurred when the Cleopatras eschewed their peculiar and traditional connotations as mothers and spouses of male rulers and became identified instead as queens regnant, the principal representatives of the ruling power in Egypt. Through several successive generations, the Cleopatras augmented, strengthened and secured the dominant role of the queen in the Egyptian monarchy, often to the detriment of the Ptolemaic kings themselves. When in 34 BCE, at the height of her power (a hair's breadth away from world domination), Cleopatra VII claimed the lofty title Queen of Kings, she believed it. Her family history had demonstrated that women were born to rule over men and she took the fact to heart. If Cleopatra VII smashed through the glass ceiling that positions women as interlopers who cannot fit into a structure that is made by men, then the hammer blows that made the glass splinter and crack were delivered by her ancestresses, the Cleopatras.

The seven Cleopatras were direct blood relatives; all of them were queens of Egypt. But there were other Cleopatras born into the Ptolemaic family too. They were not destined to be queens of Egypt but they play very important roles in this story since they became queens of the Ptolemies' great rival state, the Seleucid kingdom, which lay to the east of Egypt's border. In fact, it was in 193 BCE that the name entered the Ptolemaic tradition, when a twenty-year-old Seleucid princess named Cleopatra, the daughter of Antiochus the Great, was married into the Egyptian royal house to the sixteen-year-old pharaoh Ptolemy V. 'Cleopatra' became the staple name of the Ptolemaic royal dynasty, but its first bearer was born in Syria. The name was associated too with several important female figures from Greek mythology, such as Cleopatra the daughter of the wind-god Boreas, Cleopatra the wife of the hero Meleager in Homer's *Iliad*, and Cleopatra the daughter of King Tros, who gave his name to Troy. But most importantly, in the historic sphere, King Philip II of Macedon had, back in the past, named the daughter borne to him by Olympias, his chief consort, Cleopatra. This Cleopatra was the much-loved sister of Alexander the Great, his only full-blood sibling and the only woman in the world he had loved without uneasiness. This was reason enough why 'Cleopatra' was popularized as a dynastic Ptolemaic name; it resonated with mythical and historical prestige. Besides, the Greek penchant for bestowing names which attributed some kind of quality to the recipient (for instance, Eteoklēs meant 'one who possesses true fame'; Theodōros was 'gift of the god' and Areta meant 'the excellent woman') came into operation too. The name Cleopatra was composed of two Greek words: *kleos*, a particularly weighty term meaning 'glory' or 'renown' or 'fame', and *patēr* (genitive, *patros*) meaning 'father', 'ancestor', 'fatherland' or 'homeland'. Cleopatra therefore meant 'glory of her father', 'fame of her ancestors', or 'her country's renown'. It was a big name to live up to – although, as we will see, each of the Cleopatras did just that, even if 'glory' sometimes turned into 'infamy'. Incidentally, when used as a diminutive, in an intimate familial context, Cleopatra might be rendered as 'daddy's girl'.

It is worth drawing up a rollcall of the Cleopatras we will encounter in this book, if only to familiarize ourselves with the family dynamics of the Ptolemaic dynasty. The Ptolemies did future historians no favours in terms of their dynastic nomenclature – all the kings were Ptolemies and all the queens were

Cleopatras (with some Arsinoës and Berenices thrown in for good measure), and this fact alone makes for a bewildering family tree. Here are the chief players in the dynastic drama:

Cleopatra I Syra was the daughter of the Seleucid king Antiochus III and the wife of Ptolemy V of Egypt.

Cleopatra II was the daughter of Cleopatra I Syra and Ptolemy V. She married two of her brothers, Ptolemy VI and Ptolemy VIII (known as Potbelly).

Cleopatra Thea was the eldest daughter of Cleopatra II and Ptolemy VI. She became the wife and mother to a succession of Seleucid kings.

Cleopatra III was the youngest daughter of Cleopatra II and Ptolemy VI. She married her uncle/stepfather, Ptolemy VIII, while he was still wed to her mother, Cleopatra II.

Cleopatra IV was the eldest daughter of Cleopatra III and Ptolemy VIII. She married her brother Ptolemy IX, and afterwards went on to marry a Seleucid prince.

Cleopatra Tryphaina was the second daughter of Cleopatra III and Ptolemy VIII. She married a Seleucid king too – and killed her sister Cleopatra IV.

Cleopatra Selene was the third and youngest daughter of Cleopatra III and Ptolemy VIII. She married her brother Ptolemy IX after he had divorced her sister Cleopatra IV, and then married another of her brothers, Ptolemy X. Later she left Egypt and married a succession of Seleucid kings.

Cleopatra V Berenice III was the daughter of Ptolemy IX and Cleopatra IV. She married her uncle Ptolemy X, her father, Ptolemy IX, and the short-lived Ptolemy XI, her nephew and stepson.

Cleopatra VI Tryphaina was the daughter of Cleopatra V Berenice III and Ptolemy X. She married her half-brother Ptolemy XII, the son of Ptolemy IX and Cleopatra IV.

Cleopatra VII was the daughter of Ptolemy XII and Cleopatra VI Tryphaina. She was the wife to two of her brothers, Ptolemy XIII and Ptolemy XIV, and she was the mother of Ptolemy XV Caesar, the son of Julius Caesar. She had three more children by Marc Antony. She was the last Ptolemaic queen, the final Cleopatra.

The baffling number of shared names and title can cause confusion, and the Ptolemaic penchant for brother–sister marriage does nothing to dilute the complex blood relationships of the principal players in this royal soap opera. 'You are the descendant of generations of inbred, incestuous mental defectives,' Rex Harrison's Julius Caesar snaps at Liz Taylor's Cleopatra in the 1963 Hollywood movie. His is a fair assessment. The lives of the Cleopatras were complicated by the rules of rank and the expectations of marriage choices available to them, which were limited to a small pool of social equals. Failing to marry within the closed circle of blood relatives meant that they faced the prospect of hypogamy – marriage beneath their social rank. This is something that the Ptolemies were keen to avoid, and accordingly we see within the royal house a dependency on concomitant inbreeding. As we will go on to explore, the theme of royal incest informs and underpins this entire study and does nothing to help understand the complexities of the family tree. This book provides a clear narrative of the spectacular dynastic shenanigans that characterized the Ptolemaic period as it exposes the coagulated layers of all those Ptolemies and Cleopatras.

The Cleopatras matter. They matter because they were the first group of women in history to provide themselves with a new framework for aligning themselves with genuine, active political power. Their collective story, largely ignored until now, fascinates because it shows how royal women could, when opportunity arose, adjust, shift and refocus the long-established 'norms' of a male-controlled institution – the ancient Egyptian pharaonic monarchy – if only for one unprecedented moment in history. Cleopatra VII almost had the Roman empire at her feet; her reputation as antiquity's most impressive and celebrated queen goes unchallenged. But how exciting it is to see her as one outstanding player in a line-up of seven vigorous, impressive and authoritative Cleopatras – undisputed rulers of Egypt. As we look at Cleopatra VII, we see an exceptional personality, but when we look at the other Cleopatras, when we take them as a family of dynamic women, then we see a much larger story. Taken together, theirs is a grander, operatic narrative about the nature and importance of women's power in the overwhelmingly, stiflingly patriarchal world of antiquity. Theirs is a story of ambition, certainly, but also of ability; it is a narrative of ruthlessness, but also of determination and lifelong commitment. It is the story of a bloodline of talented, astute women. It is the unique story of the Cleopatras.

PART ONE

BEGINNINGS

Cleopatra I Syra
Cleopatra II

CLEOPATRA I SYRA

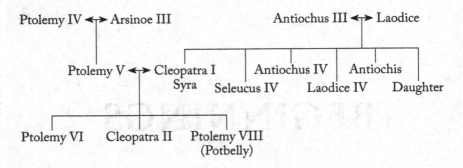

Ptolemy IV ←→ Arsinoe III   Antiochus III ←→ Laodice

Ptolemy V ←→ Cleopatra I   Antiochus IV   Antiochis
                        Syra   Seleucus IV   Laodice IV   Daughter

Ptolemy VI   Cleopatra II   Ptolemy VIII
                                  (Potbelly)

CLEOPATRA II

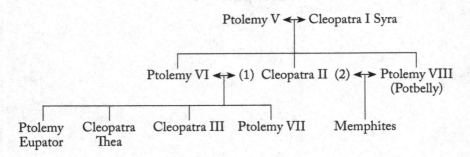

Ptolemy V ←→ Cleopatra I Syra

Ptolemy VI ←→ (1) Cleopatra II (2) ←→ Ptolemy VIII
                                                (Potbelly)

Ptolemy   Cleopatra   Cleopatra III   Ptolemy VII   Memphites
Eupator   Thea

1

The Bartered Bride

The first of the Cleopatras was a woman known to many of her contemporaries as Cleopatra Syra – 'the Syrian'. The history of the Cleopatras begins not in the Egypt of the Ptolemies but further to the east, in the empire of the Seleucids – the dynastic name given to the Greek-speaking monarchs of an empire that incorporated the modern states of Syria, Lebanon, Palestine and Israel, Jordan, Armenia, Kuwait, Iraq, Azerbaijan and parts of eastern Turkey, as well as, at times, significant portions of Iran and even Afghanistan. What was Cleopatra Syra's experience of life, growing up, knowing that, as a girl, inevitably, her birth and rank meant that she would one day be married to some king, prince or commander? To get a picture of Cleopatra Syra as she matured and edged towards a marriageable age, we must put her into the dynastic context of the time, for only then will we be able to appreciate the important political value this Seleucid princess accrued during her youth and embodied at the time of her sexual maturity. We need to explore the world into which Cleopatra Syra was raised.

*

Cleopatra Syra was born in or around Antioch in Syria sometime between 209 and 204 BCE, with the scales perhaps slightly tipped in favour of the earlier date. She was the daughter of a formidable warrior king, Antiochus III, known even in his lifetime as Antiochus Magus, 'the Great'. He was the latest scion of the Seleucid dynasty, the heirs of Alexander the Great. On Alexander's premature death in 323 BCE, his huge but flaky empire was divided among his blood-kin and his most powerful generals (known as the *diadochoi*, 'successors'), eventually giving rise to three large kingdoms that dominated the Hellenistic world: Macedon, ruled by the Antigonid monarchs; Egypt, under the Ptolemies; and Syria, the Levant and Mesopotamia (sometimes called Asia), governed by the Seleucids.

Cleopatra Syra's mother was as renowned as her father. Laodice, the third Seleucid queen to bear that name, was a princess from the kingdom of Pontus on the Black Sea and Antiochus' first cousin; she proved herself to be a good wife and an influential queen. Cleopatra had six siblings, all progeny of Laodice: there were three brothers, Antiochus the Younger, Seleucus (IV), and Antiochus (IV), as well as an older sister, Laodice (IV), a younger sister, Antiochis, and another whose name has not been preserved. The family were close and supportive, although Antiochus and Laodice were not the mollycoddling types and their children were raised at a safe arm's-distance by nursemaids and other servants. Nevertheless, the siblings often accompanied King Antiochus on his war campaigns, residing in tents erected well beyond the battlefields; it was something expected of Hellenistic royalty. Even in the rare periods of peace, the king moved throughout his realm and maintained a frantically peripatetic lifestyle that took him – and his family – from palace to palace and garrison to garrison.

The large empire Antiochus III ruled between 223 and 187 BCE had been put together over many decades by successive Seleucid kings and was the most populous part of the Hellenistic world, containing, by one recent estimate, some 15 million subjects and close to 1.5 million square miles of land. His revered great-great-grandfather had been one of Alexander the Great's successors, an efficacious and ambitious Macedonian cavalry officer named Seleucus (hence the family name), whose charisma and brutality helped him forge territorial victories in the decades following the death of the great Alexander. Having built up an empire over many decades, Seleucus and his successors set about an ambitious programme of city-building, especially in Syria, which was to be, to all intents and purposes, the 'home' of the empire. These newly created urban sites included the elegant city of Antioch-on-the-Orontes on the banks of the Orontes River (this became the primary royal residence for all successive Seleucid rulers), the garrison city of Apamea, and the beautiful Mediterranean coastal cities of Seleucia Pieria, Ptolemaïs-Ake and the port Laodicea-on-Sea. Seleucia-on-the-Tigris sprang up in Mesopotamia, and Lysimachia was constructed to make the control of Thrace (modern Bulgaria and parts of Greece and Turkey), which Antiochus III had annexed in 196 BCE, much easier. Older, well-established urban sites such as Sardis and Ephesus in Asia Minor, Susa in Persia, and Antioch on the Mediterranean coast became important royal regional centres too. Many centuries after the fall of the Hellenistic kingdoms, Libanius of Antioch, writing from a singularly partisan local perspective, waxed lyrical on the joys of living under Seleucid rule:

> And so the men of that time . . . lived in happiness in the midst of barbarians, producing a city [Antioch-on-the-Orontes] which was a true Hellas and keeping their way of life pure in the midst of so much corruption all around them . . . [Seleucus I] planted so many cities on the earth that they were enough to bear the names of the cities of Macedonia and to be named also for the members of his family . . . You may go to Phoenicia and see his cities there, and you may come here to Syria and see even more and greater ones of his. He extended this fair work as far as the Euphrates and the Tigris, and, surrounding Babylon with cities, he planted them everywhere, even in Persia; in a word he left bare no place that was suitable for receiving a city, but in his work of spreading Hellenic civilization he brought the barbarian world quite to an end.

The Seleucid empire was, in essence, a conglomerate of many different peoples and lands who happened to be under the rule of a Greek-speaking king. In fact there was no way of describing the empire apart from the person of its ruler; thus when the Romans aimed to legitimize a treaty with Antiochus III, in the paperwork they simply spoke of 'Antiochus and those under his orders'.

The Seleucid monarchy was in the first instance military in character. Simply put, the monarchy's success was dependant on the king's identification as war leader and the martial abilities of his band of followers, whose cohesion was cemented by a common interest in maintaining control of an empire from which they derived their wealth and status. Antiochus' war machine was the strongest in the world. He had under his command 120,000 soldiers and sailors, and at his stables in Apamea there were 30,000 mares, 30,000 stallions and hundreds of Indian elephants, all trained for battle. Commenting on Antiochus' eastern military advance of 212–205 BCE, the Greek historian Polybius noted: 'It was this campaign which made him appear worthy of royalty, not only to the peoples of Asia but to those in Europe as well.' Victory gave the ruler possession of territory and peoples, for the empire was 'territory won by the spear' (*doriktetos chora*), a concept the Seleucids appealed to subsequently in justification of their rule.

Wherever Antiochus went, in peace and war, his army accompanied him. He was a hard, active, dynamic man of multiple contradictions: he was a born soldier, and a very fine politician; he was, in short, the most significant king of his generation. It was a combination of blind ambition and complete self-belief which, in 217 BCE, compelled Antiochus to lead some 70,000 of his fighting men and 100 of his Indian war-elephants towards Egypt's border. His purpose was to take Egypt – or at the very least to rattle and alarm their king, Ptolemy IV, and to remind him of the very real threat which the Seleucids had always posed to Ptolemaic hegemony. By the time Cleopatra Syra was born, four generations of Seleucids and Ptolemies had fought countless wars in order to determine the dynastic supremacy of the eastern Mediterranean.

The enmity had existed between the Seleucid and the Ptolemaic kings since the time of the death of Alexander the Great, when Seleucus and his one-time battle comrade General Ptolemy had become embroiled in the vicious fight for power which erupted as soon as Alexander gasped his last breath. The rivalry continued into each and every generation of rulers and showed no sign of ending. The Ptolemaic empire had reached its apogee under Ptolemy III Euergetes (246–222 BCE), whose power briefly radiated out of Egypt and extended into (modern) Libya, Israel and Palestine, Jordan, Lebanon, Syria, Cyprus, parts of Turkey, the Peloponnese in Greece and a series of Aegean islands. Under Ptolemy III, Seleucid rule diminished as territories fell to Egypt. In fact, Ptolemy III managed to take all of the Seleucid lands west of the River Euphrates. As Polybius was to recount:

> The [Ptolemaic] sphere of control included the dynasts in Asia and also the islands, as they were masters of the most important cities, strongholds and harbours along the whole coast from Pamphylia to the Hellespont and the region of Lysimachia. They kept watch on affairs in Thrace and Macedonia . . . and of even more distant cities and, in this way, having extended their reach so far and having shielded themselves at a great distance with these client kings, they never worried about the safety of Egypt. That was why they rightly devoted much attention to external affairs.

It all sounds very coherent, but if we read between the lines, Polybius' account of Ptolemaic overseas power reveals several matters for concern: their 'empire' lacked clearly defined frontiers; it also lacked a coherent imperial administration. In all reality, the Ptolemaic 'empire' was merely composed of a string of military or naval bases, alliances, protectorates, friendly factions or 'loyal' individuals frequently bought with gold from Nubia (modern Ethiopia), forming a network of nodes through which the Ptolemies could exercise control. Yet the Seleucids in the east and the Macedonians in the north continued to hold firm their own lands and, indeed, to a large extent prevailed over the Ptolemies. By the late third century BCE, the Ptolemaic grip on the Aegean and Asia Minor was loosening. The same pattern was seen in Syria-Palestine too. This area of the Levant, with its rich trading centres along the Phoenician coast (modern Lebanon) and the inland trading centres such as Nabataean Petra (in modern Jordan), had been taken and held by Ptolemy I Soter in 320–315 BCE. But the determination of the Seleucids to maintain control over this wealthy area meant that it was a hotbed of warfare for successive generations. The area known as Coele-Syria ('Hollow Syria'), a hundred-mile stretch of rich verdant valley which divides the mountain range of Lebanon and Anti-Lebanon (the modern Beqa'a Valley), was the centre of the theatre of war between the competing Seleucids and Ptolemies, and no less than six campaigns (the 'Syrian Wars') were played out here between 274 and 168 BCE.

In 219 BCE, Antiochus III enjoyed a victory over the Egyptian king Ptolemy IV, when he drove back Ptolemaic forces who had captured Coele-Syria and the town of Seleucia Pieria, slightly to the north of the estuary of the river Orontes (in the south-east corner of modern Turkey's Argean shore), and had turned it into an Egyptian garrison. But early in the spring of 217, Ptolemy IV fought back. He left Alexandria at the head of his troops – accompanied by his sister/wife, Arsinoë III – and marched towards Raphia, a town on the coastal highland in Gaza (modern-day Rafa still serves as the checkpoint between Palestinian Gaza and Egypt). Before departing Alexandria, the queen had cut off a lock of her hair and dedicated it to the goddess Artemis in the hope of securing victory, and much to everyone's surprise, it worked: the Egyptians emerged victorious.

Ptolemy IV's shock victory over Antiochus III at the Battle of Raphia meant that the Egyptians took back wealthy Coele-Syria and the lands further north, right up to Cilicia (in southern Anatolia in modern Turkey), and put them under Egyptian administration once more. The king and queen's return to Alexandria was celebrated with a triumphal procession, and the victorious army was rewarded with 300,000 pieces of gold. In Memphis, the ancient capital of pharaonic Egypt, close to modern Cairo, the priests gathered for a synod and passed a multilingual decree (15 November 217 BCE) extolling the military prowess of Ptolemy IV. Known today as the Raphia Stele, the best-preserved stone copy depicts Ptolemy IV twice: once dressed as a pharaoh, but mounted on horseback like a Macedonian spearman, and next in the traditional pharaonic victory pose, holding a scimitar above the head of the bound and captive Antiochus who although never taken prisoner by Ptolemy Is nonetheless represented on his knees before the victorious pharaoh. Watching the action, dressed in the garb of the goddess Hathor and holding a sceptre, stands Arsinoë III, the 'heroine of the Battle of Raphia.' The text of the decree follows traditional Egyptian battle narratives in which the defeat of the enemy is absolute:

> King Ptolemy . . . pressed Antiochus so closely that he was obliged to throw away his diadem and his royal cloak. He fled with his bodyguard and only a few stayed with him after his sad and miserable defeat . . . He saw the best of his companions perish miserably. They suffered hunger and thirst. Everything he left behind was seized as booty. Only with great effort did he reach his home and he suffered bitter grief.

Remarkably, Antiochus III emerged from this defeat with a renewed vigour. He recovered very quickly from his losses at Raphia and from 216 to 205 BCE his spectacular military successes in Achios, Mesopotamia and western Iran changed the face of Seleucid rule and made Antiochus the greatest ruler of the Hellenistic age. Unbeknown to the Egyptians of the time, the Battle of Raphia was to be the last occasion when a Ptolemaic king physically led his troops into conflict. Ptolemy IV was glad to return to Alexandria and resume his indolent lifestyle, and he tried hard to avoid further conflict with the Seleucids at all costs.

*

It is not known whether Cleopatra Syra knew anything of her father's wars, conquests, triumphs and horrors; the sources are silent about her childhood and her formative years as a Seleucid princess. But it can be supposed that she was raised among her siblings in any number of palaces or tents strewn across her father's realm, living in relative luxury and having both opportunity and time to engage in study and pleasure. A princess's unmarried youth was often a happy, if not *the* happiest, time of her life.

Carefree maidenhood is a motif enjoyed by the famous Greek poetess Sappho, whose verses depict unmarried girls spending endless blissful days together stringing flower wreaths, donning garlands, wearing perfumed oil, visiting holy places and groves, dancing and playing music. We can only assume that Cleopatra Syra and her sisters would have had something akin to this happy, if fleeting, girlhood. Certainly, Cleopatra Syra's lifestyle as an unmarried girl would have been profoundly different from her life after marriage, when the burden of the expectation of fecundity was placed on her. The orthodox view of the time was that married princesses who became queens were expected to become mothers to multiple children. They were regarded as dynastic wombs, royal incubators for regal successors, and it was their fertility – not their intellect, their charitable acts, nor even their diplomatic skills – that marked them out as successes or failures. Because maternity mattered, childlessness – or its near-equivalent, the inability to bear a son – could have unfortunate consequences for a queen, for while a childless queen might not herald the end of a dynasty, it might infer a power shift within the family. And that never boded well.

Cleopatra Syra and her sisters appear in the historical record just at the moment they were thought to be useful to their royal father, as they came of age. This has been the lot of princesses through the millennia. Cleopatra Syra's elder sister, Laodice IV, first comes to prominence in 193 BCE, when Antiochus III appointed her as the chief priestess of the state cult dedicated to her mother, Laodice III, in the province of Media, northern Iran. Three years earlier, on her father's order, the princess had been wedded to her own full-blood brother Antiochus the Younger, and, for the first time, the Seleucids committed themselves to incestuous marriage in direct imitation of the Ptolemies, who had been practising this extreme form of dynastic endogamy since 276 BCE, when Ptolemy II Philadelphus married his full-sister, Arsinoë II (of which more later). Antiochus the Great's purpose was propagandistic: he used incestuous marriage for the glorification of his dynasty. Antiochus' dynastic ambitions now concentrated on the rarefying of his bloodline. He decided that his son and heir would not dilute the royal blood through interbreeding with the daughters of lesser kings. The move enhanced Antiochus' ambition to be a god-king, and his drive towards deification was made manifest through the establishment of a state-sponsored royal cult.

Records from Babylon show that as a boy of just eleven or twelve Antiochus the Younger had been promoted to a 'second kingship' by his father, but now that he had come of age (some fourteen years later), the marriage to his sister Laodice IV was intended to further legitimatize his place in the royal succession. However, Antiochus the Younger died soon after the marriage, in 193 BCE, much to his father's distress. But this was not the end of sister-marriage in the dynasty – instead, Laodice's mourning was cut short and she entered into a second marriage with another brother, Seleucus IV. She bore him three children – (another, short-lived) Antiochus, Demetrius I and Laodice V – before he too unexpectedly died. Laodice's third and final husband was the last remaining son of Antiochus III, her brother Antiochus IV, by whom she had one more son, the future Antiochus V. It is obvious that Antiochus III viewed his daughter Laodice as a transferable token to be used by the crown to advertise her brother-husbands as royal heirs; as she was transferred from one dead brother-prince to the next she acquired added value, at least by the terms of levirate marriage (a type of marriage in which the brother of a deceased man is obliged to marry his brother's widow).

Cleopatra Syra must have been keenly aware of the shifts in fortune experienced by her elder sister. She knew too that, given Laodice's fate as a perpetual bride of one brother or another, their father, Antiochus, would have to look elsewhere, beyond the immediate family, to find her a husband. He was trying to make an ally of Philip V, the clever and powerful king of Macedon, and no doubt Cleopatra Syra anticipated that her future lay as queen of the ancestral homelands of northern Greece. Alliances were in the air as Antiochus the Great geared up to take on the forces of Rome in the west, and he used his daughters as alliance-building tools, offering them to rulers he hoped would support him in a fight against Rome. Consequently, Cleopatra Syra saw her sister Antiochis packed off to Cappadocia to marry King Ariarathes IV, and her youngest (unnamed) sister sent away to the wealthy city of Pergamum to be the bride of King Eumenes II. Antiochis was later to become influential in the succession affairs of the Cappadocian court, which might account for the historian Diodorus Siculus' disparaging dismissal of her as an 'utterly unscrupulous woman'. By such means were successful women judged.

With her sisters paired off to various Hellenistic potentates, Cleopatra Syra's future was undecided. That changed due to the events which transpired in Egypt in the winter of 205/4 BCE. Ptolemy IV met his end, expiring quite suddenly of a surfeit of, if we follow Polybius' reckoning, dissipation and bad counsel. He left behind his kingdom and his wife, Arsinoë III, who was almost powerless to defend herself and her infant son, the new child-pharaoh Ptolemy V. Ptolemy IV's partners in revelry and the dispensers of his bad counsel, courtiers named Sosibius and Agathocles, kept the king's death secret for several weeks while they conspired against Arsinoë and attempted to oust her. In the late summer of 204 BCE the powerful court faction moved against the queen and had her murdered. With the young pharaoh now orphaned, the two counsellors sought to suppress any rumour of foul play and positioned themselves as his regents. Rumours of Arsinoë's murder nevertheless spread through Alexandria, but Agathocles, invigorated by his success, hurriedly had Sosibius killed as well. As he manipulated his way into sole power, he dispatched many of the experienced top figures at court on missions abroad or to the countryside and replaced them with his own amateur cronies. But it was not long before Agathocles' insolence and incompetence aroused broad resentment and resistance toward his rule, and when the soldiers in Alexandria received credible intelligence that Agathocles was planning to kill the young king, he was overthrown in a burst of popular and military violence at the end of 203 BCE. The revolution was not against Ptolemaic rule though; on the contrary, it was aimed at securing dynastic continuity through the restoration of young Ptolemy's throne against a perceived usurper.

Taking every advantage of the chaos in Egypt, in 203 BCE Antiochus III banded with Philip V of Macedon in a secret pact against young Ptolemy V – the plan was to invade Egypt and to split all Ptolemaic lands between them. Philip would receive Ptolemaic enclaves in Western Asia Minor, the Hellespont and Thrace (and thereby be able to establish for himself a new Aegean empire), while Antiochus would get Egypt, take back Coele-Syria and reverse the humiliation of the Battle of Raphia. And so, in 202 BCE, Antiochus renewed an attack on Coele-Syria, quickly captured Damascus and entered Palestine, his objective being to make a direct line for Gaza, figuring that the Gaza Strip would be the ideal place to confront an Egyptian counterattack. The Egyptians managed to deploy a field army of 40,000 men under the leadership of a mercenary general named Scopas and marched north to defend Coele-Syria. Scopas pushed his troops deep into Judaea, slashing and burning his way through the towns and villages that had shown support to Antiochus, and then advanced northward to the area of the modern-day Golan Heights. At the site of the shrine of Pan at Panium, Antiochus' troops crushed Scopas' forces and sent them packing back to Egypt. By 198 BCE, Coele-Syria was in Antiochus' hands once more, and he now concentrated on raiding Ptolemaic possessions in Cilicia, Lycia and Caria (all in modern Turkey) with his navy. The Egyptians called on Rome's support. Having finally routed and dispatched their great Carthaginian enemy, Hannibal, the Romans were already looking east with an eye to expansion themselves and, given the backing the Ptolemaic house had always shown them, Rome was only too willing to assist Egypt in her plight. In 197 BCE, the Roman armies flooded into Macedon and the ancestral home of Alexander the Great, along with the rest of Greece, fell to Rome. For all his brilliance, Philip V was defeated at the Battle of Cynoscephalae, and, much to Antiochus' chagrin, wealthy Eumenes II of Pergamon, anticipating that out-and-out war would erupt between Antiochus and the Romans – in which Rome would emerge the victor – sent his bride, Antiochus' daughter, back to Syria, unused and unwanted. Antiochus III was dumbstruck.

In October or November of 197 BCE, in Alexandria, the thirteen-year-old Ptolemy V underwent the old Greek ritual of the *anakleteria*, the 'coming-of-age ceremony'; it was a rite undertaken by all Hellenistic princes and was celebrated when new rulers took upon themselves the rulership of their kingdom. As Polybius noted, Ptolemy V's courtiers 'thought that the kingdom would gain a certain degree of firmness and a fresh impulse towards prosperity, if it were known that the king had assumed the independent direction of the government'. As his epithet, Ptolemy V chose the fitting title Epiphanes, 'The God Who Makes His Appearance'. Then, on 26 March 196 BCE, Ptolemy V Epiphanes was crowned pharaoh by the High Priest of Ptah at the ancient holy city of Memphis and, a day later, a synod of priests from all over Egypt who had gathered for the coronation passed the Memphis Decree and had it inscribed in stone. The decree, which commended Ptolemy V's benefactions for the people of Egypt and his remission of taxes on the temples of Egypt, unsurprisingly began with a laudatory paean of praise, wishing the pharaoh 'Life! Health! Prosperity!' The king was hailed as the 'living image of Amun' (the supreme god of Thebes) and as the 'beloved of Ptah' (the creator-god of Memphis), 'whose goodness is perfect'. Today, the Memphis decree is one of the best-known artefacts to survive from antiquity and is seen by the many thousands of tourists who cluster tightly around it each year in the British Museum. We know it as the Rosetta Stone.

Meanwhile, as conflict with Rome festered, Antiochus III played his last card and, as part of a peace treaty drawn up with Egypt, offered his daughter Cleopatra Syra in marriage to Ptolemy V Epiphanes. The Rosetta Stone inscription shows that as far as the Egyptians were concerned, the sixteen-year-old pharaoh was now considered a king in every respect – he was the living image of Amun and the most beloved of Ptah and he was also the embodiment of the divine Horus. Now the young god-king needed a queen.

Cleopatra Syra was about the same age as her fiancée, perhaps a year or two older. But such an issue was trivial in the international game of royal politics. She was (hopefully) fertile and would produce a brood of sons and thereby unite the warring Seleucids and Ptolemies. Early marriage was the means of optimizing the fertility of women in a society with a high infant mortality rate, even among the elite. High female fertility was required in every royal household if the dynasty was to replicate itself, and queens might be expected to have large families. But there was also the problem that a significant proportion of fertile women, including queens, would die in childbirth and, accordingly, it was necessary to distribute the burden of pregnancy as widely as possible among all the available fertile women. Permanent female celibacy was almost unheard of and practically all women married, most of them when young. Girls in Egypt, whether peasants or princesses, could expect to be married not long after menarche, often by the time they were about seventeen and certainly by their mid-twenties. For girls, marriage was indistinguishable from physical maturation. Early marriage also had the advantage of increasing the likelihood that the bride was still a virgin, an obvious concern in societies where provable paternity was of such importance.

On the face of things, the omens for a good marriage between Cleopatra Syra and Ptolemy were not propitious: the Hebrew bible's prophetic Book of Daniel, composed around the time of Cleopatra Syra's engagement, predicted future inter-state warfare, with the ownership of lucrative Coele-Syria being the most pressing issue. Daniel predicted that familial warfare would erupt as,

> He [Antiochus III] will resolve to subjugate all the dominions of the King of the South [Ptolemy V Epiphanes], and he will come to fair terms with him and he shall give the ultimate woman [Aramaic, *bat-hanašym*; Cleopatra Syra] in marriage for the destruction of the kingdom.

What did this mean? Was the author of the Book of Daniel prophesying that Cleopatra Syra, by way of her marriage to the Egyptian pharaoh, would bring down the house of Ptolemy? Would Antiochus the Great have the ultimate victory after all? Only time would tell.

Unperturbed by prophets and seers, in the spring of 193 BCE Cleopatra Syra, aged about seventeen, began her journey from Antioch-on-the-Orontes to Alexandria. She headed first for the town of Raphia, the site of her father's military defeat, where the wedding would be celebrated. Antiochus III exhibited some fine diplomacy in the selection of Raphia as the setting for the wedding, for rather than forcing Ptolemy V to lose face by travelling through Syria (territory only recently taken from the Ptolemaic kingdom), and rather than losing face himself by travelling all the way to Alexandria, the Seleucid monarch compromised by holding the wedding on the border of both kingdoms.

Antiochus and his daughter entered Raphia with the full ceremony of state. They were joined by the Egyptian delegation, headed by the young bridegroom, King Ptolemy himself. Pharaonic tradition had long seen the use of diplomatic marriages, the most prestigious of which occurred when the father of the bride was of equal status with the pharaoh and the two monarchs addressed each other as 'brother'; another type of marriage alliance occurred when the father of the bride was pharaoh's vassal and referred to the Egyptian ruler as 'my lord, my god, my sun god.' During the period of Egypt's empire, in the New Kingdom (c. 1570–c. 1069 BCE), when vast territories to the south and the north had been the pharaoh's dominions, the Egyptians had the upper hand in arranging these marriage alliances and brides were sent to Memphis or Thebes to seal the treatises, although Egyptian brides were never sent abroad. When it came to diplomatic marriage, the bride's direction of travel really mattered. As Egypt's imperial fortunes waned, however, so did its control of the foreign bride market. Famously, if fancifully, Solomon, the king of Israel, was able to claim the hand of a pharaoh's daughter and had her brought to Jerusalem, where she became the highest-ranking of his many wives.

The first four generations of the Ptolemies had avoided negotiating this diplomatic conundrum by marrying within the family or by looking for keen 'vassal' brides, like Berenice II of Cyrene who virtually ran to Egypt to climb into the bed of Ptolemy III.

When Ptolemy V and Antiochus III decided to revisit the useful-
ness of the diplomatic marriage strategy in order to ostensibly
create stability in the region in the face of Roman aggression, they
understood full well the ancient hierarchy of royal bride-exchange.

Huge tents and makeshift buildings had been erected at Raphia
for the comfort of the guests and for the rituals and ceremonials
that would take place over the coming week – for royal weddings
could be drawn-out affairs. Feasts and entertainments were laid
on, and day upon day the wedding celebrations seemed to get
ever more extravagant, for the royal retinues needed to be kept
occupied as the final touches were put to the wedding contract.

For her part, kept out of the politics of the event, Cleopatra
Syra was mainly attentive to her trousseau and to the packing and
shipping of her personal effects, which would travel ahead of her
into Egypt. She was aided in all she did by a cohort of trusted
ladies-in-waiting, *syntrophoi* or 'favourites', who, Polybius implies,
were commonplace in the households of Hellenistic queens and
princesses. When a Hellenistic princess, such as Cleopatra Syra,
found herself being shipped off to foreign lands as a diplomatic
bride, she would be accompanied by this entourage of women
whom she knew and trusted. These women helped bridge the gap
between natal family and marital home and helped acclimatize
the princess to her new surroundings while providing her with
a much-needed sense of continuity. Some of these women even
acted as aides and go-betweens, and even as spies and agents. All in
all, the *syntrophoi* had quite the potential to form a distinct power
base within the court.

With the wedding fast approaching, Cleopatra Syra appointed
one of her *syntrophoi* to be her *nymphokomos*, or 'chief bridesmaid',
and she was given the absolute authority to put together and
oversee the bride's adornment and the prenuptial bridal rituals.
It was the *nymphokomos* who prepared Cleopatra Syra's ritual
bath with waters brought from a holy spring in a special type of
water-container called a *loutrophoros*. The bride took on the symbolic role of the goddess Hera, who, according to myth, bathed
in sacred springs at Kanathos the night before her wedding to

Zeus. The bridal bath also symbolized purification as well as an expectant fertility.

Meanwhile, in the royal tent, Antiochus III and Ptolemy V took part in another ritual, the *engysis* ('giving of a pledge into the hand'), where the issues of Cleopatra Syra's dowry and guarantees of the girl's skills and purity were agreed upon. The princess's dowry-contract included a clause specifically inserted on the orders of Antiochus III. It stated that, for her own maintenance and comfort, Princess Cleopatra Syra would receive an annual revenue taken from the taxes of wealthy Coele-Syria – but that the Ptolemaic state treasury was not entitled to any of it. The money paid from the revenues of Coele-Syria was Cleopatra Syra's, and hers alone. That, Antiochus figured, would hurt the Egyptians where it mattered the most.

The next day saw the beginning of the *gamos* ('wedding') ceremony proper. Cleopatra Syra was decked out in bridal finery. An old account of the preparation of the bride Pandora in Hesiod's poem *Theogony* provides a clue to Cleopatra Syra's appearance that day. In the poem, the role of *nymphokomos* is played by the goddess Athene:

> The goddess, grey-eyed Athene, girded and adorned [Pandora]
> in a gleaming silver crown, and down over her head she placed
> an intricately woven veil, a wonder to see.
> Around her head Pallas Athene put a garland
> Fresh blossoming, beautiful, with meadow flowers.
> And she placed on her head a golden crown
> which the god himself made, the famous Lame God
>   [Hephaestus],
> making it with his hands, delighting Father Zeus.

Cleopatra Syra's costume included a red veil, the colour most closely associated in nature with ripeness and fertility. It was a highly charged, erotic colour, and because red clothing was also symbolically associated with blood, especially the blood of sacrifice, the bride's assumption of a red veil could thus be interpreted as a sign of substitute sacrifice. In Aeschylus' tragedy *Agamemnon*, therefore, the famous motif of Iphigeneia shedding her red-dyed veils as she goes off to be married is meant to evoke the image of sacrificial virginal bloodshed. The red veil may well have alluded to the colour of the blood lost during the bride's first sexual intercourse.

The bridal veil was not removed until the time came, a day later, for the groom to see his bride for the first time. With the guests gathered together (but observing strict gender division) for an enormous wedding dinner of all sorts of meats, custards, cheeses, pastries, cakes and sesame sweets, the princess was escorted into the centre of the assembly by her father, who grasped her by the wrist – the traditional gesture of 'handing over' the bride. Antiochus passed his daughter to her new husband in full view of the assembly of guests as he declared that 'in front of witnesses, I give this girl to you for the ploughing of children.'

Cleopatra Syra was escorted by her bridesmaid to the centre of the assembly and seated at the central hearth, the symbol of the goddess Hestia (the personification of domesticity), her face still covered by her veil. King Ptolemy approached and knelt in front of her, and in a ritual known as the *anakalyptēria*, the 'unveiling', he carefully lifted the veil and took a brief look at his new wife's face (Cleopatra Syra, like all good brides, kept her gaze lowered) before replacing it again. Cleopatra Syra demonstrated – albeit passively – her acquiescence to marry through her participation in the unveiling ceremony.

Finally, towards the end of the night, King Ptolemy led his bride into the specially prepared bridal chamber (*thalamos*), decorated with saffron-coloured hangings and a specific bed canopy known as the *pastos*. It was here, in intimate and less formal surroundings, that the husband and wife finally got to look one another in the eye. After the bridal couple had entered the room, the door was closed and guarded while the guests remained outside to sing the *epithalamium*, or wedding hymn, for the privacy of the chamber was respected by all concerned. Whether Ptolemy V Epiphanes and Cleopatra Syra consummated their marriage that night is unknown, but it was hoped – and expected – to have happened.

We do not know what occurred between the newlyweds in the privacy of the *thalamos*, but in the watchful eyes of the Hellenistic world, and under the piercing gaze of Rome, the Seleucids and the Ptolemies had made a public statement of peace and reconciliation.

A few days later, Cleopatra Syra, queen of Egypt, bid farewell to her father. She was never to see Antiochus III again. With her new husband, her few waiting-women and the innermost circle of the factious Egyptian court, she boarded ship; the sailors cast off and the vessel headed out on the short sea voyage. Cleopatra Syra fixed her eyes on the horizon – where her future lay.

2

A Stranger in a Strange Land

For Cleopatra Syra, as for all Greeks who lived beyond its borders, Egypt was a place of ancient mysteries. She knew of it as a realm of strange and exotic customs and curious religious practices, where animal-headed gods were worshipped with outlandish rituals, where the dead were kept looking alive, and where gold and silver burst forth from the earth. Yes, Egypt enjoyed unimaginable wealth. It had acquired the reputation for affluence early on, for already in the *Odyssey*, Homer's archaic heroes travelled there for lucrative business and with the hope of turning a quick profit. So rich was Egypt that Homer tells of many pirate raids along the country's Mediterranean coastline, all unsuccessful thanks to Egyptian vigilance. These stories were reminiscent, no doubt, of events that had really occurred back in the thirteenth century BCE, when the eastern Mediterranean was inundated with migrants fleeing their ancestral lands because of war and environmental upheavals, looking for new settlements.

Herodotus, in his *Histories*, found Egypt to be an attractive topic for an extensive excursus and he devoted the whole of Book II to it. Cleopatra Syra must have known this landmark work and been familiar with Herodotus' description of Egypt as the kingdom with 'the most wonders and deeds that defy description.' She knew too that Herodotus had found Egypt to be a place of bizarre but compelling topsy-turvydom, for as he wrote:

> Everywhere else in the world, priests wear their hair long but
> in Egypt, they are shaven ... The Egyptians knead dough with

their feet and gather mud and dung with their hands. The Egyptians (and those who have learned it from them) are the only people who practise circumcision. Every man has two garments, every woman only one . . . The Greeks write and calculate from left to right; the Egyptians do the opposite . . . Women attend market and are employed in trade, while men stay at home and do the weaving . . . Men in Egypt carry loads on their heads, women on their shoulders; women pass water standing up, men sitting down. To ease themselves they go indoors, but eat outside in the streets . . . They are religious beyond measure.

The Egypt which Herodotus encountered in the fifth century BCE followed the rhythms of life that had been established there over two millennia earlier. The Egyptians recognized distinct seasons: *akhet* (flooding), *peret* (planting) and *shemu* (harvesting). The predictable flooding of the Nile and the fertilization of the rich soil produced an abundance of crops: emmer, barley and other cereal grains, as well as flax plants, uprooted before they started flowering, grown for the fibres of their stems and used to weave sheets of linen. The country consisted of 23,000 square kilometres of fertile land which extended some 230 kilometres along the narrow valley of the River Nile from the first cataract in the south to the Delta and the Mediterranean coast. The wealth-making arable Black Land (*Kemet*) clung close to the Nile's banks, for much of Egypt was desert – the Red Land (*Deshret*), a vast zone which acted as an inhospitable boundary between Egypt and the neighbouring countries. Invading armies would have to survive long desert crossings, so they rarely tried. This arid territory also provided the Egyptians with their precious metals, such as gold, and semi-precious gemstones.

The Egyptians saw themselves as a people who occupied two lands: one, Upper Egypt, stretched north from the cataracts of Aswan right through the Nile Valley, and the other, Lower Egypt, encompassed the Nile Delta to the Mediterranean coast. As Lord of the Two Lands, the pharaoh was the ruler of a unified Upper and

Lower Egypt, and his crowns (the red crown of Lower Egypt and the white crown of Upper Egypt), titles and ritual performances emphasized the fact that Egypt was a land of duality. Dualism characterized the ancient Egyptian mindset: paired elements, or conceptual 'poles', were everywhere. Whenever there was *netet* ('what is'), there was also *djwtet* ('what is not'). In ancient Egyptian thought, paired concepts of this type served as instruments to define, and set rules for, the relationship between gods and men. The pair *ma'at* and *isfet* ('order' and 'chaos'), for instance, codified these relationships in terms of morality.

Egyptian attitudes towards foreigners were certainly structured on this concept of duality too, which gave meaning to their complete vision of the world and its functioning. In the official royal ideology, the foreigner was a symbol of *isfet*, and the pharaoh had to actively destroy chaos to preserve *ma'at*. In depictions on the exterior of temple walls, this idea is given form and the king is shown wielding a club or mace, which he smashes onto the heads of cowering foreigners; in literary compositions, foreigners were routinely termed 'vile' or 'wretched'. In other forms of imagery, they were visually interchangeable with animals: the decoration on a box from the tomb of Tutankhamun, for example, shows the young king killing both foreigners and animals alike with arrows. This visual metaphor confirms that there was little difference between foreigners and animals in Egyptian royal ideology. And yet, the 'othering' done by Egyptians towards foreigners and foreign cultures needs to be balanced by the fact that across the centuries Egypt had played host to numerous foreign groups – Nubians, Asiatics, Minoans, Libyans, Canaanites – who settled down inside its borders and lived near the Egyptians. The term 'foreigner' (*kha'as-tiw*) was never used to describe settled immigrants, however; only peoples who lived beyond Egypt were true 'outsiders'. Whoever was nourished by the waters of the Nile, Herodotus asserted, was considered an Egyptian. This, perhaps, proved to be instructional – a relief to know, certainly – for Cleopatra Syra as her ship drew ever closer to the coast of Egypt.

There had been a fixed Greek presence in Egypt ever since the
late eighth century BCE, when Greek mercenaries and merchants
were given a residential trading base at Naukratis in the Nile Delta.
The town took its Greek name from the Egyptian *niwt keredj*,
'Town of the Caraians', which clearly documents its founding as
a site with a distinct Greek character. It was the first autonomous
Greek settlement in Egypt. Excavations undertaken there between
1884 and 1903 by Flinders Petrie (which, under the focus of the
Naukratis Project, eventually extended until 1983) revealed that
the town contained no less than four Greek temples (to Apollo,
Aphrodite, Hera and the Dioscuri) alongside a 'Hellenion', an
imposing sanctuary-cum-Hellenic-social-centre, funded and built
by several Greek city-states including Cnidus, Halicarnassus and
Mytilene. Close to the Greek religious enclosures was an Egyptian
temple to the god Amun. There were manufacturing zones within
the town too, to produce pottery, faience (glazed pottery), scarabs
and the iron weapons that were unknown elsewhere in Egypt at
this time. Another sizeable concentration of Greek merchants
and mercenaries was established, at the invitation of the pharaoh
Psammetichus I (664–610 BCE), in the ancient, much-revered holy
city of Memphis, the sprawling walled Nile-side capital of ancient
Egypt (today a hodgepodge of archaeological mounds surrounded
by a group of villages, squatting at the edge of Cairo's suburbs).

The pioneering Greeks who made up these communities of
resident aliens enjoyed a prosperous life in Egypt, for work was
plentiful and trade was brisk, but they were not allowed to forget
that they were residing in a foreign land and remained there
only at the pleasure of Egypt's monarch. But all that changed in
332 BCE when Alexander the Great 'liberated' Egypt from the Persians – who had controlled it, on and off, for two hundred years
– and made it part of the 'Greek World'. Suddenly, Egypt became
a land of opportunity for all Greeks, a veritable El Dorado on the
Nile. With the equivalent cry of Mark Twain's 'There's gold in
them thar hills', Greeks flocked to Egypt, first in their thousands
and then in their tens of thousands. They came from as far east as
Sinope on the Black Sea, from as far north as Illyria, Thrace and

Macedon, and from as far west as Syracuse in Sicily, and even from Marseilles. Papyri documents tell of the presence of mercenary soldiers heading into Egypt from Malta, Crete, Ionia and Boeotia (in central Greece). All in all, migrants came from some 200 different places to join in the goldrush in Egypt. One satirical poem incites a young Greek soldier to leave his homeland and head to the Nile: 'If you are ready to clasp the military cloak on your right shoulder and if you have the nerve to plant your legs firmly on the ground and get involved in some action, then get yourself over to Egypt, double quick!' Another poem, which reads like a post-war Department of Immigration advertisement, enthusiastically sells Egypt's many attractions:

Aphrodite's HQ is down there, you know, in Egypt. They've got it all there in Egypt: money, sports, power, great weather, fame, fantastic sightseeing, philosophers, gold, sexy boys, wine – in short, everything you could ever desire. And women! By the gods, more women than the sky boasts stars!

*

Alexander the Great and his Greco-Macedonian troops had burst into Egypt and, aided by the extreme hatred for the Persians there, overcame the Achaemenid rulers almost without drawing a sword. After his victory, Alexander carefully made his peace with the powerful Egyptian priesthoods; he not only journeyed across the great Western Desert to Siwah to meet the clergy at the oracular shrine of Amun-Re but he also consulted priests elsewhere in his new kingdom, probably at Memphis and certainly at Thebes in Upper Egypt. However, Alexander's regime upset the old Egyptian establishment almost at once with the construction of the coastal city of Alexandria on a plot of land opposite the island of Pharos, between the Mediterranean coast and Lake Mareotis to the south. Its founding – the inspiration for which Alexander insisted had come to him in a dream – involved a great upheaval in the lifestyle of local Egyptians, who were uprooted from surrounding villages and conscripted into Alexander's labour force. 'A longing for the work took hold of him,' Arrian of Nicomedia, the Greek historian and philosopher, was to write centuries later. Alexander came up with plans for the site of an agora (market, business centre) and temples (mostly to Greek gods). He appointed as his chief architect Dinocrates (who had made a name for himself as the mastermind behind the reconstruction of the dilapidated Temple of Artemis at Ephesus), and his first project was to connect Pharos Island to the mainland with a causeway that divided the sea into two harbours. The city streets were laid out in a right-angled grid pattern to catch the cool prevailing breezes, and its underground drains, conduits, cisterns and sewers were a masterpiece of engineering. When the time came to create its foundations, Alexander divided the city into five sectors, designated by the first five letters of the Greek alphabet: alpha for Alexander, beta for *basileus* ('king'), gamma for *genos* ('lineage'), delta for *Diós* ('of Zeus') and epsilon for *ektisen* ('he founded'); in other words, 'Alexander, king of the lineage of Zeus, was its founder' was stamped on the very layout of the city.

No ancient historian of Alexander's campaign in Egypt fails to mention the foundation story of Alexandria. Authors such as Diodorus Siculus, Strabo, Pliny and Plutarch report that the city was designed in the shape of a Macedonian *chlamys*, a type of woollen military cloak worn by Alexander's cavalry. Plutarch records that 'as they had no chalk, they grabbed a bit of flour and marked out on the dark soil a rounded area, to whose inner arc straight lines extended so as to produce the figure of a *chlamys*, the lines beginning from the outskirts, and narrowed its breadth uniformly.' Against the black Egyptian soil (the Egyptians referred to their country as *Kemet*, 'the Black Land'), the Macedonian presence was registered in white, represented by the emblem of a warrior, the *chlamys*. It was in this symbolic context that another wondrous occurrence took place: a flock of innumerable birds of all types and sizes, coming from the river and the lake, swooped down like a cloud over the area and removed all traces of the flour. Alexander was perplexed, unable to understand what this foretold, but the soothsayers knew. For them the message was clear: the city would be very prosperous and provide the right living conditions to attract people from all around. Alexandria became the embodiment of Hellenistic culture precisely because it had no national basis.

*

Following Alexander's death in Babylon in June 323 BCE, Egypt had been taken over by a man named Ptolemy. He belonged to a Macedonian family of minor nobility related (albeit distantly) to the Aegead royal family and had won renown for himself and his kin during Alexander the Great's campaigns in eastern Iran and India. His years of loyal service were rewarded when, at Alexander's death, he was given the governance of Egypt. For twenty-three long years, Ptolemy administered Egypt as its satrap, but in 305 BCE he finally proclaimed himself Egypt's *basileus* – 'king'.

His wife and greatly loved queen was Berenice I, who bore Ptolemy a daughter, Arsinoē II, and a son and heir, Ptolemy II Philadelphus, who in January 284 BCE was appointed as his father's co-regent. Co-regency was a policy that proved popular throughout the dynasty's long history, and the Ptolemies and Cleopatras would go on to use the old pharaonic precedent of co-regencies on a grand scale in an attempt (usually unsuccessful) to check dynastic infighting. Co-regencies promoted an ideal of dynastic harmony. This concept was reflected in the propagandistic quasi-religious epithets the Ptolemaic kings and queens adopted for themselves. Starting with Ptolemy I, who grafted the moniker Soter ('Saviour') onto his name (possibly at the same time he first used the title *basileus*), the Ptolemaic monarchs regularly chose self-descriptors which were both loaded with religious connotation and hyperbolic expressions of familial love – Epiphanes ('Manifestation'), Euergetes ('Beneficent'), and even Neos Dionysus ('The New Dionysus') were mixed with Philadelphus ('Sibling-Loving'), Philopator ('Father-Loving') and Philometor ('Mother-Loving').

Ptolemy I Soter died at the beginning of January 282 BCE and was succeeded by Ptolemy II Philadelphus. He inherited a kingdom that was affluent and relatively safe from foreign threat, and his reign was seen as a time of cultural renaissance, marked by a certain opulence. The twenty-eight-year-old king was married to Arsinoē, the daughter of Lysimachus, king of Thrace (in the Ptolemaic genealogy she is known to us as Arsinoē I), and she gave him three sons and a daughter, but he repudiated her in 300 BCE and married his full-blood sister Arsinoē II, who took his royal epithet and added it to her own name: she was now Arsinoē Philadelphus, 'Sibling-Loving'. Together the king and queen were the Philadelphoi – 'Brother-Sister-Loving'.

Sibling marriage (as we will investigate more fully later) had an old pharaonic precedent, but many Greco-Roman writers believed, erroneously, that sibling marriage was a widespread Egyptian practice and that incest was the kind of thing they got up to 'down there' in Egypt. Some Greeks were certainly unsettled, if not downright shocked, by the royal brother–sister marriage. Sotades, a comic poet who was active in Alexandria during the reign of Ptolemy II Philadelphus, thought that the royal sibling marriage was comedy gold and made a notorious (and fatal) comment, stating that Ptolemy had 'put his prick into an unholy hole'. Nonetheless, the royal couple were seen as joint rulers of equal status, the first in a long line of Ptolemaic sovereigns who would follow suit. Epigraphic evidence makes it clear that Arsinoē II 'received the crowns of Upper and Lower Egypt' and, as the Lady of the Two Lands, she was given the titles of traditional pharaonic rulership with her names written in cartouches: 'Arsinoē Philadelphus, *King* of Upper and Lower Egypt'.

Arsinoē II died on the night of 16 July 268 BCE, aged forty-eight. 'This goddess has ascended to heaven,' the Egyptian scribes recorded, and Callimachus composed a Greek dirge to be performed before the grief-stricken Philadelphus: 'They cry for your sister, born of the same womb with you, it is she who has died and the cities of Egypt, wherever you look, are swathed in black.' Her body was cremated in the Macedonian fashion and her funeral was marked with athletic games and poetry competitions. Eventually, Philadelphus instituted an annual festival in her honour, the Arsinoeia, at which priestesses paraded through Alexandria to her temple, the Arsineion, for Philadelphus had wasted no time in declaring his deceased sister-wife to be a fully-fledged goddess. Temples to Thea Arsinoë Philadelphos – the 'Brother-Loving Goddess' – were constructed throughout Egypt, priesthoods were created for her, monumental statues of the late queen were erected, streets, towns and even districts were named in her honour. Ptolemy II did not marry again after Arsinoë's death, even though he was only in his early forties. His decision inevitably highlighted Arsinoë's role in his life and, to all intents and purposes, she remained his consort and co-regent from beyond the grave. Death was no impediment to Arsinoë's career.

Ptolemy II Philadelphus died in January 246 BCE, aged sixty-two. His successor, Ptolemy III Euergetes ('the Benefactor'), took as his wife his cousin Berenice II, the sole-ruler of Cyrene in Libya and the daughter of the late King Magus. In 243 BCE, the royal couple declared themselves Theoi Euergetai, 'Beneficent Gods', and Berenice II began to take an active role in her own self-promotion by advancing her identification with the Egyptian goddess Hathor. The queen presented herself to the wider Greek world with enthusiasm, and her reputation as a superlative horse-fancier (she was an active horse-breeder, with numerous stables and stud-farms to her name) was legendary.

Ptolemy III Euergetes died in the winter of 222 BCE. Berenice, who was widely popular with both the Alexandrians and the Egyptians, officially became pharaoh in his place and, following precedent, she took as her co-ruler her eldest son, the twenty-year-old Ptolemy IV, who adopted the epithet Philopator ('Father-Loving'). We know nothing about his relationship with his late father, but it is clear that Philopator had no love for his mother and was determined to curb Berenice's authority. Early in 221 BCE, the queen was murdered. Ptolemy IV Philopator married his fourteen-year-old sister Arsinoë almost immediately after becoming pharaoh, but she never enjoyed a good relationship with her husband-brother and his bed was mostly occupied by mistresses. The fact that their marriage produced only one child, the future Ptolemy V, probably born in 210 BCE, indicates the breakdown of their marriage. Ptolemy IV Philopator's death in 205/4 BCE left Arsinoë desperately vulnerable to the machinations of ambitious courtiers. Her young son was taken away from her and, considered to be too much of a liability to government, Arsinoë III was brutally murdered – the second Ptolemaic queen-consort to die through the mindless violence of a vicious and bloody court coup.

*

We have no way of knowing whether Cleopatra Syra knew anything of the bloody past of the family she had just married into when her ship approached Alexandria and inched its way towards the harbour that connected the city's palace-quarter to the Mediterranean Sea. She saw for the first time the magnitude and majesty of Alexander's metropolis. In Alexandria, buildings were constructed in glistening marble and in limestone so white that the city's fashionistas openly advised visitors and residents to wear black garments to make an impression. Everywhere there were porticos and pillared halls, very characteristic of Alexandrian architecture, and the Greek-style facades of public buildings were adorned with ancient stone sphinxes and giant granite obelisks, the work of long-dead pharaohs, which had been moved to Alexandria in order to consolidate its position as the first city of the civilized world in size, elegance, riches and amenities.

At the time of Cleopatra Syra's arrival, Alexandria, with its fine harbours, had come to dominate the social, cultural and economic life of Egypt and to effect changes elsewhere in the Hellenistic world too. It enshrined the concept of a colonialist government that saw Egypt as an alien 'spear-won' territory fit for economic exploitation. Dreams and visions aside, Alexander the Great had after all chosen the site of Alexandria for strategic reasons as much as commercial gains, because the creation of a deep-water port there clinched his domination over the eastern Mediterranean (two modern world wars have proved Alexandria's critical importance as a navy base). By and large, throughout its long and noble history, Alexandria always aligned itself towards the Mediterranean Sea and looked out to the countries that surrounded its expansive

basin; its location afforded Alexandria a more than merely symbolic separation from Egypt. Throughout the Ptolemaic age, it was
known in Greek as Alexandria pros Aegyptō (and was referred to
by the Romans as Alexandria ad Aegyptum), 'Alexandria next to
Egypt', never as 'Alexandria in Egypt'.

Just as the world-renowned Pharos Lighthouse, a scientific
marvel, was a welcome sight for weary sea travellers, Alexandria
itself acted as a beacon for merchants, curious tourists, religious
types and most importantly, the finest intellectual minds of
the times. For in Alexandria, the Ptolemaic kings had lavished
much money on the foundation of a massive research institution
known as the Museion (or Museum – the temple of the Muses,
the divine inspirers of song, music and dance). The Museion comprised lecture theatres, laboratories and an observatory, as well as
the renowned Great Library and the Lesser Library. Founded in
295 BCE, the Great Library of Alexandria was used to promote a
particular type of Ptolemaic objective – the subordination of the
Greek city-states through cultural dominance. The historian of
the Hellenistic world Andrew Erskine has noted that 'just as the
Ptolemies sought to establish control over other Greek states, so
they also sought to establish control over Greek culture' by collecting and translating their works of literature, and by attracting
scholars from around the world – often from Greek-speaking
regions. In fact, many of the most prominent early scholars of the
Library of Alexandria came from Greek domains – the geographer
Eratosthenes and the poet Callimachus came from Cyrene, Aristophanes the grammarian came from Cos, and the poet Theocritus
arrived from far-away Syracuse. The Library held texts from all
over the ancient world; the works of Socrates, Homer, Euripides,
Plato, Aristophanes, Aeschylus and even sections of the Hebrew
bible were kept there. Every ship that arrived at Alexandria was
searched by the librarians for scrolls and an intricate bureaucracy
was established to analyse all the texts which were discovered in
order to determine whether the visitors would be allowed to keep
the originals or be forced to settle for handmade copies so the
authentic ones could be archived. Highly prized Athenian texts

were taken on the promise of gold for their safe return, although the librarians were so talented at copying these texts that they often kept the originals for themselves and returned the facsimiles to the owners. The Great Library grew into the largest collection of ancient books in the world, consisting of about 490,000 papyrus scrolls.

The Library and Museion became an enormous boon to the economic life of Alexandria, since tourists from all over the world flocked to see these modern marvels. The Library of Alexandria was even copied by the upstart kingdom of the Attalids in Pergamum in Asia Minor, which tried to poach the librarian of Alexandria himself, Aristophanes of Byzantium, a man famous for his unparalleled knowledge of the Library's holdings. For most visitors and scholars, the Alexandrian Library was a symbol of modernity, for it was the physical embodiment of cutting-edge global knowledge. And for the Ptolemies, knowledge was power.

Cleopatra Syra disembarked from the ship and was taken on a lavish sightseeing tour of the capital – an opportunity for her to familiarize herself with the city which, she had to admit, clearly outrivalled anything to be found back home, even Antioch. She was carried in a litter through the crowded streets, with Ptolemy V leading the way in his own palanquin, as crowds strained forward as close as the royal bodyguards permitted them in order to view their new queen.

Cleopatra Syra, like all the successors of Alexander the Great, was aware that politics was theatre and so she played her part accordingly, gently waving to the crowds, her face fixed with a set smile. In Alexandria everything – from art and architecture to spectacular processions and ostentatious costumes – was part and parcel of the theatre of royalty. The Ptolemaic court was a stage on which their show played out to public applause and approbation or, occasionally, criticism and derision. Ancient authors themselves were not unaware of the theatrical construction of monarchy: writing of Demetrius Poliorcetes, the Macedonian nobleman and military leader who became king of Macedon (294–288 BCE), Plutarch asserts that he, like so many of Alexander the Great's successors, 'did but assume Alexander's majesty and pomp, like actors on a stage'. Plutarch went on to list just what it was that smacked of the theatrical about Demetrius' appearance – his penchant for donning purple robes shot with gold and gold-embroidered shoes of purple felt (with built-up soles for added height), and his attachment to a Ziegfeld Follies-style cloak of gold inset with semi-precious stones. Demetrius might have been a 'conqueror of cities' but he had the theatrical aesthetics of Elvis.

All the Hellenistic world was a stage, but the most overtly theatrical of the Hellenistic dynasties – or at least the most conscious of the beguiling power of spectacle to sway the masses – were the Ptolemies themselves. A century before Cleopatra Syra was paraded through Alexandria, Ptolemy II had wooed his subjects with a celebratory procession (Greek, *pompē*) of unparalleled magnificence. Connected to an Alexandrian festival known as the Ptolemaieia, the Barnum-and-Bailey outrageousness of this most celebrated *pompē* is captured in an eyewitness report by Callixenus of Rhodes:

Parades . . . passed through the city. First of all, there went the pageant . . . in honour of the several gods. In the Dionysus procession, first went the Satyrs, bearing gilded lamps made of ivy wood. After them came images of Victory, having golden wings. The Satyrs bore in their hands incense burners, six cubits in height, adorned with branches made of ivy wood and gold, and they were costumed in tunics embroidered with figures of animals, and they themselves also had a good deal of gold ornament about them. After them followed an altar six cubits high, all covered with gilded ivy leaves, having a crown of vine leaves upon it all in gold. Next came boys in purple tunics, bearing frankincense and myrrh, and saffron on golden dishes. And then advanced forty more Satyrs, crowned with golden ivy garlands; their bodies were painted – some with purple, some with vermilion, and some with other colours. They wore each a golden crown, made to imitate vine leaves and ivy leaves . . . After many other wagons came one twenty-five cubits long, and fifteen broad; and this was drawn by six hundred men. On this wagon was a sack, holding three thousand measures of wine, and consisting of leopards' skins sewn together. This sack allowed its liquor to escape, and it gradually flowed over the whole road.

An endless array of similar wonders followed: an enormous number of servants walked in the parade displaying the golden vessels of the king's palace; twenty-four chariots drawn by four elephants each followed, and then came twelve chariots drawn by antelopes, fifteen by buffalos, eight by pairs of ostriches, eight by zebras. Mules, camels and twenty-four lions were led through Alexandria's streets on harnesses of gold. Golden statues of the royal family were carried at shoulder-height and the crowds threw garlands on the palanquins bearing them and strewed the floor with petals. It was the kind of spectacle beloved by royal-watchers across the centuries.

Pompē was a key expression of a much bigger Ptolemaic concept: *tryphē*. This slippery Greek term can be loosely translated as 'magnificence', 'luxuriousness', 'extravagance', 'exorbitance', or even 'wantonness'. *Tryphē* was part and parcel of Ptolemaic self-identity because, simply speaking, they could afford to be ostentatious. The Ptolemies were unspeakably rich, vulgarly, flamboyantly, brazenly wealthy and, like latter-day Russian oligarchs, they had no qualms about putting their wealth on conspicuous display. Ptolemaic super-wealth promoted art, architecture, scholarship, court ceremonial and public entertainments of all sorts, and in putting their cash to such uses, the Ptolemies wowed their subjects and their political rivals alike. Cleopatra Syra was to become adept at self-promotion and learned quickly how to employ spectacle effectively.

*

We have a good idea of how Cleopatra Syra looked at the time of her wedding, for her portrait survives on a coin which was probably minted to commemorate the royal marriage. A unique gold *octodrachum* from Alexandria, which was purchased by the British Museum in the 1970s, affords us a glimpse of Egypt's first Cleopatra. She is a delicate young thing whose fine, narrow features work well in silhouette. Her nose is delicately retroussé and her lips are full and bud-like, whilst her chin is as round as a ball; the over-large pupil of her eye stares into the far distance with a slight upward curve (a characteristic of many Hellenistic coin portraits). All in all, despite the heaviness beneath her chin, Cleopatra Syra is doll-like in her prettiness. Her hair is subtly waved and is adorned with a large and stately *stephane*, or 'tiara'. Much of her head is covered by a wide, draped veil, but her ear is exposed and from it hangs a simple pendant earring. The Greek inscription names her simply as 'Queen Cleopatra'.

Coin portraits were the best way of creating an official image of monarchy in antiquity; they were issued on the orders, and with the direct approval, of the royal courts and were a medium that had very wide distribution, reaching to practically all strata of society. Coinage was antiquity's most effective form of mass media; coins were also part of the social media of the past, sending messages about identity, power and ownership, and monarchs enthusiastically regarded coinage as the best media in which to disseminate their images, their ideologies and their encoded messages of legitimacy. This type of self-promotion, propaganda by any other name, was endorsed by Hellenistic rulers through the development of divine epithets which appeared on coins, very often to promote civic benefactions or as indicators of success. Importantly, Hellenistic kings frequently emphasized their right to rule and their right to pass on the succession to their children, and so significance was accorded to their wives, mothers and daughters on official coinage as a way of stressing dynastic heritage and the intrinsic value of the bloodline.

As state images and political slogans, coin portraits did not necessarily give realistic reflections of a sitter's true likeness – that was not their chief function. What they did give, though, was an easily recognizable image of royalty, a kind of monarchic hieroglyph, which was accompanied by a legend, various attributes (crowns, sunbursts, diadems, sceptres) or *distinct* physiognomic features like hairstyles, noses or eyes. Some Hellenistic dynasties capitalized on this 'hieroglyphic' tendency to create distinct 'face patterns', in which family connections were stressed through commonly shared physical features, resulting in what has been termed 'portrait assimilation'. This is certainly exemplified by the Seleucid kings, for whom we have an almost unbroken succession of thirty-two coin portraits out of a line-up of thirty-four kings – all of whom resembled a family of hard-edged mobsters. The coinage suggests that Cleopatra Syra had bypassed the gene that produced the prominent hooked noses and jutting jaws which were the strong physical characteristics of the Seleucids.

*

People living in Alexandria must have felt as if they were inhabiting a paradise. Many had come from rural areas and life had really opened up for them in a lot of good ways. These new *kosmopolites* took advantage of everything Alexandria afforded them: the best housing, the cleanest streets, the choicest wine, the most pungent of spices, the finest clothing, plenty of work, fine civic architecture, great food, games, numerous theatres and a very stable economy. Immigration from the Greek-speaking world was encouraged by generous subsidies of land grants, houses and jobs in the civil service and the military.

Many of Egypt's Greek citizens visited the metropolis only rarely, for festive occasions – like the welcoming of a new queen to Egypt – but by and large they were happy to live out their days on the farms granted to them when they had arrived. The area of the Fayum, the richly fertile oases in the north-west of Egypt, had proved to be very popular with settlers, and the Ptolemies had undertaken extensive land reclamation there. Nevertheless, even for the farmer most ardently attached to his plot, the attractions of the city were intoxicating: 'Alexandria contains the most beautiful public precincts', cooed the geographer Strabo, 'for . . . each of the kings, from love of splendour, was wont to add some ornament to the public monuments . . . so that now . . . there is building upon building.' But Alexandria was also noisy, crowded and fatiguing. By ancient standards the city's population was teeming, and Cleopatra Syra found herself living cheek-by-jowl alongside around 180,000 recorded male citizens – which meant that the total population was many times greater. The historian and classicist Peter Frasier, in his monumental three-volume study of Ptolemaic Alexandria, believes that in the first century BCE the city's population was around 1 million inhabitants (and he estimates that in the early Roman period it rose to 1.5 million). No wonder that in Theocritus' idyll *The Festival of Adonis*, Alexandria is said to be simply exhausting: 'The people! The chariots! Everywhere, men in cloaks and hobnailed boots. The road seems longer each time I walk it . . . How shall we manage to find our way through this mob? . . . Get off my feet, Mister! I'm caught like you in the crowd!'

The city's two principal streets intersected at the Sema, the location of the tomb of Alexander the Great, and were said to be over one hundred feet wide. Westwards, outside the city's wall, lay a huge necropolis replete with gardens. To the north-east of the Sema was the Jewish community, overseen by an ethnarch (district governor) and their own council. Jews, Greeks and Egyptians constituted the majority of people living in Alexandria, but there were also many thousands of Persians, Syrians and Libyans, as well as many Asiatics to be found there too, making Alexandria a rich ethnic melting pot.

An area called Basileia lay at the centre of Alexandria; it was the Ptolemies' royal quarter. Temples, theatres, palaces, administrative buildings, a coin mint, the king's residence, a garden and even a zoo were to be found in this exclusive inner-space, and it was in this rarefied world that Cleopatra Syra would live out her days. Unfortunately, there is very little by way of physical remains of the palace quarter surviving these days – it has been long-submerged under the ever-encroaching Mediterranean Sea, the result of earthquakes and subsidence – but substantial underwater remains survive to tell of its former glory, and enough literary *testimonia* has come down to us to paint a vivid picture of the sheer level of wealth and ornamentation that would have filled the spaces in which Cleopatra Syra lived. Unlike the peripatetic courts of the Seleucids, the Ptolemies tended to live almost exclusively in their capital of Alexandria in the Nile Delta (with occasional trips to Memphis and luxury Nile cruises, perhaps taken on an annual basis). The palace of the Ptolemies at Alexandria is best thought of as a city-within-a-city (like the Forbidden City of Beijing) rather than a single structure *per se*. Polybius, Diodorus Siculus and most extensively Strabo provide detailed descriptions of the space constructed *de novo* for the Ptolemaic royal residence at the heart of the bustling, cosmopolitan city.

The Basileia of Alexandria covered an area that was roughly two kilometres in diameter, with access to a private harbour. There were two main sections to this palace complex: a large, public-facing area in the southern half, which was intended for highly visible state events, and to the north a more private part with residential palaces. These domestic areas were generally closed to the public and strictly reserved for the royal family and their chosen guests. According to Strabo, each Ptolemaic ruler added his or her own set of buildings to the palace quarter, which also played a pivotal role in the religious life of the city and the Ptolemaic empire as a whole: as well as the tomb of Alexander the Great, the tombs of all the deceased Ptolemies were located at the Sema, which, by the time of the Cleopatras, would already have been a large and hallowed collection. Various other sanctuaries were in the area too, namely a large temple to Poseidon and shrines to Isis and Serapis.

Underwater archaeologists have discovered the site of the submerged palace complex, and the artefacts they have rescued from the waters are revealing a long-lost world. Classical statuary found beneath the waves shows how Greek-influenced the palace buildings were, but other finds show a curiously Alexandrian blend of Greek and Egyptian artistic forms: one statue depicts a priest in a full robe holding a sacred water jar of Osiris, and another represents the protective serpent of the city, the Agathos Daemon, coiled around itself and ready to strike. They must have come from a chapel in the Basileia. Other submerged masterpieces include statues of a sacred ibis and the gigantic head of a granite falcon.

Colossal statues of Ptolemaic kings and queens in full pharaonic regalia have been brought up out of the waters, together with a colossal statue of the Nile god, Hapi; rescued too is a monumental stele inscribed in Greek and hieroglyphs, and a beautifully worked *naos* ('shrine') hewn from a single block of dark granite.

As Cleopatra Syra made her way through Alexandria's streets, heading for the palace, the Alexandrians cheered her on her way and, to return the compliment, she smiled and waved as she clung to her litter, bumping and swaying its way through the never-ending throng of admirers. From the start there seems to have developed a strong mutual bond between the Alexandrians and their young queen; even as international relations between her father and the Romans worsened and threatened to drag Egypt into the conflict, Cleopatra Syra never suffered any recrimination from her Alexandrian subjects, who seem from the get-go to have accepted her as one of their own.

3

Seeing Double

Having taken up residence in the Basileia, Cleopatra Syra faced the arduous task of fitting in to the Egyptian court and the even more demanding job of creating from scratch a good relationship with her husband, a comparative stranger still. As to the future, the young queen had two options: to disappear quietly into the shadows of the palace and produce a brood of children, stirring up no faction and causing no trouble; or to make her mark on the court, garner power and prestige, and thereby save herself from the fate suffered by her mother-in-law, Arsinoë III, whose political inaction left her unprotected and open to the machinations of powerful courtiers. Cleopatra Syra came from a line of strong Seleucid women: her mother, Laodice III, had acted as regent for her young son, Antiochus, while her husband was on campaign, and she issued benefactions to the cities of Iasos and Teos. Her grandmother, another Laodice, was the first Seleucid queen of Pontus, a foreign princess who became a queen, just as Cleopatra Syra had, while her great-grandmother, Laodice I, was the queen for whom the Laodicean War (the Third Syrian War) was named. Cleopatra Syra opted to play the power game.

At the outset it was important for her to display her loyalty to her husband and the country which she now ruled as queen. She needed to Egyptianize. After all, a foreign queen in a foreign land may in some circumstances suffer suspicion and isolation, yet by her very presence she confirmed the international standing of the family into which she married. Cleopatra Syra had been sent off to Egypt as a representative of Antiochus III, and it was presumed by the Egyptian courtiers that she would actively promote her father's interests there and that she would be his 'eyes and ears' at the heart of the Egyptian court. This was the dilemma faced by all foreign royal brides: where did their loyalty lie – with the natal family or the marital household? Was Cleopatra Syra to be invested in the new milieu into which she was thrust, working and campaigning for the Ptolemies alone? Did she feel allegiance to her husband or even have any emotional attachment to him? Such questions are impossible to answer, but to judge from her later life, Cleopatra Syra handled the hurdles of transdynastic marriage with real flair.

The previous Ptolemaic queen, Arsinoë III, had been murdered by the advisors of Ptolemy IV, and if Cleopatra Syra wanted to avoid the same fate, she had to cultivate relationships with the powerful ministers of Ptolemy V's court. Cleopatra Syra may have tried to cultivate a close network of *philoi* ('friends' or 'supporters'). Certainly, Josephus, the Jewish historian of the first century CE, mentions 'friends' of the king and queen and that Cleopatra Syra had favourites whom she defended whenever trouble arose.

Just as she strove to cultivate close relationships with the elite houses of the Alexandrian court, Cleopatra Syra also sought the loyalty of a new group of courtiers, the eunuchs. These castrated men had a long history of royal service throughout the ancient Near East, and in Assyria and Babylon they rose to positions of great responsibility in the state administration, the military and the royal household. They served the Persian monarchs too, and after the fall of the Achaemenid dynasty, Alexander the Great utilized them in his court as well. It is little wonder that they remained active in the households of the Seleucid kings, who modelled themselves closely on their Persian predecessors (they also served the kings of Pontus, Cappadocia, Bosporus, Cilicia, Judaea, Parthia and Armenia). There is little to no evidence of eunuchs serving at the pharaonic courts of ancient Egypt, however, and so the appearance of castrati at the court of Alexandria during the reign of Ptolemy V might well be because Cleopatra Syra brought them with her to Egypt as part of her entourage and thereafter had a hand in integrating them into the court. But we do have evidence that the first eunuch at the Ptolemaic court, Aristonicus, arrived slightly before Cleopatra Syra's marriage to Ptolemy. Aristonicus was, perhaps, an Alexandrian, and according to Polybius he was a *syntrophos* ('companion') of Ptolemy V when they were both children. It is unknown who or what circumstances took Aristonicus to court at a young age, and neither can we ascertain if he was deliberately castrated as an infant (as many eunuchs later were) or if he was born that way. Polybius generously records:

> [A]s he grew up, Aristonicus displayed more manly courage and tastes than are generally found in a eunuch. For he had a natural predilection for a military life, and devoted himself almost exclusively to that and all that it involved. He was also skilful in dealing with men, and, what is very rare, took large and liberal views, and was naturally inclined to bestow favours and kindnesses.

Aristonicus, who bore the title 'Beloved of His Majesty', evidently set the precedent for a successful court career for castrated servants and certainly, following his example, the period of Cleopatra Syra's queenship witnessed eunuchs becoming increasingly influential power brokers in the court of Alexandria. A eunuch named Eulaeus, who had travelled to Egypt as part of Cleopatra Syra's train, is first attested at the Alexandrian court as an overseer in the queen's bedchamber, but he quickly gained her trust and became her confidant; his presence at the centre of politics heralded a significant shift in the employment of eunuchs as councillors so that, eventually, by the close of the Ptolemaic era, eunuchs had risen to become influential politicians, military experts, diplomats and ambassadors.

Cleopatra Syra further consolidated her position in Egypt by acting the part of the supportive *basilissa*-consort to the pharaoh, her husband. A highly honorific title, *basilissa* ('queen', a compound of the Greek word *basileus*, 'king') bestowed great status, dignity and authority on any woman who bore it. Early on in Ptolemy V's reign, Cleopatra was named in dedicatory inscriptions and on some temples and stelae with this honorific title or its Egyptian equivalent, 'Lady of the Two Lands.' Some twenty-six surviving Greek inscriptions and fourteen Egyptian documents name the queen in conjunction with the king, and nine further dedicatory inscriptions bearing her name have been found throughout the Ptolemaic empire. Her name and titles are always placed after those of her husband and thus she appears in the supporting position, as was the old pharaonic tradition. A hieroglyphic stele, for example, places the queen's cartouche after that of Ptolemy V and names her the 'Lady of the Two Lands, Cleopatra,' while a set of dedicatory *phiales* ('bowls') that were deposited on the Aegean island of Delos, part of Ptolemaic territory, are inscribed 'in honour of King Ptolemy and Queen Cleopatra.' It seems that the queen had managed to work her way into her husband's affections and that he, in turn, granted Cleopatra Syra the hallmark of queenship, the title *basilissa*.

Cleopatra Syra had grown up in Syria in a cultural milieu which recognized that the Seleucid kings ruled lands which were culturally, religiously, socially and politically diverse, for there was no rulership tradition that united their subjects in, say, Babylonia with their subjects in coastal Syria. The Achaemenid Persians had never aimed at having a homogeneous empire and, to a greater or lesser extent, they allowed diversity to flourish throughout their multicultural realm. Therefore, there was no single blueprint for the Seleucids to use which would label them as 'rulers'; they approached governing different areas of their realm in diverse royal forms. But Egypt was different. Its deep antiquity had been the dominant expression of culture for thousands of years, and although many foreign invaders had fought their way into the kingdom, and had even occupied the throne of the Two Lands, they had all ultimately been conquered by the cultural power of the pharaonic tradition. The Persians had conquered Egypt in 522 BCE, but even they had been swayed by the culture of a land as old as Egypt and had become thoroughly 'Egyptianized,' building traditional temples, taking hieroglyphic throne-names and depicting themselves as bone fide pharaohs. Alexander the Great had followed suit after his conquest of the country in 332 BCE and marketed himself as a pharaoh and a son of Amun, and the Ptolemies determinedly emulated him in turn.

As the ruling house of Egypt, the Ptolemies realized that their best chance of success – and survival – as a dynasty lay in their ability to project themselves meaningfully to both their Greek and Egyptian subjects and to adopt a sort of bilingual cultural policy in which they located themselves squarely in the worlds of Egypt and Greece. In all things, the Ptolemies took a syncretic or amalgamated approach to rulership.

This was a lesson Cleopatra Syra had to learn fast. She was expected to understand and participate in an alien 'bilingual' system of royal presentation quickly and effectively, and to build up her own vocabulary of queenship too. Fortunately, she was quick to comprehend this and keenly self-motivated to make an impact in the Ptolemaic house. The years immediately following her arrival in Egypt saw her develop into a significant political and religious presence in the land she now ruled as queen.

*

The Egypt over which Cleopatra found herself queen had undergone a seismic shift in its governance since the Ptolemies had come to power. Understanding the context in which Cleopatra Syra and the other Cleopatras operated is crucial, for the mixed world of Greeks and Egyptians of the Hellenistic age brought to light unexpected possibilities and unanticipated problems. At the time Ptolemy I Soter took over Egypt, for instance, he would have, of necessity, depended on the Egyptian bureaucracy and administration to support his rule. He was also reliant on the support of the Egyptian priests and the access they had to the wealth of the temples, since the great religious institutions of Egypt owned as much as a third of the country's arable land. The priests and the temples also maintained the ancient ideologies of pharaonic kingship, with all their inscrutabilities, which could be used to bolster and enhance the status of any individual ruler – as Cleopatra Syra herself had quickly realized.

Demotic Egyptian had been the language of state during Ptolemy I Soter's reign. But gradually, as the native Egyptian scribes became increasingly – and then fully – bilingual, the administration transformed into a fully Greek bureaucracy (although it must be conceded that Egyptian scribes did not always write good Greek). Still, this non-exclusive approach to language is best seen in inscriptions that were created as bilingual statements, like the Rosetta Stone, thereby conscientiously promoting the dual identity of Egypt. Within epigraphic texts and carved into temple wall-reliefs, Ptolemaic rulers encouraged depiction of themselves as traditional pharaohs, appearing no different to any of their Egyptian predecessors. Even though an active Hellenization policy can be charted with, for instance, the championing of the Library in Alexandria, nonetheless, throughout Egypt native law-codes and courts were left as they were, an important element in the winning of native support for the Ptolemies. There was even a willingness in some parts of the Egyptian community to 'go Greek' by adopting Greek names (sometimes mixed with Egyptian ones) or Greek social conventions like wearing Hellenic dress, dining à la grecque or even building houses from Greek plans. Ptolemaic Egypt was a society with two distinct faces.

This curious balance of innovation and tradition was physically stamped upon Egypt itself. The region of Upper Egypt, usually referred to as the Thebaid in Greek administrative texts (taking its name from the ancient city of Thebes, modern Luxor), was in large part controlled by the powerful priests of the god Amun of Thebes, but early in the dynasty's history the Ptolemies created a political counterweight in the area with the construction of a large Greek city named Ptolemais Hermiou (modern el-Minshah). It effectively served as the Greek capital of Upper Egypt. Information concerning the planning of Ptolemais is shadowy (the site has never been exposed to a complete archaeological excavation), but it can be assumed that the city was based on the grid-plan seen at Alexandria, and to Strabo, who travelled there early in the first century CE, it was 'the largest city in the Thebaid

and not in any way inferior to Memphis . . . [I]t was a very large
city indeed.' Of the autonomy of the city there is no doubt, for
Ptolemais had buildings specifically associated with its city status,
with popular assemblies, a town council with a council chamber,
and a town hall for the presiding officers. The city also had courts
of justice. It even had its own theatre, and as early as the reign of
Philadelphus we find Ptolemais the place where a guild of actors
('artists of Dionysus') has its headquarters, under the patronage of
the crown. Greek temples and marketplaces dotted the city and
huge warehouses were found on almost every street corner, repos-
itories which provided the military garrisons all over Thebaid
with their food and arms. Military camps sprung up throughout
Upper Egypt, sometimes using the enclosure walls of temples,
like that still extant at Medinet Habu, the old mortuary temple
of Ramses III on the west bank of Thebes (or Diospolis Magna –
'City of Great Zeus,' as the Greeks called it).

By and large, with their non-confrontational give-and-take
policies, the Ptolemies adapted well to the practical realities of
ruling Egypt. The key to their success was balance. They ruled
over a country that already had its own well-developed administration but adapted it to suit the specific needs of the colonial
regime. For instance, the traditional division of the *chora* (Egyptian
'countryside') into pharaonic *nomes* ('provinces') was maintained
by the Ptolemies, but they replaced the ancient *nomarch* ('provincial governor') with a *strategos*, or 'general,' always a Greek official.
The Egyptian temples continued to operate as before, but the
government supervised them through the newly created offices
of temple magistrates, and although Egyptian judges remained
part of the legal system, they were placed under the command of
a government representative. Under Ptolemy IV the army, which
had once been composed only of Greco-Macedonians, became a
mix of old and new as native Egyptians were increasingly recruited
into its ranks; they proved themselves to be worthy fighters when
they emerged victorious from the Battle of Raphia in 217 BCE. All
soldiers, regardless of ethnicity, were eligible to receive a salary and
an allotment of land.

Throughout the Ptolemaic period, native Egyptians were able
to continue their traditional way of life more or less uninter-
rupted. Court cases could be heard by Egyptian judges and the
faithful could worship the old gods in their usual temples. Admittedly taxes were now levied by the state and the civil service was
centrally administered, but it was often Egyptians of the priestly
elite who served as tax officials and bureaucrats anyway, so locals
did not feel alienated from the system. As the decades passed, the
boundaries between Greek and Egyptian often blurred as mixed
marriages became more commonplace. In the early Ptolemaic
era, Greek male immigrants living in the Egyptian *chora* married
local girls, partly due to a shortage of Greek women. Thus, we
hear about a Greek (Cretan) cavalry soldier named Dryton, a
citizen of Ptolemais, who in the 130s BCE married a much younger
woman who was known by two names – Apollonia (Greek) and
Senmonthis (Egyptian). She came from a good military family
of Hellenized Egyptians (as her two names emphasize) and was
already bilingual in Egyptian and Greek, although her marriage to
Dryton brought the *kudos* – prestige – of a more ostensibly Greek
element into the family. To have a Greek cavalryman marry into
the family was a real coup and a big step up in society for Apol-
lonia/Senmonthis and her kin. For her part, young Apollonia/
Senmonthis was a natural businesswoman with impeccable skills
in estate management, which, together with her healthy dowry,
made her an especially attractive bride for Dryton.

The married couple set up home in the Egyptian town of
Pathrys, somewhat off the beaten track in Middle Egypt, and over
the course of twenty years Apollonia/Senmonthis bore Dryton five
daughters, each of whom, as was customary in the maternal family,
was given both a Greek and an Egyptian name – the eldest, Apol-
lonia/Senmonthis, was named for her mother; next there were
Aristō/Senmouthis, Aphrodisia/Takhratis and Nikarion/Thermou-
this. The baby of the family was Apollonia the Younger/Senpelaia.
The many surviving documents (tax records, wills and contracts)
that mention the family testify that Dryton and his wife, and their
daughters too, thought of themselves as – and prided themselves

on – being Greeks. This wealthy, ostensibly Greek family was apparently the only one in Pathyris that possessed female household slaves – all of whom had Greek names: Eirene, Ampelion and Myrsine. But isolated as they were in Egyptian Pathrys, far away from any Greek community, Dryton's family inevitably found themselves conforming more and more to the customs of their Egyptian neighbours. As the years passed, the papyri documents show the family tended to use only their Egyptian names – we can imagine that these were the names by which they were generally known and addressed – but they continued to employ Greek (which it must be supposed was Dryton's only language) for the family's dealings with government, and they lived in accordance with Greek law, as shown by the Greek wills drawn up for the family. Judging by the papyri evidence, though, by the time they had reached full adulthood (and following the death of Dryton himself) the Greek used by the daughters was getting a little rusty, yet they never lost their father's language entirely.

Although Apollonia/Senmouthis and Dryton's daughters had been given both Greek and Egyptian names, none of them followed in their mother's footsteps: they all married Egyptians and, consequently, did not continue the Greek traditions of their parents. They even followed Egyptian customs for their marriage contracts and divorce agreements, and they no longer gave their children Greek names. The sophisticated Greek guise enjoyed by Apollonia/Senmouthis' family, brought about by her advantageous marriage to a Greek cavalry officer, was entirely forgotten by the family's third generation, as if it had never been.

*

'Nowhere are people more religious than in Egypt,' Herodotus had reported. The Ptolemies quickly realized how true that was, and that to rule peaceably and profitably in Egypt they needed to honour the gods and – importantly – court, harness and support the powerful Egyptian priesthood and the wealthy state temples. The temples were economic powerhouses whose chief source of income was the farming of lands, which they owned in abundance, alongside the cultivation of vines, olives and palms, and the rearing of domestic animals. The temples performed multiple functions which we might class as secular, including the running of weaving workshops and papyrus-making sheds, which brought in additional wealth; the temples also produced their own oil (for lamps) and linen, including the so-called royal linen or *byssos*, with its fine chiffon-like weave. Money was also made through the sale of oracles and dream interpretations and via the employment of temple notaries, the priestly scribes whose legal services could be purchased for a price. Temples also acted as health centres where priestly doctors combined science with the arts of magic in a bid to cure everything from scorpion stings to bad dreams – there was no distinction between science and theology, and so the temple was a fitting place to practise both. Egypt's intellectual heritage could be sought out in the temple libraries, for the tradition of scholar priests was a very old one; papyrus rolls on such subjects as onomastics, theology, literary theory, geography, architecture, law and medicine were available for consultation, and in the Ptolemaic period it became customary to translate classical Egyptian texts (some dating back to the Old Kingdom, *c.* 2700–2200 BCE) into the more user-friendly Demotic and even into Greek.

Egyptian state religion was completely concentrated in the temples, which were known as *hwt-ntrw*, 'Mansions of the Gods'. The temples were giant factories of faith whose mechanisms were powered by the endless cycle of daily ritual, prayer and offerings; they spewed out enough spiritual energy to keep cosmic chaos (*isfit*) at bay by engulfing the world in a fragile bubble of divine harmony (*ma'at*). Without the temples, Egypt and the whole world would quickly be reclaimed by the pandemonium that had existed at the beginning of time, before the gods brought orderliness to the universe. The realm of the dead (which lay beneath the earth), the primal waters of Nun (waters above and waters below, which fell as rain and rose as the Nile flooded), and the deserts that stretched for many miles on both sides of the cultivated Nile Valley were the realms of the uncivilized and the demonic, and they had to be kept tamed and held at a safe distance. This is why all Egyptian temples were surrounded by enormously thick and towering whitewashed mud-brick walls, a barrier against bedlam. The clean, serene, shady and cool Mansions of the Gods stood in vivid contrast to the filthy, noisy, hot and crowded streets of the urban sprawl beyond their sacred enclosures.

Each and every day the gods renewed the act of the first creation with the splendour of the sunrise, thereby affirming their power over the dark terrors of the night; it was because of the gods that the moon followed its monthly cycle, and only because of the gods did the Nile's waters spill out each year onto the parched land to bring forth renewed life and vitality to the earth. To maintain the goodwill of the gods and to ensure their cooperation in the preservation of the universe, daily cult services (prayers, sacrifices and all other rituals) was offered to them. It was believed that the gods resided within the temples, housed there completely at the expense of the state. Each day the images of stone, wood or precious metals in which their spirits were thought to be present were clothed, fed, perfumed and entertained by cohorts of religious specialists – the shaved, circumcised, ritually purified priests who knew all the apposite hymns and incantations, the specific prayers and correct offering formulae, and the precise rituals of each liturgy. Detail mattered. And carved into the temple walls were countless images of pharaohs and queens, Egypt's chief priests and priestesses, performing holy rituals in perpetuity as an added security lest the daily rites should unexpectedly stop and, with the cessation of cult service, the gods abandon their holy mansions. If they did, then anarchy would surely return to Egypt.

The clerical elite worked closely with the Ptolemaic monarchs, negotiating with them when necessary and even overruling them at times so that the temples remained powerful. For their part, Ptolemaic kings usually cooperated with the clergy and were happy to embrace their authority, as when, for instance, they were crowned by the High Priests of Ptah at Memphis or participated in the yearly priestly synod at Alexandria, Memphis or Canopus, at which decrees were drawn up and issued. The Ptolemies undertook massive temple rebuilding programmes to legitimize their rule; under this dynasty native Egyptian society became more temple-centred than ever. Today's best-preserved temples, such as Edfu, Dendera, Kom Ombo and Esna, were constructed during the Ptolemaic age. As demonstrated by the cartouches on the buildings, almost every Ptolemy was responsible for temple construction or decoration, and the kings are shown in countless ritual scenes, often in the company of their consorts. One significant addition to temples built in this period, though, was the substantial increase of hieroglyphic signs displayed on the walls: the so-called Ptolemaic Hieroglyphs took the ancient script and cryptography to new heights of sophistication by embellishing, augmenting and elaborating on the ancient sign-system. A distinct Ptolemaic style developed in hieroglyphic epigraphy: signs were carved in high-relief with a rounded three-dimensionality which cast deep shadows on stone, thereby almost freeing the myriad birds, snakes, arms and legs, rivers, crocodiles and sunbursts from the stone.

As well as the new-builds, some older pharaonic temples were beautified or added to by the Ptolemaic rulers: an eye-catching addition to the huge Karnak temple complex, for instance, is the elegant gateway or *propylon* constructed at the Khonsu temple by Ptolemy III and named for him as the Euergetes Gate. It towers overhead and every inch of space is taken up with sacramental scenes of the pharaoh in adoration of the gods, for the gate was a place for petitioners to assemble and swear oaths and hear edicts pronounced. Not all pharaonic temples were still in use in the Ptolemaic era though, and some had already become ruins. The great Theban mortuary temples of the New Kingdom pharaohs, built to ensure the continuance of their worship long after death, had largely been abandoned by the Ptolemaic age, and some were used for less august purposes – the mortuary temple (and military camp) of Ramses III at Medinet Habu, for instance, was used as an administrative centre, and at Dier el-Bahri the ancient cult centre of Hathor was reused as a healing sanctuary with shrines to the popular curative gods Amenhotep, son of Hapu, Imhotep and the Greek Asclepius.

In the Greek cities of Egypt there were temples and cults for Hellenic or Hellenized deities, following the traditional norms of the Greek world. The same was true in the Egyptian *chora* ('countryside'): an impressive classical sanctuary has been unearthed at Hermopolis Magna (Egyptian, Khemenu; modern el-Ashmunein), for instance, which is located close to the Nile some 450 kilometres south of Alexandria, at the point where the river meets the Delta. It is one of the few Greek-style buildings to have survived outside of Alexandria itself. A Greek dedicatory inscription on a Doric-style architrave – the lintel or beam that rests on the capitals of columns – found there announces that Greek military settlers dedicated statues, a shrine and ritual equipment in the enclosure, and the temple's portico and the foundations of the building reveal that it had a fine colonnaded courtyard decorated in both the Ionic and Corinthian orders. An assembly hall for the priests and a ceremonial entranceway dedicated to Hermes has been identified too. Any number of temples and sanctuaries of this type, usually very modest in scale, were established in the *chora* in honour of the Olympian deities or the myriad lesser Greek gods. In the villages of the fertile Fayum region (a northern region of Egypt known for the abundance of plant life), for example, we find evidence of temples dedicated to Zeus, Demeter, Hera, Aphrodite, Dionysus and the Divine Twins (Dioskouroi) Castor and Pollux. The priests and priestesses who performed the temple rituals were not bound by the same strict rules as their Egyptian counterparts – they did not need to completely shave their bodies, for instance – for a Greek priesthood was a public office and could be held by a citizen for a limited period.

The temple at Hermopolis Magna provides an interesting example of the processes of syncretism in the Ptolemaic kingdom, for long before its transformation into a Greek religious sanctuary it had enjoyed a distinguished history as one of the chief cult centres of the ibis- or baboon-headed Thoth, the Egyptian god of science, learning, writing and – by extension – the patron deity of scribes and administrators. A temple to the Thoth had been constructed there during the New Kingdom (*c.* 1570–*c.* 1069 BCE) by Amenhotep III and Ramses II, and additions to it had been made in the XX Dynasty (1189–1077 BCE). When the Ptolemies began to build their Hellenic-style temple in the city, they did so by locating it near to the original pharaonic structure; both constructions were then encircled by a wall of mud brick, bringing unity to the two buildings. The Ptolemies identified the Egyptian Thoth with the Greek god Hermes, the divine messenger, and at Hermopolis Magna the god was harmoniously worshipped in his two forms – Hellenic and Egyptian – and two types of ritual were performed in his honour. To all intents and purposes, and in spite of their divergent mythologies and theologies, Thoth and Hermes morphed easily into one deity whilst maintaining their separate ethnic identities. There was no one-upmanship at the temple complex and no priesthood claimed superiority for one god over the other, so Thoth-Hermes was worshipped as 'twice greatest' of the gods.

*

Religious cults became the obvious answer to the perplexing question of how to bring the two cultures of Egypt together. The Greeks and Egyptians came to identify their respective deities in the other's religion: besides Hermes' affiliation with Thoth, Apollo was seen as Horus, Athene as Neith, and Zeus as Amun. Over time the Greeks influenced the Egyptians, and the Egyptians inspired the Greeks, and new religious cults emerged throughout Egypt which were perfectly synchronous.

Ptolemaic Egypt might be best thought of as 'a tale of two cultures' brought together by a Greek dynasty that used religious cults and temples as tools to legitimize its rule. The founder of the dynasty, Ptolemy I Soter, aided by a Hellenized Egyptian priest named Manetho, had had the foresight to create a new cult that embodied Egyptian and Greek deities in one godhead: Serapis. This new composite god embodied the characteristics of two of Egypt's most ancient and revered gods – Osiris, the fertile god of resurrection, and Apis, a sacred bull which was thought to be the living incarnation of the creator god, Ptah of Memphis. In the first

phase of Greek settlement in Egypt, the Greek god Hades, king of
the dead, had been associated with Osiris, god of the afterlife and
of the underworld; therefore the Egyptians had very little difficulty accepting Hades. But Hades quickly became directly linked
to the Apis bull too, as Osiris-Apis, or Serapis, a new deity who was
worshipped in the form of a bull wearing a sun disk and uraeus
(cobra) on its head, or else was visualized in anthropomorphic
form as a man wearing a Greek-style robe with Greek hairstyle and
full beard and a tall corn modius (basket) balanced on his head.
The modius was a symbol of abundance and fertility which, combined with the deity's afterlife associations, linked Serapis with
the concept of transformation, both in life and after death. It was
the Greek court sculptor Bryaxis, around 350 BCE, who designed
the first huge seated statue of the god – soon to become famous
throughout the Greek-speaking world. Before too long, Serapis
was also given the heavenly authority of Zeus, the great Greek god
of the cosmos, and he was therefore understood as 'Lord of All'
– having authority over everything from the underworld to the
ethereal realm of the gods in the sky. The sun god Helios, the wine
god Dionysus and Asclepius, god of healing, all added aspects of
their respective cults to the composite figure of Serapis so that the
new deity emerged as (in theory) a thoroughly Egypto-Hellenistic
god who personified divine majesty, the sun, fertility, the underworld, the afterlife, as well as healing. The mythology of Serapis
was the *mythos* of his underlying deities, but the aspects of afterlife
and fertility were always primary to his nature.

The creation of Serapis was a masterpiece of Ptolemaic state-
craft because, theoretically at least, it reconciled the Egyptians to
the fact that they were now ruled by a dynasty of Macedonian
kings. Serapis was intended to be, in Plutarch's words, 'god of
all peoples in common', and temples dedicated to Serapis were
constructed throughout Egypt, all seemingly based on his central
cult temple, the Serapeum of Alexandria, the largest and most
magnificent of all the temples in the city. Of course, Serapis was
a creation of the establishment, and the deity was soon accorded
particular importance by Ptolemaic bureaucrats, who saw him as

a god who could, if propitiated properly, give them a leg-up on the promotional ladder.

In pharaonic religious thought, Isis (Aset or Eset – 'the throne'-for the Egyptians) was the wife and sister of Osiris and the mother of Horus. She was famous for searching for and reassembling Osiris' body parts of Osiris after he had been murdered and hacked to pieces by his brother Seth, and it is from this supreme act of skill that she became associated with healing and magic. Her religious syncretism into the Greco-Roman world was particularly success-ful as she took on roles ascribed to many classical goddesses. In the Ptolemaic period, Isis became the goddess of wisdom, a lunar deity, a solar goddess, overseer of seas and sailors, goddess of magic, and much more. The full panoply of her titles and attributes is provided by Apuleius in his *Asinus aureus* (*The Golden Ass*), the only Latin novel to survive in its entirety from antiquity. In the final portion of the story, the protagonist of the novel, Lucius, is startled to witness an epiphany of the goddess Isis, who initiates him into her mysteries by revealing to him her multifaceted identity:

> I am the mother of the universe, mistress of all the elements, first born of the ages, highest of the gods, queen of the shades, first of those who dwell in heaven, representing in one shape all the gods and goddesses. My will controls the shining heights of heaven, the health-giving sea-winds, and the mournful silence of hell; the entire world worships my single godhead in a thousand shapes, with diverse rites, and under many different names. The Phrygians, first-born of mankind, call me the Mother of the gods; the native Athenians call me Minerva; the island-dwelling Cypriots, Venus; the archer Cretans, Diana; the triple-tongued Sicilians, Proserpine; the ancient Eleusinians, Ceres; some call me Juno, some Bellona, others Hecate . . . but the Egyptians, who excel in ancient learning, honour me with worship which is mine alone and call me by my true name: Queen Isis.

Accordingly, artists represented the goddess in numerous forms: when depicted in Egyptian-style as a beautiful woman she wore a headdress borrowed from the goddess Hathor, consisting of two cow horns enveloping a solar disk; sometimes a version with two additional falcon feathers was worn by the goddess. Isis could also appear in Egyptian art as a bird (usually a kite), a cat, a cow or a cobra, depending on the goddess with whom she was associated at any given sanctuary. But Hellenistic representations of Isis were common too, and in the Greek style she was shown wearing a long, fringed mantle tied with a knot between her breasts (the 'Isis Knot'). Her hair was worn in long corkscrew curls and she was often depicted holding a *sistrum* or sacred rattle, a percussion instrument frequently employed in her cult worship. Her cult quickly spread throughout the Mediterranean world, largely carried there by Egyptian sailors, and as early as 333 BCE a temple to Isis was built at Piraeus, Athens' chief port. Over the next six centuries, Isis temples, shrines and statues were to be found in every corner of the known earth and formed the basis for the cult of Mary in early Christianity.

Under the Ptolemaic policy of religious syncretism, Isis became the wife of Serapis and they appeared together in iconography as symbolic of a royal family (although this did not dislodge Osiris from mythology and ritual). In fact, this union eventually became celebrated as the so-called Alexandrian Divine Triad, composed of Serapis, Isis and Harpocrates. The Alexandrian triad was without doubt the focal point of Ptolemaic religious identity.

Harpocrates was the Greek interpretation of the Egyptian god Harpa-Khruti ('Horus the Child'), who was commonly depicted as a very young boy with a finger held to his chin, a gesture of naive infancy. This gesture actually had a convenient dual meaning: in Egypt it symbolized childhood but in Greece it was understood to be a hush for silence, and as such, Harpocrates became a favourite deity of the mystic schools of philosophy. Already known in the magical Pyramid Texts (*c.* 2300 BCE) as 'the child with the finger in his mouth', in the Ptolemaic era Harpocrates was frequently depicted sitting on top of a lotus blossom or else in the lap of his mother, Isis. His relationship to his parents was stressed through two alternative names applied to him: Horus-im-mut-ef ('Horus

Pillar of His Mother') and Har-nedj-it-ef ('Horus the Saviour of his Father'). Divine triads – a family group based on the criteria of fertility, abundance or royal legitimacy and succession, usually depicted as a god-father, a mother-goddess and a god-son – were common in the pantheon of ancient Egyptian gods and were often regarded as combining the concepts and the symbolism of 'three' and 'one'.

Alongside the Alexandrian triad of Serapis, Isis and Harpocrates, there were other divine triads: Osiris, Isis and Horus at Abydos; Ptah, Sekhmet and Nefertum at Memphis; Amun, Mut and Khonsu at Karnak; Atum, Bastet and Horhek at Bubastis; Hathor, Horus and Ihy at the important Ptolemaic temple of Dendera; and at the other great Ptolemaic temple of Edfu it was Horus, Hathor and Harsomtus who were praised as the great father, mother and son. Through these 'pseudo-families', the mythological and theological complexities of pharaonic religious thought were articulated because, in Egypt, the triad was a way to connect plurality and unity. The number three was not only a numeral for the Egyptians, it also signified the indefinite plural. This is apparent, for instance, in hieroglyphic writing: to express the plural, an ideogram could be repeated three times or else three strokes could be placed after a sign indicating a noun. In other words, the number three represented infinity. As the family unit was so important in Egyptian society, Egyptian theologians made use of the family to solve the problems of divine unity and plurality and therefore divine triads always contained *one* child and no more. The child represented the pharaoh himself, for irrespective of what divine guise he took – Horus, Nefertum or Ihy – pharaoh was the only son of all the gods.

The extent of a pharaoh's divinity is much debated but it is generally reckoned by scholars that if the pharaoh was a god, then he was a god who could die (a serious limitation, it might be thought, when it comes to divinity). The Egyptians referred to their king as *netjer* or 'god', but while a deity like Osiris or Amun was *netjer aa*, 'a great god', pharaoh was *netjer nefer*, 'the good god'. The distinction was important. A king was not omniscient or omnipotent – he could not work miracles, he was as prone to human frailties and faults as any other mortal, and his fallibility was clear to see when he was stuck by illness or disease, when he aged, weakened and inevitably expired. His body died, certainly, but it was believed that his soul returned to the gods. However, the kingship carried on for ever, passing from one ruler to the next, unchanging in nature, generation on generation. In this way, the divine nature of the monarchy, with all its supernatural powers, was seen to be real.

In effect, Egyptian kingship was divided into three components or parts: the person of the mortal reigning king; the kingship of the reigning king; and the ultimate godhead, represented by the divine Horus as the original Egyptian sun god. Horus transferred his powers to the king, who ruled as his earthbound deputy and the ritual of the coronation, when the pharaoh was acclaimed as Lord of the Two Lands, was the moment when the pharaoh partook of that divinity, when the mortal man became imbued with a divine energy – the royal *ka* or spirit – and occupied the eternal office of monarchy, the *nesu*, for the rest of his earthly days. From this perspective, it would appear that it was not the king who was honoured as a god but rather that the incarnate power of the gods was honoured in the king. The Egyptians provided a definition of what they considered the king's main tasks to be in a text which is generally known as the 'cult-theological tract'; it offers up the following expectations:

> The sun-god has appointed the King on the earth of the living
>   for all eternity
> so that he may judge humans and satisfy the gods,
> so that he may create truth and destroy falsehood.
> He gives the gods sacrificial food,
> invocational sacrifices to those who have become transfigured.
> The name of the King is in heaven the same as [that of] the
>   sun-god,
> his life is in his heart's joy as [is that of] Horus of the Horizon.
> The nobles rejoice when they see him,
> his subjects pay homage to him in his shape of a young man.

The dual nature of the pharaoh, which saw him as both mortal and divine, was not thought of as a flaw by the Egyptians, whose theological systems contained many such conundrums and contradictions (or 'mysteries', if one prefers). The theological underpinning of divine kingship was bolstered in the New Kingdom when a series of pharaohs began to stress that the legitimacy of their rule was ordained by divine origin. They created a political theology of divine birth – nothing less than an immaculate conception – which stressed that the pharaoh was not the child of the previous ruler and his wife but rather was the fruit of a union between the earlier pharaoh's wife and a god. To give legitimacy to her somewhat tenuous hold on the throne, the notorious Queen Hatshepsut (c. 1478–1458 BCE) had propagated this nativity story on the walls of her funerary temple at Deir-el Bahri, and the mighty King Amenhotep III (c. 1386–1349 BCE), who had no such worries about his legitimacy, had the same birth-cycle story carved onto the walls of the temple of Luxor. The 'Conception of Horus', as the tale is known, celebrates the occasion when the king's mother, Mutemwiya, is said to have conceived her child by the god Amun, who had visited her in her bedchamber, disguised as her husband, the pharaoh Thutmose IV. Amun and the mortal mother of Amenhotep III sit close together atop a hieroglyph depicting the sky; their knees touch, their hands clasp, their eyes meet. Tenderly, Amun lifts his hand to touch Mutemwiya's face, as if he were offering her the heady perfume of a lotus blossom. Held aloft by two goddesses, Serket and Neith, the feet of the divine couple never touch the ground. The queen is quite taken aback by Amun's presence in her bed and ecstatically cries out, 'How great is your power! How perfect you are! How hidden are the plans which you make! How contented is your heart at my body! Your dew is in all my limbs!' The postcoital Mutemwiya later notes how 'the majesty of this god has done with me all that he willed'. Later, in the XIX Dynasty (1292–1189 BCE), Ramses the Great repeated the scenes in his mortuary temple on the Nile's west bank at Thebes, in the fabled Ramesseum, where his much-honoured mother, Tuya, is shown enjoying the privileged encounter with

the lusty god. The underlying theology of the divine birth of the
king attained particular traction under the Ptolemies, who quickly
saw and harnessed its propagandistic opportunities. In numerous
small temple-like structures known as 'birth-houses' the rulers of
foreign blood were promoted as pharaohs who were the offspring
of the Egyptian gods.

Throughout Egypt, religious cults were established where the
Greek rulers were worshipped as Egyptian gods. Directions for the
creation of royal divine cults can be found in numerous priestly
decrees and temple reliefs, and these sources also describe the creation of cult statues of the ruler, sculpted images through which
they could be worshipped as gods. The royal cult focused on the
dynasty as a whole and integrated the Ptolemies as a ruling house
into the traditions of their adopted country, designating them as
the defenders and protectors of Egypt.

The first ruler to be deified (crucially, with state support) was
Queen Arsinoë II, sister-wife of Ptolemy II, who was described in
inscriptions in Egyptian temples as the Brother-Loving Goddess, a
title clearly modelled on her Greek epithet Philadelphus, 'Brother-Loving'. Ptolemy II established Arsinoë's cult following her
death, as recorded on several Egyptian stelae, the texts of which
reveal that some of the support from the priestly class came from
Ptolemy's reform of the tax on vineyards and orchards, which was
meant to favour Egyptian temples hosting the cult of Arsinoë, thus
incentivizing the support of the cult itself. Arsinoë had her special
temple at Alexandria, in which she was identified with Aphrodite
– the first instance of the practice of identifying a deified human
with one or other of the Greco-Roman gods.

A more formal state-sponsored ruler cult developed during the
reign of Ptolemy III and Berenice II, who began to honour their
dead predecessors as though they were gods. Some large sculpted
friezes, like one at the Ptolemaic temple at Tod near Thebes, portrayed the entire dynastic line-up as god-kings and god-queens,
and new temples were commissioned to enhance the divinity of
the house, with festivals established in order to celebrate dynastic
figures. In honour of the deified Ptolemy I Soter, for instance, a

festival with games was instituted at Alexandria – the Ptolemaeia. The festival was a penteteric one (it took place, like the Olympic Games, every five years) and, as in the case of the great games of Greece, envoys (*theōroi*) were sent to it by Greek city-states overseas, and athletes came from many Greek-speaking lands to compete there. With the official deification of the rulers also came the establishment of a priesthood for their worship, and their names began to appear in the 'Royal Oath' – a vow prescribed for legal proceedings throughout Egypt. The Royal Oath enumerated all the kings of the house, beginning with the reigning one: 'I swear by King Ptolemy [V],' reads one such oath, 'son of Ptolemy [IV] and Arsinoë [III], Father-Loving Gods, and by the Father-Loving Gods, and by the Brother-and-Sister Gods, and by the Benefactor Gods, and by the Saviour Gods, and by Serapis and by Isis and by all the other gods.'

To further strengthen their projection of divinity, the Ptolemies also forcefully associated themselves with the divine figure of Alexander the Great, whose body lay within the Sema at Alexandria, where it was tended by a cohort of priests who carried out daily rituals of worship in his honour. In 283 BCE, statues of the deified 'Saviour Gods' Ptolemy I Soter and Berenice I were installed in the Sema alongside Alexander, and the chief priest of the Alexander cult took over the rites for the deified Ptolemies as well. With this gesture, the Ptolemies underlined the superior position of Alexander and their own subordination to him as 'temple-sharing gods' (*synnanoi theoi*). Alexander remained the main recipient of rituals and sacrifices, but the Ptolemies partook in them too, if from the sideline. The concept of 'temple-sharing gods' was further developed under Ptolemy IV Philopator, who moved the cremated remains of the Ptolemies and their consorts to the Sema. In death, the Cleopatras literally shared a space with the great Alexander himself.

4

A Little Apocalypse

Early in her tenure as Egypt's queen, Cleopatra Syra and her husband, Ptolemy V, faced a crisis: a great rebellion in the Thebaid in Upper Egypt. Taking advantage of the youth of the rulers, a rival pharaoh suddenly appeared in Thebes, around 199 BCE. His name – chosen no doubt for its political implications – was Hor-wen-nefer (Greek, Haronnophris). The component 'wen-nefer' was an epithet of the god Osiris, and by adopting it into his royal name, Hor-wen-nefer aimed to advertise loud and clear that he was under the protection of Osiris, a god intimately linked to the richly fertile 'Black Land' of Egypt's Nile Valley. In addition, Hor-wen-nefer adopted the title 'Beloved of Amun-Re, King of the Gods' as his epithet, which was intended to set him apart from the young Ptolemy V, whose titulature proclaimed him to be the 'Beloved of Ptah'. By evoking the name of Amun of Thebes and putting it in sharp contrast to Ptolemy's affiliation to Ptah of Memphis (and to the Memphite priesthood), Hor-wen-nefer was creating a sharp south–north divide; he was splitting the kingdom. His use of the epithet 'Beloved of Amun' strongly suggests that he had co-opted the powerful Amun priesthood to his cause and, indeed, contracts dated by his name were explicitly written 'in the name of the priests of Amun'. We do not know if Hor-wen-nefer was welcomed, tolerated or actively supported by the priests of Amun, and it is possible that priestly circles composed of different families might have seen him in different ways and had diverse reasons for supporting him. Certainly, they allowed Thebes to become Hor-wen-nefer's main power centre – a limestone tablet found at Karnak states that the new king had his 'palace' there. But he was quickly recognized as pharaoh in other places as well: in Pathrys, to the south, where he gained the support of local priests; in Koptos in middle Egypt; and even as far as Abydos, the great cult centre of Osiris himself, some 200 miles from Thebes.

The first major attack of the Great Revolt was not against a military installation or an administrative position but on the Ptolemaic temple of Horus at Edfu, deep in Upper Egypt, near one of the main departure points for expeditions to the Red Sea coast. Even though Edfu was home to soldiers and served as a staging point for military (and royal hunting) expeditions, rebel attacks succeeded in shutting down construction of the temple. In addition, active construction work at the temple of Philae was abandoned. Empty of workers, it was plundered and damaged; this was also the case at the Ptolemaic temple of Montu at Medamoud, near Thebes.

Hor-wen-nefer sensed that his power was growing and that his campaign to create a new state based on the old pre-Ptolemaic order was falling into place. His was no fly-by-night fantasy but a campaign with a genuine political aim: the secession of Upper Egypt from foreign rule. Feeling secure in his success, Hor-wen-nefer changed his regnal name to Ankh-wen-nefer (Greek, Channophosis), 'May Osiris-Onnofris Live', a clear projection of his intended longevity. As far as he was concerned, Ptolemaic rule was in retreat and Upper Egypt was once more in Egyptian hands. Legal records were destroyed and the hated tax system was cancelled, and thousands of Greeks were driven from their homes, many fleeing to the security of the Delta. The city of Ptolemais was overrun by rebels.

One papyrus reports a series of linked assaults in the region of Mouchis, a village situated on the cusp of Upper Egypt and the Fayum in the north-west of the country. There, an Egyptian official named Peteminos was part of an armed 'Neighbourhood Watch' that patrolled the village every night to keep homes and lands safe from rebel attacks. One evening, at dusk, they came across a wounded royal farmer. He told them he had been assaulted on the road next to the town's main canal. There they found another wounded farmer. But neither man admitted to knowing who assaulted them, and by the time a crowd had gathered, tempers were beginning to flare and some accused the patrolling party of attacking the two farmers. The next morning, however, some of the villagers gave Peteminos the names of the attackers: four young men from the same village. By then, the suspects had already escaped, aided and abetted no doubt by the villagers who had bought time for the attackers before naming them. The assault on the two farmers at Mouchis was probably a typical form of insurgent violence during the revolt. Rebels ambushed isolated farmers in their fields (using canals and dikes for cover), and while these types of attacks appear indiscriminate, in actuality they contributed in no small way toward the insurgents' goals of instilling fear in the agents of the Ptolemaic regime and securing the compliance of Egyptian civilians. In another papyrus document, this time from Middle Egypt, some 300 miles north of Thebes, an unnamed Greek recounts the events of a night-time assault on a village patrol:

> On the night of the new moon the Egyptians ambushed the guards and pursued them back to the fort. Because the guards had been warned [that an attack might occur,] the [Egyptians] left off attacking the fort and instead attacked the houses just opposite it. They brought a siege device up to the house of Nechthenibis, which lies along the road. But when a part of the palisade threatened to crash down on them, they made their retreat. But know this: the Egyptians are not guarding the village as we told them to, because Kallias is not communicating [orders to them], nor is he submitting reports to us.

The Greek who penned this document trusted neither the fidelity nor the self-control of the local Egyptians, and he was clearly frustrated with the performance of the man named Kallias, whose job it was to act as a liaison between the self-defence forces of the locals and the military command in the region. As at Mouchis, the loyalty of the Egyptian villagers was clearly in question.

Seated in the calm of Alexandria, Ptolemy V, Cleopatra Syra and the royal advisors read the intelligence which trickled in from the south and realized that the time to act had come. Putting up with the presence of an alternative pharaoh in Thebes would have irredeemably undermined Ptolemaic legitimacy in the eyes of their Egyptian subjects, and further independence movements would no doubt have flourished, even in the north. Five Ptolemaic pharaohs had sat on Egypt's throne, but the dynasty was far from being universally popular throughout the country and it was only a matter of time before all of Egypt was attempting to break free of Greek rule. To counter this, Ptolemy V commanded his Greek troops to march south from Memphis and other bases in the Fayum to stop further insurgency before it was too late. Greek troops poured into Upper Egypt, quickly recapturing Ptolemais and laying siege to Abydos, which fell in due course. What occurred at Koptos is known only from a single grave epitaph commissioned for a Greek commander and his son, just two of the many Ptolemaic casualties in this impressive show of force against the rebels. Allowing for some epic exaggeration, the funerary poem (written in the style of epic Homeric verse) insists that the father and son 'fell during a mighty battle' and had put up a 'furious struggle' after 'striking down innumerable foes'.

Around 187 BCE, the Greek troops pressed onwards to Thebes, the centre of native discontent. The Egyptian freedom fighters soon became desperate as Greek troops swarmed through the city and quickly took it back for King Ptolemy. Even with Thebes recaptured, Ankh-wen-nefer would not give up and, daringly, he led his fighters north using desert routes until they entered the Greek-controlled province of Lycopolis (Egyptian, Sauty), over 200 miles north of Thebes. Their sole purpose was to cause as much death and destruction as they could. By plundering towns, burning houses and farms, slaughtering cattle and generally terrifying the local population, Ankh-wen-nefer aimed to isolate the Ptolemaic troops occupying the Thebaid, cut off their communications with Alexandria and deprive them of their supplies. Ankh-wen-nefer's bold campaign of terror was remarkably successful and before too long the Greek soldiers were compelled to abandon Thebes and move south to take sanctuary and find supplies in Aswan, where there was a Greek garrison that had managed to keep out of the turmoil in the Thebaid. With the Greek soldiers cowering in Aswan, the freedom fighters took back command of Thebes.

Ptolemy V now set the entire weight of his military at destroying the rebels. Led by General Komanos, tens of thousands of soldiers pushed south, retaking Thebes and forcing Ankh-wen-nefer to head towards Aswan, where he was forced to deal with the Ptolemaic troops stationed in the garrison there. Ankh-wen-nefer managed to co-opt some support from Nubia (modern Ethiopia), but he was eventually overpowered by the Ptolemaic army. The Egyptians were finally defeated on 27 August 186 BCE in what was, astonishingly, the only pitched battle of the entire revolt. Ankh-wen-nefer was apprehended and jailed, although the priests of Amun managed to persuade Ptolemy V to keep the traitor alive, arguing (with some common sense) that to execute him would turn him into a martyr for the independence movement, an outcome to be avoided at all costs. Instead, the priests recommended that Ankh-wen-nefer be declared a criminal in the eyes of the gods but should be pardoned by royal law. Ptolemy had to dig deep within himself to find the heart to accept the priests' advice, but forgive Ankh-wen-nefer he did (although the Egyptian would-be usurper curiously disappears from the sources at this point, which might suggest he met an unfortunate end anyway). On 9 October 186 BCE, Ptolemy V and Cleopatra Syra issued an amnesty decree, instructing all fugitives to return to their homes and fields:

> King Ptolemy and Queen Cleopatra proclaim an amnesty to all their subjects by the *epistatai* [superintendents] of the policemen or the chief policemen or the other officials, because they have been found guilty of theft or have been

subject to other accusations, they shall return to their own homes free from their charges, except those guilty of wilful murder or those who have plundered in temples, in other sanctuaries or in the storehouses of temples.

The Alexandrian administration, concerned as ever with the economy, held a public auction of land confiscated from the insurgents with the aspiration that the sooner lands were returned to profitable cultivation, the sooner would the taxes – which had dried up completely – flow again.

*

What was it that had caused such fierce animosity among Egyptians towards the Greeks? What was behind the Egyptian quest for independence? It would appear that the Ptolemies – who may well have sought, in theory, to promote a sense of unity between their Greek and Egyptian subjects – had little control over the lived realities of their contentious Greek and Egyptian subjects. The events of the Great Theban Rebellion (as it became known to scholars) reveal that, on the ground, ethnic tensions were rife.

While some scholars have portrayed Ptolemaic control of Egypt as relatively benign, it must be conceded that no occupation is without consequences. Under foreign occupation, a society is not autonomous because the occupying regime pervades every aspect of life and becomes the only context through which all decisions are made. The Egyptians had never been placid pushovers to any foreign invasion and rule, and had broken the shackles of occupation many times in their history; in the centuries before Alexander's conquest, they had fought against subjugation from Nubians, Assyrians and even the mighty Persians. Now that the Persians had been replaced by Greeks, the Egyptian instinct was simply to rid themselves of these latest colonialists too.

To the Egyptian mind, the colonizing Greeks lived a lifestyle contradictory to 'god-fearing' behaviour; they found the Greeks to be immoral, debased, overconfident and mutable. The Egyptians moreover claimed a natural cultural supremacy over the Greeks and maintained that since Egypt had been the place of origin of all things – arts and crafts, law and government, agriculture and animal husbandry, rational thought, humanity (in short, civilization itself) – Greek 'civilization' was a mere also-ran, a pretentious pretender and a latecomer. An especially potent form of anti-Hellenism was directed at the Greek gods, who were thought to be pale imitations of the Egyptian originals, and even the worship of the god Serapis, purposefully created to unite the Greek and Egyptian population, was predominantly a Greek cult. Even though the deity was promoted as the *kosmokrator* – 'ruler of the whole world' – the Egyptians took virtually no interest at all in the new god or his cult. In fact, the abundant dedications to Serapis which have come to light through archaeological excavations were made almost entirely by Greek worshippers, which confirms that, despite all the Ptolemaic spin of unity and synchronism, the cult of Serapis was seen as principally a Greek invention for the Greek population. As a means of uniting the peoples along the Nile, the veneration of Serapis was a miserable failure. In fact, the Egyptian priests of the traditional temples did all they could to block the worship of Serapis; they were always sensitive to competition, and it is easy to imagine how the priests of Ptah in Memphis or of Amun in Karnak looked askance at the creation of a 'deity' hastily thrown together on the whim of a foreign king. It is probably for this reason that the Ptolemaic authorities began to couple Serapis with Isis, who never lost her loyal Egyptian fan base, and brought to the worship of Serapis some much-needed Egyptian authenticity.

One of the most important Ptolemaic-period texts to have survived antiquity is known as the 'Demotic Chronicle' (although 'Oracle' would be a more appropriate term, given the tone of the work). It is an eccentric and bewildering manuscript, recording a series of enigmatic prophecies and divine judgements against Egypt's foreign rulers – those of the past (the foreign pharaohs of the XXVI dynasty as well as the Persians) and of the present (the Greek Ptolemies). The utterances are reminiscent of the famous scene from the biblical Book of Daniel where, at a banquet held by Prince Belshazzar of Babylon, a mysterious text appeared on the palace wall in supernatural circumstances; interpreting it proved too difficult for the court scholars and so an external expert (the prophet Daniel himself) was consulted about the meaning of the mysterious writing. Making sense of the 'Demotic Chronicle' is, like interpreting the intriguing otherworldly script which appeared at Belshazzar's feast, very problematic. But what does stand out from the content of the text is the abhorrence which the Egyptians had for any foreign rulers who had irreligiously taken power in the Two Lands. Because of their many sins (supplanting national god-kings, interfering with Egypt's religious festivals, and causing want and suffering amongst the people), the Chronicle stresses that the foreigners will one day be defeated and expelled from Egypt by an Egyptian-born hero or messiah-figure who will arise to champion the land. The latter part of this mystifying text – consisting of cryptic sayings and equally enigmatic interpretations – reads (in abbreviated form) like this:

> They are foreigners.
> Our sea and our land are full of tears.
> Time will bring them, the foreigners.
> The Egyptians are robbed.
> People are fallen into slaughter.
> They are coming to Egypt.
> They are the foreigners on the east and the west of the land.
> They are coming to Egypt . . .
> The foreigners will be allowed to come into all of Egypt to be
>   masters of Egypt . . .
> It is the Greeks, who will come to Egypt. They will rule Egypt
>   for a long time.
> May the hero live.
> He will be the ruler in the specified time.

A second Ptolemaic Egyptian text confirms the anti-Greek sentiment that was clearly gripping much of the native population; it is known as the 'Oracle of the Potter' or, more academically, the Rainer Papyrus and it enjoyed great popularity with the Egyptians

of the time, who knew it as the 'Little Apocalypse'. Dated to around
180–130 BCE, it purports to be an ancient prophecy made by a
potter (perhaps the god Khnum, the 'divine potter') to a pharaoh
of the New Kingdom (1570–1069 BCE) named Amenhotep and
opens with a description of the wretched conditions which are
making Egypt suffer. In reality, the 'Oracle of the Potter' was the
invention of an anti-Greek Egyptian who was intent on presenting
his opposition to the Ptolemies in the guise of a prophecy made a
thousand years back in Egypt's history. It is a timely fraud, a piece
of biting anti-Greek rhetoric. It goes on to narrate how society has
become disordered under Greek rule and then turns its attention
to Alexandria, the cursed city of the foreign sovereigns:

> The belt-wearers [i.e., Greeks] being Typhonians [followers of
> the chaotic god Typhon, known to the Egyptians as Seth] are
> destroying [Egypt] . . . And because of that, Agathos Daimon
> [the snake-guardian of Alexandria] will abandon the city . . .
> and will enter Memphis, and the foreign city will be emptied.
> And these things will take place at the conclusion of the evils
> when the falling of the leaves occurs in the Egypt of the for-
> eigners. The city of the belt-wearers [Alexandria] will be laid
> waste as in my potter's furnace, because of the unlawful deeds
> which they executed in Egypt. The statues transferred there
> will return to Egypt. The city by the sea will become a drying
> place for fishermen because Agathos Daimon will have gone
> to Memphis, so that those who pass through will say: 'This
> city, in which every race of men dwelt, was all-nourishing,
> now it is barren'.

The oracle next prophesizes a cataclysmal end to foreign rule
and the resumption of native holy rituals through the coming
of a great pharaoh sent by the god Re. The sun will break forth
from the darkened skies, heralding the return of this indigenous
Egyptian king, placed on the throne by Isis herself, and under his
rulership the country will become fertile and prosperous again so
that even the dead will be restored to life to share in the bounty
of the emancipated Egypt.

The central theme of the 'Oracle of the Potter' is no different in essence from that of the 'Demotic Chronicle' – both works anticipate the annihilation of foreign rulers and the return of a legitimate pharaoh who will put an end to Egypt's desolation. The two apocalypses lament the state of Egypt, burdened under the weight of the Greeks, and suffering their illegitimate and unwanted presence. Pharaoh, the oracles proclaim, is dead.

*

Despite its adaptation to certain traditional features of Egyptian government, the Ptolemaic bureaucracy was overwhelmingly designed as a Greek institution. As such, it brought tangible privilege to the Greek population in Egypt, a populace that was mainly comprised of military personnel and immigrants. Although the occupying Greeks settled widely, most tended to live in villages in close – and uncomfortable – proximity to well-established Egyptian settlements. Into these villages and onto landholdings all over the country, the Ptolemies sent not only their own soldiers as a standing army (a reward in the form of land was a major inducement for Greeks abroad to sign up for military service) but also prisoners of war, a rag-bag of troublesome, discontented, former Greek mercenary soldiers who went to Egypt unwillingly and hated being there. The new frontiersmen were known as *cleruchs*, and although at first their settlement allocations were meant for a single lifetime only, gradually their land allotments became permanent and heritable. In effect, the occupying pioneers came to form a hereditary class of military reservists who were at hand to facilitate official government control. Moreover, soldiers occupying cleruchic land paid no rent, only certain taxes, and since most settlers did not work the land, preferring to live as absentee landlords in Alexandria or some other Hellenized district, they leased it to Egyptians. They could, however, be closely involved in the administration and economic exploitation of their farms. Besides the *cleruchs* and other career soldiers, there was an additional class of prosperous non-military Greeks, many of whom started out with no wealth at all but made considerable fortunes in the service of the king, his courtiers or his bureaucracy. They received fine houses in Alexandria, sometimes large estates in rural Egypt (and even the revenues of towns in Asia Minor), and they may have also received salaries or supported themselves from whatever money they could extract from the Egyptians they were dealing with.

Town mayors, civil servants and most of the policemen were Greeks, even in towns where the majority of residents were Egyptian, and it was not unheard of for them to be corrupt (blackmail was rife) and discriminatory toward the Egyptian peasantry. This mindset, founded as it was on an inbuilt Hellenic tendency towards prejudice, trickled down into other ranks of Greek settlers. The colonial culture as it developed in Ptolemaic Egypt exhibited classic Hellenistic imperial bigotry in all its complexity, for while Egyptian intellectual abilities were highly regarded by the Ptolemies, in terms of daily habits and beliefs, at best the Greeks thought the Egyptians infantile, at worst, barbaric.

The Ptolemaic administration deliberately privileged Greek rights and the Greek language to the detriment of Egyptian nationals. In the many documents that survive from the period it is possible to trace a sharp decline in Greek attitudes towards indigenous Egyptians: the period of apparent stability of the third century BCE, when Ptolemy I Soter and Ptolemy II Philadelphus established a harmonious *entente cordiale* between the native Egyptians and the new Greek-speaking immigrants who settled in the Delta, did not last. By the reign of Ptolemy IV the papyri tell of how second- and third-generation Greek settlers drew a sharp dividing line between Greeks and locals. The occupiers often acted above the law: one Greek man named Nikias, for instance, is recorded as appropriating a donkey belonging to Senkhons, an old Egyptian widow; the Greek woman Satronice seized the house and lands in Oxyrhyncus that belonged to the family of the Egyptian Petesouchus; a thug named Pyrrhichus wandered the streets of Tebtunis with his gang of Greek mates, breaking and entering Egyptian homes and thieving their property; a Greek called Lykos dammed up an irrigation ditch so that the Egyptian peasant Pasis had his water cut off. Greeks intimidated Egyptian witnesses who dared appear in the courts of law, although in 141 BCE a brave peasant managed to make a formal complaint that he had been tortured by a gang of Greeks – indeed, there were other cases of illegal torture of Egyptians held in prisons too. A surviving letter of complaint found in the 'Zenon Archives' illustrates the tensions between Greeks and natives. It was sent by an Egyptian to Zenon, a Greek who worked as a private secretary for Apollonios, an influential and very wealthy royal advisor residing in a large estate in the Delta town of Philadelphia. The letter catalogues the discrimination which the (unnamed) Egyptian had suffered at the hands of a couple of Philadelphian Greeks, Crotus and Jason, who employed him as a camel driver and, latterly, as a long-distance messenger, without paying him or even feeding him. His complaint pours forth into the brush of a scribe and onto the papyrus scroll that found its way into Zenon's hands:

> I am in distress summer and winter . . . They have treated me with contempt because I am an outsider. I therefore request you, if you please, to order them to give me what is owed to me and in future to pay me regularly so that I do not die of hunger because I do not know how to speak Greek.

The document contains clear evidence for the existence of Greek prejudice against non-Greeks, since whether the speaker's particular claims were true or not, he must presumably have believed that his employers would recognize a legitimate ground of appeal. The last sentence indicates that there could be practical disadvantages in not knowing Greek.

None of this antagonism was due to a conscious policy of the Ptolemaic rulers *per se*, for the Ptolemies did not wish to inflict a harsh regime on the Egyptians, but they did fail to curb the racist activities of those Greeks who felt nothing but contempt for the Egyptian peasantry. Not surprisingly, with increasing Egyptian resentment of the superior position of the Greeks, it was sometimes dangerous to be a lone Greek among a group of Egyptians, as one Greek man, Ptolemaios, explained in a letter of complaint he sent to a local magistrate, Dionysius. A group of Egyptians, he claimed, accosted him in a sanctuary of Serapis (of all places) and violently assaulted him. He names the perpetrators: Mys the clothing-seller, Psosnaus the yoke-bearer, Imouthes the baker, Harembasnis the grain-seller, Stotoetis the porter and Harchebis the bath-attendant, together with a few others. Ptolemaios rages at how,

> They came to the sanctuary ... holding stones in their hands, others sticks, and tried to force their way in, so that with this opportunity they might plunder the temple and kill me because I am a Greek, attacking me in concerted fashion. And when I made it to the door of the temple before them and shut it with a great crash, and ordered them to go away quietly, they did not depart; but they then struck Diphilos, one of the servants . . ., who showed his indignation at the way they were behaving in the sanctuary, robbing him outrageously and attacking him violently and beating him, so that their illegal violence was made obvious to everybody ... I ask you, therefore, if it seems good to you, to order them brought before you, so that they may get the proper punishment for all these things.

Financial gain was the engine that drove Ptolemaic domestic and foreign policy, and the main goal of the regime was to collect rent and tax revenues – primarily in the form of agricultural products and animals – over an extensive tract of land, from many people whose language – Egyptian – they did not understand and who functioned in a different social and economic system from that to which the Greeks themselves were accustomed. The Ptolemies relied on a diffuse yet elaborate bureaucracy, one that seemed at times to function independently of direct royal authority. In fact, it could be said that the monarchy existed *alongside* the bureaucracy rather than being part of it. Administrators in Ptolemaic Egypt received no regular salary, so individual bureaucrats garnered their rewards primarily through exploitation of their position. The woes of the Egyptian peasants were caused less by a rapacious monarchy than by a steadily growing army of bureaucrats lining their own pockets and then covering themselves against any complaints from superiors by draining the producers to meet expectations, even in the most difficult times. And there certainly were lean years. Poor Nile floods (perhaps, it has been argued, the consequence of far-off volcanic eruptions which had a severe impact on the climate) resulted in a series of devastatingly bad harvests, leading to one papyrus reporting that 'most of the farmers have died and the land has gone dry . . . When . . . [this] . . . was registered [as] "ownerless land" . . . survivors encroached upon the land . . . Their names are unknown since nobody pays taxes for this land to the treasury.'

What emerges from such sources is an appalling picture of profound discontent amongst the lower-class Egyptians, which was as much due to the racist attitudes of the Greek settlers as to the economic and legal pressures they were under. The climate catastrophes which plagued the land and led to genuine hunger compounded the restlessness. Together, these factors formed a perfect storm of unrest which blew its destructive way through the Thebaid.

*

'It is imperative,' wrote the chief financial official of Egypt, based in Alexandria, 'that each person dwelling in the country clearly perceive and believe that all such acts have been brought to an end and they are free from the bad conditions now past.' As far as this official was concerned, the Great Theban Rebellion was over: what was past was past, and Egypt should look now to the task at hand and to a prosperous future. But it proved difficult for the Ptolemaic regime to let go of what had occurred in Upper Egypt. The official Ptolemaic political-religious decrees of the time took every opportunity to cast the Theban insurgents in a negative light and the 'rebels' were castigated for being *asebeis* ('impious' men), 'plotters of secession' and 'makers of sedition'; they were also accused of 'committing great evils' against the temples. A decree posted at Philae temple in 186 BCE, at the conclusion of the revolt, called the 'rebels' enemies of the gods and charged them with a list of impious, misanthropic and seditious crimes:

They desecrated the temples and defaced the divine statues. They molested the priests and suppressed the offerings on the altars and in the shrines. They sacked the towns and their population, women and children included, committing every depravity in the time of anarchy. They stole the taxes of the provinces and they damaged the irrigation works.

Somehow, Ptolemy V restrained his anger and in an attempt to placate native feelings he launched a lavish building programme in Upper Egypt, resuming the work on the temples which had ceased during the uprising. There was a new temple erected for the crocodile god Sobek at Kom Ombo, and extensions were added to the temple of Isis at Philae. Ptolemy commemorated the quelling of the rebellion on a stele which was erected at Memphis. Known as the 'Decree of the Priests', it depicts Ptolemy V in the standard pharaonic pose of 'vanquishing the enemy', his arm raised on high and his fist clenching a club with which he will smash in the skull of his enemies – in this case, surely, the Upper Egyptian insurgents. Cleopatra Syra is represented next to her husband in a cultic position equal to his, and the text of the decree grants her all the titles and honours of the previous queens Berenice II and Arsinoē III. Cleopatra Syra is shown as a warrior queen and her enemy was, of course, her husband's enemy: the rebellious Upper Egyptians. The iconography found on the Decree of the Priests – alongside her image on the so-called Annobeira Stele, in which Cleopatra Syra stands behind Ptolemy, her hand raised in loving salutation – is redolent with messages: in the post-rebellion world, Ptolemy V and Cleopatra Syra were consciously presenting themselves as a single ruling unit. It was their joint desire to see that *ma' at* – the special Egyptian concept of 'order' and 'justice' – was being upheld and strengthened throughout all of Egypt, finally peaceful after all the 'troubles'.

The Philae Temple Decrees mention that 'the King of Upper and Lower Egypt, the Son of Re, Ptolemy . . . and his wife, the female-ruler, the Lady of the Two Lands, Cleopatra, the two Gods-Made-Manifest, have been doing every good thing in

[Egypt]' and they gave 'much money and grain in abundance to the temples of Egypt . . . and they ordered that [grain] was to be collected from the fields of the gods and the vineyards of the divine domains of the gods should be tended? The First Decree goes as far as to specifically mention the kind benefactions of the queen, noting how 'the queen, Lady of the Two Lands of Egypt, Cleopatra, the sister and wife of King Ptolemy – may he live forever – the Beloved of Ptah, gave presents of silver, gold, precious stones in great quantity for the other statues of the goddesses of Egypt, making sacrifices, pouring libations and the rest of the ceremonies performed in the temples of the gods and goddesses of Egypt? In other words, official propaganda used Cleopatra as a potent symbol for the return of good order; she was represented as giving back to the gods and goddesses of Egypt all that had been destroyed or denied them during the rebellion. In seeking to certify the happiness of Egypt's powerful deities, Cleopatra Syra alone was represented as the intermediary of the gods, subpoenaing their benevolence on behalf of her people and promising to uphold and maintain *ma'at* so that the chaos of insurrection would never be visited on Egypt again.

The Ptolemaic victory over the 'rebels' came to be memorialized by the ruling elite as a triumph over the forces of violent politics. Other 'troubles' would periodically flare up in the south at times of dynastic instability or infighting, but none lasted very long, simply because the Ptolemaic regime had learned its lesson and always responded to insurgent movements with both aggressive military action and conciliatory politics. It remains unclear, however, whether the Ptolemies arrived at this approach out of fundamental weakness or profound wisdom.

In 185 BCE, Ptolemy and Cleopatra Syra boarded the ornate state barge – their floating palace – and sailed from Memphis up the Nile towards Thebes and on to Aswan. They wanted to give their subjects the opportunity to see them as a strong pharaoh and a devoted queen, united through their love of Egypt and its people. The journey south was supposed to be a good-will gesture, a PR exercise that would heal old wounds and unite the country again, and many subjects responded favourably. A dedication stone found by archaeologists just south of Memphis had been put up by one Damon, a local garrison commander: 'In favour of King Ptolemy, the son of the god Ptolemy [IV]', he enthused. 'And of his wife, Queen Cleopatra!' But to garner further loyal support from the more hard to please in the crowds, the king and queen had one more weapon in their PR arsenal: their baby boy, newly born. This was the golden opportunity to introduce Egypt to its future king, to yet one more Ptolemy.

5

It Takes a Woman

After seven long years, in 186 BCE, Cleopatra Syra finally fulfilled her queenly duty and gave birth to a healthy boy, the future Ptolemy VI. A celebratory dedication from the temple of Isis at Philae, erected during the king and queen's Nile cruise stopover there in 185 BCE, alludes to him simply as 'Ptolemy the son.' The need to birth copious Ptolemaic heirs, both male and female, must have put pressure on the young queen. It is possible that other children had been born to Cleopatra Syra and Ptolemy V before 'Ptolemy the son' came into the world, but they had been stillborn or expired in the first phase of life, the common fate of the major-ity of children in antiquity, regardless of wealth and status. The super-rich knew the heartbreak of the death of a baby too.

Young Ptolemy's arrival ensured dynastic durability, certainly, but the arrival of a daughter in 185 BCE (or thereabout) meant that the hallowed tradition of brother–sister marriage could be reacti-vated within the royal house. After all, it had been the scarcity of female children among the Ptolemies that had precipitated Cleopatra Syra's exogamous marriage to Ptolemy V in the first place. The new daughter was named Cleopatra for her mother; she was fated to become Cleopatra II. A final boy was born around 183 BCE. He was a red-faced and angry albeit roly-poly baby with a tremendous craving for food and attention; both these factors saw his parents employing a string of wet nurses, each of whom exhausted them-selves trying to keep him suckled, content and tranquil. That baby was to become the most notorious and unconventional of all the already eccentric Ptolemaic kings: Ptolemy VIII – known to history as Potbelly. Later critics of Ptolemy VIII (and there were many) believed in the maxim 'you are what you eat' and declared that, clearly, baby Potbelly must have been fed on the milk of goats and not of women because as an adult and a king he was so headstrong and unruly, and so uncontrollably lustful as to be more billy-goat than man. Throughout his eventful life, Potbelly retained a rapacious appetite for everything that was forbidden, out of reach or deleterious.

The birth of baby Ptolemy (VI) meant that within Egypt's religious sphere, the royal family could now present themselves as a divine triad: holy father, sacred mother and hallowed son. Thanks to her newfound station as a mother, Cleopatra Syra began to be depicted in reliefs on stelae and presented in many inscriptions as the equal in cultic status to Ptolemy V. From at least 198 BCE, Ptolemy V had been addressed as a living god and as Theos Ephiphanes – 'Manifest God', or in Egyptian phrasing 'He Who Comes Forth' – a designation which stressed the complex theological idea of divine power being made visible in the person of the pharaoh who was a living divine incarnation (or an epiphany) of a god. Cleopatra Syra was now apportioned that same epithet, concurrently with her husband's second title, Eucharistos, 'Beneficent God', so that the couple's complete royal titulary read 'King Ptolemy and Queen Cleopatra, the Manifest and Beneficent Gods'.

Furthermore, although she was only distantly related to Ptolemy V by blood, in Greek and Demotic documents Cleopatra Syra also began to be styled 'the king's sister and wife', thereby creating the illusion that the royal marriage was an incestuous union in the time-honoured style of the Ptolemaic ancestors. This fabricated incestuous union put the royal couple squarely at the centre of established Ptolemaic propaganda (we will return to the important subject of incest in due course). Cleopatra Syra's acquisition of the title 'sister and wife', and her incorporation into the dynasty's imagery, was a momentous moment in her life; with the birth of Ptolemy VI and the other children she had become the undisputed matriarch of the Ptolemies. The appellation 'sister and wife' therefore put a respectable distance between Cleopatra Syra and her Seleucid family and confirmed that she had ascended to the position of Egypt's First Lady and – almost by osmosis – had become a Ptolemy.

If Antiochus III had ever had ambitions that his daughter would promote Seleucid interests in Egypt, he was to be disappointed, for, as noted by the Christian theologian and historian Jerome (c. 347–420 CE) in his *Commentary on the Book of Daniel*, 'Cleopatra [Syra] supported her husband rather than her father.' Her loyalty displayed itself by the fact that Egypt repeatedly attempted to align itself with Rome against Antiochus, though the Romans refused the direct aid – mainly financial support – offered to them by the Ptolemies. When in April 191 BCE Antiochus' army was defeated in battle by the forces of the Roman Republic at Thermopylae in Greece (a campaign led by the consul Manius Acilius Glabrio), Ptolemy V and Cleopatra Syra sent an embassy to Rome to congratulate the senate on removing Seleucid power from the Greek mainland. By the Treaty of Apamea (188 BCE) Antiochus III was forced to abandon all the spear-won territory north and west of the Taurus Mountains, most of which the Roman Republic handed on to Rhodes or to the Attalid ruler Eumenes II in Asia Minor, both pliant allies of Rome. Ensuing rebellions in the outlying provinces of the Seleucid empire led to their liberation and the further diminishment of Antiochus' military power.

The post-Apamea era began as it would continue, with numerous embassies from the Hellenistic world to Rome, as individuals and groups sought Roman support for their own purposes. Rome had now effectively forced herself into membership of the club of Hellenistic states and was, and was perceived as, the sole arbiter of affairs, as though she was the judge and jury of the whole world. Rome now had the power to decide the outcome of wars and treaties, and by constantly seeking the support or approval of Rome, Hellenistic rulers weakened themselves and thereby weaponized Roman power. The big political story of the post-Apamea period for the Hellenistic world, then, was undoubtedly its relationship with the new Mediterranean superpower; but it was not the only story. There was another major player in the region – Parthia –

and for the Seleucids at least, it was their main problem: they succumbed not so much to Roman interference, irritating and debilitating as that was, but to the irresistible force of Parthian expansion into central Iran and Mesopotamia.

Determined to regain control of all the old territories of his empire, though, Antiochus, who still held on to central Mesopotamia, looked with ambitious eyes to the east and, having first established his son, the future Seleucus IV, as co-regent, he mounted a fresh expedition into Luristan, in north-west Iran, a territory engulfed by the titanic and menacing Zagros Mountains. Miraculously emerging from the Zagros alive, he led his troops south into the flat plains of Elam. It was there in southern Mesopotamia, while pillaging a temple of Bel-Marduk near the old city of Susa, that Antiochus the Great was killed (no source names his slayer). He died at the age of fifty-three after thirty-six years of rule, much of which was spent on active campaign. Diligently and deferentially the Babylonian priests recorded his passing in a cuneiform king-list: 'Year 125. Month 3. The following was heard in Babylon: On the 25th day, Antiochus the king was killed in Elam.' Antiochus III had been a man of vigour and impulsive brilliance, although sadly he never quite lived up to his grandiloquent public title 'Magus'. Undeniably he left his mark on the history of his dynasty though, and even if the Seleucids never again came as close to recovering the lost empire of their founder as they had under the rule of Antiochus III, the Seleucids were by no means finished yet. If Cleopatra Syra mourned her formidable, somewhat wearisome, father, we do not know about it. The sources are silent.

*

As Ptolemy V's cultic equal, Cleopatra Syra shared in his religious duties. She is mentioned in a stele on which her 'brother-husband' Ptolemy Is shown offering the produce of Egypt to the Buchis Bull, the avatar of the Theban war god Montu, and, at the temple of Horus in Edfu, Cleopatra Syra was also granted a 'Horus name' in the royal titulary. She is called the 'Female Horus', a rare and lofty title previously held only by Berenice II. In the temple of Isis at Philae she was also called 'the Female Vizier', another honorific title which had once been the sole preserve of Berenice. Queen Berenice II's former titles were further appropriated in a series of decrees from Philae in which Cleopatra Syra was titled 'Ruler' and 'Female Pharaoh' – remarkable monikers for any queen to hold, least of all a foreign-born one. In one Upper Egyptian temple-text, she is lauded as 'the Ruler, the Lady of the Two Lands Cleopatra.' The inscription records that she:

> gave plenty of silver, gold and genuine precious stones in order [to produce] a divine image among the gods of Egypt and the goddesses; she made a great offering, performing burnt offerings and libations as well as celebrating festivals for [all] the gods of Egypt and the goddesses. Her piety is great and noble.

In the temple inscriptions, the king and queen were presented as a unit, operating harmoniously both religiously and politically. But Cleopatra Syra's titulary association with Berenice II was not accidental, for the two women shared some important connections: they were both foreign princesses who had married distant Ptolemaic cousins, and they were both given invented pedigrees as 'sisters' of those husbands. Berenice II had proved her loyalty to Ptolemy III during his campaigns in Syria, and as a show of solidarity, in 243/2 BCE the royal couple declared themselves Theoi Euergetoi ('Beneficent Gods') in the cult of Alexander. For Berenice, this meant the surest confirmation that she had achieved both public and private recognition as the undisputed wife and queen of Ptolemy III. Berenice II had worked hard at promoting her cultic image, and she took an active role in her own self-promotion. She had much to live up to, of course: the cult of Arsinoē II Philadelphus, and the former queen's uninhibited exploitation of self-image, was the dominant force in the Ptolemaic ideology of queenship. Arsinoē had cast herself in the guise of the goddess Isis and, following her death, Ptolemy II had promoted his (genuine) sister-wife's association with, and assimilation into, Isis. Berenice II wanted both to exploit this resource and carve her own niche in the Ptolemaic pantheon, and so she had to forge an identity close enough to yet far enough from Arsinoē II. This was no easy task given Arsinoē's expertise in cross-cultural propaganda and the fact that even Ptolemy III continued to promote his stepmother's cultic and cultural importance. Berenice opted to promote herself as an incarnation of the goddess Hathor (whose closest Greek counterpart was Aphrodite) and when the time came for Cleopatra Syra to craft her own image of divine queenship, she too used Hathor as her divine avatar.

So, why Hathor? Of the many goddesses in the Egyptian pantheon, Hathor was one of the most easily recognizable and yet most mysterious of deities. Hathor existed for the entire history of Egyptian culture (she is attested from the pre-dynastic era, before c. 3100 BCE) as a powerful and influential goddess. She was the daughter of Re, the sun god, and was often seen as the eye of the god, and as the great cosmic goddess she was 'the mother of her father' and 'the daughter of her son'. She was one goddess and many goddesses, and was representative of all goddesses (thus she could be Hathor-Isis, Hathor-Mut, Hathor-Nekhbet, and so on). Iconographically, the goddess was usually represented as a beautiful woman, or as a cow-headed woman, or in purely bovine form, wearing a headdress of the sun disk surmounted between two elongated cow horns. In Egyptian, she was called Hwt-Hor, which is usually translated as 'House of Horus', and in hieroglyphs her name was represented as a large walled enclosure with a falcon within. From this we can surmise that Hathor was seen as the great sky itself, holding Horus within her 'womb', which was poetically referred to as 'house'. In this form, Hathor was both a solar sky-goddess and a personification of the night-time sky. As we have noted, the Ptolemies had a very close affiliation with Horus, who represented the living king, and in fact in the temple of Philae the identification was categorically made: 'The King of Upper and Lower Egypt, Ptolemy – He is Horus.' Hathor, therefore, was the protectress of the living king.

But she was even more than that, as a hymn from Dendera makes plain:

> The One, the sister without equal,
> The most beautiful of all,
> She resembles the rising morning star,
> At the beginning of a happy year.
> Shining bright, fair of skin,
> Lovely the look of her eyes,
> Sweet the speech of her lips ...
> True lapis-lazuli her hair,
> Her arms surpassing gold.

Hathor was a supremely sexual goddess and, as not only the protectress of Horus but also as his 'wife', she brought him great joy through her beauty, her love and her nurturing. The Ptolemies celebrated this divine union in the annual Festival of the Beautiful Embrace, which was celebrated at Edfu temple. It was a spectacular celebration of the god's love for his goddess. During the holiday an image of the goddess was taken by ship from Hathor's temple at Dendera up the Nile to reside with Horus for two weeks at his home in Edfu. For his part, Horus came partway up the Nile to greet his consort and escort her back to his temple. The citizens of Edfu and devotees of Hathor travelled from far afield to commemorate the great reunion, which was celebrated with feasting and music, but there was another purpose to the ritual: on the second day of the feast there was a change of emphasis as statues of the two gods were carried across the desert to the site of Behdet, the sacred burial ground of the primeval gods of Edfu. Here, priests enacted a prophylactic ritual in which wax hippopotami and fish, inscribed with the names of the king's enemies, were symbolically destroyed – 'every harmful thing that you could think of was done to them', a papyrus text records. So the purpose of the Festival of the Beautiful Embrace was twofold: to celebrate the sexual reunion of the gods and to harness the power of that sexual union, manifested through the ritual crushing and dissolving the nation's enemies.

Hathor was also the goddess most closely connected to the divine queenship; in fact, she was fundamentally representative of all royal women, and from the XVIII Dynasty queens had worn a headdress made of cow horns, which supported a sun disk, in conjunction with straight falcon plumes, representing the eyes of Re, which were all symbols of Hathor. Although it is true that Hathor could be assimilated into the important figure of Isis, in Ptolemaic times the goddess never lost her right to exist as an independent deity, a fact demonstrated by the numerous temples and shrines erected in her name throughout the period. Hathor, therefore, offered an ideal niche for Cleopatra Syra (as she had for Berenice II) to create a divine synergy. Thus the queen took on, as part of her Two Ladies name, the following lofty title: 'Her Bravery is that of Neith, Lady of Saïs, her Honour is that of Hathor in Her Love.' In her iconography, Cleopatra Syra wore a crown of Hathoric falcon plumes – just as Berenice II had done – and emulated Berenice's fashion of dressing her Egyptian-style wigs in extended ringlets. It was at Edfu that the queen's most elaborate and fulsome titles were located, for there she was eulogized as:

> The young woman, daughter of the god, created by the god,
> beloved of the gods of Egypt, adorned by Khnum, the regent
> of Thoth whose might is great, who pleases the Two Lands,
> who gives the people in perfection to the Two Ladies, who
> Hathor praises for her popularity.

The goddess Hathor clearly offered Cleopatra Syra a key to unlocking the codes of Ptolemaic queenship, for in the rich mythology of Egypt Hathor was simultaneously the lover of the king and also his divine mother; she was the gatekeeper to the kingship, and acted as pharaoh's alter ego, the feminine prototype. In effect, Cleopatra Syra played the perfect Hathor to Ptolemy V's Horus.

*

In September 180 BCE the unthinkable happened. Ptolemy V, not yet thirty years old, was found dead by his servants. He had reigned for twenty-four troublesome years, and it is probable that his death was equally tempestuous since evidence suggests that the king was poisoned. But why? The actions he took a year before he died might provide an answer, for Ptolemy had suddenly appointed his six-year-old son as his co-regent. Courtiers surmised that, following standard royal practice, this was the king's way of hinting that he was once again intent on launching a costly war against the Seleucids and that he was preparing for the succession should he fall in battle in Syria. In his *Commentary on the Book of Daniel*, the Christian theologian-cum-historian Jerome provides the details of what followed:

> Ptolemy Epiphanes . . . prepared an army to fight against [the Seleucids] and because of this was poisoned by his own generals. When someone asked this Ptolemy what money he possessed to pay for such a venture, he replied that his friends were his money-bags. When this saying became publicly known, the generals became afraid that he would strip them of their wealth, and therefore, underhandedly, they killed him.

Was Cleopatra Syra aware of the plot to kill the king? Was she, in fact, part of it? It is hard to be certain but we might speculate that Ptolemy V's death brought to a swift halt any threat of war with the Seleucid king, who was, of course, Cleopatra Syra's brother. She had nothing to gain from a costly war against her own kith and kin (and besides, she would not have wanted to jeopardize the personal income she was getting from Coele-Syria), and if she had voiced her concerns to her husband's worried ministers, then she might have had every chance of ingratiating herself with this important inner circle. The work she had done to create for herself a support network at court now paid off as Cleopatra Syra took it upon herself to become regent for her six-year-old son. We might infer from the fact that the transition of rule was so peaceful (there were no violent coups or any form of power struggle) that the queen-regent was supported by the nobility, the military and the masses, for unlike Arsinoē III, who had preceded her, Cleopatra Syra encountered no opposition to her ascension as the dominant figure on the throne. Cleopatra Syra was the first woman to become *basilissa*-regent in the house of Ptolemy, and in taking on the title and the powers devolved to it, she established a precedent for each of the Cleopatras who followed her.

In June 2010, archaeologists working at Tel Kedesh in Israel, near the Lebanon border, uncovered a gold coin dating to Cleopatra Syra's lifetime. It was reported to be the heaviest and most valuable gold coin ever found in Israel, the equivalent to 100 ancient silver drachmas (or half a year's salary for the average labourer). Weighing 28 grams, the *mnaieion* ('one-mina coin') is six times heavier than other coins from the same period, and it was probably created at the imperial mint of Kition, a city on the southern coast of Ptolemaic Cyprus. The coin was struck to commemorate Cleopatra Syra's acquisition of the regency. The inscription bears her title, 'Queen Cleopatra', but the image on the coin is not her portrait but that of the indominable Arsinoë II, the sister-wife of Ptolemy II Philadelphus, the deified queen. The coin had no doubt been commissioned and offered as a 'commemorative edition' at a sanctuary of Arsinoë II at Tel Kedesh, where she was worshipped as a goddess, and by associating herself so closely – and so extravagantly – with this ambitious, efficacious and formidable woman, Cleopatra Syra cast herself along the same lines as the Ptolemaic trailblazer: she too was now a genuine goddess-queen.

In the brief summation of Cleopatra Syra's life contained in her important 1932 book *Hellenistic Queens*, the classicist Grace Macurdy acknowledged that Cleopatra Syra 'governed wisely and well during the years of her regentship' – and indeed she did. Macurdy also noticed something else about the documents created during Cleopatra Syra's regency, and that is the fact that, without exception, the queen's name always precedes that of her son. Moreover, she used the title Thea Epiphanes ('Manifest Goddess') even though young Ptolemy VI had not yet been named Theos (god) himself. She was 'Queen Cleopatra the mother, the Manifest Goddess', while the child-king was just 'Ptolemy, son of Ptolemy [V] the Manifest God'. In other words, in matters of state and theology (two notions so interwoven in Ptolemaic thought as to be inseparable), Cleopatra Syra far outranked the pharaoh so that, in effect, she, not he, ruled the Two Lands.

Evidence from the regency period shows Cleopatra Syra to have been active in administration, governance and temple ceremonial, and it appears that no bureaucratic detail was too small for her scrutiny: in one papyrus, a prisoner, wrongfully incarcerated for crimes he did not commit, is acquitted on the orders of 'Queen Cleopatra and King Ptolemy' after the queen had personally scrutinized his case. On a broken statue base from Cyprus, a local (now nameless) dignitary was thanked by Cleopatra Syra for services rendered to 'the Manifest Goddess and King Ptolemy, and her other children.' The inscription suggests that Cleopatra Syra cultivated associations with the Ptolemaic elite far beyond Alexandria and Egypt.

Under the careful and prudent guidance of his mother, in the third year of their co-rule (178/7 BCE) Ptolemy VI was integrated into the dynastic cult as Theos Philometor ('Mother-Loving God'), and gold coinage bearing portraits of the mother and son co-rulers celebrated the youthful pharaoh's acquisition of a fitting epithet. Cleopatra Syra, it seems, was preparing Ptolemy to take on more royal responsibilities, ready for when he would sit on the throne, independent of his mother – for nothing suggests that she intended to cling to power beyond the time when Ptolemy VI would come of age and become the sole ruler of Egypt. It was the queen's intention that, once of age, Ptolemy VI should marry his full-blood sister, Cleopatra II, and thereby reactivate the age-old tradition of brother–sister union which had slipped from practice when Ptolemy V, the offspring of brother–sister marriage, had ascended the throne without a sister to wed. It is interesting to note how keen the foreign queen was to get back to the marriage traditions that had been so instrumental in forming Ptolemaic identity; no foreign bride would sit at the side of Ptolemy VI, Cleopatra Syra resolved, not while he had a sister to fill that role more fittingly.

With wedding plans in mind, the future looked good. Then suddenly, without warning, Cleopatra Syra died. The date of the queen's death is a matter of academic dispute. Early estimates placed it in 176 BCE, although more recent arguments put it in 177 BCE, meaning that her reign lasted for about three years, and that she died aged about thirty-eight or forty, depending on where one places the date of her birth. Her quick demise has also led a few scholars to surmise that, like her husband, Cleopatra Syra fell victim to some sort of court intrigue and thus met with foul play, but this is very hard to confirm or disprove. She seems to have been popular with the masses, and as queen she endeared herself to many kinds of people, and so perhaps it is best to suppose that Cleopatra Syra died of natural causes. Still, to have survived so long in the tempestuous court of the Ptolemies was nothing less than miraculous.

The posthumous establishment of an eponymous priesthood for his deified mother followed on the orders of Ptolemy VI, and in Upper Egypt the cult 'of Ptolemy and Cleopatra his mother' was activated. By 164 BCE a special priestess was put in charge of the rites and rituals of the worship of 'Cleopatra the Mother, the Manifest Goddess', as Cleopatra Syra took her place in the pantheon alongside Arsinoë II, Berenice II and the other early Ptolemaic queens. A fascinating papyrus from Ptolemaïs dated to 139 BCE records that the queen had her own priesthood at that locale too, and that her memory was held in high regard there. In the text, Cleopatra Syra is named alongside her immediate descendants, other Cleopatras. Moreover, in the temples of Edfu and Karnak Cleopatra Syra was shown alongside Ptolemy V being venerated by their sons, Ptolemy VI and Ptolemy VIII (Potbelly), her presence alongside her husband echoing thereby their joint epithet Theoi Epihaneis, and in later years coins continued to be struck showing her in the guise of the goddess Isis by her son Ptolemy VIII – an impressive display of filial loyalty from a man who fragrantly violated all other aspects of family unity.

Unlike Arsinoë III and Berenice II, who, because of the politics of the time, were prohibited from being genuine co-rulers with their spouses, the more united Greco-Egyptian country over which Cleopatra Syra held dominion was more accommodating of a public role for a woman, and so the queen rose to become Egypt's regent and co-ruler unopposed. True, Cleopatra Syra had not entered into a co-rulership with her husband (although she had been addressed on equal terms with him both inside and outside Egypt), but her compensation came in the form of her capacity to co-rule the kingdom with her son, an achievement which must be explained by the careful groundwork she had cultivated in her years as the wife of Ptolemy V, especially her careful nurturing of the most powerful and influential courtiers of Alexandria and the care she took with the Egyptian traditions surrounding her queen-ship. Cleopatra Syra set a precedent for her female successors: from this time onwards the women of the dynasty would progressively participate in joint rule with their husbands and sons.

Cleopatra Syra was a successful monarch. She took on the task of Egypt's governance as her son's regent with acumen and intelligence, and even during Ptolemy V's lifetime she had been treated as his equal, if not his superior. Her lineage was undeniably an asset to her, because the queen's direct ties to the Seleucid kings allowed the two kingdoms, which up to this point had been at loggerheads, to coexist peacefully during the era of her regency. The fact that as a bride she entered Egypt with her own dowry and her own retinue of servants and ministers meant that to a certain extent she could act independently of the Egyptian government. The ease with which she took up the mantle of power on the death of her husband must indicate that she had the cooperation and tacit approval of the highest-ranking ministers in the Ptolemaic bureaucracy. That a queen of foreign origin was able to become regent without challenge from the powerful Alexandrian families, when Arsinoë III, a Ptolemaic queen by birth, had been murdered, speaks to Cleopatra Syra's personal will and the relationships she had built at court.

She was clearly a role model for her daughter, Cleopatra II, and in turn her granddaughters Cleopatra Thea and Cleopatra III, who knew the stories of her capabilities and learned about her self-confidence. When Cleopatra Thea married into the Seleucid court herself, she might well have had her grandmother's experience as a powerful and successful foreign queen in mind as she made her own life in foreign climes. With such a shining record, it is little wonder that following Cleopatra Syra's death, 'Cleopatra' became the only female name of worth associated with the royal house of Egypt. Her legacy went further: at the time of Cleopatra Syra's regency, a woman, living in the area of the Nile Delta wrote to her daughter, for she was eager to send her congratulations on the birth of a granddaughter. Of course, the new grandmother could not resist offering some advice to the new mother and wrote to express her preference for the baby's name: 'Do not *hesitate*,' she scribbled, 'to name the little one Cleopatra.' She was clearly an admirer of the Syrian-born queen.

6

Flesh of My Flesh

Cleopatra II was born around 185 BCE, shortly after the birth of her brother Ptolemy VI. In fact, her mother, Cleopatra I Syra, must have become pregnant with her second baby almost immediately after the safe delivery of the first. Nothing survives to indicate how the royal couple viewed the birth of their daughter, but it might be surmised that having already produced a male heir, they might well have been content to welcome a daughter into the household. After all, the baby girl would make a fitting wife for her brother someday in the future.

The presence of a few girls in any royal family was good – they became potential brides in endogamous and exogamous marriage unions – but all monarchs realized that a string of female-only births could only mean bad luck: kings needed male heirs. But regarding attitudes towards female births, what were the norms in Hellenistic Egypt as a whole? Greek and Demotic tax registers from the Fayum, an area with a dense mix of native Egyptians and settled Greeks, provide a valuable database of the names and structures of 427 tax-paying Greek and Egyptian families. From these documents it is possible to access details about household sizes and the gender make-up of family units, and it has been apparent to scholars that Greek households stand out for having a marked underrepresentation of daughters, a characteristic not shared by Egyptian families. This suggests that the Egyptians tended to raise *all* children born to them (as Strabo noted, 'most zealously they raise every child who is born'). In fact, Egyptian wisdom litera-ture traditionally stressed that daughters were welcomed into a household. In areas predominantly inhabited by native Egyptians papyrus records confirm that families contained almost twice as many daughters as sons while, in contrast, in principally Greek areas daughters are sharply underrepresented within families. The Greeks had a predisposition to view infant daughters as a financial burden and they were unwanted in Greek families. As a consequence, the exposure of female infants was practised in the Greek communities of Egypt with some regularity.

Except in cases of physical deformities or illegitimacy, socio-economic reasons account for the scope of the practice of female infanticide amongst the Greek communities of Egypt, where exposure was accepted as a regrettable fact of life. Although some philosophers spoke out against it, ultimately it was not until late antiquity that imperial law enacted measures intended to discourage female exposure and encourage the rescue of abandoned girl infants. We must not assume that *all* Greek households were routinely exposing infant daughters, and we should keep in mind that the male–female ratios found in the tax-register papyri may have been skewed by the Greek notion of the worthlessness of girls, which meant that they were not valued enough even to be counted in official figures. So it is possible that the extreme sex imbalance in the documentation could be a result of the under-recording of non-adult females rather than the exposure of them – although it should be conceded that the papyrus statistics do suggest a much harsher reality. Infant exposure was likely to have been an *ad hoc* decision made by parents, dependent as much upon the success of a harvest as on the sex or health of a newborn child. If things were looking bad for a family, then the first to suffer the consequences might have been an infant daughter.

Given the affluence of the Ptolemies, the socioeconomic necessity for female infanticide within the royal family is very unlikely. Sons were generally desired as potential heirs, but the Ptolemaic kings may well have preferred to have a balanced family with sons for succession and daughters who could be put to use in dynastic marriage policies. Indeed, one text shows that it was considered a blessing for a royal couple to have both male and female children:

Provide the king and queen with life, health, long years and children: male children and female children to the first and second generations, and for the male offspring manliness and valour, and for the female offspring, womanliness and motherhood provide!

There is no doubt that in the Ptolemaic era it was assumed that daughters were integral members of the royal household. The court poet Callimachus was skilled at conveying the affectionate feelings between parents and daughters, and in his *Hymn to Artemis* he conjures up a delightful vision of Zeus jiggling his infant daughter Artemis up and down on his knee as she reaches out to play with the hairs of his beard. It is a lifelike and enduringly familiar vignette of a father–daughter relationship, and perhaps as he penned the poem Callimachus had in mind an Alexandrian king and his daughter, whom he cast in the roles of the god and his divine daughter:

Of Artemis we sing ... beginning with the time when sitting on her father's knees – still a little maid – she spoke these words to him: 'Give me to keep my maidenhood, daddy, forever ... And give me arrows and a bow ... and gird me in a tunic with embroidered border reaching to the knee, that I may slay wild beasts. And give me sixty daughters of Oceanus for my choir – all nine years old, all maidens yet ungirdled ... And give to me all mountains; and for city, assign me any, even whatsoever thou wilt: for seldom is it that Artemis goes down to the town. On the mountains will I dwell and the cities of men I will visit only when women vexed by the sharp pang of childbirth call me to their aid – even in the hour when I was born the Fates ordained that I should be their helper ...' So spoke the child and would have touched her father's beard, but she reached out in vain ... And her father smiled and bowed assent and he caressed her ...

The *Hymn to Artemis* shows the more precocious side of the toddler goddess too. The three-year-old Artemis goes on to steal a bow, quiver and arrows from the Cyclopes, and Callimachus leaves us with the image of her toddling off to the goat-god Pan to get dogs for her hunting expeditions. The point of the poem is to show how gods, even as infants, departed from the norms of life, where children are weak, incapable, fearful and ignorant. A Hellenistic Jewish wisdom text outlines the concerns any protective father might feel for his little girl:

> A daughter is a treasure that keeps her father wakeful
>   and worry over her drives away sleep:
> lest in her youth she remains unmarried or when she
>   is married, lest she be childless;
> while unmarried, lest she be defiled,
> or lest she prove unfaithful to her husband;
> lest she become pregnant in her father's house,
> or be sterile in that of her husband.
> Keep a close watch on your daughter,
> lest she make you the sport of your enemies,
> and by word in the city and the assembly of the people,
> she becomes an object of derision in public gatherings.
> See that there is no lattice window in her room,
> no spot that overlooks the approaches to the house.
> Let her not reveal her beauty to any male,
> or spend her time among married women;
> for just as moths come from garments,
> so a woman's wickedness comes from a woman.
> Better a man's wickedness than a woman's goodness,
> but better a pious daughter than a shameless son.

The overriding concern of the father – king or commoner – was his own good name, which might be defiled by a daughter's behaviour or reputation. In many 'traditional' societies, including the cultures of the Ptolemaic world, the ideal of masculinity was underpinned by a notion of 'honour' and was fundamentally connected to policing female behaviour and sexuality, since honour was generally seen as residing in the bodies of women. 'Honour' was the most powerful weapon that men wielded over women: prior to marriage, a woman, as a daughter, represented the 'honour' of her father; as sister, the 'honour' of her brother; as the beloved, the 'honour' of her betrothed. After marriage, as a wife, she symbolized the 'honour' of her husband; as a daughter-in-law, the 'honour' of her father-in-law; and as a mother she symbolized the 'honour' of her sons. Ultimately, in the case of a royal princess, she came to signify the 'honour' of the dynasty, the land and the nation.

*

As a baby, princess Cleopatra II was cared for by a wet nurse. She had retainers who chewed food before placing it into her toothless mouth, and tasters for poison were also supplied to all members of the royal family as a matter of routine. In pharaonic times the women who cared for royal offspring are mentioned in textual sources and are even depicted in tombs, for they tended to be the wives or mothers of high-ranking courtiers. They were designated with the titles 'royal nurse' or 'chief royal nurse', which, in the case of a lady whose charge grew up to be king, could be aggrandized to 'chief nurse of the Lord of the Two Lands, she who suckled the god'. It is likely that at the Ptolemaic court elite women also undertook this role, but we have no direct evidence. Nor can we state anything of worth about the ethnic mix of women residing or working within the palace domestic quarters, but it would be interesting to know if the women who were responsible for the royal children were Egyptians or Greeks and, as an extension, what languages were used in the royal nursery. The pharaonic evidence does suggest that the children of the court became closely attached to their nurses and, later, to their tutors too, and it would be logical to suppose that the same bonds might be fostered in the Ptolemaic period.

Although our knowledge is imperfect and far from complete, Egyptian evidence from the pharaonic era does afford us some glimpses of the importance placed upon princesses within dynastic ideology. We find much emphasis given to royal daughters who, in the artworks, were usually depicted near their parents.

Famously, the art of the Amarna period (1353–1336 BCE) depicted the daughters of Akhenaten and Nefertiti being kissed, caressed and cuddled by their loving parents, but even in the more formally regimented art of the reign of Amenhotep III (*c.* 1386–1349 BCE), his daughters were shown with surprising regularity in his company, alongside their mother, Tiye, too, suggesting a familial closeness or even a loving bond. Ramses II (1303–1213 BCE), who had a large number of children (between forty-eight and fifty sons and forty to fifty-three daughters), made a political statement about the unity of his family and frequently had lists of the names of the princes and princesses born to him carved into the walls of temples, such as at the Ramesseum in Thebes, at Wadi es-Sebua in Nubia and at Abydos in Middle Egypt. His efforts to have his children depicted on his monuments were in contradiction to the earlier tradition of keeping royal children, especially boys, in the background, and yet ten of Ramses' daughters were regularly depicted in line-ups in the official iconography – always in the same order, suggesting their birth dates or, perhaps, their ranking within the court hierarchy. The six eldest princesses even had individual statues at the entrance of the Greater Abu Simbel temple in Nubia. Most unusually, a series of wall reliefs found in the Eastern High Gate of the mortuary temple of Ramses III (1186 to 15 April 1155 BCE) at the site of Medinet Habu, on the west bank of the Nile at Thebes, depicts scenes of the family life of the XX Dynasty ruler. A group of young girls shares in Ramses' recreation (the king is affectionately called by his diminutive pet name of 'Sissi' in the accompanying inscriptions). Naked except for jewellery and elaborate side-locks of hair, these girls are shown playing a boardgame called *senet* (draughts) with the pharaoh (himself naked except for a crown and sandals) as he embraces them at the waist, places his arms around their shoulders or else playfully chucks them under the chin. It was once thought that these young women were concubines, but fragmentary hieroglyphs clearly call them 'the royal children'. There is no reason to take this as any kind of euphemism: the wall-scenes depict pharaoh passing time with his favourite daughters.

Did Ptolemaic princesses spend time with their royal parents? Did Hellenistic kings and queens believe in hands-on parenting? Did they feel affection for their offspring? The progressivist view held by most Victorian historians was that, until the advent of societal control over emotions in the modern era, ancient displays of emotion were primitive, violent, destructive and irrational; this view remained unchallenged until the 1960s, with the advent of cognitive psychology and subsequently, in the 1970s, of social constructionism. A general widening of the debate in the 1980s led to the 1990s being labelled 'the decade of the ancient family', as scholarly discussion of children and their role within family structures was expanded into the contemporary vogue for exploring the importance of childhood in the past. Recent scholarship confirms the centrality of the child in the familial experience of antiquity. In Ptolemaic Egypt the papyri show that adults recognized children as social beings, but at the same time the papyri alert us to the plurality of childhoods that existed in the period: all children have a childhood, and each child lives this period of its life in ways prescribed by the variables of gender, legal status, economic class, ethnicity and the 'domestic politics' of the family unit. A girl born into the ruling house of the Ptolemies therefore had a very different set of aspirations, experiences and codes of behaviour than even those girls born into noble Greek houses or elite Egyptian families, let alone those born into peasant families in the Thebaid. A daughter born into the Ptolemaic line might have experienced a young life completely unlike that of her brother: their education was segregated, and distinctive gender values were encoded in them with different expectations and outcomes. At a very young age, learning to be a man and discovering what it meant to be a woman hauled male and female siblings into separate spheres of existence.

*

In April 176 BCE the twelve-year-old Cleopatra II married her elder brother, Ptolemy VI, precisely as their mother had wished. Cleopatra II had just reached puberty by then; as a married woman she could no longer be considered a pawn in any foreign wedding negotiations and was safely out of the reach of any outsider who might aspire to wed her and press a claim to the throne of Egypt.

Sibling marriage had already been practised in the Ptolemaic house – Ptolemy II had married Arsinoë II, his full-sister, and Ptolemy IV wed his full-sister Arsinoë III – although the tradition had suddenly ceased when, out of necessity (because he had no sister), Ptolemy V had married Cleopatra Syra. The brother–sister marriage of Ptolemy VI and Cleopatra II rebooted an important dynastic institution. In fact, the marriage of King Ptolemy VI and Cleopatra II marked a significant moment in the history of the Ptolemaic house: henceforth sibling marriage (and other forms of close-kin marriage) would be a constant fixture of the dynasty's self-identity. Ptolemy VI and Cleopatra II were encouraged to con-summate their union as quickly – and as prolifically – as possible, for Ptolemaic sibling spouses were expected to have an active sexual relationship. Brother–sister marriages were not symbolic unions forged to strengthen a dynastic identity or to promote Ptolemaic propaganda, but were fully consummated marriages undertaken with the intention of begetting scores of descendants.

Throughout the ages and across world cultures, first-degree incest (sex with relatives who share 50 per cent of family genes – that is to say, parents, children and siblings) has tended to be strictly forbidden. In fact, humans have inbuilt social and psycho-logical mechanisms to deter incest, and strict taboos surrounding incestuous practices have been formed in almost every human culture; the incest taboo is about as close to a universal law as human moral rules get. Therefore the accusation of first-degree incest does not sit lightly within any society. Historically, where incest has been suspected, it has been used as an effective means of slander. The Greek historian Herodotus maligned the Persian king Cambyses II with accusations of incest as it was supposed that he had sexual relations with at least two of his sisters. Plutarch insisted that another Great King of Persia, Artaxerxes II, lusted after two of his daughters, wedded them and took them to bed, and Suetonius, the Roman historian, alleged that the emperor

Caligula bedded his three sisters while Nero was sexually aroused by his mother, Agrippina the Younger, and they often enjoyed intercourse. Indeed, the first-degree incest motif is firmly established in mythology, Greek drama, Roman literature and, down the line, in Jacobean tragedy, Romantic novels and contemporary literature. The self-loathing and self-mutilating Oedipus in Sophocles' impressively disquieting tragedy *Oedipus the King* (*c.* 429 BCE) wrestles with the realization that he has unwittingly murdered his father and had sex with his mother. His piercing cry of unearthly psychological torture intensifies the effect of these improprieties on his psyche: 'born from those who should not have borne me, laying with those I should not have lain with, killing those I should not have killed!'

The ancient Greeks had no word for 'incest'. Still, the periphrases they used were just as value-laden as the Latin term *incestum*, which means, variously, 'impurity', 'unchastity', 'defilement' and even 'pollution'. Greek idioms for 'incest' make it clear that the Greeks saw it as both irreligious and socially abhorrent, since incestuous desire implied that the instigator(s) lacked self-control (known by the Greek term *sophrosyne*, 'moderation'), one of the cardinal virtues. However, while the Greeks were repelled by the notion of first-degree incest, evidence confirms that they were nonetheless heavily endogamous in their marriage practices and that first-cousin marriage was fully acceptable and very common. Uncle–niece marriage was practised in Athens, for instance, where it was also permissible for a half-brother to marry a half-sister, provided that they were children of the same father but not the same mother.

Given the standard Greek attitudes towards incest, why did the Ptolemies promote first-degree incest within their family? The answer can be found in the dynasty's promotion and projection of its own unique concept of 'royalty'. As god-kings and goddess-queens, the Ptolemies allowed themselves to engage in behaviours not permitted to common folk and, therefore, like other royal families which have adopted incestuous practices, they did not think of themselves as breaking a taboo but rather as fulfilling the taboo by giving it meaning. Through their dynastic incest, the Ptolemies set themselves apart from the rest of society and became untouchable by ordinary standards of human behaviour. Oedipus may well be the embodiment of all the heinous miasmas we associate with incest, but it is worth noting that Sophocles' greatest tragedy is not entitled *Oedipus the Incestuous* or *Oedipus the Murderer* or even simply *Oedipus*; it is called *Oedipus the King*. Why? Because Oedipus is not any ordinary human. He is a king. And as a king, the incest he committed was crucial to his ascent to the throne. Kings and queens do not operate on the same level as mortals; they are not judged by normal codes of behaviour, for kings and queens are god-like.

It is also possible that on a more mundane and pragmatic level, incest was adopted among the earlier Ptolemies as a way for the Greco-Macedonian newcomers in Egypt to be accepted by the Egyptian population. After all, first-degree incest (typically brother–sister and father–daughter) had certainly occurred sporadically during the pharaonic age and seems to have been especially significant during the New Kingdom, Egypt's imperial period (c. 1570–1069 BCE). There is evidence to suggest, for instance, that the famous Tutankhamun married his full-sister Ankhesenamun, who gave him at least two stillborn children; she herself was the daughter of the notorious 'heretic' pharaoh Akhenaten, who married at least one of Ankhesenamun's five sisters, his daughter Meritaten. Ramses II certainly married his daughter Bint-Anath and fathered a daughter on her.

Although Egyptian pharaohs did not practise incestuous marriage to the extent that modern popular belief has it, the Greeks *thought* that they did, and this is what matters. Thus, the Greek travel writer and mythographer Pausanias notes that 'Ptolemy [II] was in love with his sister Arsinoë, and married her, flat contrary to the traditions of Macedonia, but agreeably to those of his Egyptian subjects.' In his ambitious world history, the Greek author Diodorus Siculus noted how the Egyptians 'made a law, they say, contrary to the general custom of mankind, permitting men to marry their sisters, this being due to the success attained by Isis in this respect.'

Diodorus connected the (presumed) Egyptian tradition of incestuous marriage to the Egyptian veneration of the goddess Isis, who, as we have seen, was one of the great deities of the ancient Mediterranean world. Isis was married to her brother Osiris, and stories were told that they adored each other so deeply that they made love while they were still both in the womb. When Osiris was murdered by his brother, Seth, and his body was dismembered and disbursed throughout Egypt, the grief-stricken Isis roved the length of the Nile collecting and reassembling her husband-brother's remains, and with his partially resurrected corpse she succeeded in conceiving Horus, the divine child who would grow up to have his revenge on Seth and restore order to the world. The divine triad of Isis, Osiris and Horus, as we have seen, had both religious and political significance because every pharaoh was assimilated to Horus, while each deceased pharaoh was identified with Osiris, king of the dead. Like Horus, the living pharaoh's principal job was to maintain cosmic order. As for Isis, whose name refers to the king's throne, she was literally the seat of power.

Isis and Osiris were emblematic of a deep and passionate marital love that was, at one and the same time, also a sibling love. They had counterparts in other mythologies, including that of the Greeks, whose most mighty Olympian god, Zeus, was married to Hera, his full-sister. Incest among humans might have been repugnant to the Greeks, but among their gods, who had every right to engage in whatever sexual practices they wished, it lacked any taboo. Because of this attitude, the incestuous royalty of the Ptolemaic house – who conceived of themselves as more than mere mortals – replicated the behaviour of the gods, both Egyptian and Greek, and through their incestuous behaviour they elevated their royalty to the plane of the divine.

On a decidedly earthly zone, however, the regular practice of incest through several generations of the same family had serious consequences: the problem with having sex with close relatives is that there is an extremely high chance that offspring will be born with serious birth defects. Recently, scientists at the University of Zurich studied 259 mummies for DNA analysis to secure evidence for incest within the Egyptian royal families of the New Kingdom. By calculating what is called the 'inbreeding coefficient', which determines the genetic relatedness between people, the level of incest practised within a generational group can be determined. The early XVIII Dynasty pharaoh Amenhotep I (1526–1506 BCE) was found to be one of the most obvious products of incest with an exceptionally high inbreeding coefficient, which has led scientists to think he may have been a descendant of no less than three generations of sibling marriages. But another pharaoh of the same dynasty, Thutmose III (1479–1425 BCE), scored much lower on the incestuous scale; his grandparents were siblings but his parents were not related. In October 2014, an analysis of Tutankhamun's remains suggested that his death could be attributed to genetic impairments caused by the fact that his parents were brother and sister; the sickly boy-king was plagued by malaria, had a club foot (caused by the death of bone tissue), suffered from a cleft palate and had a severe overbite. The two mummified foetuses found in the king's tomb, the infant remains of the stillborn children of Tutankhamun and Ankhesenamun, also carried genetic impairments.

Frustratingly, we do not have the osteoarchaeological remains of the Ptolemies nor any concrete evidence of their medical histories, and so it is impossible to know if they sustained genetic damage through their habit of incest, but the probability is high. It is very likely that the Ptolemies would have suffered from the adverse effects of first-degree inbreeding, but whatever genetic harm they may have borne is lost to history (and would probably not have been understood by the Ptolemies themselves as something ensuing from their breeding practices).

With these close-kin marriages came, for the Ptolemaic royal women, a curious form of polyandry in which they acquired multiple marriage partners, one after another (serial monogamy, as it were). Several of the Cleopatras found themselves married to a series of brothers (older and younger), or to fathers, uncles, cousins and nephews. The marital history of the later Ptolemaic house privileged princesses as the authorized bearers of the next generation and, because of this, significant power was placed into their hands, with the result that, in every respect, they became king-makers. As a by-product of this strange domestic set-up, the harmonious sibling unions of previous generations of Ptolemies, which promoted loyalty and cooperation, was shattered. The many dysfunctional incestuous marriages of the Cleopatras are notable for the complete collapse of familial harmony that they triggered.

The Ptolemies did not merely paddle in the shallow end of the gene pool, they dived in at the deep end. In the ancient mindset, those with extraordinary stature – gods and royalty – were permitted to breach the boundaries between civilization and the chaotic forces of disorder through their incestuous unions. Incest gave the Ptolemies an aura of divine inimitability which was strengthened with each new generation of inbreeding. The philosophy that underscored the Ptolemaic dynasty was very simple: the family that sleeps together keeps together.

7

Brothers (and Sisters) in Arms

The death of Cleopatra Syra in 176 BCE must have been swift, as she left no provision for the regency when she was gone. Young Ptolemy VI was given the lofty title 'Pharaoh Ptolemy the Mother-Loving God' (Ptolemy Philometor) but his courtiers recognized that he was too young to rule alone and that a further period of regency was required. Two royal bureaucrats ('creatures of the palace' as the classicist Edwyn Bevan calls them) made the grab for power: first there was Eulaeus, a eunuch who had been part of Cleopatra Syra's network and was already familiar to the new king, since he had been appointed the boy's *syntrophos* (personal tutor) by the late queen; then there was a Syrian named Lenaeus, who had possibly entered Egypt in Cleopatra Syra's wedding retinue. Beyond their former service to Cleopatra Syra, Eulaeus and Lenaeus had little natural talent for governance and were, in fact, totally unequipped to hold high office. Through a curious mixture of arrogance and incompetence, they quickly alienated themselves from the rest of the court, leaving them with no supporters, advisers or friends in high places and yet, probably because they were well known to young Ptolemy from his infancy, the new pharaoh placed his complete trust in them. After organiz-ing the wedding between Ptolemy VI and Cleopatra II, according to Cleopatra Syra's wish, their principal act of *kinderpolitik* was to bring forward the king's *anakleteria*, the 'coming-of-age ceremony', to show that Egypt was in steady hands. The royal titles adopted at this time are very telling: Ptolemy VI had already taken the epithet Philometor, 'Mother-Loving', into his titles during Cleopatra Syra's lifetime, but upon his marriage to his sister, Cleopatra II joined him as Philometores ('Mother-Loving-Ones'), thereby re-emphasizing their connection to Cleopatra I Syra and perhaps projecting a desire thereby to jointly claim what had originally been hers – Coele-Syria.

Seleucid diplomats arrived in Alexandria to congratulate the new king and queen on the auspicious occasion of their wedding (their reports spoke of a distinct anti-Seleucid atmosphere in Alexandria), and an embassy was sent from Rome, too, in order to renew friendship with Ptolemy. Although the sources are silent on this, it is probable that Ptolemy Philometor was crowned as pharaoh with Egyptian rights at Memphis, since Ptolemy V had set the custom for a Memphite ceremonial and thereafter it became a regular event for the later kings of the dynasty.

Wherever the coronation was celebrated, it is certain that Cleopatra II ascended the throne with Ptolemy VI as his co-ruler and the female aspect of the divine monarchy, and her image as Egypt's queen was celebrated enthusiastically. In temple scenes the new queen is depicted carrying out ritual, always standing at the rear of her husband but embodying between them the important ancient Egyptian concept of duality. On the great pylon at Philae the royal couple are shown offering wine, perfume and flowers to Isis, Horus, Hathor, Harpocrates and Meret, and another Philae scene shows Cleopatra II and Ptolemy VI offering cult to Khnum, Satet and Anuket – although the queen is shown here as a passive participant in the ritual, merely raising her hands in adoration before the divine triad and thereby emphasizing emblematically that it was always the king who, at least nominally, exercised power, never the queen. At the temple of Kom Ombo, near Aswan in the south of Egypt, Cleopatra once more plays a supporting role to her husband (who wears the Double Crown) as they both stand before Khonsu, Haroeris and Sobek.

*

Inexperience coupled with a harmless incompetence meant that Eulaeus and Lenaeus were ill-prepared for the challenges of rule, and the rise of a vocal anti-Seleucid party at court, galvanized by the death of Cleopatra Syra, who had assiduously championed peaceful relations between Syria and Egypt, put untold strain on them. As old animosities flared up once again and talk of war was reignited, the anti-Syrian movement began to openly call for an invasion of Seleucid lands and the return of Coele-Syria, lost to Egypt on Cleopatra Syra's death. Rather than stifle the incendiary rhetoric, the regents played into the hands of the anti-Seleucid party and at a mass assembly held in the city's gymnasium rashly promised the Alexandrians that the swift annexation of Coele-Syria would indeed follow on from a full-scale invasion of Syria. Cleopatra Syra's peacekeeping policy was overturned and war fever swept through the city.

Despite their total lack of military experience, Ptolemy and Cleopatra's regents quickly set Egypt on a collision course with King Antiochus IV Epiphanes, who had ascended to the Seleucid throne after the assassination of his brother Seleucus IV. In a quintessential instance of levirate marriage, he had married his brother's widow, Laodice IV, and had adopted Seleucus' young son (technically, the reigning king) Antiochus as his co-regent and heir. When news reached Antiochus IV that the Alexandrian court was making overtures of war, he seized the opportunity to echo the same sentiments and let it be known that he too was ready for conflict.

As part of their propaganda operation, in November 170 BCE Eulaeus and Lenaeus inaugurated a new form of rulership within the royal family. They established a triad of co-rulers which was comprised of Ptolemy VI Philometor, Cleopatra II and their youngest brother, Potbelly (or 'Ptolemy the brother' as he was known at the time). The three siblings became joint rulers of equal status and counterpart associates on the throne of Horus, and a document from the city of Philadelphia in Lower Egypt made at the time names the three siblings as joint sovereigns. It is marked by a distinctive renumbering of regnal years: 'the twelfth year which is also the first'.

The rationale for the unorthodox and momentous move to put three siblings on the throne together remains unknown – it certainly had no pharaonic or Hellenistic precedent, but it is possible that Eulaeus and Lenaeus were attempting to diminish the power which Ptolemy VI was beginning to accrue for himself as he grew in age and experience. Fearing Ptolemy would assume full power for himself, Eulaeus and Lenaeus decided to weaken his position by placing the young Potbelly at his side. If we are to give Eulaeus and Lenaeus the benefit of the doubt, then at best they were trying to create a sense of unity among the siblings, but if the motive of the incompetent ministers was to maintain their own tenuous grip on power by deliberately creating dissent among Cleopatra Syra's children, then it worked brilliantly. They created a recipe for disaster.

It is possible that Ptolemy VI felt indignant at having to share the throne with his younger brother, but for Potbelly himself, his unexpected access to joint power came as a delightful surprise. His sudden rise in status did little to restrain his sense of self-importance and his awareness that his primary role in life was now as a rival to his elder brother. When Potbelly was prematurely elevated to the joint throne of his siblings, a monster was born.

The official nature of the relationship between Potbelly and his two siblings is unclear, but he does not appear to have wed his sister and there is no evidence that Cleopatra II entered a polyandrous marriage at this date – that notion was too much even for the incestuous Ptolemies. Instead, Cleopatra II found herself in the role of mediator. It was a role that appealed to her ego and also provided her with a covert opportunity to exert authority over both brothers – to her own advantage. In her dealings with the brothers, Cleopatra II revealed herself to be a superb manipulator with a special skill in passive aggressivity. Her indirect expressions of hostility, which she aimed principally at Potbelly – whom she regarded as an underachieving chancer – were eventually to sabotage their relationship completely.

With the creation of the tripartite monarchy came nothing but strife. Not surprisingly, with the three rulers locked in conflict, the fortunes of the Ptolemaic dynasty began to waver: overseas territories were lost and Egypt's standing in international affairs took a marked dip. But the most noticeable feature of this period was the decaying power of the kings themselves, a truth made ever more apparent by the rise in authority of the queens. The era of the tripartite co-rule ushered in the dawn of female supremacy, an age of girl power, which was to last until the sunset of the dynasty's history. Cleopatra II built on her mother's reputation for solid governance and in future years established herself as a notable authority in domestic and international politics, but at the time of the triple monarchy not even her talents for negotiation could quell the discord within her own palace. Needless to say, with three power-hungry siblings sharing the one throne, and with two weak regents struggling to hold the royal council together, the tension at the Alexandrian court was palpable. It soon became known in Syria that Egypt was in a state of collapse.

In August 170 BCE Antiochus IV executed his nephew-stepson, who had been his co-ruler since 175 BCE, and replaced him with his own son (born of his wife, Laodice IV), also named Antiochus. The Seleucid monarch rightly regarded the farcical shenanigans in Alexandria as an opportunity to prime Syria for war. He had already sent ambassadors to Rome to request a renewal of the *societas et amicitia* or friendship pact that had been established between the two powers at the end of the reign of his father, Antiochus III, and now he sent vast bribes of money to Rome in the hope of securing favourable diplomatic relations in the face of impending war with the Ptolemies. The cash, together with 500 pounds in weight of gold tableware, helped sweeten the Romans enough to have them renew their treaty of friendship.

Given the lamentable state of government in Alexandria, Antiochus began to visualize himself as the future ruler of Egypt, safely protected and upheld on the pharaonic throne by the guiding power of mighty Rome. As the anonymous author of the Apocryphal biblical book I Maccabees put it, '[Antiochus] thought to reign over Egypt that he might have the dominion of two realms' and was intent on seizing Egypt, 'despising the youthfulness of its king and the inexperience of his tutors'.

The Sixth Syrian War was a swift and bloody affair. It was also an unmitigated disaster for Egypt. Early in 169 BCE Eulaeus and Lenaeus, full of misplaced bravado, sent their troops north-east, out of Egypt, towards Gaza. Antiochus IV was waiting for them there with his war-elephants, and at Mount Casius he successfully overwhelmed the Egyptians and inflicted on them a crushing defeat. Antiochus rapidly marched his armies south-west and succeeded in capturing the border city of Pelusium; from there he entered into Egyptian territory – it was the first invasion of Egyptian soil since the conquest of Alexander the Great 150 years before. Ptolemy VI Philometor, acting on the advice of Eulaeus, was persuaded to take all his money, abandon his kingdom to the enemy and escape from Alexandria. This Ptolemy did. His intention was to head out to sea to the safety of the sacred island of Samothrace, but he was captured by Seleucid forces and held by them as a prisoner of war. Meanwhile, Cleopatra and Potbelly, left behind in the palace at Alexandria, were flabbergasted by Ptolemy's unforeseen escape and even the level-headed Cleopatra must have realized that she did not have full control of her husband's actions. The Greek historian Polybius found himself struggling to exonerate Ptolemy VI for his actions, although in his account of the disturbances he lays the blame squarely at the feet of Eulaeus:

> Who, reflecting on this, would not acknowledge that evil company does the greatest possible harm to men? For a prince, standing in no immediate danger and so far removed from his enemies, not to take any steps to fulfil his duty, especially as he commanded such great resources, and ruled over so great a country and so vast a population, but to yield up at once without a single effort such a splendid and prosperous kingdom, can only be described as the act of one whose mind is effeminate and utterly corrupted. Had Ptolemy been such a man by nature, we should have put the blame on nature

and not accused anyone but himself. But since by his subsequent actions, nature defended herself by showing Ptolemy to have been a man who was fairly steadfast and brave when in danger, it is evident that we should attribute to the eunuch and association with him his cowardice on this occasion and his haste to retire to Samothrace.

Youth and inexperience aside, we must question Polybius' whitewashing of a young man who, it must be said, was a weak individual with little strength of purpose.

With his troops occupying a large part of Lower Egypt, Antiochus IV attempted to win over the population there (especially the Greeks) with gifts of gold coins and other forms of largess. Antiochus discussed the problem of Coele-Syria with an embassy sent from Alexandria, and he put forward the historical rationale, from the Seleucid point of view, of why the region was rightly his, refuting completely the Egyptian claims that his sister Cleopatra Syra had brought Coele-Syria to Egypt as part of her dowry when he married Ptolemy V. Antiochus marched on to Memphis and had his nephew, the captured Ptolemy Philometor, brought to him for a parley. Antiochus reminded Ptolemy of his mother's proud Seleucid heritage and posed as a kind uncle-protector, all the while, Polybius observed, deceiving Ptolemy in the most blatant fashion as he went about 'sacrilegiously despoiling most of the temples.' Under the 'protection' of his Seleucid uncle, Ptolemy was compelled to declare Antiochus as his co-ruler, 'pharaoh Antiochus', ignoring his two existing co-rulers, Cleopatra II and Potbelly.

In Alexandria, an overdue palace revolution ousted Eulaeus and Lenaeus from power (they disappear from history without further mention); they were replaced by two military men from the top echelons of Alexandrian society, Comanus and Cineas. According to the historian Porphyry, they persuaded 'the inhabitants of Alexandria [to] put the younger brother in charge', and so Potbelly became pharaoh and the short-lived rule of the three siblings collapsed. The position of queen was retained by

Cleopatra II, although there is no evidence to suggest that she married her younger brother at this time.

The promotion of Potbelly to king in Alexandria was the excuse kindly uncle Antiochus IV needed to besiege the city, for his objective was to proclaim Ptolemy VI Philometor as the sole pharaoh and to rule Egypt through his compliant nephew. The well-defended capital city, pressed up against the sea and with plentiful stores of grain in its many warehouses, held out against Antiochus' siege, and the Alexandrians sent ambassadors to Rome to ask for support (the Romans ignored all entreaties). Antiochus tried an assault on the city on three sides but failed, and when news reached him in the autumn of 169 BCE of domestic turmoil in Palestine, he quickly departed for his homeland, leaving behind in Memphis Ptolemy VI, who, he envisaged, would continue in his stead the campaign against Potbelly, Cleopatra, and the Alexandrians. For good measure, and to keep one foot in Egypt, Antiochus stationed a garrison at Pelusium, on the Egyptian side of Sinai. 'It was obvious', reported Livy:

> that Antiochus was cleaving to the king of Egypt in order to make a fresh invasion whenever he chose, but for Ptolemy [Philometor], engaging in familial strife with his brother would prove to be his ruin, since, even if victorious, he would be no match for Antiochus after an exhausting war.

One disgruntled but perceptive Egyptian priest named Hor, who was based in the temple of Thoth at Saqqara, lamented how 'Egypt had divorced itself from Alexandria'. The dangerously unstable situation could not last and so in the winter of 169/8 BCE, negotiations opened between the Alexandrian and Memphite parties to break the deadlock and find a way forward. Livy had no doubt about who must be credited for leading the negotiations and for guiding strategy: Cleopatra II. She 'helped greatly by her advice and her appeals', says Livy, and because of her diplomatic acumen 'peace was made, and [Philometor] was admitted into Alexandria with everybody's consent; even the populace manifested no opposition.' In other words, the outcome of negotiations was simply a renewal of the previous tripartite rule.

Livy's praise of Cleopatra Is notable, but it might be prudent to recognize what lay behind her reconciliatory actions: self-preservation. And who can blame her? If Ptolemy VI's weakness was to be the hallmark of his reign, and if Potbelly should gain supremacy over his elder brother, then Cleopatra's future would be dependent upon the loathsome Potbelly. So she carefully nurtured a workable relationship with her hated brother. At the same time though, as the wife of Ptolemy VI, Cleopatra still needed to appear to all and sundry as a loving and dutiful sister-consort, and so she celebrated his return to the triple-monarchy accordingly. The second period of tripartite rule, which would last until 164 BCE, witnessed the royal brothers and their clever sister operating with relative amity, but hindsight confirms that in her relationship with her siblings, Cleopatra II was prepared to play a long game.

*

In 168 BCE Antiochus IV moved against Egypt once again. His troops occupied the Delta and then moved into Memphis without a battle. His intention was to establish a Seleucid protectorate over Egypt in the name of his nephew Ptolemy VI Philometor, and therefore, after a stay in Memphis, he headed towards Alexandria with his armed forces for the second time. As a knee-jerk reaction, the Egyptians appealed to Rome for help, which was duly dispatched by the senate in the person of the venerable Gaius Popilius Laenas, who met with Antiochus at Eleusis, a suburb of Alexandria. There, at the beginning of July 168 BCE, on what is now known as 'the day of Eleusis', Popilius presented the king with a *senatus consultum* ordering Antiochus to cease and desist in his interference in Egyptian affairs. The scene that was played out that day was to be made famous by Livy:

> After crossing the river at Eleusis, about four miles from Alexandria, Antiochus [IV] was met by the Roman commissioners, to whom he gave a friendly greeting and held out

his hand to Popilius. However, Popilius placed in Antiochus' hand the tablets on which was written the decree of the senate and told him first of all to read that. After reading it through Antiochus said he would call his friends into council and consider what he ought to do. Popilius, stern and imperious as ever, drew a circle round the king with the stick he was carrying and said, 'Before you step out of that circle give me a reply to lay before the senate.' For a few moments the king hesitated, astounded at such a dogmatic order, and at last replied, 'I will do what the senate thinks right.' Not till then did Popilius extend his hand to the king as to a friend and ally. Antiochus quit Egypt at the appointed date, and the commissioners exerted their authority to establish a lasting concord . . . The work of the [Roman] commissioners won great renown amongst the nations, for it was undoubtedly owing to this that Egypt had been rescued out of the hands of Antiochus and the crown restored to the Ptolemaic dynasty.

In the broader context of Hellenistic historiography, the Roman embassy to Alexandria and the memorable image of a gnarled but experienced Roman *senex* cutting through the pomp and circumstance of Hellenistic royal diplomacy and delivering a blunt ultimatum to the Seleucid king is seen as a watershed moment in which the brute force of Rome had come to eclipse the grandeur and power of the old successor kingdoms that had replaced the empire of Alexander the Great.

The huge geographical scope of dominance already achieved by the Roman Republic by the 160s BCE was unparalleled for an ancient city-state. Monarchs like Darius and Xerxes of Persia had achieved wide and long-lasting territorial rule in the 500s BCE, but never city-state republics or democracies. Historians have long been fascinated by Roman imperial expansion, and rightly so. The reason for the fascination was explained early on by Polybius (*c.* 150 BCE), a contemporary witness:

Who is so indolent a person as not to wish to know by what means and because of what qualities of government and way of life the Romans have succeeded in subjecting almost the entire known world to their rule – and this within a period of fifty-three years?

Polybius went on to observe that there were no competitors on the Mediterranean horizon with the military, political, economic and social resources to challenge the Romans' domination – and he was right. Moreover, many scholars now argue that for Rome, war and military expansion was a social, political and economic necessity, there to satisfy the material and ideological needs of the Republican aristocracy and to resolve social and economic problems. So indispensable was war to the functioning of the Republic that the Romans looked for war when none was ready at hand. Rome was a war machine and its extraordinary rise to power in the Mediterranean can be explained only as the result of continual aggression against its neighbours. By the 160s BCE Rome had become an insatiable predator.

Much of our reading of Roman involvement in the affairs of Hellenistic monarchies is rightly coloured by the military exploits of Rome. Yet this needs to sit alongside the routine involvement of Roman statesmen in the affairs of the kings and queens of the east, who in turn played a prominent role in the factional politics of the Roman Republic. Time and again the Roman Republic displayed its preference for dispatching occasional embassies who made a show of ordering Hellenistic monarchs around rather than directly entangling themselves in long-term wars. The results were always the same though: as soon as the blustery Roman embassies returned home, the power politics of the Hellenistic monarchs returned to normal and the squabbling continued unaffected.

In Egypt, in the second period of tripartite rule, which seems to have lasted until 164 BCE, the restored sibling-monarchs appear to have operated with relative amity. Polybius describes the Ptolemies turning their attention to more pressing matters of royal government, and he records that in this period two kings wore the Egyptian crown but he makes no reference to Cleopatra II at all. Egypt's epigraphic evidence tells another story: a donation was given to a temple of Egyptian deities in Argos in the Peloponnese, for instance, by the two Ptolemies and by Cleopatra, while a papyrus from the Memphite Serapaeum dated 21 September 164 BCE begins with a formal greeting: 'King Ptolemy Is well and King Ptolemy his brother and Queen Cleopatra their sister.' More tellingly, a relief sculpture from the small Ptolemaic temple at Dier el-Medina at Thebes shows the three royal siblings offering homage to the gods Amun-Re, Amun and Anumet. Ptolemy Philometor is given the position of precedence, standing in front of his brother and sister as the eldest of the children of Ptolemy V and Cleopatra Syra; he wears the white crown of Upper Egypt (the locale of Dier el-Medina itself). Standing behind his brother and wearing the red crown of Lower Egypt is Potbelly (looking unrealistically svelte), and Cleopatra II brings up the rear. She wears an uraeus (upright cobra) on a 'fillet' (narrow strip of cloth) tied around her head, a long wig of ringlets and the towering feathered crown of Isis-Hathor. Her left hand is now missing, but she probably held an ankh, the symbol of life. The temple's iconography stresses the hierarchical relationship of the siblings (at least as a public articulation of the tripartite rule), but it says more than that: it tells us that just as each of the two brothers wears a crown of the north and the south of the country, so too the unity of Egypt is only possible when the two Ptolemies are joined on the throne. Egypt does not exist without the unity of the Two Lands, and the Two Lands cannot exist without the two brothers who jointly rule in harmony, unity and accord. Cleopatra might seem to be an adjunct to the sibling rulership, relegated as she is to the far right of the relief, but her integrity to the Two Lands is made certain when we explore the connection the three royal siblings have with the three deities enthroned before them.

It was a common device in Ptolemaic imagery to assimilate portraits of kings and queens with gods and goddesses. On the Dier el-Medina relief, the synergy between rulers and deities is accentuated since Ptolemy VI Philometor is placed in the complementary position to Amun-Re, while Potbelly stands so as to reflect the position of Amun – the essential 'self' of the composite deity Amun-Re; Cleopatra II echoes the position of Amunet, the female principal of Amun, the god's feminine aspect. The goddess's name means 'the Hidden One' although she was known by a strangely empowering title, 'the Mother who is the Father'. Thereby, through Amunet's identification with Cleopatra II, the latter's gender-fluid role as a *female* pharaoh was emphasized. Put together, the joint appearance of Ptolemy Philometor, Potbelly and Cleopatra on the temple wall was meant to underscore that the tripartite rulership brought unity and happiness to Egypt.

Interestingly, in the Ptolemaic period the goddess Amunet became associated with childbirth. She was carved on the exterior wall of the Festival Hall of Thutmose III in Karnak suckling pharaoh Philip Arrhidaios (323–317 BCE), who appears, immediately after his own enthronement, as her divine child. If this association with childbirth continued into later centuries of the Ptolemaic regime, then we cannot rule out another level operating in the visual synergy between Amunet and Cleopatra II, since the queen proved to be fertile and provided her husband, Ptolemy VI, with four children. The eldest was the son and heir, Ptolemy Eupator, who was born on 15 October 166 BCE. His arrival had been foretold in a dream sent to Hor, the Egyptian priest in service at the temple of Thoth at Saqqara, in which the removal of Antiochus IV's threat to Egypt had been reported. In Hor's dream oracle, Isis herself proclaimed Cleopatra's pregnancy:

I was told a dream: Isis, the great goddess of Egypt and the land of Syria, walks upon the face of the waters of the Syrian sea. Thoth stands before her and takes her hand. She has reached the harbour of Alexandria. She says, 'Alexandria is safe against the enemy. Pharaoh [Ptolemy VI] resides within [the city] with his siblings [Potbelly and Cleopatra II]. After him his son will wear the diadem. This son's son wears the diadem after him. The son of the son of the son wears the diadem after him, for a great length of days. The proof of this is that the queen bears a male child.'

Cleopatra II's next baby was a girl whom her parents named Cleopatra Thea. She was born in 164 BCE, a time of high political tension at the Alexandrian court, which cannot have made the twenty-year-old queen's pregnancy and delivery easy. Cleopatra II's two brothers continued to squabble. They were as different as chalk and cheese: while Ptolemy Philomator was gentle, kind and dutiful (albeit a little weak), Potbelly was naturally cruel, vindictive and petty (albeit intelligent, cultivated and oddly charismatic). Given the differences between them, there is little wonder that the latent hostilities that had bubbled out of sight for a decade began to resurface.

When Ptolemy Philometor led troops into Upper Egypt to quell a short-lived uprising, Potbelly seized the opportunity to organize his supporters into a resistance group and succeeded in ousting Ptolemy from Alexandria, declaring that the tripartite rule was over. At first, Potbelly placed his sister Cleopatra on the throne next to him (but made no move to make her his wife). She was, after all, the mother of two infants fathered by the dethroned pharaoh, who was making his way to Rome to work on gathering senatorial support for his restoration. By the beginning of 163 BCE Potbelly was ruling alone in Alexandria, his sister having made her escape, with her young children, to Cyprus, still a Ptolemaic territory. Cleopatra had probably feared for her children's lives and concluded that self-induced exile was better than life with her monstrous brother. Safe in Paphos, she was joined by her husband, Ptolemy Philometor, who sailed there from Italy, and they began to plot a comeback.

Without his sister's calming influence, Potbelly soon began to reveal his true colours, persecuting and executing his brother's chief aides and supporters and many of his courtiers. By May 163 BCE the Alexandrians had had enough of Potbelly's cruel caprices. Diodorus notes that they were 'disgusted with the king for his shameless treatment of his brother, stripped him of his royal retinue and sent to Cyprus to recall the elder Ptolemy'. They stormed the palace, overpowered Potbelly's bodyguards and ousted the fat king from the throne. He escaped with his life intact but his dignity in shreds.

So was the Alexandrian mob born. King-makers and king-breakers, operating through a terrifying collective mentality, the Alexandrian mob moved as one and dispensed immediate and resolute justice where they believed that justice had failed. Originally a small band of marginalized discontents, the Alexandrian mob went on to be comprised of merchants, servants and even members of the royal court, eventually becoming large enough to be considered as a major political force by the Ptolemies, who throughout their subsequent history considered the consequences of mob action before making any decisions.

Suddenly, Ptolemy Philometor and Cleopatra II found themselves back in Alexandria, where they were greeted warmly by the enthusiastic, if fickle, locals. Over the summer of 163 BCE, Ptolemy and Potbelly locked heads and tried to hammer out a reconciliation, under the watchful gaze of Cleopatra and, more threateningly, the eyes of an irritable Rome. During the period of Potbelly's usurpation, both brothers had repeatedly sought intercession from the Romans, begging the senate to pronounce on Egypt's internal affairs. Potbelly had gone so far in courting the senate's favour that he even created a will stating that Rome would inherit Egypt should he die as king without an heir. 'If anything human should befall me before I leave successors to my kingship,' he wrote, 'I leave the kingdom that belongs to me to the Romans, with whom I have from the beginning truly maintained friendship and alliance.' He also entreated Rome to come to his assistance should his realm be subject to attack, and invoked in his will a number of Roman gods as witnesses, among them Jupiter Capitolinus.

For modern scholars, the importance of Potbelly's will lies in the fact that for the first time in history a Hellenistic ruler made the Roman people his beneficiary in the case of his dying without a legitimate heir. It was a bold and egregious act on Potbelly's part, although it had little effect among the Romans (the will gets no mention in the histories of the period, and even Polybius seems to be ignorant of it). After all, Potbelly was still a young man and it was thought very unlikely that he would not leave a legitimate heir after him.

The real purpose of Potbelly's will was to rattle his siblings. It worked. Ptolemy Philometor and Cleopatra agreed that ousting their brother from official power would be a good thing, and once again they called on Rome to intercede. Late in the summer of 163 BCE, an embassy was sent to Alexandria by the senate to divide the remaining Ptolemaic territories into two: Egypt and Cyprus were handed to Ptolemy VI and Cleopatra, whilst Potbelly was bundled out of the palace and shipped off to Cyrenaica (in modern Libya), which he was given as his own mini-kingdom. For the next decade and more, Potbelly would continue to barrage the Roman senate with petitions to back his claims on Cyprus, but at least he was out of Egypt – out of sight if not exactly out of mind.

In October 163 BCE Ptolemy VI, aged about twenty-three, and Cleopatra II, a year younger, departed Alexandria and arrived in the ancient capital of Memphis. There they resided in a palace adjacent to the old temple of Ptah and received petitions and accolades from their subjects. In a well-organized piece of PR, the royal couple went on a city walkabout and visited the temples, as pharaohs had always done, making the requisite offerings and sacrifices at these holy shrines. They showed themselves too at the palace's Window of Appearances, the forerunner of the 'balcony appearance' beloved by modern royal-watchers; it was a nice pharaonic touch which endeared the royal couple to the clergy and the populace. A priestly synod was called, and the king was careful to court the priests as a means of assuring the loyalty of the temples. The message conveyed during the Memphite visit was clear: now that the chaotic force that was Potbelly had vanished, good order had been restored in Egypt. As living symbols of the restoration of harmony, little prince Ptolemy Eupator and baby princess Cleopatra Thea had their parts to play at Memphis too, and they accompanied their parents on all their official visits – after all, everyone loves a royal baby.

Two more offspring can be ascribed to Cleopatra II and
Ptolemy Philopator: another daughter, Cleopatra III, whose date
of birth is unknown but is estimated at 160–157 BCE; and one
more son, Ptolemy, born probably before 4 April 152 BCE – he
was destined to be Ptolemy VII Neos Philopator. Neither of the
sons would live long enough to rule as sole pharaoh, but both
daughters – Cleopatra Thea and Cleopatra III – had long and (as
will become apparent) eventful lives.

With Potbelly gone, the royal titulature changed again: the
king and queen were known as 'the pharaohs Ptolemy and Cleopatra, the Mother-Loving Gods', a designation they would retain
for the next eighteen years of their married life. In every known
example of the royal titulature, Cleopatra II was listed by name
after her brother-husband as his equal in governance; in fact, Cleopatra II was the first Ptolemaic queen to be granted this accolade.
The queen appears in all Greek and Demotic protocols directly
behind Ptolemy Philometor and is often referred to as the 'sister'
or 'sister and wife' of the king. In addition, she officially participated in the management of Egypt: the two sovereigns are invoked
in the oaths of Egyptians, and they received petitions and reports
in both their names and co-signed all royal orders and letters to
bureaucrats. These factors add up to show that Cleopatra was
clearly understood as the co-ruler with her spouse and that she
achieved complete equality with Ptolemy VI as Egypt's god-king
and goddess-queen.

*

Ptolemy Philometor and Cleopatra II were great builders. They
undertook repairs of existing temples throughout the Nile Valley
and even created new ones. They completed works at Dendera
(the erection of the birth house of Isis), at Karnak (where the huge
gate of the second pylon was restored), at Armant near Thebes,
and on the island of Elephantine (which saw the completion and
decoration of the temple of Khnum), as well as at the Isis temple
at Philae.

An exquisite little temple at Kom Ombo (Egyptian, Nwbt, 'City of Gold'), close to Edfu and Aswan, was built anew on the orders of the king and queen. There the crocodile was held in especial honour by the people, and the new temple was dedicated to the worship of the crocodile-headed god Sobek, as well as to Haroeris ('Horus the Elder'). For the ancient Egyptians, the crocodile was a force to be reckoned with; it was a common but dangerous creature which frequented one of the busiest and most important spheres of human habitation: the water's edge. And yet the Nile crocodile was a sacred beast, closely associated with the god Sobek, whose major cult-centres were located at both Kom Ombo and in the richly fertile marshes of the Fayum. Sobek had few myths, but his epithets, linking him to the powerful amphibious reptile, were plentiful. Sobek was hymned as 'pointed of teeth', 'standing on his claws', 'who lives on robbery', 'who eats while he mates', 'who impregnates females', who is 'alert-looking, broad-chested, sparkling' and 'who is in splendour'. Given the close affinity between the god and the crocodile, unsurprisingly Sobek's temples have yielded solid proof that crocodiles were kept in large numbers by the god's priests and that they were mummified and venerated after death. Several crocodile necropolises, mainly dating to the Ptolemaic period, have been found in the Fayum and Upper Egypt; at Kom Ombo crocodile mummies were discovered still in their clay coffins and, remarkably, crocodile mummies have often been found alongside eggs and hatchlings. Newborn crocodiles were reared in temples like Kom Ombo and then, while still young, they were sacrificed, mummified and sold to pilgrims, who could then dedicate them to Sobek in the chapels of the temple. The site of Kom Ombo offers excellent evidence for a lucrative business in the breeding, slaughter and sale of reptiles to satisfy the needs of a mass pilgrim-tourist industry which developed rapidly throughout the Ptolemaic period.

Such was the popularity of Ptolemy Philometor and Cleopatra that at the military garrison in Aswan a club was formed to celebrate the annual festival in honour of the king, the queen and their children. In the wider sphere of the Hellenistic world the royal couple were admired too, for both gained notable victories in the chariot races they sponsored in the Olympic Games of 162 BCE and were hailed by the Greeks as 'beloved by the gods'. Much of the goodwill the king and queen incurred from others was down to their personalities, for (at her best) Cleopatra was rational, highly capable and generous, whilst Ptolemy Philometor was mild and easy-going, at least as Polybius portrays him:

> [H]e was a gentle and good man, if ever there was one among the preceding kings. There is very strong proof of this. Firstly, he did not execute any of his friends on any charge. And I think that no Alexandrian either was put to death because of him.

*

It was during the joint reign of Ptolemy Philometor and Cleopatra II that the Jewish community of Egypt grew in size and standing. There had been a Jewish military colony on the island of Elephantine in Aswan since the early fifth century BCE, and it had flourished under Persian rule. Because of his open-door policy, under Ptolemy I many Jews flooded into Egypt, and Alexandria quickly established a considerable Jewish community. The first synagogues are attested in Egypt in the reign of Ptolemy III and, with the passage of time, the number of Jews in Egypt grew ever larger, especially after Coele-Syria was lost to the Seleucids and the Jewish inhabitants there were displaced. Jewish communities of significant size appeared in Memphis, in the Fayum, the Delta and in the Thebaid, where they were recognized as a separate ethnic group possessing a distinct nationality and religious identity and benefitted from the privileges which the Ptolemies accorded to such groups.

In the Seleucid empire, however, the Jewish experience was decidedly different. In the years after the Sixth Syrian War Antiochus IV adopted a violent policy against the Jews, fuelled by his commitment to a programme of Hellenization, for he thought that the independent national identity of the Jews and the practice of their monotheistic faith was in direct and dangerous opposition to his vision of a homogenous Greek realm. In 168 BCE Antiochus launched a vicious attack on Jerusalem, in which, as the Bible's Book of Maccabees recalls:

> Raging like a wild animal, he . . . ordered his soldiers to cut down without mercy those whom they met and to slay those who took refuge in their houses. There was a massacre of young and old, a killing of women and children, a slaughter of virgins and infants. In the space of three days, eighty thousand were lost, forty thousand meeting a violent death, and the same number being sold into slavery.

Antiochus issued decrees forbidding many traditional Jewish practices and began a campaign of persecution against orthodox Jews. Diodorus Siculus records how:

> [Antiochus] sacrificed many pigs [which Jews regard as unclean] at the image of Moses, and at the altar of God that stood in the outward court of the Temple, and sprinkled them [the Jewish elders] with the blood of the sacrifice. He commanded likewise that the books, by which they were taught to hate all other nations, should be sprinkled with the broth made of the swine's flesh. And he put out the lamp [called by them immortal] which burns continually in the temple. Lastly, he forced the high priest and the other Jews to eat the flesh of swine.

A series of decrees in 167 BCE led to Jerusalem's transformation into a Greek polis; the cult of YHWH, the ancestral God of the Jews, was prohibited and his holy Temple of Zion was reconsecrated to the worship of Olympian Zeus. The Hasmonean family, a powerful dynasty of Jewish priests, established themselves as defenders of the Jewish faith, and through successful guerrilla attacks against the Seleucid military they provoked a national and religious war of liberation – the so-called great Maccabean revolt. After several brilliantly coordinated military operations, in

164 BCE Judas Maccabeus, the third son of Mattathias the Hasmonean priest, succeeded in taking Jerusalem from Antiochus and re-establishing the cult of YHWH. Some scholars suggest that the Maccabean revolt prompted the writing of the prophetic Book of Daniel, in which a villain called the 'King of the North' is generally considered to be a reference to Antiochus IV; his portrayal as the attacker of the holy city of Jerusalem would eventually influence early Christian depictions of the Antichrist. When Antiochus IV suddenly died of disease on a campaign in Parthia in 164 BCE, the Jewish sources attributed his swift demise to his earlier impiety at the Temple of Jerusalem. According to 2 Maccabees, he died from a divinely inflicted ailment:

> But the all-seeing Lord, the God of Israel, struck him with an incurable and invisible blow . . . he was seized with a pain in his bowels, for which there was no relief, and with sharp internal tortures – and that very justly, for he had tortured the bowels of others with many and strange inflictions . . . He, who only a little while before had thought in his super-human arrogance that he could command the waves of the sea, and had imagined that he could weigh the high mountains in a balance, was brought down to earth and carried in a litter, making the power of God manifest to all. And so, the ungodly man's body swarmed with worms, and while he was still living in anguish and pain, his flesh rotted away, and because of the stench the whole army felt revulsion at his decay.

Perhaps fearing the power of the Jewish God, the new nine-year-old Seleucid ruler Antiochus V Eupator (164–162 BCE), appointed as king by the Romans, accepted the liberation of Jerusalem without opposition.

One of the consequences of the upheavals in Jerusalem was the appearance in Egypt of a man named Onias, the heir of the Zadokite line of High Priests of Israel. He arrived in Egypt at the end of the 160s BCE with a large following and was permitted by Ptolemy Philometor and Cleopatra to settle in Leontopolis

in the Delta and to erect a temple to YHWH on the site of an
abandoned temple of the cat-goddess Bastet; the area became
known as the 'Land of Onias', and the Jewish temple of Leontopolis (today known as Tel el-yahudiya, 'Hill of the Jews') remained
an important centre for the Jewish community in Egypt well
into Roman times. A short while after the establishment of the
YHWH temple, Onias, his two sons Chelkias and Ananias, and
one of his followers, Dositheus, received by royal decree high
positions of command in the Ptolemaic army. It is certain that
Ptolemy Philometor and Cleopatra took personal interest in the
Jews, and it is quite likely that the Jewish community in Alexandria benefitted from some kind of formal organization during
their joint reign. Jewish literature from Alexandria in the third
and second centuries BCE demonstrates the extent to which Greek
culture was keenly adapted by Jewish communities. One of the
most important representatives of the Jewish intelligentsia was
the philosopher Aristobulus, who dedicated an exegesis of the
books of Moses to Ptolemy Philometor and Cleopatra. In the years
after the death of Ptolemy VI, Onias and his sons were to remain
faithful to Cleopatra II and even went on to serve her daughter
Cleopatra III. Their devotion to the two queens suggests that the
kindness shown to Onias and the Jews by the Egyptian crown was
never forgotten.

PART TWO

EXPANDING HORIZONS

Cleopatra II
Cleopatra Thea
Cleopatra III
Cleopatra IV
Cleopatra Tryphaina
Cleopatra Selene

CLEOPATRA II

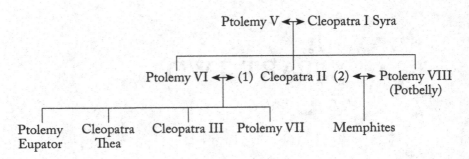

Ptolemy V ←→ Cleopatra I Syra

Ptolemy VI ←→ (1) Cleopatra II (2) ←→ Ptolemy VIII (Potbelly)

Ptolemy Eupator | Cleopatra Thea | Cleopatra III | Ptolemy VII | Memphites

CLEOPATRA THEA

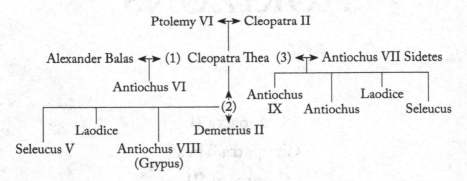

Ptolemy VI ←→ Cleopatra II

Alexander Balas ←→ (1) Cleopatra Thea (3) ←→ Antiochus VII Sidetes

Antiochus VI

(2)

Antiochus IX | Antiochus | Laodice | Seleucus

Seleucus V | Laodice | Antiochus VIII (Grypus) | Demetrius II

CLEOPATRA III

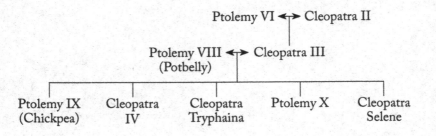

Ptolemy VI ←→ Cleopatra II

Ptolemy VIII (Potbelly) ←→ Cleopatra III

Ptolemy IX (Chickpea) | Cleopatra IV | Cleopatra Tryphaina | Ptolemy X | Cleopatra Selene

CLEOPATRA IV

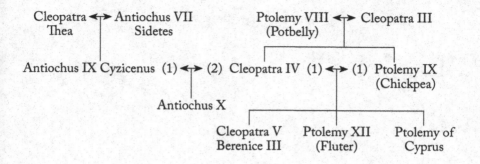

CLEOPATRA TRYPHAINA

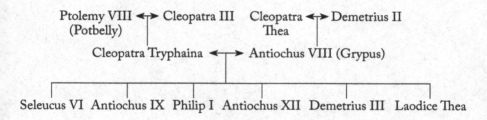

CLEOPATRA SELENE

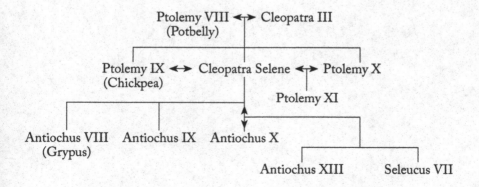

8

Bridal Showers

Ensconced in Cyrene, irate and discontented, Potbelly continued to make trouble for his siblings by directly – and incessantly – involving Rome in Egypt's affairs, so much so that in 154 BCE the exasperated senate granted him military aid in order to invade and secure his hold of the island of Cyprus. However, Ptolemy VI and Cleopatra II, who had the loyal support of the Cyprian cities, quickly and effortlessly drove Potbelly from the island. As a placating gesture to the Romans, whom they recognized as the fastest-growing power in the Mediterranean, they decided to be both lenient and magnanimous to their youngest brother, taking Cyprus from Potbelly but allowing him to keep the territory of Cyrenaica. Polybius wrote: '[Ptolemy VI] was so far from punishing his brother as an enemy that he loaded him with gifts in addition to what he already possessed under treaty and promised him his daughter in marriage.' The daughter in question was almost certainly Cleopatra Thea, given that her sister Cleopatra III was unlikely to have been much more than a toddler at this time. Cleopatra Thea, however, may have been around thirteen and was therefore considered ripe for marriage and childbirth. By offering marriage to his eldest daughter, Ptolemy Philometor was inviting his bother back into the inner sanctum of the royal family and stressing, perhaps that given time, and through his marriage union with his niece, Potbelly (or his decedents) might sit on the throne in his own right.

More practically speaking, though, Ptolemy Philometor obviously wished to prevent any political developments that his younger brother might undertake through an arranged marriage with the princess of some foreign house; keeping Potbelly securely within the family fold was desirable. Probably realizing that this was his brother's tactic, the ever-devious Potbelly superciliously rejected the offer of marriage. It was an insult to both Ptolemy Philometor and Cleopatra II, but they were able to capitalize on this loss of face by appealing to the Romans: the king and queen had demonstrated goodwill towards their younger brother, they stated to the senate, and had looked for harmony but had been spurned. From then on, the Romans were less enthusiastic in their support of Potbelly, who now had to be content with ruling Cyrenaica, although he remained active in Rome's politicking, even offering himself as a husband to Cornelia, the widow of Tiberius Sempronius Gracchus, Rome's war-hero statesman, in about 152 BCE. She refused him.

It is probable that before she was offered in marriage to her uncle, Cleopatra Thea had been intended as a bride for her brother Ptolemy Eupator. Potbelly's rejection of Cleopatra Thea as a bride meant that she was once again Eupator's intended spouse, and that meant she would one day rule by his side as Egypt's queen. But politics intervened one more time as Ptolemy Philometor, like all Ptolemies before him, began directing his attention back to the Seleucid kingdom and the former Ptolemaic territory of Coele-Syria. When Ptolemy VI and Cleopatra II had offered their daughter to her uncle, the king and queen had thereby advertised Cleopatra Thea's availability in the royal bridal market, all but announcing that she had come of age to be used in political matchmaking. Potbelly's rejection of the princess was, in dynastic terms, therefore quite inconsequential since Ptolemy Philometor now realized that he had an enormous asset in his eldest daughter. Breaking with the tradition of marrying the eldest daughter of the house to the heir apparent, Cleopatra Thea became instead the chief transferable 'king-maker' in her father's policy towards the Seleucids.

In Syria, Demetrius I, the eldest son of Seleucus IV and Laodice IV, had become king in November 162 BCE – but not without considerable effort on his part. By all accounts, Demetrius should have succeeded his father to the throne, but Rome's (surprising) direct intervention in favour of his younger brother, Antiochus, had put paid to that. Moreover, when his uncle then speedily usurped power and had himself crowned as Antiochus IV, Demitrius was even further removed from power – he had been taken as a child to Rome, where he remained a royal hostage. After the death of Antiochus IV in 164 BCE, the new child-king, Demitrius' younger brother, Antiochus V Eupator, came under pressure when the Roman senate heard that the Syrian kingdom kept more warships and elephants than was allowed by the Treaty of Apamea, made in 188 BCE. Accordingly, a Roman embassy was sent to travel around the cities of Syria, attempting to cripple Seleucid military power by sinking the Seleucids' warships and hamstringing their fighting elephants.

In Rome, the impatient twenty-two-year-old Demetrius twice petitioned the Roman senate to restore the Syrian throne to him, but twice was he rejected, since the Romans preferred to oversee a weak Syria ruled by an inept child. But Demetrius had his supporters in Rome, including the Greek philosopher Panartius and the historian Polybius (both of whom were part of the intellectual circle of Scipio Aemilianus, the Roman general and statesman noted for his military exploits in the Third Punic War against Carthage), and it occurred to them that there was a man in Rome who could help Demetrius gain the throne: Menyllus of Alabanda. This Menyllus was in Rome as the ambassador of Ptolemy VI and Cleopatra; Polybius knew him well and trusted him implicitly. Polybius introduced him to Demetrius and Menyllus was told about the prince's ambition to take the crown of Syria into his own hands. The quick-thinking ambassador recognized that any trouble in the house of Seleucus would be of benefit to his royal master and mistress, and so he agreed to help Demetrius by commandeering a Carthaginian ship at the port of Ostia, just outside Rome, smuggling the prince aboard and setting sail for Tyre on the coast of Phoenicia (modern Lebanon). By the time the senate realized Demetrius was missing, he had already sailed through

the Straits of Messina and into the Mediterranean. A Roman delegation was dispatched to Syria to watch the events there unfold.

Demetrius' invasion of Syria in 162 BCE (which can be seen
as the catalyst for the complex Seventh Syrian War) was swift and
wildly successful. Everywhere the people rose in support of him,
and at Antioch even the royal troops declared allegiance to him.
He put an end to the brief reign of Antiochus V Eupator, and
after seizing Antioch, Demetrius massacred what remained of the
family of his uncle, Antiochus IV, purportedly without even seeing
them: 'Do not show me their faces', he commanded his soldiers as
they led his cousins in chains towards their execution spot. The
Seleucid *Ancien Régime* collapsed instantly on the reappearance
of Demetrius, and for the Romans this was a matter of intense
anxiety; they began to offer surreptitious support and encouragement to any state or individual who would challenge Demetrius
and weaken the newly energized Seleucid kingdom. The Jewish
Maccabees and the anti-Seleucid kings of Armenia, Rome hoped,
would crush Demetrius' plans for a Seleucid military renaissance once and for all, but in the end, Rome found its answer in
Attalos II of Pergamon.

King Attalos decided to capitalize on the turmoil in Syria by
championing a young man named Alexander Balas as the true
Seleucid king and setting him up as a rival to Demetrius I. Seleucid
propaganda (spread by Polybius, who was ardently pro-Demetrius,
of course) claimed that Balas was an out-and-out nobody, 'a man
of low birth', but in all probability the young man was a son
of Antiochus IV and a royal concubine named Antiochis. The
support Balas enjoyed from the Attalids, and the acknowledgment
of legitimacy he received from the Roman senate, indicate that
the charismatic Balas was widely regarded as a legitimate heir of
Antiochus IV. For this reason, Demetrius I, who took the epithet of
Soter ('Saviour'), decided to anchor his claim to the throne via the
begetting of heirs and so married his sister, Laodice V; she was the
mother of his three sons, Demetrius (II Nicator), Antiochus VII
(Sidetes) and Antigonus, born in conveyor-belt fashion between
162 and 158 BCE.

The chief players in the overthrow of Demetrius I, however, were Ptolemy Philometor and Cleopatra II, who were horrified that Menyllus had acted without their consent to give Demetrius an opportunity to establish himself as king in Syria. They could see for themselves, even if Menyllus could not, how dangerous a re-energized Syria under the rule of an ambitious and enterprising king would be to Egypt. They did everything in their power to block Demetrius' success and soon declared their support for Balas by sending troops into Syria, where, at a decisive battle near Antioch in 150 BCE, they helped bring about the death of Demetrius I. The new Seleucid king, who took the royal name Alexander Theopator Euergetes – 'He Who Comes from a Divine Father, the Benefactor' – purged the court of the former king's favourites and murdered Demetrius' wife, Laodice V, together with her eldest son, Antigonus (her two other sons, Demetrius and Antiochus, managed to escape death). Balas then asked his ally Ptolemy Philometor for his eldest daughter's hand in marriage:

> I have returned to my kingdom and taken my seat on the throne of my ancestors. I have taken over the government, and I am now in control of the country. I made war on Demetrius, defeated him and his army, and I have taken over his kingdom. Now I am ready to make an alliance. Give me your daughter in marriage, and I will give both of you such gifts as you deserve.

King Ptolemy was quick to reply:

> It was a great day when you returned to your country and took the throne of your ancestors. I agree to your proposals, but first meet me at Ptolemaïs-Ake. We can get acquainted there, and I will give you my daughter in marriage.

Ptolemy's promise to give Cleopatra Thea to Balas as his wife must have been regarded by all as implicit royal recognition of the usurper king's legitimate right to the Seleucid throne, since no Ptolemaic ruler would ever have contemplated marrying one of their princesses to a mere commoner, no matter how politically useful. After all, Ptolemaic princesses carried with them a latent claim to the kingship, which could become active in a husband whenever they married. This makes it likely that in the eyes of Ptolemy VI and Cleopatra II, Alexander Balas had at least some shred of royal legitimacy through the blood of Antiochus IV.

We know nothing of the negotiations which underpinned Cleopatra Thea's marriage to Balas, but there must have been some kind of formal agreement between the Egyptian and Seleucid parties, with special attention given to the size of the princess's dowry and its terms and conditions. Without a doubt, Ptolemy Philometor would have used the occasion of his daughter's wedding to 'splash the cash' and celebrate the union of the two houses with all the pomp he could muster. Exogamous weddings demanded this kind of display. In a marriage of international importance, such as that between Balas and Cleopatra Thea, ritual, display and ceremonial were fundamental elements, and the pageantry of Ptolemaic *pompē* – that Egyptian love of spectacle – would have been employed to full effect. When in the 170s BCE the Seleucid bride Laodice (daughter of Seleucus IV) had married Perseus of Macedon, her journey to the Attalid court included an escort of dignitaries and, according to the historian Appian of Alexandria, the whole Rhodian fleet, but we know that Ptolemy VI did better for his daughter: he himself escorted Cleopatra Thea to Ptolemaïs-Ake, an ancient port city on the coast of Palestine, as part of what must have been a very splendid procession indeed, akin, no doubt, to the splendid bridal progresses of Renaissance and Enlightenment Europe.

When a princess was chosen for marriage by a prince from another territory, or was told by her father that she would have to travel far from home to fulfil her matrimonial duty, she was cast in a central role in a huge political and dynastic drama whose script had been written by others. The marriage was conceived behind the scenes in confidential negotiations, and was promulgated in public court announcements, perhaps panegyric poetry, and through spectacular displays of wealth. Cleopatra Thea's marriage to Balas, intended to be the cornerstone of Ptolemy VI's Seleucid policy, was, in the words of I Maccabees, celebrated 'with great splendour as the manner of kings is ... with gifts of silver and gold, and ... many donations to the high officials who had accompanied them. Everyone was favourably impressed.'

Hellenistic royals were trained to be adroit actors; performance was key to their ruling strategy. Cleopatra Thea had no doubt ingested important performative techniques in her mother's milk, and had learned from Cleopatra II the 'job description' for the role she would be expected to play in cult and ritual, royal ceremonials, and the intricacies of court etiquette. Her marriage to Alexander Balas meant that she had to learn to act the role of a queen according to the Seleucid understanding of what that entailed. Cleopatra I Syra had very successfully played the role of a foreign princess in the Egyptian court by assimilating herself into the manners and mores of the Ptolemaic household, and now her granddaughter, Cleopatra Thea, had to find her way in the Seleucid system. Once she arrived in Syria, Cleopatra Thea needed to become absorbed into the Seleucid court as quickly as possible. Cleopatra Thea was expected to integrate herself visibly and fully into the Seleucid system because it would have been fatal for her chances of success if in her new environment she came across as too 'foreign.' Of course, Cleopatra Thea's parents expected, indeed, would have demanded that she further Ptolemaic interests at her marital court, and they must have wished her to keep in mind at all times the family and culture into which she had been born and to which her loyalties belonged.

Royal courts were dangerous environments, and especially so for new royal brides, yet Cleopatra Thea could, if she so chose, exert considerable influence upon the court if she could negotiate her way through its key relationships. The most important of these, of course, was with her husband, the king. Cleopatra Thea never forgot that providing her husband with an heir was her pivotal function within the dynastic system. This was the one and only thing that could give a queen importance and status. At her marriage to Balas, Cleopatra Thea gave her body over to her marital dynasty, to serve its needs by producing the proverbial 'heir and a spare' and as many daughters as might be useful in constructing future international (or domestic) marriage alliances. A successful biological performance was the ultimate role played by any queen, and a year (or thereabouts) after the marriage, Cleopatra Thea gave birth to Balas' heir, Antiochus VI, a prince in whose veins was remixed the blood of the Ptolemies and the Seleucids.

As they settled into their new routines at court and beyond palace life, the young royal couple became aware of the expected division of labour which was paramount to a successful royal partnership. In his new position of ruler, Alexander Balas was responsible for war and government; as queen, Cleopatra Thea was supposed to show piety and loyalty. He built fortresses while she undertook conspicuous acts of civic benevolence and handed out charity; he conquered territories by force of arms while she was responsible for connecting them by brokering marriage alliances. He had to be loved and feared by his people, she had to demonstrate her love for them. Balas could philander with courtesans and concubines, Cleopatra Thea had to be the model of chastity. He needed to be handsome (Balas was certainly that, with chiselled good looks – at least to judge from his coin portraits) and look imposing on horseback, she needed to impress in the palace with her beauty and elegance and sparkling conversation. How all this worked out for royal husbands and wives in reality must have varied greatly, depending much on personalities and personal dynamics, for while some Hellenistic royal marriages were certainly physically and emotionally close, others were disasters. To all intents and purposes, the marriage of Alexander Balas and Cleopatra Thea veered towards the latter. It was pretty much a debacle from the beginning.

*

For all his smouldering good looks and magnetic charisma, Alexander Balas proved to be a profoundly ineffectual ruler at a time when what the Seleucids needed most was a 'strong and stable' leadership. He enjoyed an easy life full of pleasure, neglecting his royal duties for the company of courtesans and allowing the territories of the Seleucid realm to dwindle rapidly. The date of the loss of Mesopotamia to the Arsacid rulers of Parthia can be placed sometime between 155 BCE and 140 BCE, but it is almost certain that Media was lost to the Seleucids in 148 BCE and that the king of Elymais, Camnascires, took the great city of Susa from the Seleucids around 147 BCE. In the same year, Demetrius II, a surviving son of Demetrius I, landed in Cilicia and made his way into northern Syria to claim his father's throne. The presence of the vigorous sixteen-year-old Demetrius in the realm came as a rude shock to Balas, whose life of self-indulgence suddenly came under threat. He hurried from Ptolemaïs-Ake, close to the present-day city of Acre on the Palestinian coast, the seat of his pleasure-loving court, to Antioch only to find that the once-enthusiastic garrison there had was at the point of insurrection and that the governor of Coele-Syria, Apollonius, had declared his support for prince Demetrius. All seemed lost for Balas.

But Balas' father-in-law, Ptolemy Philometor, rushed to Syria to help him, riding at breakneck speed to Ptolemaïs-Ake. There one of the strangest events in Hellenistic history occurred when, for some unfathomable reason, from a safe distance north of Antioch, Balas tried to have Ptolemy assassinated. Did Balas misread the situation and think that Ptolemy Philometor had hurried to Syria to activate his Seleucid birth right and seize the throne for himself? Whatever the rationale, the assassination attempt failed and a furious Ptolemy VI renounced his friendship with Balas and marched his army north towards Antioch, where he was joined by his daughter Cleopatra Thea, who had abandoned both her dead-weight husband and her child, Antiochus VI, who was handed over to an Arab chieftain, Yamlik, for fostering. The boy's parents prepared themselves for open hostilities. It is important to note how Cleopatra Thea did not wait for events to overwhelm her but proactively abandoned her spouse and infant son and sought out her father, thereby declaring her marriage over and giving Ptolemy VI carte blanche to employ her again as a Ptolemaic bride. It is important to acknowledge, too, that this move was made by Cleopatra Thea *herself*, acting in accord with her father. She was to a large extent the maker of her own destiny.

While Ptolemy Philometor and Cleopatra Thea were ensconced in Antioch, the city revolted against Balas and offered the crown to Ptolemy, who was taken by surprise by the enthusiasm of the crowd as citizens and soldiers alike called on him to ascend the throne. Wisely, he graciously declined it. Instead, he persuaded the citizens of Antioch to support Demetrius II, to whom he proffered his support and the hand of Cleopatra Thea. Demetrius promptly became Ptolemy's new son-in-law. Cleopatra Thea's second marriage (a bigamous one) to her second Seleucid prince must have been conducted in considerable haste, without the panoply of splendour which had accompanied her marriage to Balas. Instead, she was hailed as Demetrius' queen when, in 145 BCE, he entered his capital and was acknowledged as the rightful Seleucid king. That night the sixteen-year-old king consummated his marriage with the nineteen-year-old queen.

With this swift transfer of his daughter into Demetrius' bed Ptolemy Philometor was effectively writing Alexander Balas out of dynastic history, as though Balas had never existed in the first place. It appears that Ptolemy Philometor was willing to ignore the existence of his first-born grandson too. Cleopatra Thea's only son was now far away, out of sight and out of mind in Arabia; there would be others to replace him, Ptolemy Philometor thought, born of a proper union between Cleopatra Thea and her lawfully recognized new husband.

King Ptolemy VI Philometor threw himself, body and soul, into a campaign to bring down Alexander Balas, following the latter's bungled assassination attempt against him. The Jewish historian Josephus records how, during a battle with Balas' forces,

> Ptolemy's horse, upon hearing the noise of an elephant, cast him off his back, and threw him on the ground . . . [and] his enemies fell upon him, and gave him many wounds upon his head . . . For four days he was not able either to understand, or to speak . . . On the fifth day he died.

The last date for which we have a text mentioning the king is 15 July 145 BCE, but it is probable that he died several weeks before that. In spite of Ptolemy VI's death, by the high summer of 145 BCE Balas' troops had abandoned him and each of his foreign allies had deserted him – only the Jews continued to support him, since he had allowed them to reclaim a greater degree of religious and political independence than his predecessors had done. The exact circumstances of Balas' death late in August 145 BCE are uncertain: either he was killed by Demetrius' forces or he was murdered as a refugee in Arabia. Either way, he was out of the picture and Cleopatra Thea, simultaneously a young widow and a new bride, was now set to enter again the formidable world of Hellenistic politics. She embraced its challenges with brio.

9

Death on the Nile

King Ptolemy VI's death in battle was a tragic ending to the life of a fine ruler. He had achieved the greatest military success of any pharaoh of his house since the time of Ptolemy III and had effectively taken control of the whole of Syria; Demitrius II, the new Seleucid king, was no more than a puppet in his hands. But at his premature death, the fabric of his power simply frayed away to nothing. The Egyptian forces in Syria were hopelessly lost, without a leader or direction. At the court of Demetrius II, it was decided that invaders should be repelled before they could consolidate their hold over Seleucid territory any further. Demetrius ordered a massacre of the Egyptian forces, and the population of the coastal towns and cities obligingly rose to annihilate the foreign garrisons. Cleopatra Thea, playing the part of a patriotic Seleucid queen, made no attempt to block the attacks on the Egyptian troops. Those fugitives who survived managed to limp home to Alexandria, abandoning on the way any hope of Seleucid conquest. The brief ascendency of the house of Ptolemy in Syria was over.

In Egypt, Ptolemy's beloved wife, Cleopatra II, shed many tears and raised the ritual cries of lamentation as she began the lengthy process of leading the public mourning period. Tearing her clothes, throwing dust on her head and lowering herself into the dirt of the palace courtyard, Cleopatra performed the part of the grieving Isis and wailed aloud for days on end. Formal royal mourning was always accompanied by conspicuous displays of misery, and Cleopatra would have employed the services of professional mourning women to help her in the grieving process.

Their well-rehearsed lamentations of anguished cries, groans and piercing screams were amplified by the rending of their garments and the exposure of their breasts, stomachs and even genitals. Cleopatra smeared ashes, symbolizing the insignificance of life, on her face and breasts to highlight the tearstains that ran down her face – emphasized too by the smudged kohl eye make-up; it made a striking impression. Like Isis mourning for the dead Osiris, Cleopatra stood watch over her husband's body, now returned home from Syria, as it underwent the long funerary rites. All the while a lector priest recited the sacred texts and the professional mourning women took turns in the vigil: 'They enter and mourn', one funerary text documents, 'two women at a time, eight women in all, performing the purification which is incumbent on them.' They stand inside the door of the courtyard.' Finally, as the body of the pharaoh was moved into the family vault, close to the body of Alexander the Great, Cleopatra spoke in the sombre voice of the goddess Isis and chanted the 'Songs of Isis and Nephthys':

> Behold me, I am your beloved sister,
> You shall not part from me!
> O good youth, come to your house!
> Long, long have I not seen you.
> My heart mourns for you, my eyes seek you,
> I search for you to see you!
> Come to your beloved, come to your beloved!
> Come to your wife, come to your wife,
> Weary-hearted, come to your house-mistress!
> I am your sister by your mother,
> You shall not leave me!
> Gods and men look for you,
> Weep for you together.
> While I can see you, I call to you
> Weeping to the height of heaven!
> But you do not hear my voice,
> Though I am your sister whom you loved on earth,
> You loved none but me, the sister, the sister.

Ptolemy and Cleopatra had been married for thirty years and she felt the ramifications of his death acutely. Yet in those years of marriage, she had proved herself to be a strong woman and a very capable ruler. She had shared the throne of Egypt with both of her brothers, regardless of which of them had actual control of the kingdom, and during much of that time she had stayed in Egypt, fending off enemies and cultivating her power base. If anything, in the years following Ptolemy VI's death, during the next phase of her life, she would emerge as an even more formidable politician and an increasingly accomplished sovereign.

*

The eldest of the two sons of Cleopatra II and Ptolemy VI, Ptolemy Eupator, had occupied the throne alongside his father as a co-ruler for three or four months in 153/2 BCE. He is recorded as such in an epigraphic dedication to the god Apollo on Cyprus, where he is named as 'King Ptolemy, the god Eupator' alongside his parents, the Philometores, which is evidence, at least, for the continuation of the policy of projecting the image of family unity and the subsequent public consolidation of the dynastic line. Ptolemy VI Philometor obviously intended his son Eupator to be his heir, and there is nothing to suggest that he ever anticipated that his brother, Potbelly, would sit on the throne after him. But Eupator had died suddenly in 152 BCE (no suspicious circumstances were ever voiced about the death and the young prince seems to have expired from natural causes), and following her husband's death in 146 BCE, Cleopatra acted quickly and promoted her second son, the only remaining male heir, a fifteen-year-old boy, as pharaoh. The relatively smooth transition of power to this teenage ruler is testament to Cleopatra's authority at court, for the calm accession of the new king, Ptolemy VII Neos Philopator, following his father's death, went unchallenged. Cleopatra quickly confirmed herself as the boy's co-ruler and set about instructing him in the art of government. Yet within days of hearing news of his brother's demise, Potbelly was hurrying back to Alexandria from his Roman-sponsored mini-kingdom of Cyrene. In late

August 146 BCE he entered Egypt – just a month after the death of Ptolemy VI.

Because the troops loyal to Cleopatra II were still making their way back to Egypt from Syria, where they had been fighting alongside Ptolemy VI, it seems that Potbelly entered Alexandria without much opposition. However, Cleopatra's champion, the Jewish commander Onias, had brought a small force of loyal Jewish soldiers from Leontopolis in the Delta to support the queen in her bid to hold the throne for her son. Although there was no clash of troops, according to Josephus, writing in the first century CE, as soon as Potbelly got to Alexandria his reaction to the display of loyalty for the queen was nonetheless brutal: he rounded up all the Jews in the city, regardless of sex or age, and attempted to massacre them all. They were supposed to be trampled to death by elephants, but, according to tradition, the animals turned on their own mahouts and killed them instead. No doubt this is a fabricated 'miracle' tale but it shows how the legend of the cruel, tyrannical Potbelly was propounded in the centuries after his death.

The Roman historian Justin asserts that some people at the Alexandrian court were happy to have Potbelly back in Egypt, preferring the rule of an experienced adult (Potbelly was close to forty at this time) to that of an adolescent. Moreover Potbelly's presence in Egypt guaranteed the reunification of Ptolemaic lands, since he brought Cyrenaica back into the orbit of Alexandria. He had also courted the Romans with repeated embassies and gained influential friends in the senate, including Lucius Minicius Thermus, whom, Josephus says, had always been partisan to Potbelly and actively helped him regain the throne of his dead brother.

Potbelly assumed the title of Ptolemy VIII Euergetes II to associate himself with his popular ancestor Ptolemy III Euergetes I, but the ever-inventive Alexandrian mob, with a keen eye for satire, soon took hold of the lofty aspirations of the Euergetes title ('Benefactor') and twisted it into Kakergetes ('Malefactor'). To the mob he would never be Ptolemy Euergetes anyway; as far as the Alexandrians were concerned, he was destined to be Potbelly (Greek, Physcon) the Malefactor.

Morbidly obese, with a stomach so large that its circumference was wider than two arms extended, Potbelly was hated and feared in equal measure. Short almost to the point of dwarfism, he deliberately played on and exploited his less-than-perfect body shape and courted controversy. During a visit of a Roman delegation to Egypt in 139 BCE the king was described by one stunned observer in this way:

> Through indulgence in *tryphē* his body had become utterly corrupted with fat and with a belly of such size that it would have been hard to measure it with one's arms; to cover it he wore a kaftan (*kalasaris*) which reached to his feet and which had wrist-length sleeves; he never walked anywhere on foot . . .

Potbelly was almost unable to walk and tended to be transported around in a litter; he was rarely seen on his feet, and there were even reports of daytime somnolence. But despite the grim picture of slovenly inertia, Potbelly was also an intellectual and an active scholar with a flair for philology. He is reported to have written poetry, a fine study of Homer, and twenty-four books of *Hypomnemata* ('Notes'), a miscellaneous collection of paradoxography, including stories about historical and contemporary monarchs, as well as exotic wildlife, geographic marvels and myriad other topics. He was a true gastronome and a connoisseur of rare fine wines – although he was also content to bulldoze his way through a banquet with little regard for presentation, flavour or quality.

For more than a century the Ptolemies had been the butt of Roman jokes. They thought of the ostentatious Ptolemies as the antitheses of the manly and disciplined *mors maiorum* (literally, 'ancestral custom') that defined the Romans or of the natural *severitas* and *dignitas* through which culture found its meaning; they regarded Potbelly especially as the blubbery embodiment of the kind of effeminate eastern excess that was so reviled by card-carrying Republicans like Cato the Elder. One Roman deputation witnessed the king wearing a transparent moo-moo, red-faced from puffing and panting his way through the streets of Alexandria, anxious to meet and greet no less a Roman than Cornelius Scipio Aemilianus, the destroyer of Carthage,. It was only because of Scipio's presence, one observer recalled, that the Alexandrians got to see their fat king walk. Potbelly was deemed to be the very personification of Hellenistic grotesqueness, more monster than monarch.

*

To be fair, most of the Ptolemies were fat: Arsinoë II was morbidly obese, and her brother-husband, Ptolemy II, was enormous too. He was not an energetic man – he disliked all forms of physical exertion, and although he lived to the age of sixty-two, he was troubled by ill health throughout most of his adult life. Ptolemy IV was described as fat and licentious even by the standards of his contemporaries, and he languished in habitual lethargy, perhaps because of chronic illness too. Ptolemy V Epiphanes also developed extreme obesity and used to fall asleep during social and political events, and even good Ptolemy VI Philometor was portrayed by Polybius as 'apt to be lethargic and inert'; Justin describes him as extremely obese and sluggish.

But let us put a Ptolemaic spin on fatness. For a king like Potbelly, his bulk, his excessive eating and his consequent immobility were marks of high prestige: they represented, through his person, the high regard the Ptolemies had for *tryphē* – 'immoderation'. Ptolemaic dinner parties, Ptolemaic processions, Ptolemaic dress, the arts and literature of Ptolemaic Egypt, Ptolemaic royal incest, and fat Ptolemaic kings and queens were all political advertisements for dynastic opulence. To the Ptolemies, *tryphē* was a measure of wealth and power and *tryphē* was the logical consequence of a dynastic propaganda that emphasized the generosity and beneficence of the monarchs. This dynastic ideology of excess was manifested in the prominence of the image of the cornucopia – the horn of plenty – which was frequently seen in Ptolemaic royal iconography, and even in the exaggerated fat cheeks and necks of the Ptolemies on their coin portraits. It means that Potbelly's own exaggeration of his fatness and excesses, with his see-through gown, were meant to *impress* Scipio Aemilianus. In his portraiture, Potbelly's facial features swell and his chin disappears into his neck; his eyes bulge in their fatty sockets and his excess fat renders him as a kind of living cornucopia, a symbol of his realm's wealth.

Few people in the ancient world could afford to be fat. Most of Potbelly's subjects ate only a subsistence diet, and many people were malnourished and only one meal away from starvation. The elite could afford better food and had a more regular intake of meat and fish, but they rarely ran to fat. So to be obese in antiquity was the ultimate display of success. Thus Ptolemy VIII was not a fat loser, he was an aspirational role model – and it was likely that he had consciously cultivated this Rubenesque image as a further manifestation of his family's *tryphē*.

Naturally, Ptolemaic queens had a role to play in dynastic extravagance as well. The Cleopatras were all in tune with the potential power of *tryphē*. Indeed, they shared similar constructions of that image with their menfolk: their fleshy coin portraits and their bloated 'Greco-Egyptian' statues played upon the Ptolemaic penchant for fatness as an ideal. Even Ptolemaic royal incest was an expression of the dynasty's devotion to *tryphē* and, like all forms of *tryphē*, it was publicly fêted. As the Canadian scholar of the Hellenistic period Sheila Ager emphasizes:

> Ptolemaic incest should . . . be considered in the context of the Ptolemaic philosophy of excess in general . . . Ptolemaic freedom to indulge, and to do so ostentatiously and deliberately, is representative of power. Incest, as the most illicit of sexual acts, is almost demanded by a royal philosophy of power that recognizes no limits or restraints and that is prepared to overstep all boundaries. The particular Ptolemaic dedication to *tryphē* may indeed be why this dynasty was more determinedly incestuous than the native pharaohs had been. The Ptolemies may first have adopted sibling marriage because of reports about native Egyptian behaviour; but it

would have resonated so well with the rest of their philosophy that it inevitably became central to it.

If Egypt was the gift of the Nile, then the corpulent statues of the Cleopatras were almost representations of the fertility of the Nile's black land itself. The Nile flood was personified by the fertility god Hapy, who was shown with a full, fat belly, male genitals and full female breasts. On a Ptolemaic stele from Sehel, in the cataract region, he embraces the land of Egypt like a lover and impregnates her:

> He brings up the flood
> Bounding up as he copulates
> As man rejoices with woman
> Renewing his manhood with joy . . .
> Hapy embraces the field
> An embrace that fills each nose with life;
> For when embraced the field is reborn!</verse>

Images of sex, fatness and abundance speak of how these concepts were inextricably woven into the whole fabric of society in Hellenistic Egypt. The rhythms of life and regeneration were in tune with the fertile regenerative force of the Nile and the *tryphē* of its benefaction. For the Ptolemies, obesity, wealth and fertility worked in harmony. Fatness was not something to be ashamed of but to be indulged in.

*

The Roman historian Justin tells how '[Potbelly] rejoiced at having recovered his brother's throne without a struggle (for which he knew that his brother's son was intended, both by his mother, Cleopatra, and the inclination of the nobles), but being incensed at all that had opposed his interests, ordered, as soon as he entered Alexandria, the partisans of the young prince to be put to death.' Justin's account misses the fact that Ptolemy VII Neos Philopator, groomed by his mother and her supporters to challenge his uncle, had already been recognized as king (at least by

Cleopatra's inner-circle), but we cannot be unequivocally certain how far Cleopatra was prepared to contest her brother's claim to the throne. After all, if she were to marry Potbelly, her own position as the sister-wife of the new pharaoh would, in theory, give her greater status than that of queen dowager or queen mother, and given the threat that Potbelly had always posed to the harmony of the realm, she might have been prepared to endorse his rule if only for the stability of Egypt. By 14 August 145 BCE Cleopatra had married Potbelly; that date is the first surviving attestation of the joint names of Ptolemy VIII and Cleopatra II in the historical record. There is no mention of young Ptolemy VII. Cleopatra II's feelings towards her new husband are not recorded either.

On Ptolemy's part, the reactivation of the brother–sister marriage with Cleopatra II was of paramount importance, and the occasion was celebrated in a stone relief in the East Temple of Amun-Re-Who-Hears-Prayers at the temple of Karnak, where an unrealistic portrait of an impossibly slender Potbelly is accompanied by that of Cleopatra II. Both are shown offering cult to the gods: he holds out a vessel of *shedeh*-wine and she proffers bouquets of papyrus.

It is a strange fact that in all his years of exile Potbelly had not taken a wife. He certainly had a long-standing mistress, Eirene (sometimes called Ithaka), who had a good influence on him and did her best to curb his natural cruelty; by her he had a bastard son, Ptolemy Apion, who, when he came of age, became the king of Cyrenaica (when he died without heirs in 96 BCE he would bequest Cyrenaica to the Romans, which proved to be the first step towards the annexation of Egypt by Rome and the break-up of the Ptolemaic empire just sixty years later). Yet it seems that Potbelly had never been interested in looking for a bride outside of the immediate family, and even his rejection of his niece Cleopatra Thea as a child-bride suggests that he was not willing to compromise on marriage even within the dynasty. There could only be one wife for him: his sister, Cleopatra. But why?

Still a handsome woman, Cleopatra was around thirty-seven at the time of her second marriage. Her portrait sculptures reveal her to have had a round face with a prominent chin, a small mouth and fleshy lips. Her eyes were large, deep-set and hooded, and they sat beneath well-defined brows which accentuated the shape of her eyelids. Physically, she was still in remarkably good health (even among the Ptolemaic aristocracy the average lifespan was between thirty-five and forty; the generations came and went quickly). She was already the mother of four children (three of whom were alive at this time), and although her years of fertility were drawing to an end, there was *perhaps* hope that she might bear future offspring – although this might prove perilous at her age. This alone might have been a draw for Potbelly. But of more importance to him was Cleopatra's longevity as a queen, for she was a resounding symbol of successful hereditary rulership. Potbelly needed to capitalize on that fact.

Moreover, the union of Ptolemy VIII and Cleopatra II was a pragmatic attempt to avoid civil war. Because both parties had their adherents and loyalists, a reciprocal engagement was advantageous for all, and especially so for Egypt itself. Cleopatra had proved to be a good consort, ruling with both of her brothers (together and separately), and by the time he returned to Egypt Potbelly might have been regarded by her as the proper transmitter of legitimizing power. Her personal charisma – the fact that she reigned with the support of the army and the Jews, and the love of the mob – coupled with the biological and propagandistic advantage of sisterhood, made Cleopatra II the only feasible matrimonial candidate for Potbelly. So marry her he did.

There is a notable absence of information on the act of getting married – the wedding ceremony itself – in Egypt. Legal papyri always identify a woman as the 'wife of so-and-so', and there are many documents attesting to divorce, so an official union was certainly acknowledged, but the papyri give no support to the occurrence of anything like a wedding ceremony *per se*. We may assume that there was a moment before which a couple was *not* married and after which they *were* married, but we have no clear evidence to tell us what actually happened to make a woman a wife.

Egyptians loved a party and it is hard to imagine them ignoring such an obvious excuse as a wedding, but not only is there no evidence of a ceremony, there is no evidence of a celebration either. A woman was considered to have married if she simply took her belongings from her parents' house and moved them and herself into the home of a man who was not already married to someone else. There are records of parents using the occasion to transfer property to the bride or the groom, but there are no other signs of anything approaching either a ceremony or a party.

What about Ptolemaic kings and queens? Did they have endogamous wedding ceremonies where the custom of marrying only within the limits of the family was followed? Was there a Greek-style *gamos* ceremony which confirmed them as husband and wife? Given that we hear nothing of royal wedding ceremonies, nor even of wedding feasts within the Ptolemaic household, it is best to assume that they simply did not happen. Most probably a newly married Ptolemaic royal couple just emerged in public as man and wife and their union was expressed and acknowledged through the official joint titles they thereafter adopted and propagated.

Whatever form of ceremonial was or was not used, the period around the marriage of Potbelly and Cleopatra was memorable. Justin's macabre account of what happened next centres on one significant but much overlooked character in the royal drama: the boy-king Ptolemy VII Neos Philopator. In Justin's story the boy steps into the limelight one last time just as his mother and uncle tie the knot:

> On the day the king [Potbelly] was taking his [Ptolemy VII Neos Philopator's] mother as wife, Ptolemy [Potbelly] killed him in his mother's arms ... and entered his sister's bed still dripping with the gore of her son.

The story makes for gruesome – if compelling – reading but is probably more fictitious than factual. That Ptolemy VII was murdered by his uncle-stepfather Potbelly is highly likely, however, given that the boy was an unwanted accessory and an awkward reminder of the popularity of the late Ptolemy VI. Ptolemy VII

Neos Philopater does not resurface in the epigraphic evidence after 21 August 145 BCE, just one week after Potbelly had entered Alexandria. That the lad was killed in his mother's arms is less probable – this is more likely to have been Justin's way of spicing up his theatrical history to satisfy the bloodlust of his audience, the rapacious Roman elite.

Ever the gentleman, what puzzled the great Edwardian classicist Edwyn Bevan about the incident was not so much that Potbelly murdered his nephew but Cleopatra's subsequent behaviour:

> That she can have consented to cohabit with her brother after the murder of her son is hard to believe . . . One might say, of course, that she was compelled by fear to live with Euergetes [Potbelly] as his wife, but when one thinks what these Macedonian princesses were, that seems hardly plausible. It is more likely to have been the desire to remain queen at all costs.

Bevan may be right in suggesting Cleopatra II was motivated by her own ambition and love of power, but there may have been a deeper, more psychological explanation at work too. Even with his success in Syria, Ptolemy VI had been a weak and gentle king, always somewhat in the shadow of his younger, aggressively ambitious brother. So on one level, Cleopatra might always have been attracted to her younger sibling's drive and determination and, despite his many, many shortcomings, at this point in her life she may have regarded him as the only secure route available to her to maintain her long-lived role as queen of Egypt. The fact is there was no alternative.

*

Within a year of her marriage to Potbelly Cleopatra II was pregnant – for the first time in over a decade. As the pregnancy developed, so Potbelly began to plan his coronation; his intention was to have the child born at the holy city of Memphis at the time of the religious ceremony itself. Cleopatra duly travelled to the city and based herself in the Memphite palace to prepare for her confinement. Childbirth was the exclusive domain of women – largely nameless, likely older, experienced birth assistants who were labelled 'servants of Heqet' (the frog-headed goddess of child-birth) – but the queen was also surrounded by the familiar faces of her loyal ladies-in-waiting. Her teenage daughter, Cleopatra III, was in attendance too. When the time for the delivery of the baby arrived, the queen was led into an inner bedchamber which had been blessed to provide magical protection for the mother and infant, and she was helped to lower herself into a squatting position, supporting her arms on 'birth bricks' decorated all over with magical images. As Cleopatra's contractions got stronger and more excruciating, she cried out in discomfort and the women in attendance screamed out in sympathy as they chanted incan-tations to the deities of childbirth: the hippopotamus-bellied Taweret; the frog-headed Heqet; the dwarf Bes, who was addressed as 'the great god of women's wombs'; Eileithyia and Baubo, two prominent Greek birthing-deities; as well as the great goddesses Isis and Artemis. Finally, the *hrw wadja*, 'day of separation', arrived – that remarkable moment when the child left the womb and was placed in its mother's arms.

Cleopatra's healthy baby boy was born early in 143 BCE, at Memphis as planned. The birth coincided with Potbelly's decision to massacre a delegation of well-wishers from Cyrene because they had allegedly spoken disrespectfully of his mistress Eirene. That aside, Potbelly was delighted at the arrival of the healthy boy, whom he named Memphites. On the eastern external wall of the *naos* or shrine of the temple of Horus at Edfu, Potbelly celebrated his paternal success in stone in a series of elegant low-reliefs that depict him seated on his throne, wearing the Double Crown of Egypt, in the presence of the god Thoth, who records the phar-aoh's good fortunes for posterity. Potbelly is accompanied by Memphites (shown as Potbelly's 'mini-me' doppelganger, com-plete with royal Double Crown) and Cleopatra II, wearing the horns, feathers, and the solar disk of divine queenship. Cleopatra's prominence in the relief is a clear indicator that as a reward for birthing a new heir, her position as queen of Egypt received a reboot. The Edfu images, which were probably created when Memphites was declared Crown Prince shortly before September 142 BCE, encode the message of dynastic harmony and union and a return to stable governance now that Egypt was once more under the authority of a divine triad: king, queen and prince – Osiris, Isis and Horus. The world, the temple relief stated, was back in order.

*

The harmony promoted on the temple wall at Edfu was bogus. Even before the birth of Memphites, the family was being torn apart from the inside, for during the time of Cleopatra II's confinement Potbelly had turned his sexual attention to his sixteen-year-old niece-cum-stepdaughter, Cleopatra III.

Unusually for a princess of her age, Cleopatra III was unmarried. It is probable that she had been betrothed to her elder brother, Eupator, but his death had foiled any plan for marriage; she may then have been all set to wed her younger sibling, Ptolemy VII Neos Philopator, until the dramatic events of 145 BCE put paid to that too. As the only remaining daughter of Ptolemy VI in Egypt, Cleopatra III must have envisaged her future as one in which she would sit next to a brother on the throne. Her uncle's marriage to her mother and the murder of her brother had deprived her of this dynastic right, and it looked as though Cleopatra III could have no future in Egypt.

When Potbelly married Cleopatra II, the traditional succession formula was thrown out of synch, and the murder of Ptolemy VII and the birth of Memphites served to twist the established rules even further, but what happened next threw everything into chaos. According to Justin, Potbelly, 'repudiated his own sister [Cleopatra II] after forcibly committing adultery with her virgin daughter [Cleopatra III] and taking her to him in marriage'. The story is reiterated by another Roman historian, Valerius Maximus, who states that Potbelly 'had adulterously ravished' the virgin daughter of Cleopatra II. Both authors suggest that the girl was sexually assaulted by her uncle, although, needless to say, we must exercise caution when assessing the subject of rape in this story simply because, no matter how hard it is for us to accept, the application of modern categories or definitions of rape are unserviceable when evaluating an ancient account of sexual assault. In antiquity there was no such thing as the idea of consent. Instead, the taking of a woman through a violent act was seen as a male right that was limited only by the rights of other men. Women were never regarded as the victims of rape; the crime's victim was either her father or, in the case of a married woman, her husband. It was the men of the family who suffered the 'shame' of the attack and who needed legal (that is to say, financial) recompense. So, although Potbelly may well have raped his niece (in the modern sense), at the time it would never have been understood that way, as there was no such thing as forced rape in the Ptolemaic legal system – there was merely 'illicit' or 'transgressive' sex – and we see that Justin and Valerius Maximus both highlight Potbelly's *adultery against Cleopatra II* in their assessment of his misdeed. The Roman authors encourage us to think of Cleopatra III as a victim of unnatural lust and as an innocent participant in a degraded *ménage à trois*. Is this fair?

Cleopatra III was around sixteen years of age when her mother married Potbelly and her brother was – most probably - murdered by the hand of the same man who now shared her mother's throne. The killing of Ptolemy VII left Cleopatra III in a quandary: without a full-blood brother to marry, there was no prospect that she could become Egypt's queen. Of course, she could wait patiently, keeping out of danger, and marry her little half-brother-nephew, Memphites, but it would be at least fifteen years before he came of age and was capable of begetting children, by which time Cleopatra III would be around thirty, far from being an ingénue, ripe for marriage. There was no foreign prince available for her to marry either – her sister, Cleopatra Thea, was working her way through the choicest of those – and so Cleopatra III was forced to acknowledge that in dynastic terms she was defunct.

To judge from her actions as a mature woman, the teenage Cleopatra III was already an astute manipulator of circumstance.

By the time her mother was pregnant with Memphites she had come to realize that she needed to act with resolution, and so, drawing on her status as a blood-princess, Cleopatra III allied herself to the only man of power who mattered: Uncle Potbelly. By virtue of her own dynastic pedigree, Cleopatra III turned a hopeless situation into a personal triumph. She was an independent and strong-willed young woman who probably played more of an active role in climbing into Potbelly's bed than the passive 'rape stories' suggest. The fact is Cleopatra III realized that the only security she had in life came in the ample shape of her uncle, and she willingly became his bride.

For her part, Cleopatra II, now aged about forty, knew that she was running out of time to give the king further sons. As the only Ptolemaic adult male capable of fathering children, Potbelly could not be content with one single male heir; there was no security in that. He needed to father more boys, and this meant that it was essential for him to take a new bedmate. Mistresses and concubines would not do, because any sons born to him by such women would have only a diluted version of the divine blood of the Ptolemies. Cleopatra III was the last unmarried daughter of the royal house and her pedigree made her the perfect choice for a wife.

In marrying his niece, Potbelly sought to neutralize the authority of Cleopatra II. Future heirs would not be dependent on her but rather on him and his younger wife, Cleopatra III. And so it was that Potbelly and Cleopatra III joined together in sexual union, not out of lust (Cleopatra III was no Lolita figure) but out of political expediency and dynastic necessity. Nevertheless, the news that her daughter had fallen pregnant to her own husband must have struck Cleopatra II like a lightning bolt.

*

In 142 BCE Cleopatra III gave Potbelly a son. Known throughout his life by the endearing nickname Chickpea (Greek, Lathyrus; coincidentally, its Latin equivalent was Cicero), he was destined to be the future Ptolemy IX. With the boy safely delivered and healthy, Potbelly acknowledged Cleopatra III as his second wife and pronounced her his second queen.

Chickpea's birth was recorded on the western external wall of the *naos* of the temple of Horus at Edfu, where the baby prince was shown accompanying his father and mother in the presence of the god Thoth. It mirrors the scene created in the same temple at the time of the birth of Memphites, where the elder prince is depicted in the company of his father and his mother, Cleopatra II. In both scenes, Thoth, the divine scribe, is shown recording the regnal years of Ptolemy VIII and jotting down the details of the births and lineage of the two princes, born of the two Cleopatras, the mother-daughter-queens. Egypt now had one king, two queens and two potential male heirs. Potbelly was clearly enjoying himself, behaving very much like an old-school polygamous Hellenistic king, flaunting his unconventional harem of wives and offspring, but beneath the smiles and the celebrations he must have realized that his matrimonial choices were certain to bring trouble to the throne.

Justin and Valerius Maximus insist that Potbelly repudiated Cleopatra II when his second wife gave birth to Chickpea, but this is not supported by the Egyptian evidence, where a kaleidoscopic array of approaches to the royal family's oddities emerge. On 8 May 141 BCE, for instance, a Theban document tells of Pharaoh Ptolemy (Potbelly) and 'Queen Cleopatra [II] and Cleopatra [III]' alongside priestesses who held the titles 'Priestess of Queen Cleopatra' (Cleopatra II) and 'Priestess of Cleopatra the Daughter of the King' (Cleopatra III). Another Demotic text of September 140 BCE declares Ptolemy VIII to be ruling alongside 'Cleopatra, his sister, his wife, the goddess' and that cult was also performed by priestesses of 'Queen Cleopatra'. This interesting little text suggests that Cleopatra III was not yet being recognized everywhere in Egypt as queen, although a Greek papyrus of July 141 BCE lists the same priestesses as serving the cult of 'Queen Cleopatra and of Queen Cleopatra the daughter', inferring an increase in status for the king's younger wife.

Potbelly's newest queen was not a woman to be ignored. She had shown a steely determination when she made a move on Potbelly's bed and throne, and as queen she was determined never to be kept in the background and never to be overshadowed by her mother as a 'senior queen'. It was probably during the period of her ascendancy that the lofty, imperious and often chillingly resolute Cleopatra III acquired a particularly savage yet memorable nickname from the Alexandrians: Kokkē. The classicist Edwyn Bevan drew a polite veil over the meaning of the word in his 1927 study of the Ptolemies, insisting that 'what Kokkē meant in the Alexandrine slang of the day it is idle to conjecture'. Actually, the meaning is very clear. It is double entendre playing on the Greek word for 'scarlet' and the low-slang word for female genitalia. To cut to the chase, the queen was known to her irreverent Alexandrian subjects as Cleopatra the Cunt. It says a lot about her.

During this formative era of the strange and uneasy tripartite marriage Cleopatra III, Kokkē, developed from a wilful adolescent into a very powerful and accomplished woman. The long and sophisticated power games played by her husband and her mother must have provided Cleopatra III with a model for politicking, one-upmanship and scheming, and their ceaseless machinations furnished her with a blueprint for successful strategies which she might adopt for herself and a dossier of ignominious failures she could avoid. Over the next few turbulent decades, as mother and daughter fought against each other with a hatred that was irreconcilable as it was implacable, Cleopatra III nonetheless benefitted from watching her mother's methods of rulership. She recognized that in her mother she had the best example of what a woman might achieve in life. For despite all the wrangling that had passed between them, Cleopatra II was still able to maintain precedence over her daughter, a fact that was well attested in the inscriptions of the time. Whether the elder queen's success was due simply to her own charisma or to the powerful supporters she maintained both within Egypt and beyond its borders (or a combination of the two) is hard to say, but that Cleopatra II managed to maintain her preeminent position as Egypt's female ruler is undeniable. The tenacity with which she clung to power must have provided inspiration for her irritated daughter, who hated playing a subordinate role to her mother and who, when her turn came, was to maintain an unflinching precedence over all her own offspring.

At the end of 140 BCE the royal triculture finally settled down into a regular pattern which would continue in use until 132 BCE. A Greek royal circular provides us with its earliest attestation: 'King Ptolemy and Queen Cleopatra the Sister, and Queen Cleopatra the Wife.' A little later, around 138 BCE, the fuller formula was concocted: 'Pharaoh Ptolemy, Beneficent God, Son of Ptolemy [V] and Cleopatra [I], the Manifest Gods, with Queen Cleopatra [II] his Sister and with Queen Cleopatra [III] his Wife, the Beneficent Goddess.' And that is how the two Cleopatras came be known thereafter: Cleopatra II was 'the Sister' and Cleopatra III was 'the Wife.' Significantly, Cleopatra II's title 'Sister' did not indicate a diminution of her status, for there is no evidence to suggest that Cleopatra II ceased to be Potbelly's spouse; it can be explained by the fact that amongst the Ptolemies, the honorific titles 'Sister' and 'Wife' were used quite interchangeably.

In the iconographic repertoire, though, precedence was easier to identify. In standard pharaonic art importance was attached to the order in which individual figures were portrayed in any line-up. Thus, at Philae, a relief depicting the white-crowned Ptolemy VIII worshiping Isis shows his two wives standing behind him in line; Cleopatra the Sister is placed immediately after her husband and Cleopatra the Wife brings up the rear. Identified by their titles, the queens are dressed alike, although there are subtleties of difference in their poses: with both hands, Cleopatra II offers *nu*-jars of ointment to the goddess, whilst Cleopatra III presents the goddess with a burning oil lamp and raises her right hand in supplication. Some meaningful attempt at distinguishing the two women is at work in the relief, although this is more apparent on a similar scene at the temple of Kom Ombo. This scene focuses on the deity Horus, who presents an ornate scimitar of victory together with palm staffs (representing long life) to an elaborately costumed yet lithe Potbelly. He is again followed by Cleopatra II and Cleopatra III, identified as 'Sister' and 'Wife' respectively, and, as at Philae, the queens wear modius crowns, sun disks, cow horns and the tall plumes of feathers of Isis-Hathor; they carry papyrus sceptres and ankhs, the symbol of life, but this time their garments, though quite uniform in appearance, are not quite identical. Cleopatra II's gown is the more elaborate, with an over-robe worn on top of her dress (one can see clearly the lines of the robe's opening depicted at the front of the queen's torso). However, Cleopatra III's sheer gown hints at her belly button beneath the diaphanous linen, which draws attention to her fertile body. Cleopatra II's dress is more matronly and statelier, but it is the simplicity of the younger queen's figure-revealing frock that solicits the of the eye of the beholder.

*

It must have been around the time, in 140 or 139 BCE, when the Kom Ombo relief was erected that Potbelly decided to cease having a sexual relationship with his sister-wife, Cleopatra II. She would bear the dynasty no more heirs. In her place, Cleopatra III would become the dynastic mother. Cleopatra II was probably experiencing menopause by this stage of her life, and she cannot have been slow to realize that her barrenness put her in an unstable position in the dynastic hierarchy and that the chief threat to her perceived rank as senior queen lay in her daughter's productive womb. The youthful Cleopatra III held the best cards: the more children she could bear for Potbelly, the greater the chances that the dynasty would continue through her.

In the period 140–132 BCE Cleopatra III proved her worth by giving her husband at least four more children: Ptolemy IX's birth in 142 BCE was followed by that of Ptolemy X Alexander (c. 140 BCE). Calling their second son Ptolemy Alexander was a notable break with family tradition and probably reflected his parents' desire to align themselves to the past – not just to the founding of the dynasty by Ptolemy I but to Alexander the Great himself. Next came a brood of healthy daughters – Cleopatra IV

(c. 138 BCE), Cleopatra Tryphaina (c. 137/6 BCE) and Cleopatra Selene (c. 133/2 BCE).

Potbelly and his two Cleopatras somehow managed to co-exist on the throne together for nine unhappy years, but family life was far from harmonious. Seething tensions simmered beneath the surface of an exasperating political stalemate in which the mother–daughter feud was escalated with every newly perceived breech of etiquette, slight of rank or hierarchical *faux pas*. The rival queens worked hard at one-upmanship, finding any excuse to pull rank or obtain privileges, and they delighted in causing their opponent humiliation or dishonour. Yet the mother–daughter hostility was merely the symptom of a much deeper malaise which had infected the royal family for decades: the hatred that Cleopatra II had long harboured for Potbelly. *That* was the real source of contention. She had watched Potbelly lie, cheat, maim and murder his way to power, and during his dramatic ascent it was she who had sacrificed the most – her royal title, the life of her son, and even the love of her daughter. Cleopatra II must have been very embittered.

A frustrating silence in the sources makes it difficult to know what ignited a new spate of hostilities between Potbelly and Cleopatra II in the late 130s BCE, but the alarming rate with which Cleopatra III was bearing him children might well have prompted the older queen to take control of a situation which was fast becoming dangerous. Memphites, she knew, was slowly being eclipsed by his half-brothers, Potbelly's younger sons. In 132 BCE, just as Memphites was coming of age, Cleopatra II made her move. She sent Memphites off to Cyrene for safekeeping while she herself took an active part in inciting the Alexandrian mob, who still adored her, to oust Potbelly from the throne. This was easily done: Cleopatra only needed to recite a list of Potbelly's crimes and misdemeanours to get the mob at frenzy point. The Alexandrian palace was stormed and Potbelly, Cleopatra III and their brood of infants fled Egypt and took refuge on Cyprus.

With them gone, Cleopatra II established herself as the sole ruler of Egypt, and she was recognized as such with comparative ease – a testimony, surely, to the support she had been able to garner at court, in the military, and from the mob during the difficult proceeding decade of hostile deadlock. No doubt Ptolemy's fits of cruelty and general bad government had contributed to Cleopatra's popularity in Alexandria, and it seems that the bulk of her supporters came from the Greek and Jewish populations, who had suffered the most under Potbelly's unhinged regime. It is difficult to know how far into Egypt her new title, Cleopatra Thea Philometor Soteira ('Cleopatra the Mother-Loving Saviour Goddess'), penetrated, but no doubt the Greek-speaking elites of Lower Egypt recognized the significance of the queen's new titulature, which proclaimed her affinity with her deceased brother-husband Ptolemy VI Philometor, her mother, Cleopatra I Syra, and the dynasty's founder, Ptolemy I Soter. At long last, Cleopatra II was queen in her own right. She was pharaoh.

10

Third Time Lucky

In Syria, Cleopatra Thea learned about the events unfolding in her native Egypt from her ambassadors. She was getting regular reports of how first her mother and now her younger sister were producing children for her uncle, the man who had rejected her as a potential bride when she was barely a teenager. The domestic carryings-on in the Egyptian royal household must have bewildered the young Seleucid queen, although, as time would tell, the high jinks in Alexandria would present Cleopatra Thea with lucrative opportunities. Her first marriage to the ineffectual playboy Alexander Balas had not exactly been a picture of domestic bliss, and the antagonistic actions of her second husband, Demetrius II, did not augur particularly well for the future either.

Cleopatra Thea felt isolated and disconnected by the events that had rapidly unfolded around her, but she was eminently aware of the strategic role she had to play in Syria following her father's death and the installation of the unique new regime in Alexandria. Potbelly was not interested in reviving the conquest of Syria when he faced more pressing matters at home, and this fact left Cleopatra Thea somewhat adrift. Both of her marriages had been in the service of political alliances that no longer existed, and yet there was no prospect of her returning to Alexandria, given that her second husband had massacred her father's Egyptian troops. Any marriage alliance that might have united the Egyptian and Syrian kingdoms had been summarily dashed to pieces in the summer of 145 BCE with the battlefield death of Ptolemy VI. Now, in her early twenties, already a mother and a widow, and married to the relatively unknown Demetrius II, Cleopatra Thea felt very much alone.

Cleopatra Thea did have one ace to play, however: her fertility. This was her greatest asset; her track record for producing healthy sons was good and she was still at an age when she would be able to produce yet more heirs and spares through her second marriage. Added impetus for securing her own position in Syria came from her second husband's less than astute handling of power, for Demetrius had, at best, a tenuous grip on authority and was reliant on the support of Cretan mercenaries, who were the backbone of his army, and on his new allies, the Hasmonaeans in Judaea. When, around 144 BCE, Demetrius attempted to demobilize the Syrian portion of his army by disbanding several contingents and diminishing the pay of others, Antioch erupted in violence and Demetrius was forced to barricade himself inside his palace in the city, guarded by his Cretan forces, as the population of Antioch occupied city streets. Cleopatra Thea, for her part, quit the city as soon as the violence began to escalate and made for Seleucia-in-Pieria on the coast. He was saved by the arrival of battle-hardened Jewish troops from Judaea, but the whole shambolic affair left Cleopatra Thea underwhelmed by her husband's lack of political acumen.

While Demetrius was busy alienating the most prominent city in his kingdom, Cleopatra Thea's infant son by Alexander Balas, Antiochus, suddenly reappeared on the scene. He had been established as the silent figurehead of a new regime, led by a man named Diodotos, a native of Casiana, a village near Apamea, northwest of modern Hama, Syria, overlooking the Ghab Valley. He had been a *philos* or 'companion' of Alexander Balas and perhaps also one of the generals who had been in charge of Antioch when it was handed over to Ptolemy VI. At some point, Diodotos had managed to take under his wing the young son of Alexander Balas and Cleopatra Thea, a child of (at most) four or five years of age. This did not prevent Diodotos from proclaiming him as the new king – Antiochus VI Theos Epiphanes Dionysus – at some point in late 145 BCE; coins were minted in his name early in 144 BCE.

With an impressive band of supporters, Diodotos marched on Antioch and was able to secure the city, forcing Demetrius to flee to his wife in nearby Seleucia-in-Pieria. There, Demetrius II began to organize his resistance to the infant king.

Cleopatra Thea found herself in a very awkward situation. She was married to a man who was waging war against rebels who were using her own son by her former husband as a figurehead, for she probably saw Diodotos' exploitation of her child for what it was – an attempt to legitimize his insurrection against Demetrius II, which was actually driven by his own naked ambition. Instead of repudiating Demetrius as she had Alexander Balas, Cleopatra Thea decided to remain loyal to him. By this point, Cleopatra Thea must have either been pregnant with or already given birth to two boys, Seleucus (V) and Antiochus (VIII), the sons of Demetrius II.

At any rate, a year or so later, in 142/1 BCE, little Antiochus VI apparently (and conveniently) contracted some sort of disease that required urgent surgery; it proved fatal and the child died. Undoubtedly the usurper Diodotos had done away with the boy-king as soon as he felt secure enough to rule in his own right. One wonders what Cleopatra Thea's reaction to the news of the death of her first-born son would have been as she waited, safely ensconced in Seleucia-in-Pieria, for the conflict between Demetrius and Diodotos to play itself out. Her second husband was not destined for greatness, she came to realize, and it must have seemed increasingly apparent to her that as both a husband and as a king, Demetrius was a dead end.

With the struggle against Diodotos at a stalemate, at the close of the 140s BCE Demetrius II suddenly and inexplicably set his sights on the reconquest of the former eastern territories of the old Seleucid realm. Nearly a decade of internal conflict in Syria had provided plenty of opportunities for the Parthian king Mithridates I to invade Iran and expel the last vestiges of Seleucid influence in the region. Babylonia had been occupied by the Parthians too, and in 141 BCE Mithridates had captured Seleucia-on-the-Tigris. Yet Demetrius believed he could retake these lucrative territories and reunite them with his kingdom. Demetrius' departure to the east would have been worrisome for Cleopatra Thea, and in the summer of 139 BCE the news she did not want to hear reached her: the forces of Demetrius II had been smashed by the Parthians and he himself had been taken captive and carried off into Mesopotamia, where he was to be held hostage.

Given his less-than-stellar strategic performance so far, it would seem safe to surmise that Cleopatra Thea was not surprised to learn of Demetrius' capture. But it meant that there was an uneasy vacancy on the Seleucid throne. Diodotos would have been all too happy to fill that space, of course, blocked only by the presence of Cleopatra Thea and her two sons. Diodotos still commanded the loyalty of several prominent cities, and for a while it looked as though he might be the only feasible choice to put on the Seleucid throne. But Cleopatra Thea had the legitimacy of royal authority behind her; she managed to engineer a mass defection of soldiers from Diodotos to her side and hunkered down for a long fight. Cleopatra Thea meant to show herself as a power to be reckoned with.

It was just at this moment that Demetrius II's younger brother, Antiochus, suddenly appeared in Syria. He had come to claim his ancestral throne, driving out the usurper Diodotos and putting himself in place of Demetrius, who was far off in Persia – maybe even dead by now. Cleopatra Thea had been surreptitiously working behind the scenes for such a moment and had sent copious messengers to her brother-in-law, inviting him into Syria to claim his brother's throne. It was therefore at Cleopatra Thea's instigation that Antiochus VII arrived at Seleucia, accepted the royal diadem and married his sister-in-law in the spring of 138 BCE. Cleopatra Thea had decided that she would sooner think of herself as a widow than a waiting wife. She was twenty-nine years old at the time of her marriage to her third husband, who was aged about eighteen when he was recognized as the new Seleucid king by virtue of his descent from Demetrius I and through his marriage to Cleopatra Thea, the king-maker.

Who was this new young hero who had gallantly arrived in Seleucia in the nick of time? Antiochus VII was nicknamed

'Sidetes' – 'the man from Side' – due to the fact that as a child he had been sent away to the Pamphylian city of Side on the southern coast of Turkey, near modern Antalya. He had stayed there for safekeeping during the reign of Alexander Balas and had lingered on when his older brother, Demetrius II, had taken the throne. He was something of a swashbuckling man's man, more at home among pirates and hill people than the eunuchs and intellectuals of the royal court. Certainly Justin paints a picture of a man of singular will and determination:

> Antiochus Sidetes, remembering that his father had been hated for his pride, and his brother despised for his indolence, was anxious not to fall into the same vices, and having married Cleopatra Thea, his brother's wife, proceeded to make war, with the utmost vigour, on the provinces that had revolted because of his brother's ineffectual government and, after subduing them, reunited them to his dominions.

Although it is difficult to unravel the dynamics of Cleopatra Thea's third marriage, it does seem that, comparatively speaking, she had the upper hand this time. Her power base was well established in Syria – she had been residing in the region for a decade by this point – and she had matured as a ruler and was more au fait with politics than Antiochus, who was at least ten years her junior. Cleopatra Thea had repeatedly shown herself to be a shrewd ruler in her own right and had weathered the storms of the 140s BCE alive and unscathed. Her marriage to Antiochus VII therefore marks the beginning of a different chapter in her life because, in a basic sense, Antiochus VII owed his kingdom and his throne to her; in this marriage Cleopatra Thea was more than just a dynastic vessel or a legitimizing token – she became a strategic force in her own right. For his part, Antiochus VII came to Cleopatra Thea's bed with a strong dynastic pedigree, a powerful navy and a large and effective army. Within a span of barely five years, Cleopatra Thea's third husband accomplished what her first two husbands had been unable to do: he brought peace to Syria and established through his own authority a remarkable kind of *pax Antiochana*.

Through her marriage to Antiochus VII, Cleopatra Thea gave birth to five children: two daughters, both named Laodice, a son named Antiochus (who would become Antiochus IX Kyzikenos), a second son called Antiochus and another, a short-lived son named Seleucus. Besides the children by her third husband, she had her two sons by Demetrius II – Seleucus (V) and Antiochus (VIII) – who were quickly growing up. Cleopatra Thea had produced a veritable herd of male heirs and spares along with a gaggle of daughters, who would follow in their mother's footsteps and whose marriages would steer the fate of the dynasty. Cleopatra Thea's fertility, particularly in her third marriage, made her dynastic future secure (although truth be told, the next century or so of Seleucid history would be shaped in no small part by the conflicts among her children).

Like his brother Demetrius II, Antiochus VII was anxious to launch an expedition to the east to reconquer Seleucid territories lost to the Parthians; if he could free Demetrius from captivity, should he be alive, then so much the better – he could then have his elder brother executed by his own authority. In March 131 BCE Antiochus began his own advance out of Antioch at the head of a massive army of 80,000 men and tens of thousands of civilian hangers-on. Before he departed, Antiochus VII, perhaps at Cleopatra Thea's instigation, had designated their four-year-old son Antiochus as his co-regent - just in case anything untoward should happen. It was Cleopatra Thea who, in reality, held the power during her husband's absence.

Antiochus VII's campaign initially enjoyed great success as it steamrolled through eastern Syria, entered Mesopotamia and recaptured Babylonia and Media; he was the first king since Antiochus III to invade the old Persian satrapy of Parthia in eastern Iran. A failed attempt at peace negotiations in the spring of 130 BCE led Antiochus VII to a second incursion across the Tigris, and it was at this point, as his campaigns were getting the results he desired, that he was ambushed and killed by Parthian guerillas. The scattered Seleucid army was either slaughtered, enslaved or fled into the mountains, and the offensive came to an ignominious end. At some point during the fighting, the Parthian king, Phraates, decided to release Demetrius II from captivity, apparently hoping that unleashing his incompetence on Syria would once more make ripe the country for Parthian conquest further down the line.

News of the expedition's defeat preceded Demetrius' arrival in Syria. To secure her family against any reprisal Demetrius might take on them, Cleopatra Thea – genuinely grief-stricken by the death of Antiochus VII – promptly sent her sons by Antiochus Sidetes out of Syria, while she remained in Antioch to face the arrival of her wrathful second husband. By the autumn of 129 BCE Demetrius II was back in Syria and revenge was in the air. He arrived there precisely as the power struggle in Egypt was reaching its climax, just at the point when Potbelly and Cleopatra III had been forced into exile in Cyprus and Cleopatra II had established herself as the sole pharaoh. The world held its breath. What would happen next? Surely, the time had come to settle old scores on all fronts? The Hellenistic kingdoms waited anxiously, poised for the fallout.

11

'Oh, what a tangled web we weave'

Cleopatra II sat on the throne of Egypt as its sole monarch. But even a queen as beloved as Cleopatra II did not have the capacity to bring the *whole* of Egypt under her sway, and although papyri documents bearing her name have been found in Alexandria and at the Upper Egyptian cities of Thebes, Edfu, Herakleopolis, Dios Polis and Hermonthis, Potbelly's titles still appeared in documentation from Memphis and the Fayum in the Nile Delta region, where he was still being recognized as king. Cleopatra's support network was strong though, for the continued presence in Upper Egypt of its old *strategos*, or 'army-leader', Boethos, who had been a *philos*, a 'companion', of Ptolemy VI and Cleopatra II during their reign together, galvanized the queen's position in the region; in fact, a papyrus dated to 132 BCE demonstrates that Boethos was in the process of founding a military city, Euergetis, named for the queen, shortly before the expulsion of Potbelly. Cleopatra also had the unwavering support of the Jews of Alexandria and the wider *chora*, the 'countryside', and thanks to the loyalty of the Jewish military leaders Onias and Dositheos her independent reign was sufficiently bolstered for her to feel a modicum of security. Nonetheless, she sent her beloved young son Memphites away from Alexandria, out of Egypt to the relative security of Cyrene, far from trouble.

Safely ensconced in his palace on Cyprus, Potbelly – who started referring to himself by the telling title Tryphon ('Furious', 'Wild' or 'Warlike') – wasted no time in counteracting his sister's claims to Egypt's sovereignty. He too had a support network in

Egypt, as an inscription from the Thebaid dated to 130 BCE reveals: it tells of the presence of soldiers loyal to Potbelly and of how, in the same year, Cleopatra's loyal Boethos was replaced as *strategos* there by a steadfast supporter of Potbelly, an Egyptian named Paos. Even in exile, it appears, Potbelly still maintained the support of the military, especially the many mercenary soldiers that he paid with the state funds he had illegally taken with him to Cyprus, as well as the corrupt officials he had bribed to support him.

To goad his sister and hurt Cleopatra II where it really mattered, Potbelly began to load his younger, fertile wife with divine honours. In this period of exile, Cleopatra III was awarded a new religious cult of unprecedented status, a remarkable creation established for adoration of the 'Holy Foal of Isis, Great Mother of the Gods'. This religious institution, replete with male priests and its own rituals, was invented from scratch for the young queen, and Cleopatra III was worshipped as the living epiphany of the goddess Isis on earth. The meaning behind the title 'Holy Foal' (*hieros pōlos*) is, admittedly, difficult to discern. It might refer to the youthfulness of the high priest who held the chief office in the cult (a foal is a young horse), or (sticking with the equine theme) it might have alluded to the stable of boys Cleopatra was birthing for the dynasty; if so, then the title reflected her glory as a divine mother. What is clear, however, is that Cleopatra III alone of all Ptolemaic women was honoured with a cult administered by a priest rather than a priestess, reflecting the structure of the Isis cult itself, which was also ministered by priests and not by priestesses. The creation of the cult propelled Cleopatra III into a new league of dynastic celebrities and left Cleopatra II lagging sluggishly behind as a royal also-ran. Through the identification of his second wife with Isis, an Egyptian goddess of such high status, Potbelly cleverly sought the support of the indigenous Egyptian population in the conflict with his sister, who herself primarily leaned on the Greek stratum. Cleopatra II was no doubt disturbed by the installation of a religious cult for her daughter. By taking Cleopatra III as his second wife and conferring an exceptional priesthood upon her, Potbelly added insult to injury. His obvious preference for his second wife must have made Cleopatra II realize that the chances of her son with Potbelly, Ptolemy Memphites, being designated as heir to the throne were seriously threatened.

Twisting the knife deeper, Potbelly had Memphites escorted from Cyrene, where he had been sent for his own safety by his mother, to Cyprus so that he might join his half-siblings on their island sojourn. A curious little inscription from the sanctuary of Apollo at Delos can be dated to this precise moment: it presents a scene of domestic harmony between the father, the son and his stepmother-half-sister, for in the text Memphites declares that,

> I, [Ptolemy Memphites], son of King Ptolemy Euergetes [i.e., Potbelly] in honour of Queen Cleopatra Euergetis [i.e., Cleopatra III], my father's wife, my cousin, on account of my gratitude towards her [have dedicated this statue] to Apollo, Artemis and Leto.

What is the meaning of this remarkable piece of epigraphy? Does it show that Memphites favoured his father over his mother, even as Cleopatra II was busy fighting for his inheritance? It certainly reads that way, and it appears as though Memphites had thrown in his lot with his father and stepmother. But this is unlikely. It is more probable that Memphites had nothing to do with the Delian inscription and that it was created on Potbelly's order in an attempt to project to the rest of the Hellenistic world the image of a happily unified royal family. It was especially intended as a message to Cleopatra II, telling her that her dynastic ambitions were futile and that her son had abandoned her. In effect, Potbelly had taken Memphites hostage, and his master plan, no doubt, was to use the boy's capture to force Cleopatra II to capitulate and consent to his return to Egypt. But she did not. In fact, she dug her heels in deeper with a bold act of *lèse-majesté* and took on board a new title, Philometor Soteira, 'Mother-Loving-Saviour'. Furthermore, in Upper Egypt, Theban scribes now began a policy of double-dating all documents: 'year 39 [of Ptolemy VI and Cleopatra II] which is also year 1 [of Cleopatra II]'. Simultaneously, in Alexandria Cleopatra II ordered the destruction of all statues, reliefs and inscriptions of her fat brother. She wanted him erased from history. Potbelly's reaction to this was swift and shocking.

*

Events came to a head in 130 BCE, as Cleopatra II celebrated her fifty-fifth birthday. The great banqueting hall of the Alexandrian palace had been decorated for an enormous party, an especially lavish one, for the queen wished to celebrate the beginning of her sole rule as *basilissa*-regnant. She and her many guests – courtiers, the aristocracy, dignitaries and foreign ambassadors – reclined à la *grec* on soft couches and drank fine wine from Chios from gold, silver and bronze cups. They feasted on hare cooked with mint and thyme; lamb and pork skewers soaked in coarse salt, wine and oil; flour sweets sprinkled with honeyed wine and sesame seeds; savoury rolls, roast quail, cheese from Achaia, figs, honey from Attica, grapes from the Mendi of Pallini, eels and fish from the Nile, seafood from Euboe, and barley bread from Pylos. The very world was spread out on the banqueting tables. Musicians entertained the queen's guests with the sound of lyre, *aulos* (a double-reed flute) and *sistrum* (a metal rattle); others played cymbals, the harp, bag-pipes, conch and triton shells, the trumpet, and the horn.

From across the world, birthday gifts poured into the palace, and Cleopatra delighted in examining the many curiosities which had been sent to her: a rhinoceros horn from a merchant based at Berenice on the Red Sea, stained purple and gilded with intricate chase-work; a parrot – a talking bird! – from a Jewish family in Alexandria; fine cotton cloth from India, the gift of one of her military generals. When a very large ebony box decorated with exquisite ivory marquetry was brought to her, carried by four slaves, the queen sat up, full of curiosity. 'From King Ptolemy and his wife Cleopatra,' the steward announced, to the surprise of everyone gathered. Cleopatra II was mystified and ordered the box to be opened. Peering inside, her eyes met with a bloody spectacle, for there, piled one on top of another, were the arms, legs, torso and head of a boy. It was the dismembered body of Memphites.

Diodorus Siculus wrote that the gruesome spectacle 'mimicked the savagery and bloodthirstiness of Medea', the infamous mythical child-murderer immortalized by the Athenian playwright Euripides in his most compellingly bloody tragedy. Justin's descriptive account noted that Potbelly 'stacked [Memphites'] body parts into a chest'. The accounts of Memphites' dismemberment are not beyond the bounds of probability given Potbelly's propensity for violence, for when threatened, Potbelly always resorted to thuggery – and if Memphites presented a block to him regaining the power which he felt to be his, then there was little chance that the boy would have been allowed to live. The murder and mutilation of Memphites was probably carried out with the knowledge (perhaps even the encouragement) of Cleopatra III, whose own future success depended upon her own sons' accession to the throne.

Never one to let personal grief get in the way of political gain, Cleopatra II put the dismembered limbs of her son on public display in Alexandria in order to rouse the anger of the mob. In fact, the whole of Egypt dissolved into chaos; indeed, a papyrus of c. 131/30 BCE speaks of a time of *amixia* – 'a breakdown of civil order'. In the midst of all this chaos, and in spite of Cleopatra II's best efforts, around 15 January 130 BCE Potbelly managed to return to Alexandria but failed to quell the country. Disorder continued unabated in every part of Egypt. Cleopatra II, realizing that her life was in danger now that Potbelly had returned, took ship and sailed to Syria, hoping to find refuge with her son-in-law, Demetrius II. Alexandria was finally quelled by Potbelly's general Hegelochus, and the names and titles of Cleopatra II were erased from all official documents. Ptolemy VIII was back in control, and he had a well-paid army at his disposal.

Cleopatra III and the children had remained on Cyprus until Alexandria was settled, and they now returned to the capital to take up residence in the palace again. Potbelly rewarded his supporters and capitalized on native support by promoting Egyptians to offices of state, the first occurrence of such a thing in two hundred years. One such beneficiary was Wennefer, whose sarcophagus inscription echoed in its content the standard hyperbole of count-less bureaucrats who had lived for centuries before him:

> I was true-of-heart, impartial, trusted . . .
> I was one praised in his town,
> Beneficent in his district,
> Gracious to everyone.
> I was well-disposed, popular:
> Widely loved, cheerful.
> I was . . . sweet-tongued, well-spoken.
> I was a good shelter for the needy,
> One on whom every man could lean.
> I was one who welcomed the stranger.

But the coffin text takes an unexpected twist when Wennefer owns up to having lived a life of dissipation – drinking, hunting and whoring – all of which signalled the decay in morality and decline in traditional values which seem to have accompanied Potbelly's return to power:

> I was a lover of drink, a lord of the feast day,
> It was my passion to roam the marshes.
> I spent life on earth in the King's favour,
> I was beloved by his courtiers . . .
> Singers and maidens gathered together . . .
> Anointed with myrrh, perfumed with lotus,
> Their heads garlanded with wreaths,
> All together drunk with wine,
> Fragrant with the plants of Punt,
> They danced in beauty, doing my heart's wish,
> Their rewards were on their limbs.
> I followed my heart inside the garden,
> I roamed the marshes as I wished.

Very much a sign of the times, Wennefer's inscription sug-gests that Potbelly's officials were simply taking their cue from the monarch himself and were behaving without restraint or decorum. Unsurprisingly, once Potbelly had retaken Alexandria, he enacted his revenge against the disobedient population and ordered his soldiers to indiscriminately round up groups of locals, put them into the gymnasium, surround it and put the building to the torch, burning alive everyone inside.

*

With a humiliating diminution in her status, Cleopatra II's natural grief over Memphites' grisly murder was mixed with a burning rage against her brother and his niece-wife. In 129 BCE Cleopatra II did the unthinkable and offered her son-in-law, Demetrius II of Syria, the Egyptian throne. Egypt, she affirmed, would be his in exchange for his military assistance in ousting and killing Potbelly. How serious she was about this as a long-term strategy is hard to know (could she really give up the throne she had fought for so easily?), but Demetrius, now completely estranged from his wife, Cleopatra Thea, threw in his lot with his mother-in-law and keenly accepted her proposition. But his troops got no further into Egypt than the border town of Pelusium, where they clashed with Potbelly's forces, and in 128 BCE his soldiers retreated into Seleucid territory.

Cleopatra II followed Demetrius deeper into Syria and there she met with her eldest daughter, Cleopatra Thea, for the first time in decades. Following his release by Pharses, king of Parthia, Demetrius had not taken revenge on Cleopatra Thea and they had been masquerading as a normal married couple since his return from Persia, overlooking the interlude in which she had married his brother, Antiochus VII Sidetes, and had given him children. Their reunion had not been easy, however, and the queen spent her time as far away from Demetrius as was possible in her palace at Ptolemaïs-Ake.

We have no evidence of what passed between mother and daughter at their reunion – we cannot know if they were affectionate or if time had diminished any bond which they once might have had, but we can suppose that Cleopatra Thea listened with attention while her mother decried the actions of her duplicitous youngest daughter and her wicked husband.

What we do know, though, is that Potbelly was determined that Cleopatra II would find no safe harbour in Syria, and he plotted to once again outmanoeuvre her by playing on the hostility which the Syrians still felt towards the weak Demetrius II. Potbelly, taking it upon himself to play king-maker, offered the Syrians a brand-new ruler in place of Demetrius. He offered them an inconspicuous man of low birth named Alexander Zabinas.

Born around 150 BCE, the boldly aspirational Zabinas was probably the son of a Hellenized Egyptian trader named Protarchus. He had gained some notoriety in Syria during the period of chaos following the Seleucids' loss of Mesopotamia to the Parthians, when he claimed to be an adopted son of Antiochus VII. Justin maintained with some plausibility that 'Alexander' was his assumed regnal name while his epithet Zabinas – 'The Bought One' in Hellenized Aramaic – arose from the justified rumours that he was simply in the pay of Potbelly. Backed by Potbelly's money, Zabinas presented a threat not just to Demetrius II but to Cleopatra Thea as well, although the chances of her allying herself with Demetrius were thin. With the support of Potbelly, Zabinas arrived in Antioch at some point in 128 BCE and captured the city. By the end of the year he had won control of territory in northern Syria and had begun minting coins in the region. With Antioch made secure, Zabinas marched on to meet Demetrius, who was just about clinging onto Coele-Syria. In early 125 BCE Demetrius and Zabinas clashed in battle near Damascus and Zabinas emerged victorious. The defeated Demetrius fled the battle and sought refuge in Ptolemaïs-Ake at the court of his estranged wife, but Cleopatra Thea neither needed nor wanted to give Demetrius another try at being king or a husband and she ordered the gates of the city to be shut in his face. By the time Demetrius II came a-calling at Ptolemaïs-Ake Cleopatra Thea had lost all patience with the incompetent men under whom the Seleucid kingdom was going to pieces.

With Ptolemaïs-Ake shut off to him, Demetrius II fled to Tyre, on the coast of Phoenicia, where, according to the Jewish historian Josephus, he was slain by his enemies after suffering many tortures; according to Justin, though, Demetrius tried to hide himself in the sanctuary of a temple but was killed on the order of the city's governor. In either case, it is probable that Cleopatra Thea issued the order to have him murdered. Her second husband thus met a curiously similar fate to that of her first – repudiation followed by an ignominious death. Thrice widowed, Cleopatra Thea no longer needed a husband, and she resolved that the next Seleucid king would be one of her sons. In fact, she favoured her youngest boy by Demetrius II above all others. His name was Antiochus but he was known to all as Grypus – 'Hook-Nose' – on account of his strikingly memorable profile.

Cleopatra Thea had already toyed with putting Grypus on the throne during the time his father had been preoccupied fighting skirmishes with the forces of Potbelly at the Egyptian border, but now the queen decided that Grypus' moment to shine had come. Much to her chagrin, however, her elder son, Seleucus V (also Demetrius' heir), had other ideas. Inclined more to support his father than his overbearing mother, he managed to corral Demetrius' remaining troops to keep Grypus off the throne so that he could take it himself. On hearing of the revolt, Cleopatra Thea promptly put an end to it by having Seleucus V murdered. The Roman historian Appian reports that Cleopatra Thea 'killed Seleucus by shooting him with an arrow immediately after he took the diadem after his father Demetrius, either because she was afraid on account of the treacherous murder of his father, or because she had an insane hatred for all people'. Clearly, Appian did not know *why* Cleopatra Thea had Seleucus V killed, although the inference is that she killed him with her own hands – with a bow and arrow. Justin too was only able to conjecture that 'because he had assumed the diadem without the authority of his mother, Seleucus was killed by her', once more inferring that Cleopatra Thea herself murdered her son. Even in late antiquity, historians were still debating why Seleucus V had to die and what form that death took. Centuries later, Eusebius, bishop of Caesarea Maritima in the Roman province of Syria Palaestina, was rather circumspect in his assessment, writing that 'Seleucus [V] . . . succeeded

Demetrius [II], and then straight away died from the accusations of his mother? Eusebius' suggestion was that the murder was done at Cleopatra Thea's command, under accusations of treason, rather than by her own hand. Regardless of the method or the actual identity of the murderer, the queen was clearly the agent behind the killing of her son.

In 125 BCE, sixteen-year-old Prince Grypus was elevated to the Seleucid throne as Cleopatra Thea's co-regent; the queen was forty-two or forty-three when Antiochus VIII Grypus joined her on the throne. During her time in Syria she had outlasted five kings and a prominent usurper, but now, with Antiochus VIII governing the realm with her, there was finally a realistic prospect for her to rule over a peaceful Syria. The only thing that this king needed to secure his hold of the country was a queen of his own.

*

While Cleopatra II was in Syria, conditions in Egypt declined badly. Potbelly had been unable to establish a stable government, and crime was rife, harvests were poor and the morale of ordinary working Egyptians had descended to an all-time low. An anxious uncertainty permeated the whole country. To help alleviate the disorder and dissatisfaction, Potbelly decided to put on a brave face and attempt a reconciliation with his sister. For that to work, compromise was needed, and Cleopatra Thea, looking to institute a rapprochement between the Seleucid and Ptolemaic kingdoms, acted as mediator between her mother and uncle. Her intervention worked; by 124 BCE Cleopatra II had been reinstated as queen in Egypt and Potbelly had reversed his Syrian policy by withdrawing all support from Zabinas – he gave it instead to Cleopatra Thea's chosen son, Antiochus VIII Grypus.

Cleopatra II returned home to Alexandria to be grudgingly reunited with her brother-husband and her daughter. The last papyrus citing only Ptolemy VIII and Cleopatra III as rulers dates from August 125 BCE, and the first papyrus that lists the newly reconciled ruling trio, placing Cleopatra II back in the second position, is dated to January 124 BCE. Thereafter, prescripts from

November 123 BCE to January 121 BCE once again contain the names and titles of all three rulers, with Cleopatra II once more addressed as the sister of Potbelly and Cleopatra III as his wife. Cleopatra II's secondary placement in the dating protocol was retained until Potbelly's death in 116 BCE, revealing that even after all the troubles of the proceeding years Cleopatra II was nonetheless able to resume her former status in the official hierarchy. She was routinely listed after Potbelly but always before her daughter – a clear indication that the senior queen still held significant authority.

Egypt was in a bad way. So grave was the situation that civil disruption did not dissipate even with the homecoming of the much-loved Cleopatra II. Extensive unrest broke out in towns such as Gebelen and Hermonthis, as well as in the urban centres of the Thebaid, where there was a shocking (but failed) attempt to set up a native Egyptian king. Egypt was rapidly deteriorating into anarchy.

With fields gone to waste, houses and farms destroyed, dangerous unrest rampant in all the towns and cities, and native Egyptians ready to throw off the shackles of a foreign government, the country was set to collapse. A radical solution to the country's many problems was sought and, in due course, found. In 118 BCE Potbelly and the two Cleopatras attempted to redeem the troubles of the recent decades by passing a series of revolutionary reforms and ordinances, including the so-called 'Amnesty Decree' which, at its outset, stated the following:

> King Ptolemy and Queen Cleopatra the Sister and Queen Cleopatra the Wife proclaim an amnesty to all their subjects for errors, crimes, accusations, condemnations and charges of all kinds up to the 9th of Pharmouthi of the 52nd Year, except to persons guilty of wilful murder or sacrilege. And they have decreed that persons who have gone into hiding because they were guilty of theft or subject to other charges shall return to their own homes and resume their former occupations, and their remaining property shall not be sold.

In the decree, the crown made many significant concessions to its Egyptian subjects. In addition to the return of confiscated properties, the decree set terms for the forgiveness of tax and selected other debts, and requirements concerning fair pay for labour. Although the Amnesty Decree further impoverished the administration, it was nonetheless a carefully designed attempt to stabilize the country and restore order. The way in which it addressed the crookedness of the government and sought to protect Egyptians from possible Greek corruption, as well as the emphasis given to land settlements, may reflect active policy-making on the part of Potbelly and Cleopatra II to satisfy their various groups of followers, while the safeguarding of revenues of temples to members of the dynastic cult was clearly beneficial to all three rulers. Bevan was one of the first scholars to point out the importance of the decree, noting that the reconciliation of the royal brother–sister pair meant that Potbelly had to recognize and accept the grants of land which were made to Cleopatra II's supporters and she the property-grants Potbelly made to his. Potbelly was clearly not the unequivocal champion of dynastic war; he was compelled to cooperate with Cleopatra II, who still had considerable leverage with the Alexandrian mob. We cannot be sure how much of the credit for the settlement should go to Cleopatra II and how much we must recognize Potbelly's hand at work; it might be that credit belongs to neither of them but to some nameless bureaucrat in the royal service, given that royal decrees were rarely composed by sovereigns themselves.

Part of the reconciliation strategy of the rulers was to launch into a mammoth new building programme, and up and down the country Potbelly and his two queens built and adorned Egyptian temples on a prolific scale. It was under the triple monarchy that the temple at Edfu had its formal dedication, some ninety-five years after the foundation stone had been laid by Ptolemy III Euergetes I, and the temples at Medinet Habu, Kom Ombo, Dendera, Medamud and El-Kab all benefitted from fulsome royal attention too. At Philae temple a triple shrine and a pair of 7-metre-tall obelisks were dedicated to the three rulers, whose serene images decorated the temple walls too, conveying absolutely nothing of the reality of the maelstrom they were living through. The svelte figure of Potbelly depicted within the shrine is a wonderful spin on lived reality. At Aswan a stele mentions the *philanthropia* Potbelly and Cleopatra III ('the Wife') conferred upon the temple of Khnum of Elephantine, and even further south at Dakkah a *naos* (shrine) of red granite was set up in the names of 'King Ptolemy and Queen Cleopatra the Sister, Beneficent Gods'. Significantly, the reconciliation of the royal family was celebrated through the deification of the late Ptolemy VII, the murdered son of Ptolemy VI and Cleopatra II, and the addition to his title of the cult names 'Theos Neos Philopator'. Poor Memphites, conversely, received no such posthumous divine honours; his name went unspoken, no doubt too much of a trigger to be mentioned.

Meanwhile, the children of Potbelly and Cleopatra III were beginning to reach maturity and were fast turning ripe for marriage, or whatever other duties were thought appropriate by their parents. In fact, by 124 BCE, aged around eighteen, the eldest son, Chickpea, had been married to his full-sister Cleopatra IV, aged about fifteen, a proud and haughty young woman keenly aware of her rank as pharaoh's eldest daughter. Chickpea adored her, and she him, for theirs was a love match – as disturbing as that might be, given the incestuous context of the romance – and from the outset the prince relied on his young wife's tenacity and bravado to give him the confidence which he lacked. In around 118 BCE, Cleopatra IV bore Chickpea a daughter, the future Cleopatra V Berenice III. She was born on Cyprus, where the young husband and wife had been sent to learn the arts of governance; Chickpea did such a good job there that he became the official governor of the island in 116 BCE. Cyprus suited Chickpea. It meant that he was far away from his mother, Cleopatra III, who despised him, although he really never understood why. It was the second son on whom she doted. Ptolemy X Alexander was unmarried and resided close to his mother at the Alexandrian court, where she mollycoddled and spoiled him and, as a consequence, the Alexandrians began to refer to him flippantly as Ho Kokkēs, 'Son of a Cunt'.

Potbelly's middle daughter, Cleopatra Tryphaina, aged about fourteen, was being trained for marriage to some Hellenistic sovereign
and was taking to her lessons very well – being naturally haughty
and given to fits of temper like her mother – whilst her younger
sister, Cleopatra Selene, the baby of the family (but already a bit
of a schemer), was still more interested in her girl friends than in
dreaming about the beds of powerful potentates.

*

By 125 BCE Potbelly was looking to put an end to any further
involvement in costly Seleucid-driven wars. His interference in
the dynastic fortunes of the Syrian house and his championing
of Alexander Zabinas had been expensive and ultimately unsuccessful, and because of this he had agreed to pull his support of
Zabinas and enter peace negotiations with his niece, Cleopatra
Thea. She knew her price. She insisted that concord between the
two royal houses be demonstrated publicly with a lavish wedding
of a Ptolemaic princess to her son Antiochus VIII Grypus. Potbelly
and Cleopatra III gladly obliged, agreeing to send their second
daughter, Cleopatra Tryphaina, to Antioch to retrace the footsteps
of her aunt Cleopatra Thea on her journey to the Syrian throne.

The marriage of Grypus and Cleopatra Tryphaina took place
in Antioch in 124 BCE. Cleopatra III felt an intense satisfaction that
her daughter had been put to such productive use, while Cleopatra Thea saw in her niece something of her old self, for if any
woman had been born to be queen it was Cleopatra Tryphaina,
whose inflated sense of self-importance informed every move she
made. If she had any anxiety at the thought of coming face to face
with her revered and powerful mother-in-law, Cleopatra Thea,
then she showed no hint of it. After all, alongside her dowry, Cleopatra Tryphaina brought Ptolemaic military and financial support
to aid her new husband in his fight against the usurper Zabinas.

Shortly after the wedding, in the first half of 123 BCE, Grypus
and Zabinas clashed on the battlefield. Grypus emerged victorious and Zabinas fled to Antioch, where, according to Justin, he
quickly ran out of funds with which to pay his soldiers. A desper-

ate gambit to plunder the Temple of Zeus and steal the massive golden statue of the god was exposed, which provoked the wrath of the Antiochenes, who accused Zabinas of impiety and chased him from the city. There are various accounts of the usurper's end. According to Justin, he fled north towards the south-eastern coast of (modern) Turkey but fell into the hands of robbers and was taken before Grypus, who ordered his execution. Josephus relates that he was killed in battle with Grypus, while Porphyry insists that Zabinas killed himself with poison (possibly at Grypus' command) after the defeat. Whatever the method, Zabinas was out of the way and Grypus could enjoy his first stint of peace as king. It did not last long.

We will likely never know precisely what caused the relationship between Cleopatra Thea and Grypus to deteriorate so rapidly in the aftermath of his victory against Zabinas, but downhill it went. Mother and son no longer communicated and entered an unfortunate period of self-inflicted cold war. The cause of the breakdown was possibly the domineering presence of Cleopatra Tryphaina. Never one to take a back seat, Grypus' imperious wife was not content to play the part of second lady to her influential mother-in-law. The apple did not fall far from the dynastic tree, for Cleopatra Tryphaina showed all the backbone and fight that had defined her aunt's own apprentice years in Syria two decades before.

With his power base secure, a resourceful Ptolemaic bride at his side, and his defeat of the usurper having earned him the epithet Nikephoros – 'Victory-Bringer' – Grypus' star was ascendant. Perhaps he began to see his mother as the final impediment to self-rule, for her overbearing presence loomed large at court. He understood that in her role as king-maker, a part she clearly relished playing, Cleopatra Thea had other dynastic spares dotted around the Eastern Mediterranean whom she could – and would – bring in and champion if she thought that Seleucid Syria needed a replacement king, one more malleable than he. Cleopatra Tryphaina may have reminded Grypus that his mother was a threat to his power and that his rulership would not be complete until

Cleopatra Thea had renounced power, willingly or not. Justin provides the narrative of what transpired next:

> With his father's kingdom recovered and free from external threats, Grypus became the target of his mother's snares. Having previously betrayed her husband Demetrius and killed her other son on account of her desire for power, because she [Cleopatra Thea] was suffering from the slight of her inferior dignity after his victory, she offered Grypus a cup of poison as he was returning from exercise. But Grypus had been warned of the plot previously, and as if he was competing with his mother in politeness, he begged her to drink it herself. When she refused, he pressed her again, and finally he accused her of the crime outright and argued that the only defence against the alleged crime was if she drank the cup she had brought to her son. The queen, being thus defeated by her own wickedness having been turned against herself, was extinguished by the same poison which she had prepared for Grypus.

Appian recounts the story in rather more laconic detail, stating: 'After ... Grypus became king, he compelled his mother to drink some poison that she had mixed for him,' but even Appian cannot resist a bit of moralizing as he reflects how 'she was delivered at last to justice.'

The famous Alexandrian medical researcher Herophilos once called poison 'the hand of gods' and thereby pointed to an association of poison with absolute power, divine prestige and fatal force, and tales of its death-dealing capabilities led to a common view that poison was a popular weapon for the court assassin. Certainly, the Hellenistic dynasties demonstrated an intense interest in acquiring toxicological knowledge, and poison had much to recommend it – there was its invisibility, the difficulty in attaching it to a particular agent and the fact that the agent does not need to be present when poison is put into effect, all of which made it a murder weapon of choice. Physical strength was not needed to administer poison, and its secretive and devious nature helped to characterize poison, in both ancient and modern sources, as typically a woman's weapon, but on this point we must be cautious. It is probable that Cleopatra Thea had plotted to remove her son Grypus – after all, her career had been built on a remarkable flair for court intrigue and the disposal of threats to her power – and now she had good reason to fear her eclipse by the Egyptian-backed royal couple, Grypus and Cleopatra Tryphaina. Although our ancient sources attribute the poison initiative to Cleopatra Thea, modern historians have been less convinced. Her ignominious failure to assassinate her son is incompatible with her previous skill in strategy, and indeed the figure of the solicitous mother offering her son a refreshing drink after exercise is not in keeping with her character at all, nor with probable court practice. If anything, it was Grypus and not his mother who had the reputation for employing poisons and drugs in his political machinations, suggesting that he was the more likely candidate to deploy it against his family. He could not have been under any illusion that he would be exempt from his mother's ambitious plans and may well have thought to forestall them with a pre-emptive strike. The story does contain the two motifs aimed at persuading the court: an eyewitness testimony (Grypus' informant) and supporting evidence (a potion which is proven to be poison). Concern about court and popular reaction to royal deaths and murders was evident throughout the Hellenistic kingdoms, but it became critical in the turmoil of the civil wars between the last Seleucids. It is entirely possible that our sources reflect a court-promoted version of events in which Grypus' matricide is justified because he was merely taking defensive retaliation against the mother's threat.

It is feasible to think that Grypus was keenly aware of a potential plot against his life by his mother. Tensions between the two were at breaking point and it seems that when push came to shove, Grypus simply managed to kill his mother before she got to him. Again, one wonders what role Cleopatra Tryphaina might have had in this. Was she following in her family's footsteps by neutralizing the threat Cleopatra Thea posed to Grypus, particularly with other male relatives lurking just over the horizon? The most likely explanation for Cleopatra Thea's murder is that the Seleucid court was simply not big enough to accommodate all three royal players, and given that Grypus and his wife felt that their star was on the rise, they had to ensure that Cleopatra Thea would not try to extinguish its brilliance.

Cleopatra Thea breathed her last at some point in late 121 BCE. This remarkable woman, the teenage princess who managed to forge a position of the highest authority over a foreign kingdom, drank from the cup of her death as she had done with the royal chalice in life: in deep draughts, right down to the dregs. But Cleopatra Thea's legacy did not perish with her, much to the consternation of Grypus and Cleopatra Tryphaina. Her fertility had always been Cleopatra Thea's strongest asset, and in death it was her fecundity that haunted Grypus and Cleopatra Tryphaina. Soon after Cleopatra Thea's murder, a spectre arose in the form of another Antiochus, yet another would-be Seleucid king.

Antiochus IX – nicknamed Kyzikenos, 'the man from Kyzikos' – was the son of Antiochus VII Sidetes and Cleopatra Thea. He had been sent as a boy to the Mysian city of Kyzikos in northeast Anatolia for protection from his uncle, Demetrius II, after the death of his father, and now in his late teenage years he was ready to throw his hat into the ring. Over the next few years, he was to be the chief threat to Grypus and Cleopatra Tryphaina: he would challenge them over possession of the Seleucid throne and threaten to tear their world apart. At his side would be his wife, another Ptolemaic princess, another of Potbelly's daughters. For it was through the offspring of the sister-queens, Cleopatra Thea and Cleopatra III, that discord reared its ugly head once more and tore its way into the royal houses of Seleucus and Ptolemy.

12

'Après moi, le déluge'

By 117 BCE, Potbelly's dynamic and dramatic life was slowly but surely ebbing away. His character had become calmer of late; he was less given to outbursts of violence and was trying to live up to his godly title, Euergetes, 'the Beneficent', by building temples and generally doing good works. He had drawn up a will back in 161 BCE, when he was busy going back and forth to Rome in order to secure senatorial support for his claim on Cyprus, and the will, which had been inscribed in stone as a public document, stated Ptolemy's desire to bequeath his kingdom to the Romans should any mortal fate prevent him from leaving heirs to the throne. Entrusting the Roman senate to protect his interests, he called upon Rome's chief god, Capitoline Jupiter, together with the sun god Helios, and Apollo Archegetes, the eponymous founder of the city of Cyrene, to witness his intentions. The will was never executed; in fact, it was revoked by another – secret – document.

A building inscription from Edfu temple tells us that Ptolemy VIII Euergetes II – Potbelly – died on 26 June 116 BCE. Outlived by his rival sister-queen, Cleopatra II (which must have brought her some wry satisfaction), he was succeeded as ruler by his niece-wife, Cleopatra III. Like much of his life, the death of Potbelly was played out as a glorious black comedy in which a crowd of grief-stricken courtiers gathered in the king's bedchamber to watch their monarch die. All wept quietly. None could possibly match the theatrical lamentations of Cleopatra III anyway, so none tried. Through her crocodile tears, she embraced her dying husband and kissed his fat cheek. Everyone at court knew that

Potbelly would leave the throne to her and, they assumed, that she would be Egypt's co-ruler with her eldest son, Ptolemy IX, Chickpea, at her side. They all assumed wrong. In his dying hour Potbelly declared that he had written a new will (legally witnessed), which was read aloud to the assembled courtiers. In it he left Cleopatra III the throne, as expected, but the will contained a striking new caveat: Cleopatra III was permitted to choose whichever of their two sons she thought the fitter for the role of king. Everyone was speechless. Potbelly made Cleopatra promise that she would choose between the two, guided only by wisdom and knowledge of what the country needed and desired, and that she would not be swayed by any consideration of personal like or dislike. Humbly, Cleopatra acquiesced. When Potbelly died, aged about sixty-five, 'after years of unbroken possession of the desirable things for which he had intrigued and murdered', as Bevan put it, he went with a smile on his face, knowing full well that his widow would be partisan towards her favoured youngest son. Potbelly's last joke was a masterstroke of mischief, and the dynasty would reel from it for decades to come.

Potbelly's reign had begun inauspiciously – one might say grotesquely – with the murder of his nephew, yet it turned out to be one of the longest in Ptolemaic history and was by no means inconsequential. Notwithstanding his insufferable and obsessional character, he was no clown, although his indubitable intellect was for too long squandered on the pursuit of acrimonious private scheming – so much so that it is sometimes hard to know how Egypt's government functioned at all. Everything wrong with the Ptolemies was present in the vulgar person of Potbelly: the steadfast quest for physical pleasure (the food, the booze, the sex, the violence), which went unconstrained by any ethical limits, culpability or fear of payback; the acts of wanton (indeed merciless) cruelty against his subjects; the treatment of Egypt as a vast private royal estate to be drained of resources for personal profit. There was also, less often noted by scholars, a strong and palpable component of make-believe in Potbelly's megalomaniacal character. He convinced himself that he was loved and that he was a great pharaoh. More harmfully, his fantasy projected the illusion of Egypt's immunity to invasion by foreign enemies. In the decades after his death, it would become clear that the mirage of Egypt's invincibility was fading fast as the country opened its eyes to the dark reality of Mediterranean politics.

The kingdom Potbelly left to Cleopatra III was on the cusp of decline, and the coming decades would show how the Ptolemies failed to unite as a family and instead put their relentless dynastic quarrels ahead of everything else. Slowly they began to bankrupt the once wealthy realm, a fact which worried the Romans, who had long seen Egypt as a valuable cash cow. Rome's increasing influence in the Eastern Mediterranean was becoming more apparent year upon year, and by the time Potbelly died the Romans had begun to impinge on the liberty of the old Hellenistic kingdoms of Macedon, Syria, Asia Minor and Egypt, threatening their very existence. Potbelly, however, had deemed Egypt to be his personal possession, and no Roman had any right to it. Egypt was his to gift away, and at his death he chose to give it to his younger wife. The question is, why? Bevan thought Potbelly did so to gratify Cleopatra III, who had been 'made dear to him by his lusts'; other scholars have suggested that Potbelly was simply worn down by her nagging or by her passionate desire to extend her own authority.

But the picture of a henpecking wife beleaguering a frail old man in his dotage does not match with the image of the energetic, pitiless Ptolemy VIII who had stirred up trouble in Syria only a few short years before his death. During the proceeding decade, Cleopatra III had demonstrated a remarkable level-headed ability to handle the autocracy of her husband (as well as the demanding nature of her mother), and after some twenty-four years of marriage not only had his lust for his second queen no doubt faded but his regard for her political acumen had grown. Potbelly's will, for all the fun he had in making it, did in fact ensure that Egypt was placed in the capable hands of Cleopatra III, recognizing her as the most outstanding of women.

*

Following a mourning period that was as brief as Clytemnestra's, Cleopatra III began ruling Egypt and its territories. The Greek historian Strabo suggests that she ruled unaccompanied in the period immediately following Potbelly's death. This ought not to come as a surprise as time was needed to select a new king, and although it was certain from the start that Cleopatra III desired to make Ptolemy Alexander her co-regent, for appearances' sake protocol needed to be followed and the royal council would have to be appraised of the queen's decision. The army and the Alexandrian mob had their own ideas as to who should be their king, though, and before Cleopatra could put her case to the council, they began to bellow for Chickpea to be appointed as their king. Cleopatra, fearing a full-scale riot, was forced to acknowledge her reviled eldest son as her co-regent. She was incensed at being outmanoeuvred at the very moment when she had finally been given the ultimate authority to rule.

Cleopatra III had no love – and hence held no loyalty – for Ptolemy IX. Even his nickname may have been an invention of Cleopatra's, given to him 'in sarcastic mockery', as Pausanias noted. In fact, the Greek historian stated categorically, 'I know of no other king who was so hated by his mother', and went on to explain that 'among the reasons assigned for Cleopatra's enmity towards her son is her expectation that Ptolemy Alexander, the younger of her sons, would prove more subservient'.

Cleopatra's reluctance to accept her elder son's co-rule might be explained by the presence of Chickpea's dangerously strong-willed sister-wife, Cleopatra IV, her eldest daughter – and in many respects her mother's equal in terms of ambition – whom Cleopatra III rightly feared would demand her own place on the throne as wife and queen of Ptolemy IX. Chickpea and Cleopatra IV, much in love, had a daughter too, and it is likely that Cleopatra III viewed this ready-made ruling triad as a threat to her own authority. As Chickpea and his little family made their way from Cyprus (where he had been conveniently sent to be out of sight, out of mind – and out of the running for the throne too) to Alexandria, Cleopatra III's mind must have been spinning: something would have to be done to keep Chickpea off the throne.

As Chickpea's ship advanced ever closer to the Egyptian coast, Cleopatra still had to deal with her ageing and increasingly cantankerous mother, who, at almost seventy years old, remarkably still clung to life and to the throne. A ruling triad was thus created, consisting of Cleopatra III, Cleopatra II and Ptolemy IX Chickpea, and it was first attested in a papyrus document dated 29 October 116 BCE, four months after Potbelly's death. Cleopatra II's presence is recorded with all due official protocol and decorum:

> Year 2 second month in the season of *akhet* the female-pharaoh Cleopatra [II] and the female-pharaoh Cleopatra [III] and the pharaoh Ptolemy [IX] her son, whom she loves.

The text reveals not just that Cleopatra II was alive and still being acknowledged as queen; her inclusion at the head of the dating protocol was an honorary reference to the prestige she had earned during her long years as queen and her period as *basilissa*-regnant. The papyrus also shows that, much against her will, Cleopatra III had been obliged (by that baying Alexandrian mob) to welcome Chickpea back from Cyprus and to establish him as Egypt's king. He arrived home with his wife, Cleopatra IV, his toddler daughter, an infant son (born on Cyprus around 117 BCE) and a baby boy who arrived on the scene just before Chickpea arrived back in Alexandria, late in 116 BCE. Chickpea's own dynastic line was increasing quickly – and Cleopatra III could not help but observe its steady growth.

Just as Chickpea set foot in the Alexandrian palace, Ptolemy Alexander boarded a ship bound for Cyprus where, it had been agreed by his mother, he was to become the *tropheus* (governor) of the island in place of his brother. Once comfortably installed in the Cypriot palace though, in 114 BCE the pushy prince proclaimed himself 'Ptolemy X Alexander, King of Cyprus', and began to live the high life commonly associated with the greatest Hellenistic monarchs, even awarding himself a make-believe crown and coronation. It was as egregious an action as had ever been committed by Potbelly, but back home in Egypt, Cleopatra III let it pass. If her favourite boy wanted to be the king of Cyprus, then the king of Cyprus he would be.

The new pharaoh of Egypt, Ptolemy IX, was given the cultic title Philometor Soter – 'the Mother-Loving Saviour' – the masculine version of the powerfully expressive epithet assumed by Cleopatra II during the era of her sole rule. It must have been Cleopatra II who bestowed this name on her grandson, and it was another twist of the knife for Cleopatra III. In fact, the long-drawn-out rivalry between royal mother and royal daughter which had played out decade after decade only ceased when the seventy-year-old Cleopatra II, ill, enormous and panting under the weight of her golden necklaces and bracelets, died late in the autumn of 116 BCE. In her life she had been obtuse, stubborn, wilful, crafty and calculating; she had known great happiness and gut-wrenching despair; she had tasted victory and had known bitter defeat. Cleopatra II had also been quick-witted, self-reliant, brave and utterly brilliant. She had played the long game and, to all intents and purposes, she had won it. Cleopatra II was a truly great princess of the Ptolemaic house and the longest reigning Ptolemaic queen. How sad it is that in the years after the queen's death the hostility that had scarred the lives of mother and daughter was played out beyond the grave. Cleopatra III omitted her mother's names and titles from all new inscriptions, so that after her death Cleopatra II was never allowed to be venerated as a goddess in the temples of Egypt, and eventually even her priesthoods ceased to function. Only then could Cleopatra III finally claim her victory. If we were to write an imaginary epitaph for Queen Cleopatra II – denied one in real life – it should, perhaps, read like this:

> Here lies Cleopatra Philometor Soteira
> Queen over her brother-husband Ptolemies,
> Great by birth and great through rule,
> But greatest through her own Cleopatras, goddesses all.

*

With her mother finally out of the way, Cleopatra III turned her attention to her ambitious, equally defiant daughter Cleopatra IV, whose spirit she was determined to curb. According to Justin, Cleopatra III 'took away [Chickpea's] wife, compelling him to divorce his sister Cleopatra [IV], whom he very much loved'. It is likely that Cleopatra III had made the divorce of Cleopatra IV a condition for Chickpea's accession to the throne. Unwillingly, Chickpea acquiesced.

Although quite common in Ptolemaic society, divorce itself often went unrecorded – as with marriage, a public proclamation of divorce usually sufficed without the necessity of lawyers or judges or priests. All the known Demotic divorce documents we possess come from Upper Egypt and were drawn up to certify that the husband of a divorced woman no longer had any claims over her (financial, legal or moral) and that she was free to remarry without hindrance. Such a process probably occurred within the royal household too, although we cannot be certain. What is sure, however, is that no matter how distressed Chickpea was by his separation from Cleopatra IV, he nonetheless conformed to his mother's command – what option did he have but to agree? In tearing Cleopatra IV away from Chickpea's side and by demoting her from the queenship, however, Cleopatra III made for herself an implacable enemy. Cleopatra IV turned out to be every inch her mother's daughter – forceful, unyielding, totally fearless and driven by a quest for power and revenge.

The precise timing of the divorce is unknown, but it was probably at some point in 115 BCE since the narrative of events suggests that the three momentous happenings of the period – the death of Cleopatra II, the accession of Ptolemy IX and the divorce of Cleopatra IV – all followed very closely on the death of Potbelly. Throughout history, succession periods have almost always been times of turmoil because in such moments the transfer of power has the capacity to quickly become a flashpoint to be seized on by usurpers at home or enemies abroad. But Cleopatra III had acquired enough sole power to be able to exercise a prerogative usually reserved for kings without opposition: she became, in effect, the 'living law', with the ability to sanction (demand) divorces and marriages. Chickpea had no control over his own matrimonial status, so dominant was Cleopatra III, whose next move was to force the king to marry his youngest sister, Cleopatra Selene. The queen supposed she would be more malleable than Cleopatra IV and would prove to be a loyal and compliant daughter. Aged about sixteen, Cleopatra Selene played the role of the yielding ingénue to perfection – though later events would show she was anything but mailable. She took no formal part in the institution of queenship and was glad to be marginalized from all royal ceremonial; she did not even warrant a presence in prescripts or inscriptions of the time, even though she bore Chickpea two short-lived boys. For now, Cleopatra Selene took a back seat and made no attempt to challenge her mother's role as queen.

With Chickpea remarried, Cleopatra IV had no chance of occupying the Egyptian throne and so she turned her attention elsewhere. Cut free from the fetters of her position as a queen-in-waiting, Cleopatra IV swiftly made for Cyprus, where, with her own resources, she raised an army of mercenary soldiers with the intention, it would appear, of securing her return to the Egyptian throne. We have no idea if her brother Ptolemy Alexander was party to her ambitions, although as 'king' of Cyprus he would have been hard pressed not to have known. There is even a likelihood that the siblings might have contemplated marriage and a joint invasion of Egypt – after all, both were unscrupulous, unafraid and addicted to power. But rather than go for the Egyptian throne by a direct route, Cleopatra IV plumped for a more subtle way to avenge herself on her mother and, in 115 BCE, she sailed with her army to Antioch. Once there, and with all eyes fixed on her, in a flagrant act of self-will she offered herself in marriage to her cousin, the Seleucid rival king Antiochus IX Kyzikenos, Cleopatra Thea's son by Antiochus VII. Kyzikenos had set his mind on the Seleucid throne ever since the death of Cleopatra Thea and in his quest for power had embarked on an apocalyptic collision course with his half-brother Antiochus VIII Grypus, who was married to Cleopatra Tryphaina. She was horrified that her manipulative elder sister, Cleopatra IV, had come to Syria and accused her of deliberately wishing to stir up trouble within the royal family and to threaten her own status as queen.

Kyzikenos' marriage to Cleopatra IV represents the genuine coming-of-age of the Ptolemaic princess. Kyzikenos was delighted when his new wife handed the soldiers of her private army over to his command – full-out war between the two half-brothers was now inescapable. Open warfare was briefly delayed when Grypus, acting through agents, made an unsuccessful attempt on Kyzikenos' life (poison was once again his chosen weapon), but a full-blown struggle for the Syrian throne quickly followed.

The good-looking Kyzikenos – his coin portraits show him sporting a mop of long curly hair and a sexy little beard – fell in love with his new bride and she with him. Soon she bore Kyzikenos a son, Antiochus (X) Eusebes, although her rival, her sister Cleopatra Tryphaina, had produced for Grypus no less than five healthy sons – Seleucus (VI), Antiochus (XI), Philip (I), Demetrius (III) and Antiochus (XII) – as well as a daughter, Laodice Thea. The Seleucid realm now found itself in the bizarre situation of having two rival Ptolemaic princesses married to competing half-brother-kings, with two sets of heirs promising to prolong conflict into the next generation. Because of Ptolemaic interference in Seleucid affairs, there now emerged a power struggle of epic proportions in which the ferocity of the battlefield fighting was amplified through the mutual hatred of the sister-queens themselves.

*

In Egypt, early in their uncomfortable joint reign, Cleopatra III and Ptolemy IX took their required titles: they were styled Theoi Philometores Soteres, 'the Mother-Loving-Saviour-Gods'. Cleopatra's hand in the choice of epithet is clear to see, and Pausianias, the Greek historian-cum-travel writer, later wrote that Chickpea was given the title Philometor by his mother out of mockery. He must have recoiled at being addressed as 'Mother-Loving' but nonetheless he tried to make the best of things and establish his own identity as pharaoh. From 117 BCE to 107 BCE Chickpea was recorded assuming the annual office of priest of Alexander in the dynastic cult, and we know that in August 115 BCE he travelled to Elephantine to celebrate and officiate at the Nile's flooding, and where he granted privileges to the priests of Khnum. But even the traditional religious role reserved for the pharaoh was hijacked by his mother who, during this period, assumed for herself more religious and cult titles than ever before. Thus in the hieroglyphic temple inscriptions found at Dakka and Philae she is given traditional female titles such as 'Mistress of the Two Lands' and is addressed as the 'daughter of Re', but more unconventionally she is also termed 'the female Horus' and 'the female ruler'. At the temple of Nekhbet at El-Kab, just south of Thebes, Cleopatra III was given the strangely androgynous titles 'the Female Horus, Mistress of Two Lands, Strong Bull', which suited her non-binary self-presentation very well. By fully embracing the old pharaonic theology of amorphous sexuality, Cleopatra was able to embody both a 'masculine' aggression as a pharaonic and Hellenistic warrior-king and a 'feminine' sensibility as a nurturing mother and a living goddess.

Cleopatra's most notable honorific acquisition, though, was her personal attachment with the rites of the Alexander cult, the rituals of which focused sharply upon the worship of the deified Alexander and the successive Ptolemaic kings and queens. During the reign of Chickpea, it was Cleopatra herself, not the king, who procured and utilized the title 'Priest of Alexander' – an unprecedented achievement for a woman – but the possession of honours escalated when Cleopatra awarded herself a priest for her personal worship as a living deity, and no less than three priestesses, each recruited for her ritual adoration. In earlier generations, the Ptolemaic rulers had been integrated into the Alexander cult under their own names and titles and were given the honorific epithet Theos – 'God' – or Thea – 'Goddess' – as a way of marking clearly their transition into the divine realm. The women of the dynasty had always identified as Isis but their roles as queens had remained clear and separate. Cleopatra III changed all that. She was 'Isis, Great Mother of the Gods', as if the mortal woman Cleopatra had disappeared to be replaced as the living incarnation of divinity, Isis herself. The queen elevated herself as a goddess outside Egypt too – in the form of Aphrodite, whose incarnation she adopted within Alexandria also, she was said to be intermingling with the gods of Olympus.

Throughout the joint reign with Chickpea, Cleopatra III preceded her son in all official prescripts – Greek, Demotic and hieroglyphic – and she was inevitably given first place in dating formulae too, a significant indication of her superiority and dominance. Sculptors carefully described the queen's privileged rank, and her carefully regulated image appeared in a variety of artistic media. A fragmented relief found in the Temple of Khonsu at Karnak, for instance, shows Cleopatra III occupying the place of honour, standing in front of Chickpea, and a huge well-preserved relief on the Mammisi (Birth House) at the Temple of Hathor at Deir el-Medina, on the west bank of Thebes, portrays Cleopatra III in the frontmost position, offering a papyrus posy to the Theban triad of Amun, Mut and Khonsu, while Chickpea, who stands in the hierarchically enfeebled position behind her, offers the gods the symbol of *ma'at* ('justice'). In other relief scenes, such as on columns at Kom Ombo, Chickpea and his mother were even represented in separate acts of worship. The facade of the temple of the vulture goddess Nekhbet at El-Kab in the Thebaid represents Cleopatra III alone in an act of worship without the king, and the Greek epigraphic evidence from Chickpea's reign echoes the Egyptian material, for in the documentary prescripts the name of Cleopatra III always appears alone, without that of her son, and she is routinely addressed as the Goddess Euergetis.

Beyond Egypt's border, the name Cleopatra III was synonymous with the country she ruled, but it is hard to say that Cleopatra pursued an active foreign policy because (as we will see) her political ventures into the wider Hellenistic world were usually forced upon her by circumstance. Her focus was on the internal affairs of Egypt. Nevertheless, Cleopatra III kept a close diplomatic eye on Rome, which she understood to be a fast-growing world power; although it was not – as yet – a direct threat to Egypt, she found it judicious to at least court the Romans. Her diplomacy chiefly focused on inviting influential Roman senators to Egypt and dazzling them with upmarket Nilotic tours. In the summer of 116 BCE, for instance, a party of four illustrious senators came to visit the temple of Philae and left behind two inscriptions – the oldest known Latin texts to have been discovered in Egypt – recording the bounty and largess of the queen. The itinerary for these Roman state visits was always the same: a senator would arrive at Alexandria to be shown the Pharos Lighthouse, the tomb of Alexander and the Great Library, before being loaded onto a Nile cruiser and shipped upriver to Memphis, via the Delta, to do some sightseeing. He would visit the temples of the ancient city, the Serapeum, the many pyramids in the surrounding area and the Great Sphinx at Giza – which was always a hit with Roman visitors. The cruise would continue through Upper Egypt with stops in Abydos and Thebes, where a tourist tradition of scratching names and verses onto the Colossi of Memnon (the enormous, ancient, twin seated statues of Amenhotep III) began in earnest. Back on board the cruise ship, the senator would drift up the Nile to Aswan and on to Philae, where the party would marvel at the temple of Isis, turn around and make their way back to the Mediterranean coast.

The Ptolemaic royal family and their guests would often travel the Nile on what might today be called a 'superyacht', a floating royal palace constructed for the most opulent of cruises. According to the poet-historian Callixenus, the royal yacht was known as the *thalamēgos* – 'carrier of the bedchamber'. It was a behemoth of a vessel: nearly 100 metres long and 20 metres wide, it had a double hull and its two prows and two sterns sat high above the Nile's waterline, supporting a massive two-storey palace complex that rose from the ship's middle. Its mast of 70 cubits (37 metres high) supported a topsail made from purple linen. The building materials of this floating pleasure-palace were a physical testament to the royal family's sumptuous wealth: fragrant Milesian cypress and Lebanese cedar beams extended across the roof between supports made of ivory and columns of Indian alabaster capped with Corinthian-made capitals adorned with ivory and gold. From one of the many elegant dining couches a reveller could glimpse scenes of animals carved in ivory and gold at the tip of the columns or marvel at the gilded carvings adorning the cypress-wood roof. Towards the head of the vessel was an apartment dedicated to Dionysus that featured thirteen dining couches placed beneath a gilt canopy, and on the right-hand side of the room was a cave made from actual stone and gold, and placed within it were statues carved from Parian marble. Alongside the ship's massive main banqueting hall was an apartment for the queen and her retinue, sumptuously decorated of course, which led to a private *symposion* (party space) for the queen, with nine dining couches placed in a square. The *thalamēgos* was a floating symbol of Ptolemaic royal *tryphē*, and Cleopatra III dazzled the Roman aristocracy with it whenever they came to Egypt to play. Her policy of diplomacy-through-dazzle worked well, for while Cleopatra III reigned Rome kept up very friendly relations with wealthy Egypt.

Sometimes a Roman visitor had particular requests. When Lucius Memmius joined Cleopatra III for a tour of the Delta, for example, he requested especially that at Tebtunis he might feed the sacred crocodiles at the temple of Sobek. A well-preserved papyrus letter, written perhaps on the queen's instructions and dated 5 March 112 BCE, survives to tell the story:

> To Asklepiades. Lucius Memmius, a Roman senator, who occupies a position of great dignity and honour, is making the voyage from Alexandria to the Arsinoite *nome* [province] to see the sights. Let him be received with special magnificence, and take care that at the proper spots the chambers be prepared and the landing-places to them be got ready, and that the gifts of hospitality below written be presented to him at the landing-place, and that the furniture of the chamber, the customary titbits for Petesouchos and the crocodiles, the necessaries for the view of the Labyrinth, and the offerings and sacrifices be provided; in general take the greatest pains in everything that the visitor may be satisfied, and display the utmost zeal.

The letter is perhaps symbolic of Egyptian weakness in the attitude of deference to a Roman senator, yet it would be a mistake to read too much into the hospitable reception of an important person. But throughout the second century BCE institutional recognition and acceptance of Roman domination is increasingly evident. The cult of the goddess Roma, the patron goddess of Rome, developed and spread round the Greek east in this period, as is illustrated by an inscription from Miletos of about 130 BCE, which outlines a regular timetable for sacrifice to 'the People of the Romans and to Roma'. Indeed, 'The people of Rome' crop up on inscriptions from all over the Hellenistic world and increasingly they are referred to as 'the common benefactors'.

*

Meanwhile, a less-than-happy Chickpea was thwarted by his mother in every attempt he made to assert sovereignty; each time he reached out for control, she managed to curb his ambition. Serious struggles for power developed until, in 107 BCE, Cleopatra decided that Chickpea had to go. She had her servants spread a malicious rumour throughout Alexandria that Chickpea had tried to assassinate her and, conjuring up all her skill in amateur theatricals, she made a public appearance in front of the Alexandrian palace, weeping and wailing and showing off her self-inflicted wounds. According to Pausanias, the drama queen put on quite a show:

> She even covered her eunuchs (those she thought best predisposed to performing) with cuts and bruises and presented them to the people, making out that she was the victim of [Chickpea's] aggression, and that he had thrashed the eunuchs in a similar fashion. The people of Alexandria rushed to kill [Chickpea], and when he escaped on board a ship, made Ptolemy Alexander, who returned from Cyprus, their king.

Although it had never been Cleopatra's intention to let Chickpea escape with his life, he nevertheless returned to Cyprus and took cover there. She had failed to kill her thankless son but at least she had, after nine years, finally expelled him from the throne. In his haste to escape Alexandria, Chickpea left behind his children by Cleopatra IV – they were put into their grandmother's care – and his second sister-wife, Cleopatra Selene, was separated from him through divorce, at the command of Cleopatra III.

In 107 BCE Ptolemy Alexander emerged in Alexandria as Pharaoh Ptolemy X Alexander I, his mother's new and much-beloved co-regent. To cement his status as king, Cleopatra III had Ptolemy X marry his brother's ex-wife Cleopatra Selene, his own youngest sister, who in 105 BCE bore the king, her second husband, a son. Within months of his birth, the boy was sent out of Egypt to the sanctuary of the god Asclepius on the Aegean island of Cos for safekeeping; he was never to see his parents again. With the baby went two more of Cleopatra III's grandsons, the sons of Chickpea, together with much of her treasure and her last will and testament. The times were dangerous and even with her favourite son installed next to her as her joint ruler, Cleopatra III knew no peace of mind for she felt threatened by Chickpea, whom she envisaged to be malignantly sitting on Cyprus plotting how best to take revenge on her. And indeed, her instincts were correct – that was just what he was doing. Soon reports reached Alexandria of how Chickpea was gearing up for war and of how, having crossed into Syria, he was intent on advancing on Egypt, retaking his throne, and destroying his mother's power for once and for all.

Late in the summer of 103 BCE Cleopatra III dispatched Ptolemy X and a fleet of warships to Syria to fight and defeat Chickpea, where he succeeded in getting his men as far north as Damascus. She herself travelled overland with her infantry troops to Ptolemaïs-Ake, but when she was denied entry to the city, she began, in September 103 BCE, to brutally besiege it. With most of the Egyptian troops occupied in Syria, Chickpea took his chance to regain his sovereignty and marched on the Egyptian border town of Pelusium; Ptolemy X got there first and managed to drive his brother back to Gaza, where he and his army were forced to spend the winter. With a large garrison stationed to keep watch at

Pelusium, Chickpea had no choice but to retreat with his troops back to Cyprus. He had tried to counter his mother but had failed. From then on, he lived peacefully as Cyprus' 'king'. It was only in early 102 BCE that Ptolemaïs-Ake surrendered to Cleopatra's troops (they were still there in September 102 BCE, long after Chickpea had returned to Cyprus). In a neat piece of autobiographical hyperbole, one of Cleopatra's generals, a man named Petimuthes, son of Psenobastis, from Semabehdet in Lower Egypt, recounted the capture of Ptolemaïs-Ake in a dramatic inscription which he had carved into his statue, found centuries later at Karnak where Petimuthes promoted the construction of a storehouse in the temple of Amum. In it he boasted how:

> Heroic like [the war god] Montu, lord of valour, I reached the land of Khor [Syria], being in the company of the queen [Cleopatra III]; I entered foreign countries like a divine hawk; I seized the town and the fortress of Psy-of-Ptolemy [Ptolemaïs-Ake]; I massacred tens of thousands of enemies, I trampled underfoot hundreds of thousands of enemies; I made a great massacre among the 'children of the revolt'. The Great Royal Wife (Cleopatra III) gave me many presents, as well as to my father and my troops.

Some historians have suggested that Cleopatra III's war with Chickpea was pointless, since he went back to Cyprus and she returned to Egypt, but the fact that Chickpea made no attempt to reopen hostilities suggests that Cleopatra's victory was viewed as decisive – at least by him. Scholars have been quick to condemn Cleopatra's eagerness to engage in hostilities with her son, labelling her a cruel, overbearing woman. But perhaps we can read Cleopatra's military exploits during the 'War of the Sceptres' – as it has been grandiloquently termed – in a different light, for not only was there an established convention for royal women to participate in warfare (we might recall the galvanizing presence of Arsinoë III at the Battle of Raphia a century earlier), but Hellenistic kings had to be seen as successful warriors if they wanted to be taken seriously as efficacious rulers. Cleopatra III put herself squarely in the masculine sphere of war to prove that her reputation for strong rulership was completely justified. Yet, as noble and as valiant as that might sound, when all was said and done, Cleopatra III achieved nothing of worth during her Syrian campaign; she simply increased the amount of fighting and destruction that was already raging in the Syrian civil war. Unbeknown to her, two of its most prominent casualties were to be her own daughters.

*

The war between the two Seleucid half-brothers had taken on an extra dimension of ferocity as the Ptolemaic sisters, Cleopatra IV and Cleopatra Tryphaina, locked horns over the ever-diminishing, fatigued Seleucid empire. And when their youngest sister, Cleopatra Selene, entered the fray, it brought a fresh level of enmity to Syria. Between 116 BCE and 113 BCE, the three Ptolemaic princesses participated in the bloodiest, goriest and greatest *grand guignol* spectacles of Hellenistic history.

The marriage of Cleopatra IV to Kyzikenos had certainly improved the competitor king's standing – both in the eyes of the global community, which regarded his marriage with the impressive Ptolemaic princess an obvious advantage, and by the presence of Cleopatra IV's substantial mercenary militia. It was because of these ruthless soldiers of fortune that Kyzikenos managed to gain the throne in 113 BCE and take control of Antioch, which became his military base and the site of his court. When he led his troops out of the city on campaign, he left Cleopatra behind in the safety of the palace, but in a remarkably short time, Grypus surrounded and besieged Antioch and trapped his hated sister-in-law within the palace walls.

When, in 112 BCE, Antioch fell to Grypus, his wife, Cleopatra Tryphaina, appeared in the city and demanded that her husband give her complete authority over her sister Cleopatra IV, now a prisoner of war. Her wish, no doubt, was to gloat over her sister's bad fortune and so aggravate the woman's humiliation, to torture her and, finally, to have her executed. Even Grypus, who was never reticent about punishing or executing his enemies, was surprised by his wife's appetite for retribution, and when he refused to comply, Cleopatra Tryphaina suspected him of holding a guilty passion for her sister (probably with some justification). Her vindictiveness was therefore sharpened by a feverish jealousy. In his account of the episode, Justin tried to rationalize Cleopatra Tryphaina's murderous impulses:

> The wife of Grypus ordered that the highest priority be given to hunting down her sister Cleopatra [IV]. Not that she wished to help her if taken prisoner, rather it was to ensure that she escape none of the miseries of her captivity. For [Cleopatra] Tryphaina believed that it was from feelings of jealously towards herself that Cleopatra [IV] had entered this kingdom rather than any other, and that she had declared herself her sister's enemy by marrying her sister's foe. She then accused Cleopatra [IV] of introducing foreign armies into the dispute between the two brothers and of marrying outside Egypt, against her mother's wishes, after she had been divorced from her brother [Chickpea]. For his part, Grypus begged [Cleopatra] Tryphaina not to force him to do such a dreadful deed. None of his ancestors, he said, had ever unleashed his wrath on women after a victory, their sex itself sufficed to spare them the perils of war and the cruelty of the victors. And in the case of this woman there was moreover . . . a blood relationship, for the woman who was the object of her vindictive fury was her own sister, his cousin, and the aunt to all the children they shared . . . Grypus refused to give way, the more stubbornly the sister was fired with a womanly single-mindedness, for she thought all these words derived not from human compassion but from sexual desire.

If Cleopatra Tryphaina's hunch was correct and Grypus was indeed infatuated by his sister-in-law, then what was going on in

Grypus' mind? Was he prepared to replace one sister with another? Would he repudiate Cleopatra Tryphaina and take Cleopatra IV to his bed – willingly or otherwise? Cleopatra IV was a magnet for men. Both Grypus and Kyzikenos found her desirable, and let us not forget that Chickpea had been fervently in love with her also. Their devotion implies, perhaps, that Cleopatra IV had a more winning disposition than the average Cleopatra, and perhaps she was thought to be beautiful too. It is certain that she had charisma, and her nerve and stamina cannot be doubted, and so kings were prepared to fight wars over her, like a latter-day Helen of Troy.

What Justin's account of Cleopatra IV's capture provides, though, is the choicest psychoanalytical discussion of sister-envy found in the whole of ancient literature. He manages to articulate the acute consciousness of sibling rivalry that was operating between the two royal sisters, and he demonstrates that the dark side of their relationship was rooted in jealousy, the most destructive of emotions. Cleopatra Tryphaina's malevolence, Justin makes clear, arose from her lack of confidence and her obsessive fixation that her husband found her sister more desirable than her; her anger was fuelled by the jealousy she had for her charismatic sister, whom she knew to be sought-after. Justin asserts that Cleopatra Tryphaina found other excuses to present Cleopatra IV as worthy of rebuke. She was a bad daughter, it was stressed, and she had willingly stirred up agitation in Syria. But at the heart of the matter lay Cleopatra Tryphaina's dread that her sister would rob her of her man. Envy, after all, is sharpest when the qualities of someone close to us – and very much like us – are its focus, and this makes the ferocity of envy even more terrifying. Even though Cleopatra Tryphaina admired the sister that she envied (she was more beautiful, charismatic and easier to like than she herself), she wanted to obliterate her completely. Cleopatra Tryphaina had tied herself up in a 'sister knot', as contemporary sociologists put it. Sisters who are at odds with one another face the guilt of wanting to annihilate someone they love and identify with. In the case of Cleopatra IV and Cleopatra Tryphaina, two women who shared an intimate and overlapping history, the psychology is clear and the drama of the two sisters – so very alike in character and ambition – was played out in the way we might expect, in the style of a bloody revenge tragedy.

Justin tells that while the husband and wife squabbled, Cleopatra IV managed to escape Antioch and fled south-west to the nearby town of Daphne, a place celebrated for its fine olive grove, planted in the sanctuary of Apollo. The place was one of extreme beauty, with perennial fountains and abundant woodland, and its holy sanctuary had been founded with the privileges of asylum, which made it famous throughout the Greek world. The asylum laws of the Greeks maintained that refugees forcibly ejected from their places of habitation needed to be protected and given shelter in another location. When individuals claimed asylum in a religious sanctuary or temple, it meant that they were putting themselves under the protection of the gods, foremost among whom was Zeus Hikesios, the general overseer and champion of *hiketeia* or asylum-seeking. The asylum seekers were not subject to arrest and were under the protection of the law; nobody had the right to carry them off as slaves or use any force against them. At Daphne, Cleopatra IV invoked the sacred laws of asylum and entered Apollo's temple, taking refuge at the god's altar, where she would be guaranteed divine protection.

Grypus and Cleopatra Tryphaina soon arrived at the holy site and, acting on her own authority and against all laws civic and sacred, Cleopatra Tryphaina commanded her soldiers to enter the temple and take her sister's life. The troops dutifully dragged Cleopatra IV out of the darkness of Apollo's shrine and into the sunshine of the sacred precinct where, it was thought, the execution could be done without offending the god. Struggling for all her worth, Cleopatra IV managed to clutch onto a statue of the goddess Artemis, Apollo's divine twin, and with a determination that shocked all who heard it, she screamed out aloud to the priests of Apollo that the laws of asylum were being debased. A soldier informed Cleopatra Tryphaina that because her sister was grasping the sacred statue of the goddess she was safe from harm and could not be removed from the confines of the sanctuary. Cool Cleopatra Tryphaina issued another command: 'Hack her hands off,' she said. Then, approaching the trembling Cleopatra IV, the soldiers struck through her wrists with their swords. She died in that holy safe house, cursing her assassins. As Justin put it, 'Cleopatra [IV] died, enjoining revenge for her death from the deities who had been violated.'

Late in 112 BCE, Cleopatra IV's ghost got its bloody retribution. Justin tells the story:

> Shortly afterwards another skirmish found Kyzikanos victorious. He captured Grypus' wife [Cleopatra] Tryphaina, who had just murdered her sister, and, by executing her, he appeased the phantom of his dead wife.

So died two Cleopatras, the Ptolemaic queens of Syria, victims of civil war and casualties of their own sibling jealousies. The Syrian civil war dragged on for a further eight years, during which neither Grypus nor Kyzikenos managed to get a decisive grip on power: 'Both those kings were like wrestlers,' says Josephus, 'who finding themselves deficient in strength, and yet being ashamed to yield, put off the fight by lying still as long as they can.' Punch-drunk and drained of energy and resources, they let their competition drag on.

*

In Egypt, Cleopatra III does not seem to have mourned her two daughters. Instead, ever the political pragmatist, she hurried to reconfirm the Ptolemaic presence in Syria by sending her sole surviving daughter to follow in her sisters' footsteps into the Seleucid kingdom. Cleopatra Selene, it will be recalled, on her mother's command had first married her bother Chickpea (Ptolemy XI) and latterly had wed her other brother, Ptolemy X, but with Cleopatra Tryphaina dead a vacancy opened up for a candidate to step into the role of Seleucid queen and Cleopatra III decided this would be perfect for Cleopatra Selene. Putting her to better political use, in 102 BCE Cleopatra III had Ptolemy X divorce Cleopatra

Selene, who, putting up no resistance, was dispatched to Syria where she quickly married Grypus, the Seleucid king whom her mother most favoured.

Aged between thirty-two and thirty-seven years old, Cleopatra Selene had decided that being queen of Syria was preferable to playing second fiddle to her mother as a neglected queen in Egypt, so she slipped easily into Cleopatra Tryphaina's marital bed and found herself the stepmother to five sons and a girl, all born to Grypus by her deceased sister. Even though Selene had proved herself fertile with Chickpea (and would do so again), her new marriage did not last long enough for her to add to Grypus' impressive progeny because, out of the blue, in 96 BCE Grypus was murdered by his ambitious disciplinarian chief-of-staff, Heracleon, who claimed the throne for himself. He was immediately challenged by Grypus' eldest son who, as Seleucus VI, managed to raise an army in Cilicia to claim back his rightful throne.

Cleopatra Selene turned out to be as skilled an operator as her mother: in 95 BCE, after the death of Grypus, not wanting to be embroiled in the war between Heracleon and Seleucus VI, she went to Antioch and gave herself in marriage to Kyzikenos, the widowed husband of Cleopatra IV. In a barefaced act of self-preservation, Cleopatra Selene switched husbands and now settled into the bed of her former brother-in-law, who enthusiastically accepted her in wedlock – albeit as a fourth-time bride. But war was brought to her anyway when young King Seleucus, having finished off Heracleon, advanced towards Antioch and challenged Kyzikenos, who, after a long and distinguished life of fighting, was finally killed in pitched battle. Cleopatra Selene was widowed for the second time in two years, but within months of Kyzikenos' death the now-forty-year-old Cleopatra Selene accepted a marriage proposal from his heir, her eighteen-year-old stepson, Antiochus X Eusebes, who was also her nephew by her sister, Cleopatra IV (Cleopatra Selene was also the niece of his maternal grandmother, Cleopatra Thea). Two sons were born of this marriage, although the sources only name one of them, Antiochus XIII Asiaticus, the man destined to be the last of the Seleucids.

With Cleopatra Selene at his side, and Ptolemaic financial support guaranteed, Antiochus X Eusebes launched into a violent campaign against Seleucus VI and quickly forced him out of Syria and into Anatolia, where he died. Seleucus' twin brothers, Philip I and Antiochus IX, then appeared as the champions of Grypus' throne, although the latter brother quickly disappeared from the scene when he drowned in the River Orontes. Philip I turned out to be more of a problem though, for he was a fine solider and politician, but just as Antiochus Eusebes began a campaign against Philip, news arrived that his eastern borders were under attack from the Parthians and Antiochus Eusebes rushed off to secure his territories. It was in the east that he died, in 89 BCE, fighting bravely against the Parthian cavalry, just as his grandfather, Antiochus VII, had done before him.

Widowed yet again, Cleopatra Selene put her considerable energy into fighting for the accession rights of her two sons. Her whereabouts during the reigns of Philip I and Demetrius III – Antiochus X's successors in Antioch – is unknown, but she evidently took shelter with her children somewhere in the kingdom; she possibly fled to Cilicia or Coele-Syria, and almost certainly to the city of Ptolemaïs-Ake, which she held until her death. Antiochus XII, another son of Grypus, was ruling in Damascus, but he died in 82 BCE and so, with the Seleucid throne finally vacant, Cleopatra Selene declared her son Antiochus XIII the new king (his younger, unnamed brother was possibly a co-ruler), although in reality it was she who held all the power. The sources show that in 69 BCE Cleopatra Selene was still alive and politically active; she visited Rome with her sons, for instance, where she prevailed upon the senate to recognize her boys' claims to the throne of Egypt. She was known to the great Roman orator Cicero, who in one of his letters to his friend, Atticus, recorded that:

The kings of Syria, the boyish sons of King Antiochus, have lately been at Rome. And they came not on account of the kingdom of Syria; for that they had obtained possession of without dispute, as they had received it from their father and their ancestors; but they thought that the kingdom of Egypt belonged to them and to Cleopatra Selene their mother. When they, being hindered by the critical state of the republic at that time, were not able to obtain the discussion of the subject as they wished before the senate, they departed for Syria, their paternal kingdom. One of them – the one whose name is Antiochus – wished to make his journey through Sicily.

In 69 BCE, shortly after Cleopatra Selene's return from Rome, the ambitious Armenian king Tigranes II invaded Syria and besieged Ptolemaïs-Ake, where Cleopatra Selene held court. The queen was taken prisoner and, to deny other ambitious men from acquiring influence through her, Tigranes had her executed. Following Tigranes' defeat by the Roman Lucius Licinius Lucullus, a close ally of the Roman dictator Lucius Cornelius Sulla, at the Battle of Tigranocerta, the residents of Antioch hailed Antiochus XIII as their ruler, and Lucullus approved his appointment as Rome's client-king of Syria. Just five years later, in 64 BCE, the Roman general and statesman Pompey had him deposed and Syria became a province of the quickly expanding Roman empire.

Cleopatra Selene, the last surviving daughter of Potbelly and Cleopatra III, had lived an extraordinary life, even by the standards of the other Cleopatras. It is a great pity that beyond the rudimentary details of her four marriages, we know little else about her, for she must have been a remarkable woman. She went from being the compliant wife of two Ptolemaic kings to an unstoppable force in the dynastic history of the Seleucids. She was a decisive opportunist, and for this reason alone, by the end of her life Cleopatra Selene had crafted herself into a symbol of Seleucid continuity. Two of her husbands, the half-brothers Grypus and Kyzikenos, sons Demetrius II and Antiochus VII, were fully Seleucid on the male side of the family, but by their mother, Cleopatra Thea, they were of Ptolemaic descent too. When she married them, Cleopatra Selene strengthened the Ptolemaic dominance over both branches of the Seleucid family tree, which could be traced back to the time of the great Cleopatra I Syra, 'the Syrian', through whom the Seleucid-Ptolemaic connection had been established. As the sons of Cleopatra Thea, Grypus and Kyzikenos embodied the line of ancestry from Ptolemy VI and Cleopatra II, offspring of Ptolemy V and Cleopatra Syra, while Cleopatra Selene herself, as the daughter of Ptolemy VIII Potbelly, the younger son of Ptolemy V and Cleopatra Syra, and his niece Cleopatra III, stood in a direct relationship to the dominant line of the Ptolemaic house. Therefore during her long Syrian sojourn Cleopatra Selene had been the single most important chance of creating a true union between the Ptolemaic and Seleucid houses. She was, in her time, the most eligible bride in the world.

The integration of Egypt and Syria had been tried often enough in the past – through the brute force of conflict – but it had always failed. By the time the two royal families recognized that a peaceful unification was possible, should it be looked for, both must have grasped the fact that the Romans would never have tolerated a union of the whole of the east through the rule of one commanding dynasty. Throughout the first century BCE the Romans were growing in their awareness of the east and its vast riches, and as political power in the Roman Republic became ever more reliant upon the acquisition of incalculable amounts of wealth through military exploitation, it suited Rome to see the east fragmented, broken and powerless. The disintegration of Seleucid Syria and Rome's procurement of its rich resources would make the Romans hungry for more eastern territories.

13

Death Becomes Her

The earliest dated document of Cleopatra III and Ptolemy X is 30 October 107 BCE – year 1 of the joint rulership, year 11 of Cleopatra III and year 8 of Ptolemy X, who counted his regnal years from the beginning of his governance of Cyprus in 114/13 BCE. Cleopatra continued to use her title Euergetis ('Beneficent') and shared the epithet Philometores ('Mother-Loving') with her son, although she maintained a hold on the premiere position in all titles and images. As in the reign of Chickpea, there were instances in the new co-regency where Cleopatra III appeared alone in the temple reliefs, as the Goddess Philometor, in complete and splendid isolation from her son.

Early in the new joint reign, Cleopatra began to implement innovations in her personal cult, first through the establishment on Cyprus of a priest of Queen Cleopatra the Goddess Aphrodite and later with the creation of a second male 'priest of Queen Cleopatra the Goddess Aphrodite, also called Mother-Loving.' The goddess Aphrodite's ancient association with Cyprus had been harnessed by Cleopatra III as far back as 131 BCE, when she resided on the island with Potbelly and her five children during their temporary exile from Alexandria. The outcast king and queen had carefully fostered their association with the chief goddess of Cyprus so as to make a politically expedient statement about their control of the island and stake their claim over the whole of Egypt's territorial orbit. But now, back in Alexandria, the ageing queen elevated herself as a goddess within Egypt too and took the form of Aphrodite's Egyptian avatar, the great goddess Hathor, as her chosen deity. The queen's new cult was serviced by a priest of 'Queen Cleopatra-Hathor the Goddess Philopator' and by a priestess of 'Queen Cleopatra the Goddess Euergetis Philometor.' In promoting herself as Hathor, Cleopatra III claimed a prerogative adopted only by her illustrious ancestress Queen Berenice II, who had employed the goddess's image and mythology to stress her identity as the guardian of Egypt's throne (Hathor had long embodied this symbol) and as the partner of the living Horus, the pharaoh (in Cleopatra's case, her son Ptolemy X).

Cleopatra III championed the royal cult of her own divinity as her chief mode of establishing her precedence in the dynasty. The rich panoply of cultic titles the queen heaped upon herself were reflected in public celebrations, festivals and elaborate street parades. Cleopatra III understood the benefits of religious spectacle very well and, with her loyal priests and priestesses in tow, she regularly employed carnival-type spectacles as part of her self-promotion. Dressed in ritual robes, a great Egyptian wig plonked on her head and rouge smothered all over her pantomime face, she processed through the streets of Alexandria, affording the citizens a holiday, a religious experience and a patriotic pageant at one and the same time. Such cavalcades were designed to win the hearts and minds of the people, with free food and drink, street entertainments and a view of the goddess-queen herself, magnificent and magnanimous in her royal bounty. Cleopatra III's showy cultic innovations – with their splashy links to divinity, rulership and celebrity – easily outstripped the more modest religious titles and festivals of even Arsinoë II and Berenice II, and Cleopatra's rich accumulation of epithets reached a point where they resembled, when read aloud, nothing short of a hymn. And why not? She was, after all, a living goddess, worthy of praise.

The most striking of Cleopatra III's Egyptian-style portraits is a portrait sculpture of intense presence and power, and it tells us much about how she wished to be known to her contemporaries. Cleopatra's narrow eyes, complete with crow's-feet creases, squint at the viewer, almost challenging the observer to break the queen's penetrative gaze; heavy bags droop beneath the eyelids and deep furrows extend from the side of her nose to her thick lips. There is no sphinx-like smile on this statue, but neither is there a grimace. In profile the fat queen is shown to have a slightly arched narrow nose (the tip is broken off the sculpture) and a weak chin which blends seamlessly into the thick masculine neck – in fact, we see essentially a man's portrait in the guise of a queen. In another, closely related portrait sculpture, the queen's head twists dramatically to the left, as though she is shooting a killer look at some poor emasculated courtier or feeble co-ruler. It speaks volumes.

It has been suggested that whereas Potbelly's self-promotion had expressed itself through extravagant expenditure, Cleopatra III's manifested itself in the grandiose religious conceptions that she loved so much. With all her priesthoods and godlike titles, it is not surprising to learn that her divine agenda was amplified through the creation of multiple portrait statues too. Often incorporating Greek-style facial features with pharaonic-type bodies and the use of tripartite wigs and the triple uraeus (three cobras) associated with Isis and other goddesses, Cleopatra III's portraits are memorable representations of a woman of unlimited authority. Two standing statues of the queen (now in San Jose, California, and St Petersburg, Russia) have heavy facial features but curvaceous bodies; they are bulky in appearance, with a great deal of fleshiness under the dimpled chin and fat folds (politely termed 'Venus rings' by art historians) circling the squat neck. On both sculptures the queen is given full breasts, fatty deposits around the belly button and love handles at the waist, all there to emphasize Cleopatra III's role as Egypt's fertile mother. Another, more elegant statue of the queen was carved from steatite and shows her wearing a figure-fitting gown and carrying a lily sceptre (a pharaonic symbol of queenly authority); she wears an Egyptian tripartite wig that is crowned by a modius of uraeuses and a triple uraeus hangs low over her brow. The rounded, chubby face, narrow eyes and full lips make the statue a strong yet strangely seductive image of Cleopatra III.

Ptolemaic royal statuary occupied two specific contexts in Egypt: the temple and the metropolis. Within both spaces, royal sculpture tended to be placed in courtyards, squares and at the entrances to temples, theatres and gymnasia, and in porticoes within towns and cities. Royal sculptures needed to be placed in the correct context in order to fulfil their roles, for they were supposed to represent the power of the individual and encode messages about the status of the royal dynasty itself, as well as reflect something of the relationship which was fostered between kings and queens and the gods. Statues placed within temples became part of the rites and rituals of the place, and it was via their statuary that Ptolemaic monarchs were able to direct their cultic status. The sculpted images of Cleopatra III therefore projected positive messages of dynastic rulership. Cleopatra appears in her perfected form: her body emanates strength and vitality; her posture encodes both masculine prowess and female sensuality; her head is covered in thick curls of hair, which are luxuriant and radiate health and vitality; her face, with its well-defined profile, penetrating eyes and thick eyebrows, is as powerful as it is magisterial. These images are royal pronouncements. We must 'read' them as codes through which the queen's body took on cultural meaning: it was the wholeness, beauty and physical strength of the monarch's body which guaranteed her right to rule, and the strange assimilation of the tough masculine and the soft feminine in each of these images endorsed and publicized Cleopatra's idiosyncratic style of rulership. These statues defined Cleopatra's power through her physiognomy, which was itself tempered by and constructed around the imagery created for Ptolemy VIII and his sons. The statues of Cleopatra III are not portraits of an individual woman *per se*, but rather they are powerfully evocative icons of the unique form of female power which was channelled into and through the persona of Cleopatra III herself.

*

Cleopatra's co-ruler, Ptolemy X, shared much of his father's personality and all of his physicality, as recalled by the Greek sophist Athenaeus of Naucratis:

The master of Egypt, a man who was hated by the masses, though flattered by courtiers, lived in great *tryphē*; but he could not even go out to ease himself unless he had two men to lean upon as he walked. And yet, when it came to the rounds of dancing at a drinking party he would jump from a high couch, barefoot as he was, and perform figures in a livelier fashion than those who performed them professionally.

But unlike Potbelly, Ptolemy X had no taste for governance and no head for rulership. It would have been better for everyone if his mother had left him on Cyprus to drown in drink. Ptolemy's laziness and addiction to pleasure soon put a strain on Cleopatra's relationship with her youngest son who, according to Justin, was 'terrified of the ruthlessness on his mother's part' and therefore 'abandoned her, preferring a secure and stable life to a throne fraught with danger.'

Fearing that his mother was plotting against him and would take his life – as his aunt Cleopatra Thea had done to one of her two sons – Ptolemy X absconded from Alexandria and settled in Memphis. His flight, which has been dated to 102 BCE, might well have been precipitated by his mother's acquisition of the priesthood of the dynastic Alexander cult which had, until that time, been the prerogative of the king alone. And yet, even though she could have ruled alone (she was more than capable), Cleopatra recalled Ptolemy X to Alexandria to resume the rulership with her again. It is hard to know why, but among Justin's rather jumbled re-creation of events is an indication that the queen feared that her eldest son, Chickpea, might regard his brother's absence from Alexandria as an opportunity to recover Egypt for himself and bounce her off the throne. If this was the case, Cleopatra thought that there was safety in numbers and that she was better off with her youngest son beside her, no matter how feckless he might be as a king and a man.

In a complete reversal of fortune, as Ptolemy X entered Egypt, so Chickpea left for Cyprus, happy to put the Mediterranean Sea between himself and his mother. Chickpea quickly settled into a comfortable, quiet, life, choosing the seaside city of Paphos for his home. There he governed the island competently and carefully, avoiding, as far as he could, any contact with Alexandria.

Upon Ptolemy X's return to the throne of Egypt in 101 BCE, with an eye to his immediate future, Cleopatra III arranged for him to wed his niece, the fifteen-year-old daughter of Chickpea and Cleopatra IV. Princess Berenice III was an intelligent young woman, a quick learner and a keen observer, who had already proved herself to be popular at court and with the people of Alexandria. When Chickpea and Cleopatra IV had been forced to separate and both had left Egypt to pursue their separate destinies, Berenice had remained behind in Alexandria with Cleopatra III, her grandmother. As Chickpea's daughter, she was much loved by the infamous Alexandrian mob, who had watched her grow up and simply adored her. In many respects, Cleopatra III's grand-daughter was her trump card, and she considered Ptolemy X's marriage to the popular princess a triumph of her invention, since it redirected support in Alexandria to Ptolemy X through the person of his pretty young bride. In October 101 BCE, with the consent of Cleopatra III, Berenice was named as co-ruler alongside her husband-uncle and was incorporated into the dynastic cult as the 'Brother-Loving Goddess'. She was co-ruler in name only, for all authority still rested with her grandmother, Cleopatra III.

The young bride had been called Berenice throughout her childhood (perhaps because of the superabundance of Ptolemaic women holding the name Cleopatra) but upon her marriage to Ptolemy X she adopted the name Cleopatra and added it to her birth name. She became Cleopatra V Berenice III (or, according to one papyrus document, simply 'Cleopatra, known as Berenice'). Fittingly, Cleopatra Berenice adopted 'Cleopatra' as a throne-name to demonstrate continuance from her grandmother Cleopatra III and great-grandmother Cleopatra II, as well as to propagate a belief in the dynastic stability of the new ruling couple. Following their marriage, Ptolemy X's name was coupled with that of Cleopatra Berenice in governmental documentation – with his name listed before hers – with the young queen often referred to as Ptolemy X's 'sister' although she was biologically his niece. This honorific title had fallen out of use while Cleopatra III was ruling with her sons, but it was now resumed by Cleopatra Berenice, who was also incorporated into the dynastic cult as one half of the Theoi Philometores – 'Mother-Loving Gods' (or, more rarely, as the Theoi Philometores Soteres – 'Mother-Loving Saviour Gods').

Ptolemy's marriage to his niece somehow galvanized him. He began to act independently of his mother, and a rift developed between them as the king began to mull over the many slights Cleopatra had perpetrated against him over the course of their co-rulership. His resentment grew, perhaps thinking of how his mother had hijacked the cult of Alexander and its priesthood for herself (it should have been the king's prerogative, as it always had been), how Cleopatra III had forced him to divorce his wife, Cleopatra Selene, so that she could send her as an alliance-bride to Grypus in Syria, and how she had taken the credit for the overall victory in the War of the Sceptres herself, even though he had played an important part in ousting Chickpea from the throne. Usurping Cleopatra's power, he reckoned, would not be enough: his mother had to die. Ptolemy decided to assassinate Cleopatra – before she killed him.

The murder of Cleopatra III occurred between 14 and 16 October 101 BCE, and although the sources are silent on the exact cause of her death, it was certainly brought about by foul play – rumours had it that Ptolemy, drunk after one of his interminable all-night banquets, had strangled her with her own belt, grappling Cleopatra to the ground until the breath was wrung out of her. We do not know for certain if Cleopatra Berenice was involved in her grandmother's death – she had nothing to gain by it – but she might have witnessed the killing.

Cleopatra III died at the age of sixty or thereabouts. Few people mourned her. She experienced a partial *damnatio memoriae* when, at her death, her string of elaborate priesthoods was disbanded. They soon disappeared from all official documents as all traces of her reign were quickly suppressed, and even the pretentious titles she had amassed in her lifetime as the Goddess Euergetis

Philometor, the Female Horus, the Living Hathor, the New Isis and the Living Aphrodite were allowed to fade into obscurity. The blackening of Cleopatra III's memory, which started at the time of her murder, was carried on across the centuries by Roman authors like Justin, who later wrote about her life and characterized her as an archetypal oriental villainess. 'She richly deserved her infamous death,' Justin was to write, 'because she had driven her own mother from her marriage bed.'

Because of the Roman portrayal of Cleopatra III, the scholarly tradition has not been kind to her either. Cleopatra has been interpreted as daring, certainly, but unscrupulous, a woman whose drive for power spread war and ruin among her children. Scholars often regard her as a worse woman than the earlier Cleopatras, chiefly because she was an officious despot. She is chiefly remembered for hungering after power, even though, ironically, she was murdered by a son who was just as ambitious – although he lacked any of his mother's political shrewdness. Potbelly was as tyrannical as Cleopatra III – and made many more harmful choices for his children than she ever did; in order to cling to power, Potbelly had been willing to murder one of his sons, yet in modern studies he is never portrayed as a bad father. If Cleopatra III were to be judged as a man, then her yearning to rule, the questionable raising of her children, her warmongering, her brutality and the numerous power-plays she undertook in her lifetime would not look out of place. But Cleopatra III was not a man and therefore she has been written into history as an egregiously transgressive female, blasted for withholding rightful power from her sons and derided for being overly ambitions and heavy-handed in her abuse of a power which, because of her sex, should never have been hers.

But Cleopatra III should be viewed through a different, less patriarchal lens. She ruled as queen of Egypt for thirty-nine successful years, second in longevity only to her mother, Cleopatra II. During the early years of her reign, Cleopatra III was the inferior of three co-rulers, the individual with the least authority. Her image was exploited for dynastic propaganda and her presence was permitted in the triad of rulers because she was of a fertile age and was expected to produce heirs. Whilst taking the back seat, she used her time profitably and learned from her senior co-rulers – especially her mother – what it meant to rule, and she began to grow in confidence and capability. During the ensuing fifteen years in which she reigned as dominant co-ruler with both of her sons in succession, she was an excellent queen with a keen eye for bureaucratic detail. She carefully maintained her kingdom, and even protected it by leading troops – in person – into battle in Syria, and she efficaciously negotiated the international politics of the day by knowing when to make war and when to stop; she even managed to keep Roman intervention in Egyptian affairs at a minimum. In Egypt she was a brilliant propagandist and decided that instead of trying to rule alone as a woman – flouting centuries of Ptolemaic tradition that required a joint king and queen – she would fuse masculine and feminine royal titles and put them to her use, even contorting the traditional forms of iconography to create her own unique form of rulership. Finally, Cleopatra III used her children to create successful alliances which supported her dynasty and protected her kingdom, just as capable male monarchs of the Hellenistic world had always done. What it comes down to is that the real problem history has had with Cleopatra III is not that she was a wicked queen but rather that she was a successful king – a king who happened to be a woman.

Happily, amongst the later Ptolemies Cleopatra III was not utterly forgotten: when Cleopatra VII, *the* Cleopatra, emerged as the most powerful woman in the world, she took as one of her chief titles 'the New Isis' and she presented herself to Marc Antony at Tarsus in the guise of the living goddess Aphrodite too. To her Egyptian subjects Cleopatra VII was also the Female Horus. In other words, the great Cleopatra VII appropriated the titles of, and moulded her greatness on, her great-grandmother, the ineffable, incomparable Cleopatra III, a woman who ruled like a king.

PART THREE

TERMINAL DECLINE

Cleopatra V Berenice III
Cleopatra VI Tryphaina
Cleopatra VII

CLEOPATRA V BERENICE III

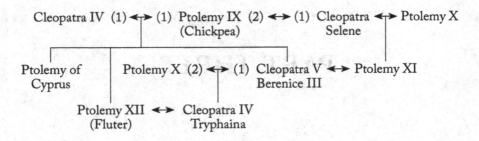

Cleopatra IV (1) ←→ (1) Ptolemy IX (2) ←→ (1) Cleopatra ←→ Ptolemy X
(Chickpea) Selene

Ptolemy of Cyprus   Ptolemy X (2) ←→ (1) Cleopatra V ←→ Ptolemy XI
Berenice III

Ptolemy XII ←→ Cleopatra IV
(Fluter) Tryphaina

CLEOPATRA VI TRYPHAINA

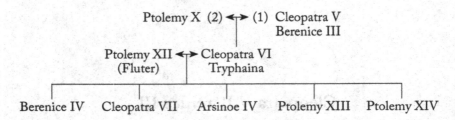

Ptolemy X (2) ←→ (1) Cleopatra V
Berenice III

Ptolemy XII ←→ Cleopatra VI
(Fluter) Tryphaina

Berenice IV   Cleopatra VII   Arsinoe IV   Ptolemy XIII   Ptolemy XIV

CLEOPATRA VII

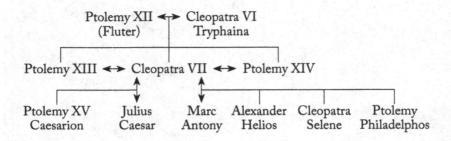

Ptolemy XII ←→ Cleopatra VI
(Fluter) Tryphaina

Ptolemy XIII ←→ Cleopatra VII ←→ Ptolemy XIV

Ptolemy XV Caesarion   Julius Caesar   Marc Antony   Alexander Helios   Cleopatra Selene   Ptolemy Philadelphos

14

Waiting for the World to Change

Many scholars regard the fifty-odd-year period that stretched from the death of Cleopatra III to the rise of Cleopatra VII as Egypt's period of terminal decline, an era when the realm lurched its way inescapably, inevitably – and inelegantly – towards the finish line. Certainly the once mighty Ptolemaic empire was shrinking fast. When Ptolemy Apion, Potbelly's bastard son and half-brother of Ptolemy X, died in 96 BCE, the gigantic territory of Cyrenaica and Cyrene (much of modern Libya), over which he had governed since his father's death, was bequeathed to Rome. Ptolemy Apion had no say in the matter, for Potbelly had preplanned that Cyrenaica's secession from Egypt into the hands of the Roman Republic would occur upon Ptolemy Apion's death. For the first time, Egypt found itself sharing a land border with the Romans. Of course, our conception of the moribund state of Egypt is largely coloured by subsequent Roman sources that liked to exaggerate the moral depravity and uselessness of the last Ptolemies. For moralistic Latin historians like Livy or Tacitus, making comparisons with the decadent regimes of other nations was imperative; these contrasts provided the Roman authors with a measuring stick against which the moral probity and dignity of the Roman people might be highlighted and admired. Still, even with this caveat, we cannot get away from the reality that Egypt was not the place it had been a century earlier.

If, in the eyes of the Romans, Potbelly had been a corpulent waste of space, then his youngest son barely warranted a second thought. Ptolemy X was disliked by everyone. The desperately feckless king courted popularity by emphasizing links with his namesake, Alexander the Great, and many of his official documents began with the opening credit 'On behalf of King Ptolemy who is also Alexander.' He even went as far as to pilfer the great conqueror's military helmet from his tomb and wear it in public, but to no avail – no amount of fancy dress could hide the fact that Ptolemy X was a hopeless, embarrassing ruler. He was a loser.

Ptolemy's reputation in Upper Egypt was poor, and among the powerful priests of Thebes he was particularly disliked and mercilessly denigrated. Accordingly, the offended king took no interest in the maintenance of the Theban temples, nor did he commission any building work south of the Delta. This was a dangerous move. The south of Egypt became so out of touch with the north that even the temple stonemasons still working on old temple projects opted to keep the cartouches blank rather than carve in the wrong name of whoever it was who might be ruling in Alexandria; they simply had no idea. In 91 BCE Upper Egypt briefly broke away from Ptolemaic control, and although it was back under Ptolemy X's jurisdiction by 88 BCE, the rebellion highlighted that the central government was weak and close to collapse. The Lower Egyptian clergy were kinder to the king though, especially the priests of Memphis. It was the High Priest of Ptah, Petubastis II, who had crowned Ptolemy in a ceremony of grandiose splendour and, after completing the ancient rites, the king and priest switched places as Ptolemy installed Petubastis into his high office. The priest, we are informed by an eyewitness report,

> drank in the presence of the king. He [the king] handed over to him the golden crook, mace, robe of linen from the southern house and the leather garment according to the ritual of Ptah's festivals and solemn processions. He [the king] placed the golden ornaments on his head according to the custom of his forefathers.

Ptolemy continued to hold Memphis dear to his heart and made the city one of his power bases. Records show that he visited the great Memphite Serapeum many times, and on several occa-

sions he met with Peteese, the chief embalmer of the sacred bulls
there, and even awarded him 'royal protection' – meaning that, for
his services to the city, Peteese was safeguarded against assault or
any form of misbehaviour on penalty of death. Ptolemy X wanted
to be liked and went out of his way to reward anybody who
showed him any respect.

The one thing Ptolemy X had in his favour was his brilliant
young niece-wife, Cleopatra V Berenice III. She was the antidote
to Ptolemy's ineptitude. Very little evidence has survived about
the nature of their reign, but there is just enough to hazard a
guess about the couple's power dynamics. It does not seem that
she wielded much personal power at first, and she appears to have
acted more as a *basilissa*-consort than co-ruler during the initial
period of their joint reign. But over time Cleopatra Berenice grew
in importance and visibility, especially after she bore the king a
daughter sometime around 100–95 BCE. By the mid-to-late 90s BCE
she had given birth to a second child, attested in an inscription
from Philae which suggests that the king and queen visited the
temple of the goddess with their children. To get to Philae, just
south of modern Aswan, roughly 1,000 kilometres south of Alexandria, would have been a substantial journey for the royal family
to make. They traced their way up the Nile and into the heart of
Upper Egypt, passing by the major Pharaonic sanctuaries of the
kingdom, perhaps as an atonement for Ptolemy's earlier neglect
of the southern half of his kingdom. This southern sojourn might
have been at Cleopatra Berenice's instigation, for we know that in
later years she became an important patron of the Upper Egyptian temples and gained enormous popularity amongst her Upper
Egyptian subjects.

Curiously, Cleopatra Berenice is absent from many inscriptions
and documents where we might expect to find her. For instance,
four Greek inscriptions from the Delta oasis known as the Fayum,
which record donations and dedications made on behalf of the
king to the crocodile deity Sobek in the 90s BCE, fail to mention
her at all. This is a strange departure from the regular inclusion of
royal women in Greek inscriptions from the reigns of Ptolemy VI

and Potbelly, and even from Cleopatra III's co-regencies with her two sons. Why was Cleopatra Berenice overlooked in these documents? Was it because Ptolemy X was trying to marginalize his popular wife? Do we sense an air of jealousy on Ptolemy's part? Perhaps, although sadly the epigraphic sample is too small to be sure, but much like the Seleucid king Demetrius II before him, Ptolemy X seems to have had the remarkable ability to alienate nearly all the constituent groups of his kingdom. His profound unpopularity among the populace of Alexandria, for instance, can be juxtaposed against the city's deeply held affection for Cleopatra Berenice, a detail even mentioned by Cicero in his now fragmentary work *Alexandrian Kings*, where he notes that she was 'dear to her people and well-established in their affections'. Such reports fuel the inkling that Cleopatra Berenice was more popular than the king, despite his efforts to ostracize her from public consciousness.

Ptolemy X had become so hated by his own military that during the period of unrest in Upper Egypt he was forced to bring into Egypt foreign mercenary soldiers to quell the rebellion. This proved to be a costly decision for, without thinking of the consequences, Ptolemy Alexander turned to his legendary namesake for salvation; repeating an age-old Egyptian practice of plundering the wealth of royal tombs, Ptolemy stole Alexander the Great's golden coffin from its resting place and had it melted down and turned into gold coins with which to pay off the mercenaries. On learning of the violation of the tomb of the founder of the city, the Alexandrian mob turned wild, rioted through the streets and made for the palace, aiming to lynch the king. As the crowds gathered on the steps of the palace, Ptolemy, Cleopatra Berenice and their children fled the city and sailed to Myra in Asia Minor, from where the king attempted to assemble enough naval and ground forces under his banner to take control of Cyprus – perhaps, he hoped, with the financial support of the Romans. Ptolemy's desecration of the tomb of Alexander the Great stands as a fine metaphor for his rule: through uninterest and shocking incompetence, he had squandered and decimated his glorious ancestral inheritance for ever.

On Cyprus, Ptolemy allegedly drew up a will that bequeathed his kingdom to Rome as collateral for a loan. Late in the summer of 88 BCE, the small fleet of ships he had managed to pull together with Rome's financial aid met with the larger naval squadrons sent by Egypt off the coast of Cyprus. In the short sea battle that ensued, Ptolemy X lost his life, drowning in the ocean.

If Ptolemy X's will was in fact genuine, then Rome found itself facing the awkward question of exactly *how* it was to be involved in Egypt's affairs. The Romans had already hesitated to make Cyrene a Roman province even after it had been given to them on the death of Ptolemy Apion in 96 BCE, and they were not at all keen to make the whole of Egypt a proconsular province upon the death of Ptolemy X either. Roman Republican politics got in the way of that notion – any Roman man who was appointed to be proconsul of all Egypt would have become an individual of such wealth and influence that he might easily compromise the delicate (and quickly unravelling) aristocratic balance of power in Rome itself. The great elite families of Rome (known as the Patricians) were as immersed in the complex game of politics as their Ptolemaic neighbours, and because of the incessant (and murderous) spats among the aristocratic houses, the Republic itself was in a very fragile and perilous state. Schisms and factions arose from political or personal causes as the leading Patrician families of Rome found themselves falling into cliques. Political support in Rome was primarily mobilized by patronage – the relationship fostered between wealthy Patricians and their poorer dependents, which was often implemented with the kind of techniques employed by latter-day Mafia kingpins – which frequently led to interfamilial vendettas pursued to violent ends. Too engaged with its own dynastic skirmishes, when it came to the Egyptian question Rome was more inclined to maintain the loose status quo that had existed for a century by remaining an outsider – albeit an *interested* outsider – to the Ptolemaic game of thrones.

*

From his island home, Chickpea had been carefully watching affairs unfold in Alexandria. When the Alexandrians unexpectedly invited him to retake a seat on Egypt's throne, he was only too happy to accept their offer. He was back in control of Alexandria and of the kingdom itself by mid-88 BCE. Once he was back, Alexandrian wits tagged him with a new nickname – Potheinos, 'Much-Missed' – although whether this was coined out of genuine affection or cutting sarcasm is hard to know. According to Porphyry:

> [T]he inhabitants of Alexandria were unable to completely delete [Ptolemy X's] reign from the records, but as far as was in their power they erased all mention of it . . . So they do not count the years of his reign, but attribute the whole thirty-six years to the elder brother.

The widowed queen Cleopatra Berenice, for her part, also returned to Alexandria in the summer of 88 BCE, accompanied by her one surviving daughter (the other child, we must presume, died during the period of exile) and settled into the palace along-side her father, Chickpea. Her return to Egypt almost immediately following her husband's death might have been motivated by a desire to see her estranged father again or simply because she had nowhere else to go. In the distant past, when Cleopatra II had been forced into exile, she had fled to her daughter Cleopatra Thea at the Seleucid court, but during her exile Cleopatra Berenice had no such serviceable networks in other Hellenistic courts; her only Ptolemaic relations outside Egypt were not in positions to aid her – Cleopatra Selene, Cleopatra Berenice's aunt, was in a similarly vulnerable position in Syria, where she had just lost Grypus, her third husband. So Cleopatra Berenice figured that returning to Egypt was her only option.

It seems that Chickpea and his daughter developed a close relationship; she had been with him throughout the first period of his reign as king, silently observing how her grandmother Cleopatra III had bullied and disdained him, and she had seen her father flee for his life in the post-war period when her uncle-husband Ptolemy X had been given the throne instead of him.

Now, back in Alexandria, she resolved that she would be at his side to help him.

Chickpea needed all the help he could get. On his return to Alexandria, the Thebaid revolted again. Chickpea decided that the only way to quell it was with quick and blunt military action, and so forces under a general named Hierax were dispatched south and the region was quickly and brutally brought back in line. A letter from the miliary general, or *stratēgos*, of Thebes to the people of Pathyris dated to 1 November 88 BCE announced both Hierax's success in quelling the rebellion and the arrival of the king in Memphis for his re-coronation. Ptolemy IX was crowned pharaoh for the second time at Memphis in a gesture clearly meant to broadcast the message that order had been restored. Although she is not explicitly attested at the event, Cleopatra Berenice was no doubt present at the ceremony. Chickpea was unmarried and needed a Ptolemaic royal female by his side in order to rule Egypt, and just as Cleopatra III had required one of her sons to rule alongside her, so too Chickpea needed a royal woman at his side, for appearance's sake at least. Even if Cleopatra V Berenice III was not strictly a co-regent in a manner understood by the Egyptians, she nevertheless had a prominent ritual role to play alongside her father, and he relied on her many capabilities to steer him through the choppy waters of state politics.

Little evidence survives for the second reign of Chickpea, although the kingdom seems to have been restored to some measure of tranquillity by him. Elsewhere in the Mediterranean, however, unrest and fraction surged, and the problems of other kingdoms began washing up on Egypt's shores with alarming regularity. Cleopatra Berenice's stepson, the surviving boy of Ptolemy X through his former marriage to Cleopatra Selene, was in the hands of Mithridates VI of Pontus, along with Chickpea's two sons – the queen's full-brothers – held as hostages. All of the boys had been captured by Mithridates in 88 BCE, at the outset of his war with Rome, when he had kidnapped them from the island of Cos, where their grandmother Cleopatra III had sent them for safekeeping. Now, Ptolemy X's sole surviving son, whom

Mithridates brought up for a short while as a young prince in Pontus, had escaped to Italy. There Lucius Cornelius Sulla, the Roman proconsul and future dictator, having in his possession Ptolemy X's will, sent the prince to Rome as a potentially useful pawn in future politicking.

After marching on Rome and infamously gaining his command at the tip of a spear, Sulla set out in 87 BCE to avenge the massacre of the Asiatic Vespers (Roman and other Latin-speaking peoples living in parts of western Anatolia) by forces loyal to Mithridates VI. Realizing that he needed whatever naval support he could muster, Sulla dispatched his *quaestor* – the title given to an elected official who supervised the state treasury and conducted audits – Licinius Lucullus to Crete, Cyrene and Alexandria, seeking a fleet of warships for Sulla's campaign. While Lucullus imposed some form of constitutional order in Cyrene, his clashes with pirates allied with Mithridates in the winter of 87 BCE cost him the few ships he was able to muster, and so in the summer of 86 BCE he followed the Egyptian coastline towards Alexandria, in the hope of gaining support from Chickpea. The situation called for delicate diplomacy. One the one hand, Chickpea was aware of the powerful factional divisions that existed between Sulla and his rival, Gaius Marius, in Rome (they would soon explode into outright civil war) and was naturally hesitant to throw in his lot entirely with Sulla. Antagonizing Mithridates through a display of support for the Romans would have likewise been ill-advised, Chickpea thought, for he feared (with good reason) that the king of Pontus would take reprisals against his captive sons. And yet Chickpea could not afford to snub the Romans outright either, because Ptolemy X's last will and testament was still in Roman hands and could be used to oust him from the throne. Besides, Sulla was not a man to toy with. Guided by the necessity of juggling these strategic concerns, Chickpea received Lucullus with all due pageantry, giving him fine guest rooms in the royal palace and inviting him to numerous lavish banquets, as well as to private strolls in the grounds of the royal menagerie, where they might discuss philosophy, as befitted a guest of his status. In place of ships, though, he loaded Lucullus with lavish gifts and bundled him off on his merry way back to Rome, along with a Ptolemaic naval escort that went no further than Cyprus. Chickpea played the perfect host and managed to avoid any recriminations from any of the parties involved simply by doing nothing.

Just how Cleopatra Berenice fared during those tumultuous events is unknown, but, as a woman of keen intelligence, she must have kept herself abreast of these curious diplomatic comings and goings. This is probably why she was appointed as Chickpea's co-ruler for the last months of his reign (August to December 81 BCE), as well as to prepare her for rulership, as had been done previously for male heirs. In late December 81 BCE, Chickpea died at the age of sixty-two. He had reigned for thirty-seven troubled years, although no less than eighteen of those had been spent in semi-exile on Cyprus. His children by Cleopatra Selene seem to have died in infancy, and his two teenage sons by Cleopatra IV were far away from Egypt in the custody of the Romans, so it was his daughter, Cleopatra Berenice, who ascended the throne as a sole female-pharaoh. It was the first time a woman had gained rulership this way in the whole, long history of the dynasty. Cleopatra V was accordingly incorporated into the royal cult as the Father-Loving Goddess, while the Egyptian titles created on behalf of the queen praised her as 'the Great Ruler, the King's Wife, the King's Sister Who is Beloved of Re, the Noblewoman, Mistress of Two Lands, and the Female Ruler.' Her most profusive set of royal titles are to be found at the temple of Edfu, where Cleopatra Berenice contributed much time and expense to the building programme. The rear wall of the temple was decorated with a stupendous 20-foot-high image of the queen in traditional pharaonic dress, proffering perfume jars to Horus, the principal god of the temple. There Cleopatra V Berenice III is depicted wearing the towering horned and plumed crown of the goddess Hathor, perhaps in reference to her dynastic namesakes, Berenice II and Cleopatra III, who in their time had presented themselves as the 'new Hathor.'

Cleopatra V's brief period of independent rule (March–August 80 BCE) was brought to an abrupt halt when the Romans interfered in dynastic policy on the instigation of the Alexandrian mob, who, despite their genuine affection for Cleopatra Berenice, felt unnerved by the presence of a sole female ruler on the throne. The Ptolemies had always regarded the monarchy as a dual entity that required a male and female presence, and it was probably unnerving even for Cleopatra Berenice herself to rule alone as an unmarried woman. In fact, according to Appian, the queen actively 'wanted a man of the same lineage' to sit on the throne beside her. The correct and obvious thing for Cleopatra Berenice to do, in terms of both dynastic policy and cosmic order, was to take another husband.

At this point, Sulla – having decided in the boredom of his semiretirement to get involved in Roman foreign policy – concluded that the time was ripe to put a submissive pro-Roman puppet-king on the throne of Egypt. His choice was his protégé, the son of Ptolemy X and Cleopatra Selene, who dutifully arrived in Egypt bearing the title Ptolemy XI Alexander II – although the Alexandrians knew him only as Pareisactus, 'the Usurper'. His mandate required him not only to wear the crown but to marry his middle-aged stepmother-aunt Cleopatra Berenice. No one, at this point, thought it prudent to argue with Sulla and the marriage duly took place sometime shortly before the end of April 80 BCE. After more than twenty years away from Egypt – in Cos during his childhood, then at the court of Mithridates and then in Rome – the boy was completely ignorant of Egypt's royal traditions; he had no concept of Alexandrian courtliness and had nothing whatsoever to recommend him as either a Hellenistic king or an Egyptian pharaoh. Cleopatra Berenice loathed him at first sight, and he her. He may have been shocked when he arrived in Egypt, expecting to rule under Sulla's protection but discovering that instead he was a very junior associate to an authoritative and experienced older woman.

After nineteen days of marriage, young Ptolemy XI murdered his stepmother-bride in cold blood (perhaps he took a page from Ptolemy X's book and assassinated his female senior co-ruler in order to take power by force). Ptolemy XI Alexander II may have committed the crime because he felt threatened by her power, for Cleopatra Berenice certainly seemed set to become as commanding as her grandmother Cleopatra III had been. Because Cleopatra Berenice's life was cut short, it is impossible to know what kind of ruler she would have become, although even in her brief period of rule she continued to promote female authority – she certainly became an inspirational model for her immediate female successors.

The Alexandrian mob, hearing of the murder of the people's princess, stormed the royal palace and, according to Appian, dragged Ptolemy XI 'to the gymnasium and put him to death; for they too were still without fear of foreigners, either by reason of the magnitude of their own government or their inexperience as yet of external dangers'. Ptolemy XI Alexander II's body was torn limb from limb and he suffered a complete and thorough *damnatio memoriae* – his name was never mentioned in the hieroglyphic inscriptions and he swiftly became a 'non-person'. Interestingly, once his candidate was dead, Sulla showed no further enthusiasm for Egyptian affairs and did not attempt to hit back at the boy's murderers or to implement the will of Ptolemy X.

The cruel murder of Cleopatra V Berenice III brought about an unexpected vacancy to the throne. As was so often the case, the Romans decided to play the waiting game and see how affairs in Egypt played out. The annexation of Egypt, according to the 'right' Rome had acquired through Ptolemy X's will, was a possibility, of course, but nobody in power seemed to be in a rush to occupy Egypt; better to wait and let the Egyptians find a successor to the vacant throne. But who might it be?

15

The Magic Flute

After the deaths of Cleopatra Berenice and Ptolemy XI, the Alexandrians realized that they needed to move quickly to choose another king because Rome could, at any time, hold them to the terms of Ptolemy X's will and move in to annex Egypt. Potbelly's daughter Cleopatra Selene was regarded by the Alexandrians as the most competent living member of the Ptolemaic family, but at the time the widowed queen was far away in Cilicia. Nonetheless, hearing of the events in Egypt, she laid claim to both the Seleucid and Ptolemaic thrones on behalf of her two sons by King Antiochus X. This stopped the Alexandrians in their tracks – they had no desire to unite Egypt with Syria, nor to see a Seleucid prince on the throne of Egypt. So they rescinded the offer and looked elsewhere for their much-needed monarch.

It was then that the Egyptians remembered the sons of Chickpea. His two boys had been sent off to Cos by their grandmother Cleopatra III at the outbreak of the War of the Sceptres in 103 BCE, alongside their cousin, the now-dead Ptolemy XI. The eldest of Chickpea's sons was another Ptolemy (of course), although from a young age he was known to all as Auletes ('Fluter') because of his love for, and skill at, playing the *aulos* or double-reed flute, on which, says Strabo, '[H]e prided himself so much that he would not hesitate to celebrate contests . . . and at these contests would come forward to vie with the opposing contestants.' He had been born around 117 BCE, a few years after his elder sister, Cleopatra V Berenice III. His mother was Cleopatra IV, the adored sister-wife of Chickpea, who had been driven out of Egypt by Cleopatra III at the time of her divorce from the king. When Cleopatra IV left for exile, Fluter and his brother, Ptolemy the Younger, had been kept behind in the Alexandrian palace, all but ignored by their grandmother, who had no love for either of the boys' parents and so gave little thought to them either. Indeed, Cleopatra III aimed to deny the boys any opportunities to claim the Egyptian throne, since she was reserving that space for her beloved Ptolemy X and his future offspring; it may have been Cleopatra III herself who began a smear campaign, tarring the boys with the epithet *nothoi*, 'bastards'. The name stuck, and several years later, after Fluter had been acclaimed as pharaoh, the Roman orator Cicero was able to write: 'I see that is agreed upon by *nearly* all men [*inter omnis fere*], that he, who is at this present moment in possession of the kingdom [of Egypt], is neither of the royal family nor of any royal disposition'. Cicero's turn of phrase '*nearly* all men' is illuminating, and one can conclude that the illegitimacy slur against Fluter, although widely accepted by most Romans, was also disputed.

Fluter's rise to the throne was swift. From Cos, Fluter and his brother had been taken to Pontus as prisoners of Mithridates VI, who treated them with kindness and even planned for them to marry two of his daughters, Mithradatis and Nyssa. It was here at the court of Mithridates that Fluter, in his twenties, received the news that the Alexandrians had invited him to become their king. In April 80 BCE he and his brother returned to Egypt. Fluter was hailed as Ptolemy XII by the mob while his brother was made king of Cyprus – it was the first and only time that a Ptolemy was given the legal right to rule Cyprus as a separate kingdom, and this was probably done to appease the Romans, whom the Alexandrians thought would be more inclined to accept an independent successor to the throne if Cyprus were officially disconnected from Egypt. The reign of Ptolemy XII was claimed to date from the end of Chickpea's last year as king; the short sole-rule of Cleopatra V Berenice III, and her even shorter co-reign with Ptolemy XI Alexander II, were officially disregarded in the documentation.

The new king needed a wife, and a bride was conveniently located in the royal palace: born between 100 BCE and 94 BCE,

Tryphaina was the daughter of Ptolemy X and Cleopatra V Berenice III, expediently making her Fluter's half-sister and therefore highly suitable for the needs of the dynasty. (In fact Tryphaina, who could claim legitimacy from both her ruling mother and father, was a more direct heir to the throne than Ptolemy XII.) Depending on where one places her date of birth, the bride was anywhere from fourteen to twenty years old at the time of her prestigious marriage, which took place before 17 January 79 BCE.

In all the surviving sources, Fluter's sister-wife is distinguished as 'Tryphaina', which may have been her personal name before she became queen, but on her marriage to the new king she assumed the traditional royal name 'Cleopatra' – there is no known instance where she is called 'Tryphaina' without also being called 'Cleopatra' – just as her mother had been 'Cleopatra Berenice' some years previously. Cleopatra VI Tryphaina was appointed as a co-ruler with Fluter, and both were crowned at a ceremony in Memphis, where they were incorporated into the dynastic cult as Theoi Philopatores kai Philadelphoi, 'the Father-Loving and Sibling-Loving Gods'. The epithet Philadelphus ('Sibling-Loving') had been employed by Chickpea and by Cleopatra V Berenice III, and so Fluter probably took it as part of his titulature to evoke their memories and strengthen his ties to his late father and his murdered sister. At his coronation, if not before, Fluter also took the lofty title of New Dionysus (or the Young Osiris to his Egyptian subjects) – the only Ptolemy to give himself a cultic title at a coronation. He lived up to his Dionysian aspirations, being totally 'corrupted by luxurious living . . . [and] general licentiousness', as Strabo observed. 'He was not so much a man', wrote a contemptuous Athenaeus, 'but more of a flute-blowing charlatan'.

Ptolemy XII's reign was marked by troubles, mostly arising from the encroaching power of Rome and its desire to bring the wealth of Egypt under its control. Cicero, upfront in saying that '[e]veryone knows the story that Egypt has been left to the Roman people by the will of the king of Alexandria', spoke for many Romans of his day. Yet Fluter and his kingdom somehow managed to survive. His success in maintaining an independent

Egypt can be put down to two factors. First, Fluter had no serious rivals for the throne – after all, the closest contender for the throne, Cleopatra Selene, had been killed in 69 BCE, and Rome had no interest in recognizing her two surviving sons as Ptolemaic heirs – that really would have been scraping the bottom of the dynastic. Secondly, Fluter energetically shopped around the Roman elite for political backing, since his principal aim was to secure his hold on the Egyptian throne and eventually pass it to his heirs. To achieve this goal he was prepared to sacrifice much – including rich Ptolemaic lands, most of his personal wealth and even, according to Cicero, the very dignity on which the mystique of kingship rested. The Romans found in Fluter the living image of the dissolute spendthrift Oriental potentate. They gladly took and enjoyed his protection money, but they despised him for it too.

*

Fluter's queen, Cleopatra VI Tryphaina, gave birth to at least five offspring. The first was a daughter, Berenice IV, born around 79–75 BCE; the second child was also a daughter, Cleopatra VII – *the* Cleopatra, who would become Egypt's last queen. Her birthday came in regnal year 12 of Ptolemy XII, probably in December 70 BCE or early January 69 BCE. There followed a third daughter, Arsinoë IV, in 63 BCE, and finally two longed-for sons – the future Ptolemy XIII, born in 61 BCE, and Ptolemy XIV, who arrived in 60 BCE, shortly before the queen died, perhaps from postnatal complications. All five siblings were hailed as 'Our Lords and Greatest Gods' from birth, yet, curiously, each of them met with a violent death (although at least Cleopatra VII got to choose the manner of hers).

Oddly, debates over the parentage of Cleopatra VII have raged for decades. Some scholars have fancifully claimed that her mother was a Greek courtesan or else an Egyptian concubine, or that, at any rate, she was 'non-Ptolemaic'. Cleopatra VII may be the most studied woman of antiquity, but the amount of misinformation that continues to be written about her is astounding. True, the name of Cleopatra's mother is not given in any of the classical Greek or Latin sources, but references to Cleopatra VI Tryphaina are preserved in the Egyptian evidence, where, in fact, they are quite plentiful. An inscription at Edfu temple, for example, dated 69 BCE, mentions her with Fluter and 'their children', and the date of the text chimes precisely with the arrival of Cleopatra VII into the family, so that the 'children' referred to in the text must equate to the first-born girls, Berenice IV and Cleopatra VII. As late as December 57 BCE in the temple of Edfu, in the passageway between the entrance pylons, a scene depicts Fluter making an offering to Horus; he is followed by the goddess Seshat and Cleopatra VI Tryphaina, who stands behind both her husband and the goddess in the traditional queenly regalia and pose of hands raised in greeting. The name of the queen appears with that of her husband on the temple's pylons as 'Ptolemy, the Young Osiris, with his sister queen Cleopatra named Tryphaina'. The pylons were decorated with enormous figures of Fluter smiting the enemies of Egypt in traditional pharaonic manner, but his queen is not represented at all; she had probably died earlier that year and the inscription which named her was almost certainly commemorative. Cleopatra VI Tryphaina ostensibly made no impression on the course of events of her time, when Rome was intimidating Egypt and her husband was beleaguered by debts and political problems, finding his distraction from his troubles in flute-playing. And whilst she comes across as a woman of little authority, it is nonetheless a pity we do not know more about the mother who bore three daring, bold and single-minded daughters. Significantly, the Romans never brought a charge of illegitimacy against Cleopatra VII or her four siblings, a detail which can only be explained by the fact that Rome saw them all as the legitimate offspring of Fluter and Cleopatra VI Tryphaina. If Cleopatra VII had been a bastard child of Fluter, it is inconceivable that the Roman propagandists would not have seized on that fact in the ensuing character assassination of the queen immediately after her death.

By 65 BCE the Romans began to call for the annexation of Egypt, and it was only by offering increasingly elaborate bribes to the Roman senate and the aristocracy that Fluter managed to cling to his kingdom and keep it free from a complete Roman takeover. He paid out enormous sums of money to help the campaigns of the Roman general Gnaeus Pompeius Magnus, better known as Pompey the Great, when in 63 BCE he launched into the Third Mithridatic War; Fluter funded no less than 8,000 cavalry for Pompey's war in southern Syria, and yet when he begged the Roman general to come to Alexandria to aid him in crushing a revolt which had broken out in Egypt, Pompey refused. Later that year Pompey brought an end to Seleucid rule and claimed the whole of Syria and the Levant as Roman territory, and Egypt found itself blocked on its eastern and western frontiers by Rome: Fluter's kingdom was surrounded.

The money needed to sustain Pompey's wars and to keep the Roman senators sweet was a burdensome worry for Fluter, whose first instinct was to raise taxes throughout Egypt, but a strike by farmers on the royal estates around Herakleopolis in 61 BCE was an early indication of the widespread displeasure at the tax rise around the country. An increasingly desperate king turned more and more to Roman bankers, such as the unscrupulous Gaius Rabirius Postumus, for high-credit loans, which gave the Romans even more leverage. The governance of Egypt became a progressively urgent issue in Rome's politics, and sensing a change in the political winds, in 60 BCE Fluter sailed to Rome to meet with Pompey, Marcus Licinius Crassus (undeniably the richest man in Rome) and the ambitious and resourceful Gaius Julius Caesar (the three men had recently formed a governing Triumvirate) in order to negotiate official acknowledgement of his kingship. At the cost of 6,000 talents – the equivalent of 1.5 million pieces of gold, a sum that represented Egypt's entire annual revenue – Fluter was awarded the title 'friend and ally of the Roman people' (*amici et socii populi Romani*), the closest thing he could secure to a guarantee that Egypt would not be taken over by Rome. A year later, the Romans seized and subjugated Cyprus.

The Roman excuse for the invasion of the island was that Fluter's younger brother, King Ptolemy of Cyprus, had been

aiding and abetting the pirates who milled around the Mediterranean Sea disrupting the Roman shipping trade. The Romans
allowed Ptolemy to stay on Cyprus and gave him the honorific
title of High Priest of Aphrodite but stripped him of power and
took away his title of king. Preferring death over the ignominy of
Roman occupation, Ptolemy drank poison and died. Cyprus was
joined to the province of Cilicia; its status as a Roman province
lasted approximately ten years until Julius Caesar gave the island
back to Cleopatra VII in the summer of 48 BCE.

Tensions were running high in Alexandria. Diodorus Siculus
described the edgy situation when he visited Egypt around 60 BCE.
He himself had witnessed a Roman visitor being killed in the
street after he had inadvertently killed a cat, an animal considered
sacred by the Egyptians, and had watched the agents of the crown
inertly standing by as the Roman was bludgeoned to death, even
though it was their duty to put an end to such violence. Religious
fanaticism was possibly a very welcome pretext for the people
to kill a hated Roman. Later, when news reached the mob that
Fluter had refused to aid his brother on Cyprus because he feared
jeopardizing his new title 'friend of Rome', they were incensed by
his passivity and ran amok. They regarded Rome's annexation of
Cyprus as an attack on Egypt, and for this reason the Alexandrian
courtiers forced Fluter to give up his throne and stay out of Egypt.
Late in the summer of 58 BCE the dejected New Dionysus took
himself off to the island of Rhodes, and sometime during 57 BCE
he limped back to Rome, where Pompey received him and loaned
him his villa in the Alban hills. Fluter was accompanied there by
his eleven-year-old daughter, Cleopatra VII.

*

The Alexandrians did not know nor care where Fluter had gone,
and they even entertained the pleasant thought that he might be
dead, but in his absence it was the mild Cleopatra VI Tryphaina
who did her royal duty and ascended to her husband's throne.
More of a place-holder than a usurper, the queen invited her
politically gifted daughter, Berenice IV, to be her co-regent, and

she contented herself with being Berenice's legitimizing figure-head. Intelligent, ambitious and very able, Berenice accepted without hesitation. In little more than a year, however, after careful management of Egypt's affairs, Cleopatra VI Tryphaina was dead, leaving Berenice IV as the sole ruler. To uphold Ptolemaic tradition, Berenice should have married one of her two brothers, but at that time, in 57 BCE, they were mere toddlers and could not be associated with the kingship, and so, in a scenario that follows closely the experience of Cleopatra Berenice some years previously, a husband hunt was launched on behalf of the virgin queen.

The first candidate for the queen's hand was the youngest son of Cleopatra Selene (whose name has not been preserved), the final scion of the house of Seleucus. But no sooner had marriage negotiations begun than he died of a fever. The Alexandrian government next approached the sole-surviving heir of the Seleucid line descending from Grypus and Cleopatra Tryphaina, their grandson Philip II, who had reigned as the last monarch of an independent Syria (65–64 BCE) and was keen to do his dynastic duty by becoming Egypt's pharaoh. The Romans put a block on that idea. Aulus Gabinius, the proconsul of Syria, was less than keen on a union of the royal houses as it would fly in the face of Roman interests, and besides, Gabinius had received a personal bribe of 10,000 talents from Fluter, who was still in Rome pursuing political backing for his restoration.

That Queen Berenice IV's advisers were getting more desperate is revealed by their third choice for a husband: casting their net wider than ever, they eventually found a very minor Seleucid princeling of bastard stock. His name was Seleucus, but upon his arrival in Alexandria, the mob nicknamed him Kybiosaktes, 'Salt-Fish Seller', because of his inferior birth. Berenice did not find the joke funny. She was appalled at the vulgarity of this subordinate outsider, completely lacking in courtesy, intellect and panache. Worse than provincial, Kybiosaktes was parochial, and the thought of sharing this low-life's bed disgusted the queen so much that, breaking all family records, Berenice had him strangled to death just hours after the wedding.

The Alexandrian courtiers finally found a willing and more suitable husband for the freshly widowed queen in the person of Archelaus, the supposed son of Mithridates the Great of Pontus (although it is more likely he was the son of Mithridates' general Archelaus – the clue is in the name). Archelaus bribed the Roman proconsul Gabinius to let him go to Egypt to take up the queen's offer, and in April 56 BCE he arrived in Alexandria, married Berenice IV and became her co-ruler. From the spring of 56 BCE until the spring of 55 BCE, Egypt was ruled by the newlyweds and, accordingly, the papyri date their joint reign as 'year 2 which is also year 1.'

In Rome, Fluter had found an ally in his host, Pompey, who brought the concerns of the exiled king to a debate in the senate. The 'Egyptian question' was of great concern to Fluter's Roman creditors, who had a vested interest in the success of the king's restoration to the Egyptian throne; only then could Fluter pay off his astronomical loans. After Fluter had again either spent large amounts of money for bribes or had promised such sums, he was able to obtain letters of support from Pompey addressed to the Syrian proconsul Gabinius, who was exhorted in a most high-handed fashion to lead the king back to Alexandria at the head of his Germanic and Gallic cavalry, led by Marc Antony, its commander. The mission was to get rid of Berenice IV and Archelaus and put Fluter back on the throne. Antony's chivalrous conduct towards the king and his fourteen-year-old daughter, as he led Fluter and Cleopatra from Ephesus on the west coast of Asia Minor, through Syria and towards the Egyptian border, was to be remembered fondly by the princess. For his part, the young Antony, Appian insists, was dumbstruck at the sight of Cleopatra's beauty at that time, but nothing came of that attraction just then, if it ever existed. Cleopatra always went for the top brass, and Antony still had to make a name for himself.

Archelaus was defeated and died in a battle on two fronts led by Antony and Gabinius. On 15 April 55 BCE, with Gabinius' army clearing the way, Fluter marched into Alexandria and reclaimed the kingdom as Ptolemy XII. For the first time in history, a Roman army had taken hold of Egypt. When Gabinius and Antony left Egypt, a few Roman troops remained behind in Alexandria to protect the king. Known as the Gabiniani, the Gallic and Germanic cavalrymen were to leave their mark on the city's history. They were deployed multiple times thereafter to counter revolts by native Egyptians but were responsible too for much lawlessness and violence in the city's streets and bars. They formed a major Roman presence in Alexandria, although over the years they gradually lost their ties with Rome and eventually formed the core of the army which would fight against Julius Caesar in the Bellum Alexandrinum, the Alexandrian War.

Within days of his return to Alexandria, Fluter had his daughter Berenice IV killed, as well as many of her supporters. Because of the *damnatio memoriae* she consequently suffered, no monumental depictions or titles survive for Berenice IV. Details of her life are sadly lacking, although from what little we know of her, she can count as a major political figure of the period, a capable woman who capitalized on the exertions of her precursor queens and set a precedent for her own sister's queenship by demonstrating that a royal woman could inherit the throne and efficaciously rule in lieu of a male heir.

The execution of Queen Berenice still left Fluter with two boys named Ptolemy (aged about six and four) and two girls – Cleopatra, who would soon be fifteen, and Arsinoë, who was several years younger – and all four were named by the king as Theoi Neoi Philadelphoi, 'The New Sibling-Loving Gods', in a public statement of family unity. The king had no need to worry about potential heirs, and not being inclined to take a new wife, he decided to make his eldest daughter his co-regent. Cleopatra VII is represented in this role in the crypt of the temple of Hathor at Dendera where she is shown in procession, standing behind her father, bearing the titles 'Ruler' and 'Lady of the Two Lands'. In fact, Cleopatra accompanied her father to lay the official founding stone for a new temple dedicated to Hathor-Isis at Dendera on 16 July 53 BCE – a date which commemorated the accension of their ancestress the great Arsinoë II to heaven. At the same time, Fluter and Cleopatra carried out an official visit to Memphis and were warmly greeted there by the leading representative of the native aristocracy, Pasherenptah, the High Priest of Ptah. On 31 May 52 BCE, in recognition of her loyalty and her capabilities, Ptolemy XII bestowed a new honorific title on the sixteen-year-old Cleopatra, declaring her to be Thea Philopator, the 'Father-Loving Goddess'; through the acquisition of this prestigious title, she became her father's divine female counterpart.

At the beginning of 51 BCE, Fluter's health took a sudden turn for the worse and he went into a sharp terminal decline until, on 7 March, a partial solar eclipse heralded his end. He died in Alexandria, aged about fifty-five; he had been the most tenacious of kings and had clung on to the crown of Egypt despite having spent more than half of his life abroad. The clever policies of Ptolemy XII Neos Dionysus had provided Egypt with a certain autonomy but had also decisively opened new doors for Rome's involvement in Egypt's affairs. The Ptolemaic empire had now declined almost to the borders of the old satrapy which Ptolemy I Soter had inherited upon the death of Alexander the Great.

16

(Un)Civil Wars

At the age of eighteen Cleopatra VII found herself the ruler of Egypt, being the only possible candidate in the royal family old enough to take up the reins of government. She had witnessed much in her young life, and a sense of the weight of history might have already been awakened in her early on as she saw her father ceaselessly begging Rome for recognition as king of Egypt. She had witnessed how Rome toyed with her father, took his money and set him up as a puppet-ruler; under Roman pressure, she had experienced the killing of a king-consort, the husband of her sister, the queen, and she had seen that sister humbled and executed. Little wonder that the image of Rome dominated Cleopatra's later life.

In his will, read at court in Alexandria, Fluter made Cleopatra VII a joint ruler with her ten-year-old brother, Ptolemy XIII. A copy of that will was kept by Pompey in his house in Rome, and was opened at the king's death. In this way the pharaoh shrewdly made Rome responsible for protecting the continuity of his dynasty through the management of his heirs. Cleopatra, Fluter determined, would not sit alone on the Egyptian throne; she would have to continue the Ptolemaic practice of sibling marriage.

Immediately, Cleopatra went into action to secure the throne for herself. There is no evidence that suggests the marriage between Cleopatra VII and Ptolemy XIII took place at this point, although when, on 22 March 51 BCE, just days after Fluter's death, a sacred Buchis bull died, the event was commemorated with the erection of a burial stele at the animal's tomb. It records the 'Female Ruler, Mistress of Two Lands, the Father-Loving Goddess', confirming that Cleopatra ruled alone, at least nominally, without her brother, contrary to what her father had determined. Fully aware that Rome would intervene and force her to accept her brother's joint rule, she hastily proceeded to put together a council of advisors whom she could trust. She found support in Pasherenptah, High Priest of Memphis, who encouraged Cleopatra to continue with her late father's temple-building projects to solicit the support of the Egyptians, who were, at this time, still being heavily taxed.

As part of a forward-thinking PR strategy, Cleopatra decided to leave Alexandria to tour the southern part of her realm. Ptolemy XIII was left behind. She began her trip with a state visit to Memphis where she was given the official (masculine) title 'King of Upper and Lower Egypt' and was declared to be the 'Female Horus, the Great One, Mistress of Perfection, Brilliant in Council, Lady of the Two Lands, Cleopatra, the Father-Loving Goddess, the Image of her Father.' She travelled further up the Nile to Dendera, where she inspected the works on the temple of Hathor-Isis, and moved on to Thebes, where she attended the installation ceremony of the newly chosen Buchis Bull, which was celebrated with full Ptolemaic pizzazz; Cleopatra herself, costumed in pharaonic finery, led the processions. When the Theban ceremonials came to an end, she travelled on the state barge of the god Amun nine kilometres further up the Nile towards Hermonthis, to the temple of the war god Montu, where the Buchis Bull would thereafter reside. The sacred animal was led onto the queen's barge and the flotilla headed off. The Egyptian sources record:

> The Lady of the Two Lands, the Father-Loving Goddess, rowed him in the barque of Amun, together with the royal boats, all the inhabitants of Thebes and Hermonthis and the priests being with him as he reached Hermonthis, his dwelling-place . . . Hermonthis and Thebes were united in drunkenness and the noise was heard in heaven . . . As for the ruler, everyone was able to see her.

Safely installed in his penthouse-like paddock (equipped with a harem of heifers), the Buchis Bull was eulogized in prayer by Cleopatra: 'I adore thy majesty and give praise to your soul, O great god,' she intoned, continuing by addressing him as the 'self-created lord.' The fact that she spoke the ritual prayers in the Egyptian language, and then spoke to the locals in their native tongue, further endeared her to the crowds. Cleopatra VII was the first ruler in more than 300 years who spoke Egyptian (we need to look back to Nectanebo II, 358 to 340 BCE, for the previous example), and her ability to speak the language bonded Cleopatra with the people – their cause was her cause, and they would not forget it.

To cut her brother out of the kingship completely, Cleopatra had documents from the first half of 51 BCE dated to the thirtieth year of Fluter's reign and her first year of rule, while the cult title of Thea Philopator, which she had used from the beginning of her co-regency with her father, made it clear that she would continue his administration and policies. When Wennefer, the chief priest of Isis in the in the Fayum, erected a Greek stele on 2 July 51 BCE, it was done 'on behalf of the female king Cleopatra Thea Philopator' – no mention was made of the queen's brother at all. The limestone relief portrays the queen as a bare-chested male pharaoh making an offering to Isis, alerting us to the fact that the stele was originally prepared as a dedication to Cleopatra's father and that she simply appropriated it and had it dated year 1 of her sole rule.

Cleopatra alone was mentioned in the official documents as late as August 51 BCE, but forces were gathering against her, and by early 50 BCE not only did the Romans know of Fluter's death and of Cleopatra's appropriation of the throne but, closer to home, supporters of Ptolemy XIII had started to gain the upper hand by getting hold of Egypt's food supply. The Nile floods of 51 and 50 BCE had been disappointingly low, which meant a decrease in the country's grain harvest. The populace of Alexandria had their food rationed because of the low floods, but Ptolemy XIII and his ministers managed to divert transportation of all wheat cargos which were meant for different parts of Egypt into the enormous warehouses of Alexandria in order to feed its citizens, as they wanted to counteract the hunger riots which were looming large in the capital. The diversion of resources was recorded in a royal order of 27 October 50 BCE, which commanded the sellers of grain and legumes in Middle Egypt to transport all their goods to Alexandria on pain of death. The order placed King Ptolemy at the head of the document, and the queen, his sister, is named only after him. Other documents dating to June 49 BCE name 'Pharaoh Ptolemy and Pharaoh Cleopatra, the Father-Loving Gods' in 'year 1 which is year 3', demonstrating that, to Cleopatra's great consternation, Ptolemy XIII's tenure as senior ruler had begun in earnest.

'Pothinus the eunuch, governor to the young king, had the chief management of affairs during Ptolemy's minority', wrote Julius Caesar in his *De Bello Civili*, his memoir of the vicious civil war he fought against Pompey and the Roman senate. In the eyes of the Roman leader, Pothinus was the palpable power behind the throne and held a Svengali-like hold over the twelve-year-old Ptolemy, whose 'nurse' and tutor he had been since the boy's infancy. The influential old eunuch had control of Egypt's purse-strings and held onto them so prudently that no great financial transactions could be done without his direct participation; he worked hard, too, to turn the Romans against Cleopatra and did his best to bypass her in all matters of government. In this ploy he was supported by two acolytes – Achillias, a competent enough military general, and King Ptolemy's rhetoric tutor, Theodotus of Chios. 'All of them alike', wrote Caesar of this unlikely triad, 'found it shameful to be ruled by a woman.'

And yet it was Cleopatra who took on the job of curbing the Gabiniani, those Roman soldiers who had been left in Egypt by Gabinius, when the need arose in 48 BCE. The Roman proconsul of Syria, Marcus Calpurnius Bibulus, had sent his two sons to Egypt to petition the Gabiniani to aid him in his war against Parthia, but the sons met with unbridled violence as the cavalrymen first tortured and then killed them. It was generally believed in Alexandria that Ptolemy XIII's advisors, most notably Pothinus, had ordered the double murder because he was reluctant to lose the services of what was, in essence, a private (if undisciplined) army.

Cleopatra saw things differently and had the murderers extradited from Egypt and sent to Syria for trial, her intention being not just to challenge her brother's cronies but to demonstrate to Rome that she was a law-enforcing monarch who acted with vigour and determination. It had taken enormous courage to stand up to Pothinus and his circle, and this incident made Cleopatra the chief target of the eunuch's schemes for reprisal.

*

In the early hours of 11 January 49 BCE, Julius Caesar led his troops across the Rubicon River in northern Italy, heralding the beginning of the Roman civil war. Soon afterwards, as Caesar rapidly advanced on Rome, Pompey and his men withdrew from Italy to build up armed forces in the east. The Hellenistic dynastic houses allied to him – chiefly the Ptolemaic house – were expected to take part in the war and fight for his cause, and so, in the summer of 49 BCE, Pompey's eldest son, Gnaeus Pompey, arrived in Alexandria seeking military support for his father's war against Caesar. Given that Egypt was duty-bound to assist Pompey (since Fluter had carefully cultivated a special relationship with him), 500 troops of the Gabiniani were bequeathed to the war effort, together with 60 Egyptian warships. Later accounts state that Gnaeus Pompey and Cleopatra began a sexual relationship at this point; they knew each other well, for sure, since Cleopatra's adolescence had been spent in Rome at her father's side, and it was probably the developing bond between them (sexual or not) that spurred a fearful Pothinus into action. Before the summer had ended Ptolemy XIII's privy councillors succeeded in having Cleopatra ousted from the throne. Pothinus' generosity towards Pompey's arms race was rewarded when the general recommended to the senate that Ptolemy XIII should be formally thanked for his gift of military aid and recognized as Egypt's sole ruler.

Fearful for her life, Cleopatra fled south (taking her sister Arsinoë with her) to the Thebaid, where she was still recognized and loved as ruler. She crossed the Eastern Desert to the Red Sea and took ship to Arabia, from where she travelled north into

Judaea, eventually establishing a court-in-exile at Ashkelon, near Gaza in Palestine. Here she took advantage of the presence of a royal mint to issue coins, stamped with her image, to pay for an army of her own, for she knew that conflict with her brother's forces was inevitable. In the autumn of 49 BCE, a rival branch of the Roman senate held a meeting in Thessaloniki, in northern Greece, where the high command was given to Pompey for the coming year and allies who had distinguished themselves were awarded due honours. Ptolemy XIII was hailed as king and legitimate ruler of Egypt while Cleopatra was excluded from the throne – in other words, at Thessaloniki, the Roman faction, feeling hard-pressed by trying circumstances, chose to completely disregard the will of the late Ptolemy XII.

At Pharsalus, in central Greece, on 9 August 48 BCE, in a scorching heat, the forces of Julius Caesar and Pompey the Great clashed in the biggest battle ever fought between Romans. It was a landmark event in history. The Pompeian defeat was crushing: Caesar's own report lists 15,000 dead and 24,000 captured against merely 200 killed on his side. Pompey managed to escape to Larisa, the capital city of the Thessaly region in Greece, and then to Mytilene on the west coast of Asia Minor, and eventually to Tyre on the Phoenician seashore, where he took refuge. Caesar meanwhile made a grand victory procession east (mainly to find money to pay his soldiers), marching to Ephesus, where, in exchange for leaving intact the treasury of the goddess Artemis, he was hailed by the priests as the 'Manifest God, offspring of Mars and Venus, Saviour of Mankind.' Divine honours, he found, were very much to his taste. They resonated too with an anxious Cleopatra, who was following the news of Caesar's victory closely – and no doubt cheerfully. She sent Caesar a missive, congratulating him on his victory and on his procurement of divine titles, while alerting him to the fact that she was readying her army to retake Egypt and reclaim the throne. She would be glad, she wrote, if great Caesar would support her. Soon after, she and her forces embarked on the six-day march towards Pelusium, and it was there that they encountered Ptolemy XIII and his army, under the leadership of

Achillas, with the Gabiniani at his side. The armies of the rival siblings faced off on 28 September 48 BCE and, as the two armies eyed each other with hatred, all set for the fight, an insignificant flotilla of ships was seen drifting along the coast. Upon enquiry it was revealed that the defeated Pompey, his wife, Cornelia, and their youngest son, Sextus, together with the loyal remnants of his forces were sailing towards Alexandria, set on a mission to ask for more Egyptian cash to buy new troops. Until the generals arrived, as was often custom in ancient warfare, the battle was put on hold.

Pothinus was less than enthusiastic about doling out yet more gold to a man whose star was clearly fading and, resolving that 'a dead man cannot bite', decided that Pompey would no longer find a friend in Egypt; the future security of Ptolemy XIII's throne lay in the hands of Julius Caesar, who was heading to Egypt in hot pursuit of his enemy. It is the Roman historian Cassius Dio who presents the most detailed (and rather beautiful) account of what happened at Pelusium next:

> Bringing the ships to anchor, [Pompey] sent some men to remind the king [Ptolemy XIII] of the favour shown his father and to ask that he be permitted to land under certain guarantees of safety. Ptolemy gave him no answer – for he was still a mere boy – but some of the Egyptians . . . came pretending to be friends, but they wickedly plotted against him . . . After many friendly greetings they implored him to come over to their boats, saying that because of its size and shape his ship could not draw close to land and that Ptolemy was very eager to see him.

Cornelia warned him not to go, but Pompey stepped onto the skiff, thereby sealing his fate. Watching from the dockside, arrayed in his diadem and purple robes, Ptolemy XIII witnessed Pompey's murder. The Roman 'veiled his face' as knives plunged into his abdomen and back. Then his head was struck off from his body and his corpse was thrown into the sea (it was later retrieved by one of his men and cremated on a modest funeral pyre). Pompey's severed head was given to King Ptolemy, who ordered it to be pickled and safely stored away. Pompey died the day before his fifty-eighth birthday.

Caesar arrived on the scene only two days later. Before he landed in Egypt, the tutor Theodotus of Chios brought Ptolemy XIII the head and signet ring of Pompey the Great, for it was assumed that this would satisfy Caesar and persuade him to continue his journey back to Rome without stopping in Egypt. Instead, as Plutarch recorded, Caesar deeply mourned the loss of his former friend and ally (and one-time son-in-law): 'From the man who brought him Pompey's head, Caesar turned away, as from a murderer, and when he received Pompey's signet ring . . . he burst into tears.' Julius Caesar entered Alexandria on 2 October 48 BCE, accompanied by his *lictors* or bodyguards, as a Roman consul with military imperium and set up his quarters in the royal palace, whether the Egyptians wanted him there or not. Caesar's conduct was viewed as an insult to the sovereignty of the state and to royal dignity, and from the beginning he and his troops faced hazardous disgruntlement in the streets of Alexandria. Caesar ordered reinforcement troops from Asia, but generally he downplayed his authority and took the role of an educated and peaceful tourist; he visited the sights of Alexandria, pondered the tomb of Alexander the Great and took part in the intellectual life of city.

However, Caesar made it clear to the Egyptians that, since he was consul once more, it was his duty to settle the quarrel between the two royal siblings, and he enjoined Ptolemy XIII and Cleopatra VII to dismiss their soldiers and appear before him in Alexandria, where, he decreed, they should settle their differences by negotiation. He also asked for part-payment of the 17 million drachmas that he was owed (Fluter had borrowed heavily from Caesar) so that he might maintain his troops. Pothinus proposed to pay everything later if only Caesar would leave Egypt. He got a sharp rebuke for the suggestion.

Dutifully, Cleopatra dismissed her troops and left Pelusium for Alexandria, accompanied by her bodyguard-cum-confidant, the utterly loyal Apollodorus of Sicily. Aware of the presence of her brother's troops there (Ptolemy had decided against disbanding them), she contrived, with Apollodorus' help, to sneak into the palace under the cover of darkness, smuggled through these hostile lines like a piece of contraband. It is Plutarch, perhaps drawing on the memoirs of Apollodorus himself, who gives us the most vivid account of the iconic scene that (allegedly) played out that night:

> It being impossible to escape notice otherwise, [Cleopatra] placed herself in a bedding sack and lay full-length. Apollodorus tied the sack with cord and carried it inside to Caesar. We are told that it was by this ingenuity of Cleopatra's that Caesar was first captivated by her, for she showed herself to be truly beguiling. So overcome was he by her graciousness and her company that he reconciled her to her brother, Ptolemy, on condition that she rule as Ptolemy's equal in the kingdom.

Here these two extraordinary individuals, both of whom were characterized by their political flair, their fierce determination and a great love of taking risks, met in the flesh as man and woman. Caesar was fifty-two years old, Cleopatra was twenty-one.

The following morning, Cleopatra and Ptolemy were both directed to appear before Caesar to hear his judgement, but by then Caesar had been completely smitten by Cleopatra's insistent charm and had already made her his lover the night before, as she had intended all along. The not-completely-naive Ptolemy immediately grasped the situation and stormed out of the throne room, tearing the diadem off his head and ranting about how he had been betrayed. Pothinus began to spread the unfounded rumour throughout Alexandria that Caesar planned to make Cleopatra the sole ruler of Egypt and an eager puppet of the Romans. Caesar himself made a conciliatory public speech, stressing to the mob that he had every intention of upholding the will of their late liege lord, Fluter, and to show that he was serious, he not only put Ptolemy XIII and Cleopatra VII back on the throne as co-rulers but established their younger brother and sister, Ptolemy XIV and Arsinoë IV, as joint rulers of Cyprus, which was returned as a

Ptolemaic possession. By giving up a province which had contributed much to the wealth of Rome, Caesar paid a very high price to secure peace in the royal house. It was done, of course, for the sake of Cleopatra.

Pothinus attempted to block the reconciliation of the siblings. With an army of about 20,000 men under Achillas' command (the core of which was again formed by the Gabiniani), he initiated the so-called Alexandrian War. Caesar took Ptolemy XIII and the young king and queen of Cyprus into custody as hostages as the war quickly escalated into a national movement of protest against the Roman presence in Egypt. A people's militia was established and anyone capable of bearing arms was levied from every corner of the country to fight the foreigners. Caesar managed to shut off the palace district in Alexandria and occupied the island on which the Pharos Lighthouse stood; he kept the city's large harbour open, docked ships there and had them set on fire to prevent his enemies from commandeering them. But the conflagration quickly got out of control and spread to the dockyards and into the city, setting the Great Library ablaze. Something in the order of 400,000 papyrus scrolls went up in flames that night, late in the summer of 48 BCE, and the incalculable loss still gives classicists sleepless nights thinking about what vanished forever in the inferno.

All through the winter the fighting and the intrigue continued. The Cypriot queen, Arsinoë, the younger sister of Cleopatra, escaped from the royal palace with her tutor, a eunuch named Ganymedes, and fled to Achillas' army, where she was acclaimed queen of Egypt by the troops. She declared herself an enemy of Cleopatra VII and swore to the army that she would not be seeking Roman favour. In any event, her relationship with the armed forces quickly soured when she and Achillas wrangled over tactics. When Caesar intercepted communications between Achillas and Pothinus, he accused Pothinus of treason and finally had him executed.

Shortly afterwards, Ganymedes, who was the driving force behind Arsinoë's success, murdered Achillas and thereafter skilfully managed the troops himself. He tried to use an early form of chemical warfare against Caesar when he (unsuccessfully) attempted to contaminate the drinking water in the palace quarter. One of Ganymedes' more successful ruses, however, was to request from Caesar the presence of Ptolemy XIII as a peace envoy to Arsinoë; liberated from the palace, Ptolemy promptly joined the side of Arsinoë and her soldiers. All looked lost for Caesar, but reinforcements began to arrive from Asia and the Levant, and the final struggle began just as, early in 47 BCE, Ptolemy XIII and Arsinoë had established their headquarters along the Nile, close to modern Cairo. Here the Roman reinforcements successfully routed their troops in battle. Ptolemy XIII, resplendent in his heavy gold armour, managed to flee the battlefield, but as he attempted to wade through the waters of the riverbank, he fell into the Nile and drowned. Arsinoë was taken captive and brought back to Alexandria in chains.

After celebrating his victory with games and banquets, Caesar once again settled down to work. He synchronized the succession to the throne by reinvoking Fluter's will and placing Cleopatra on the throne at the side of her youngest and only surviving brother, the thirteen-year-old Ptolemy XIV. In actuality, Caesar handed over complete control of Egypt to his lover, but for appearance's sake the brother–sister couple took on the title Theoi Philopatores Philadelphoi, 'Father-Loving, Sibling-Loving Gods', which was the cult title that Cleopatra had shared with Ptolemy XIII.

Cleopatra looked to Julius Caesar to be her advocate, her chief supporter and her lover. But lest we become *too* embroiled in the love story, we should remember that Cleopatra would have appealed to Pompey in the same way if he had won the civil war instead of Caesar. However, we must concede that it was the romance which played out between Caesar and Cleopatra that prevented Egypt from becoming a Roman province.

Caesar's stay in Egypt was seen as unusually long by his fellow Romans. There were lavish feasts and entertainments to keep him occupied – the sorts of thing which made Egypt such a morally treacherous place in the eyes of some Romans, but which were no more than the usual diplomatic exchanges between Roman leaders and Hellenistic rulers. The complex and fraught situation in Egypt had taken time to sort out and Caesar certainly deserved some leisure time to explore Egypt – and its queen. Like countless thousands of couples ever since, Caesar and Cleopatra sealed their love with a Nile cruise – a lavish high-end vacation, ostensibly for the queen to show her new boyfriend the wonders of Egypt but more perhaps because Caesar wanted to make direct contact with this newly procured land, which was now so intimately bound up with his own person. For Caesar and Cleopatra, politics and passion were always intertwined. By the time they returned to Alexandria from their honeymoon-like cruise Cleopatra had conceived Julius Caesar's child.

17

Sons and Lovers

On 23 June 47 BCE, just as the Nile's rise heralded a season of
plenty, Cleopatra VII gave birth to a boy. According to a Demotic
inscription on a Serapeum stele said to have been written on his
birthday, straight away he was addressed as 'Pharaoh Caesar'. The
message was clear: Cleopatra's son was a future pharaoh and the
heir of Julius Caesar too, and henceforward he was Ptolemy XV
Caesar. In the Egyptian hieroglyphic titulary he was frequently
called 'Ptolemy named Caesar', and in Greek nomenclature he
was 'Ptolemy and Caesar', although since Caesar was one of
Ptolemy XV's official names, he was also addressed by that term
alone (Cicero, for instance, in a letter dated 11 May 44 BCE,
referred to him as '*Caesar ille*', 'that Caesar'). But in Egypt, where
the hieroglyphic monuments proclaimed loudly that Caesar was
the father of the boy, the Alexandrians expressed his paternity with
the affectionate patronymic Caesarion ('son of Caesar').

Julius Caesar was not present at the birth of his son. He had
departed Egypt, after nine months spent in the country, in the
spring of 47 BCE, when Cleopatra was in the seventh month of
her pregnancy. His farewell gift to Cleopatra was the permanent
installation of three Roman legions in the Nile Valley. They were
there because (as he recorded):

> [He] thought it beneficial to the smooth running of our
> empire that the king and queen [Ptolemy XIV and Cleop-
> atra VII] should be protected by our troops, as long as they
> [the king and queen] remained loyal to us; but if they were

disloyal, they could be brought back into line by the same troops.

Cleopatra's parting gift for Caesar was more sentimental: the construction of a fine monument in his honour, the Caesareum or – as it was known in Greek – Kaisaros Epibaterios, 'the Embarking Caesar'. Standing on the Alexandrian seaside site now occupied by the once-grand Hotel Metropole, the Caesareum was an homage to Ptolemaic Egyptomania: a riot of pylons, colonnades and obelisks, two of which, both antiquities, had been taken from their original home in Heliopolis to flank the entrance to Caesar's temple. Today known as Cleopatra's Needles, one stands on the Embankment in London, while its companion is in New York City. Along with the construction of the Caesareum came the promise of Egypt's unfailing fidelity to Rome.

Although Caesar remained publicly silent about the birth of Caesarion, it is probable that in private circles in Rome he quietly accepted the boy's parentage. Conversely, throughout Egypt Cleopatra made a great show of the birth and in repeated official pronouncements made it known that Caesarion's father was unambiguously Julius Caesar the Roman. Coinage issued by Cleopatra to celebrate Caesarion's birth forwarded an important tripartite message, for she appears on them with her baby boy in her arms. Mother and son play the triple roles of Isis and Horus for the benefit of her Egyptian subjects; for the wider Greek-speaking world they were no less than Aphrodite and Eros, and for the Romans the queen crafted herself as Venus, the divine ancestress of the Julii, the family of Julius Caesar, which made Caesarion Cupid, the divine offspring of the Roman goddess of desire. Because they made no mention of the child's father, the coins hinted too at an auto-generational type birth story for the young prince. But it was the mother–child image which impacted so powerfully on the viewers of the coins. The iconography informs us that Cleopatra never needed to follow the traditional life path of a Hellenistic (or Roman) woman and, just like the goddesses Aphrodite and Venus, the coins declare how she had bypassed the *nymphē* ('bridal') stage of life to emerge at Caesarion's genesis as a fully-fledged mother and queen.

In Egypt, where Julius Caesar had no official position (after all, he was no king-consort or co-ruler), Cleopatra VII publicized herself as the sole progenitor of her dynasty on the walls of the temple at Iuny (Greek Hermonthis), a few miles south of Thebes, where she had herself depicted as Mut, the great mother goddess. She was represented watching herself give birth to Caesarion, aided by numerous divine midwives. In the New Kingdom (1570–1069 BCE), pharaohs had enjoyed a vogue for showing their divine conception in temple wall-reliefs, and some monarchs went so far as to represent their mothers pregnant with the post-coital blessing of Amun, but Cleopatra's iconography was far more revolutionary. Never – not even in the ingenious Cleopatra III's self-promotion – had a queen of Egypt thought of representing herself in the throes of childbirth, but that is what she did at Iuny. Squatting close to the ground, her arms held aloft by birth-goddesses, Cleopatra was shown birthing the prince. The message was clear to all who saw the image: Cleopatra's part in the production of a divine child, Egypt's new Horus, was down to her alone. Caesarion, it was announced through the propaganda channels, had been generated through Cleopatra's own divinity, without the aid of a male god; he was a miracle-child, sent by the gods.

The birth of Caesarion was the pivotal moment of Cleopatra VII's life, for the boy gave the queen her purpose for living: her sole ambition was to love him, guard him and see him established as king. If we want to do justice to Cleopatra VII as a ruler, then we must acknowledge the fact that from the moment of his birth until the hour of her suicide, Caesarion was Cleopatra's greatest love; he alone gave her purpose. Cleopatra did not anticipate that the Ptolemaic dynasty would end with her, of course, and she looked forward to a future when her son would be the next Golden Horus, sitting on Egypt's throne and ruling over an empire even bigger than that of Alexander the Great. In her ambitions for Caesarion, Cleopatra VII replicated – knowingly or unknowingly – the mindset of Cleopatra Thea and Cleopatra III in their drive to secure the throne for their (favoured) sons and, consequently, consolidate their own power base. The birth-relief at Iuny helps us to understand Cleopatra's self-conception, for it is composed *entirely* of female figures and its powerful message is of female self-generation. Nothing like it had been done before. In effect, the Iuny birth-scene is a paean of praise for single mothers.

*

Following his departure from Alexandria and a successful campaign in Africa – picking up treaties, allegiances, gifts and hostages – Caesar arrived back in Rome in June 46 BCE. Once there, he spoke about his son only within the tightest circle of friends, and even then with extreme discretion. His sexual relationship with Cleopatra had been the stuff of gossip in Rome for some months already, but as a 'couple' they had no legal status in Roman eyes. This was about to change. Caesar's wife, Calpurnia, was barren and so, with an eye to the future of his dynastic line, Caesar passed new legislation which would allow him, as the dictator of Rome, to have more than one legal marriage – precisely for the purpose of begetting male heirs (the low birth rate among the Roman aristocracy was a matter of official concern at the time). The question of Caesarion's paternity was obviously a pressing one, particularly for Octavian, Caesar's grand-nephew (his mother, Atia, was the niece of Caesar) and adopted son, who had expected to inherit Caesar's rank, titles and wealth without contention. Now that his automatic inheritance was put in jeopardy, Octavian needed to discredit the claim emphatically upheld by his enemies that Caesarion was Caesar's legitimate son, and he did so with such vigour that many doubts were expressed about Caesarion's paternity, both in his lifetime and in later eras. Cassius Dio, for example, insisted that Cleopatra 'pretended the boy was her son by Caesar, and she was therefore wont to call him Caesarion', although Suetonius took a more neutral stance, writing that 'this child was very like Caesar in looks and carriage', although he added that Gaius Oppius, Cleopatra's secretary, 'published a book, to prove that the child of Cleopatra was not fathered by Caesar? None of these statements can be completely trusted. There is no reason to doubt Caesar's paternity. Caesarion's birth date, in the summer of 47 BCE, alone qualifies Caesar as the father; the rest is pure Roman obfuscation and propaganda.

Around July 46 BCE, Cleopatra, the one-year-old Caesarion and Cleopatra's brother Ptolemy XIV arrived in Rome on a state visit as the invited guests of Julius Caesar, and they were assigned luxurious quarters in the gardens of one of Caesar's villas close to the Tiber. Conservative Republicans shuddered at the arrival of the flamboyant Oriental court and gave the royal retinue a frosty reception. Their hostility towards the Egyptians was not thawed by Cleopatra's *de haut en bas* social manners as she swanned about Rome in her curtained litter, snubbing Rome's great aristocratic ladies and courting their influential husbands instead. Rome buzzed with gossip. Whatever they said about her in private, anyone who was anyone in Rome swarmed to see the goddess-queen – even Cicero, whom Cleopatra completely ignored. He fired off a letter to his friend, Atticus bemoaning his treatment by the uppity Egyptians: 'I cannot stand the queen . . . and I cannot recall her impertinence without a twinge. I will not have anything more to do with that lot.'

Cleopatra and her party had arrived in Rome in time to celebrate a series of four military triumphs, parades held in Caesar's honour by the Romans. Military triumphs had a long history in Rome since, after all, the city had been established through military expansion. During the period of kings (750–509 BCE), it was the monarch himself who headed expeditions and held command in times of war; his military power was, in fact, the foundation of his 'civil' power. But following the expulsion of the kings from Roman society, there was no longer a single absolute authority and the notion of kingship became associated with detestable tyranny – the sort which they saw operating throughout the Hellenistic kingdoms. Although the Romans had completely changed their political system in founding the Republic in 509 BCE, they continued their military campaigns against their neighbours, and in order to do this they found it necessary to empower a single man with the king-like privileges to wage wars in the name of the Republic. An individual commander – a consul – was granted a significant amount of power during military campaigns – the *imperium*, as the Romans called it, which reflected the power of the ancient Roman king – while the holder of that office had only a limited amount of power in Rome itself, which was under the charge of his co-consul (there were always two consuls at any time). At the beginning of each year of office, the Roman senate defined the provinces which would be the seats of war for the newly elected consuls and an army was granted to the commander himself. With this army, he was to leave the city of Rome to fulfil his task on conquering and quelling the chosen provinces. Once the commander had crossed the pomerium, the sacred boundary of the city, he was in possession of the absolute authority of the imperium and was responsible for all the decisions made during the campaign. In short, he was a 'Republican king'. True, the senators – the politicians – tried to temper the actions of the commander during his campaign and he was expected to report to the senate on a regular basis, although this was not always possible, above all because very great distances between the place where the military action was happening and Rome itself. There was a tendency among the commanders, therefore, to make important decisions without consulting the senate.

If the campaign was successful, the soldiers under their commander won battles, beat the enemy, gained booty and captured prisoners of war. The commander would send a message to Rome that was decorated with a sprig of laurel as a symbol of victory. In due course, after the commander and army returned to Rome, the senate assembled to receive the victorious chief. The commander reported his achievements in war and asked the senate to grant him a triumph for them. If the senators voted in favour of the triumph, the commander was allowed to cross the pomerium with his army, with the booty and with the prisoners of war, and to pass through the entire city up to the Capitolium, where he made a sacrifice to the god Jupiter Optimus Maximus. He was celebrated by all the citizens, the people of Rome. For one day only the commander was elevated above his peers; he wore the costume of Jupiter and was thus seen as a god. But at the end of this day, at the conclusion of the triumph, he had to lay this role aside. Every commander tried to show as much war booty as possible in the triumphal procession, and a triumph over a Hellenistic king could obviously yield more booty than a triumph over, for instance, one of the Spanish provinces or hill tribes. In 46 BCE, Julius Caesar's triumphs were pulled off with particular Ptolemaic-style panache. In one, in imitation of the god Dionysus' triumph over India, Caesar paraded no less than thirty elephants, twenty-two camels and countless other exotic animals through the city (he used the popularity of the cult of Dionysus to foster his own political myth). In another – celebrating the overthrow of Ptolemy XIII – there were floats carrying enormous models of pyramids and sphinxes, and even of a towering Pharos Lighthouse. In each of the parades, Caesar's royal war captives were led in chains through the crowded and jubilant city: there was Pharnaces, the son of Mithridates VI of Pontus, wearing around his neck a placard proclaiming Caesar's great victory exclamation, 'Veni, vidi, vici!'; the four-year-old prince Juba of Mauretania was there too, part of the exotic cargo Caesar had taken from Numidia (in North Africa), who, in a twist of fate, was destined to marry Cleopatra's only daughter. Cleopatra's wearisome teenage sister, Arsinoë IV, representing the subjugation of Egypt, was led in chains at the triumph's big finale. Cleopatra watched unmoved and pitiless as her sister was led in front of the temple of Jupiter on the top of the Capitoline Hill, the place where foreign hostages were executed. But, as Dio tells us, 'the sight of a girl once considered a queen in chains – a spectacle which had never been seen, at least in Rome', was too much, even for the Romans, who shouted for Caesar to show pity and have mercy on the princess. A compassionate Caesar displayed his famous clemency and freed all his prisoners; he even allowed the humiliated Arsinoë to leave Rome and take quiet, trouble-free sanctuary in the great temple of Artemis at Ephesus. We are not told of Cleopatra's reaction but she cannot have been unaware that, had the Alexandrian War turned out differently, she might have suffered the same disgrace.

The impact of Cleopatra's presence in Rome and her effect on Caesar cannot be overestimated. She influenced his growing sense of superiority and ramped up his desire for complete power (in February 44 BCE he declared himself dictator for life) – 'she aroused his greed', said a hostile Lucian, the Roman author – and it was with her encouragement that he began to behave like an old-style Hellenistic ruler, especially regarding his religious outlook. Caesar began to see in himself a form of latent divinity. He was unconcerned by the fact that his soldiers ridiculed his devotion to Cleopatra, for as far as Caesar was concerned, he w as the lover of a living goddess. Coins of the queen with the epithets and head-dress of Isis appeared in Rome in 47/6 BCE, and Caesar was able to turn these to his advantage by directly connecting the figure of Cleopatra as Isis to his triumph: at the end of his victory celebrations he dedicated the Forum Iulium, which had been constructed in 54 BCE. In the centre of the Forum Caesar erected a temple to Venus Genetrix – the goddess from whom his family had always claimed decent – which he had pledged to do at the battle of Pharsalus. Inside the temple he mounted, next to the cult statue of the goddess herself, a magnificent life-sized chryselephantine statue of a naked Cleopatra. In effect, through the installation of Cleopatra's statue, Caesar, who was said to be devoted to the worship of Venus, made both a public declaration of his love for the Egyptian queen and an open acknowledgement of marriage between a descendant of a prestigious Roman dynasty and a living goddess. He not only publicly accepted the divinity of Cleopatra but associated her with (and made her) the ancestral mother of his own family. All the fears of the traditional Republicans were being realized: Rome was being corrupted by Oriental cults, and, under the enchantment of the treacherous Egyptian queen, Julius Caesar was turning native.

To many observers, the assimilation of the Venus Genetrix of the Julii, Caesar's family, with Isis-Aphrodite, the earthly manifestation of whom was now living in Caesar's house in Rome, was anathema enough, but when Caesar himself began to play the part of the divine ruler, a much-lauded Theos Soter, 'Saviour God', hostilities quickly bubbled to the surface. Cleopatra was at least partially to blame for the speed with which the Republican opposition, led by Cassius Longinus and his brother-in-law, Marcus Brutus, moved to overthrow Caesar. Rumours that he nursed ambitions to be crowned a king and a god unnerved them and made them jumpy, to the point where they began to believe the widespread tittle-tattle that a coronation ceremony was already being organized. They began to band together and plot Caesar's assassination.

Cleopatra was in Rome on the Ides of March (15 March) 44 BCE when, in the Curia of Pompey, Julius Caesar's grandiose dreams of conquest and rulership died with him. He perished from twenty-three individual stab wounds. According to Suetonius, after the murder all the conspirators – some sixty senators in all – fled; even Caesar's loyal next-in-command, Marc Antony, though innocent of any crime, went into hiding. Maybe Antony feared being implicated in, or falsely assumed to be part of, the plot to kill Caesar, or perhaps he feared he would be assassinated himself, given that his loyalty to Caesar was so well known. All the while, Caesar's body lay on the floor of the Curia untouched, and it was several hours later that three slaves put the mutilated corpse on a litter and carried it home, where it was met by the anguished cries of Calpurnia. We have no reports of how Cleopatra received the news of Caesar's murder, but it must have been traumatic on both a personal and a political level. The news of Caesar's murder travelled fast and soon his great-nephew, Octavian, who had been in Macedon, was back in Rome. His presence there exacerbated Cleopatra's unease as she realized that Octavian was now a direct threat to Caesarion's life.

After the initial hysteria had subsided, Julius Caesar's will was read aloud at Marc Antony's house on 17 March. Cleopatra, who was in attendance, was not surprised that, as foreigners, neither she nor Caesarion warranted a mention (even the villa they were staying in was bequeathed to the citizens of Rome), although

Antony himself later informed the senate that Caesar had a cknowledged Caesarion's paternity. To this the senators turned a deaf ear. The eighteen-year-old Octavian was declared Caesar's heir, with Antony installed as his guardian. Cleopatra had not accomplished her political goal of having Caesarion confirmed as Caesar's only male heir, and with nothing to keep her in Rome and having every reason to leave (and quickly), Cleopatra and her court sailed from Italy – with more speed than dignity. 'The queen's flight doesn't bother me one iota,' Cicero snipped as he revelled in Cleopatra's humiliation and drank to the well-overdue departure of Caesar's hated, if bewitching, Oriental trophy bride.

*

After three years in Rome, Cleopatra returned to Egypt via Cyprus (she made a brief stop on the island in order to confirm its return to Ptolemaic control). Arriving at Alexandria, she wasted no time in having her docile and compliant sibling-husband, Ptolemy XIV, murdered (poisoned, according to Josephus). He had caused her no trouble and had been happy enough to quietly trot along at her side, but that was no guarantee for the future when he might prove troublesome to Caesarion's accession. The last thing Cleopatra wanted was another family-focused civil war. The last mention we have of poor Ptolemy XIV comes from a papyrus dated 26 July 44 BCE, although he had probably died late in June. A stele from Memphis records that Caesarion was recognized as Ptolemy XV Caesar, and Cleopatra's co-ruler, on 14 February 43 BCE. Retaining the title 'Father-Loving Goddess' but happily disposing of the now obsolete epithet 'Brother-Loving,' Cleopatra VII emphasized her new dual role through Caesarion's titles: he was known as Theos Philopator Philometor, the 'Father-Loving-Mother-Loving God.'

Cleopatra quickly turned personal catastrophe into a propaganda triumph when the murdered Julius Caesar was commemorated throughout Egypt in the guise of the slain god Osiris. The ancient Egyptian saga of the murder and resurrection of Osiris was prized by the Ptolemies, who had long enjoyed this piece of Egyptian theological doctrine and had lovingly (and at high expense) rendered the story of how Osiris had been killed by his wicked brother in several 30-foot-high reliefs carved onto the walls of the temple of Edfu, their spiritual home. The painted walls included images of the assassination and showed how the goddess Isis, Osiris' lamenting widow, took refuge in the papyrus marshes of the Nile Delta in order to escape death. There the goddess was shown cradling her son, the child Horus, to her breast. Cleopatra hijacked this age-old story and dexterously modified it, casting herself in the role of Isis, weeping for the murdered Julius Caesar. Ever vigilant, ever watchful, Isis was shown safeguarding her son Horus, the 'avenger of his father' – who, in Cleopatra VII's propaganda programme, took on the form of Caesarion, Pharaoh Ptolemy XV Caesar. In the shade of the great entrance pylon of Ptolemy XII Fluter at Edfu, where the late pharaoh was shown in the act of vanquishing Egypt's enemies, two elegant granite Horus falcons were placed to flank the entrance doorway; the majestic birds protected a diminutive male figure placed between their legs. He has recently been identified by Egyptologists as Caesarion.

Fragmentary Greek inscriptions from the Caesareum at Alexandria, the temple built in honour of the now deified Caesar, describe a marble statue of Cleopatra as the goddess Venus that once graced the inner sanctum of the building – suggesting that the statue of Cleopatra from the temple of Venus Genetrix in Rome had been replicated for Alexandria. Next to the Cleopatra-Venus statue was 'the image of the god Julius', probably carved in Osirid (mummified) form, while a recently found granite statue of Caesarion may have come from the same family group – a divine triad for Alexandria. Cleopatra ordered work to start on a companion temple for the Caesareum – it was to be known as the Cleopatrion – along with her own tomb, a monument 'of wonderful height and very remarkable', according to ancient reports. Breaking with the family tradition of burying kings and queens in the dynastic tomb alongside the body of the Great Alexander, Cleopatra decided to erect her own on Alexandria's Cape Lochias; despite regular crackpot claims that it has been discovered beneath the sands of the Western Desert, today the tomb lies deep beneath the Mediterranean Sea.

The queen's building activities were even more prolific in Upper Egypt. At the Theban temple of Hathor-Isis at Dier el-Medina, where her father had undertaken work, Cleopatra erected a large granite stele with an inscription in Greek and Demotic and an image of Caesarion worshipping Amun-Re in the presence of Cleopatra, who wears a crown of horns and feathers usually associated with Monthu, god of war. But it was at the Hathor temple at Dendera that Cleopatra VII left her most lasting mark, for on the 100-foot exterior walls, taking their place amongst the multitude of gods who circle the building, is the dyarchy of Cleopatra and Caesarion, who appear not once but twice on the temple's rear wall. The two scenes are carved as mirror images, as was traditional in pharaonic times, and although Caesarion was but a boy when the images were completed, he is depicted as an imposing adult man wearing a very elaborate pharaonic crown and offering incense to the gods. Cleopatra, in an Egyptian wig and towering Hathor-headdress sporting an uraeus (cobra), and carrying Isis' attributes of *sistrum* (rattle) and *menet* (a bead necklace also used as a percussion instrument), stands behind her son, affording him the place of honour. In both scenes the royal pair face five deities, to whom they offer incense, perfume and wine – Hathor, Horus, Harsomtus, Ihy and Hathor again on the east part of the wall, and Isis, Harsomtus, Osiris, Horus and Isis again on the west part. At the centre of the wall is a monumental head of the temple's patroness, Hathor. The iconographic emphasis on Hathor and Isis suggests that Cleopatra herself played a significant part in the design and implementation of the temple's visual programme.

While the gods were being happily placated on the walls of Dendera, they seemed to be far from content with Egypt itself, for between 43 and 41 BCE the country suffered from severely low Nile floods, bad harvests and growing civil unrest. As she struggled to cope with the domestic crises, international affairs pressed heavily on Cleopatra too, as Egypt came ever closer to being drawn into the new Roman civil war that was starting to erupt between Caesar's assassins, Brutus and Cassius, on the one side, and Marc Antony, who had allied himself with Octavian, Caesar's lawful heir, on the other. With the aid of the exiled Arsinoë, out of Cleopatra's reach in Ephesus, Brutus' legions seized Egyptian ships stationed at Cyprus and demanded that Cleopatra supplement them with further vessels from Alexandria. When Cleopatra refused, Brutus and Cassius threatened to invade Egypt but were distracted by Antony, who was busy marshalling troops in Greece. Cleopatra managed to hang on to Cyprus, and Antony's victory over the assassins at the Battle of Philippi, which saw the deaths of both Brutus and Cassius, justified her decision not to send Egyptian ships anywhere.

In the aftermath of battle, the fragile Octavian went back to Italy, so sick that people feared he would die, leaving Antony in charge of the victorious forces and to be hailed as the New Dionysus in Athens. He began the process of organizing Rome's eastern provinces and soon realized that to secure the east he would need the support of Egypt and its still-wealthy queen. In the summer of 41 BCE, hoping to develop the *entente cordiale* that had existed between Cleopatra and Caesar, Antony, through his envoy Quintus Dellius, invited the Egyptian queen to meet him at the port city of Tarsus in Cilicia, in south-east Asia Minor. She agreed to go there, to what was destined to be an appointment that rewrote history.

18

History Stops Here

The barge she sat in, like a burnish'd throne,
Burned on the water: the poop was beaten gold;
Purple the sails, and so perfumed that
The winds were lovesick with them; the oars were silver,
Which to the tune of flutes kept stroke, and made
The water which they beat to follow faster,
As amorous of their strokes. For her own person,
It beggar'd all description: she did lie
In her pavilion, cloth-of-gold of tissue,
O'erpicturing that Venus where we see
The fancy outwork nature: on each side her
Stood pretty dimpled boys, like smiling Cupids,
With divers-colour'd fans, whose wind did seem
To glow the delicate cheeks which they did cool,
And what they undid did.

William Shakespeare's evocative description of Cleopatra's love-boat, taken from his magnificent 1607 tragedy *Antony and Cleopatra*, which was inspired by Thomas North's 1579 English translation of Plutarch's *Lives*, captures to perfection Cleopatra VII's unrivalled flair for the whimsical and the theatrical. The meeting between Antony and Cleopatra at Tarsus marked a pragmatic shift in her style of governance, as the carefully coded use of pharaonic myth and image she had employed during the Caesar years gave way to an ostentatious use of spectacle. Flashy Ptolemaic-style *pompē* was the hallmark of the Antony and Cleopatra era: lavish

Mediterranean cruises, epic banquets, hard drinking, dressing-up, passionate breaking-up and making-up, city-centre parades and water pageants all sent out a message to the Roman world in which the lovers declared: 'We are doing it our way.' Once, with Caesar, Cleopatra had played the role of a highly educated and fascinating urbane woman (which indeed she was), but with Marc Antony, the other Roman in her life, she opted to perform a very different sort of role and acted the part of a razzle-dazzle showgirl – it spoke to Antony's taste.

Ever the politician, by the time she sailed up the River Cydnus Cleopatra had carefully weighed the evidence and had come to the cold-hearted conclusion that Antony's star was in the ascendancy and that he was worth pursuing. Following Caesar's murder, Antony was indeed following his own path and was slowly but surely separating himself from the clan of the Julii – and its new leader, that priggish, aspirational boy Octavian. Cold, prissy, yet motivated by an intense desire to be the best at everything, Octavian was a nasty piece of work; he had recently been named 'Son of the Divine Julius', and his inflated ego caused Antony to increasingly recoil from his company. Equally, Octavian's antagonism towards Marc Antony, whom he considered base and ignoble, drove Antony into Cleopatra's corner.

For her part, Cleopatra understood what made Antony tick. He was popular with his troops; he drank copious amounts of wine and liked to party; he was an inveterate womanizer; he was poorly educated and lacked intellect; he was a Philhellene but only superficially so; he was vulgar, ambitious, sexy and – as Cleopatra realized – he was completely strapped for cash. She had long been aware of Antony's designs on the east, and although she was not intrinsically invested in eastern affairs *per se*, she knew that she could get Antony on her side if she were to offer him the finances that he needed to invade Parthia – his chief goal in life. In the extraordinary *pompē* with which she wowed Antony at Tarsus – the gilded poop of the ship, the silver oars, the purple perfumed sails, the fancy-dressed extras fanning her with colourful ostrich plumes – Cleopatra played the oriental queen to the letter. 'Venus was come to feast with Bacchus', wrote Plutarch, 'for the common good of Asia'. Antony bought into it all. The twenty-eight-year-old queen, at the height of her charms, dressed as the goddess Aphrodite herself, won over the forty-two-year-old Anthony, dressed in the leopard-skin cloak of the god Dionysus, in an instant and bedded him on the first night. He awoke the next morning a man completely smitten. According to Suetonius, sometime later Antony wrote to Octavian asking why he had turned so hostile – '*Quid te mutauit? Quod reginam ineo?*' 'Why are you so changed towards me? Is it because I fuck the queen?' Marc Antony, who had pursued tepid affairs with a string of rather stolid middle-class Roman mistresses (including one whom he made his wife, the intimidatingly forceful Fulvia), loved the idea of romancing a genuine blue-blooded and passionate queen. He was mesmerized by her and by all the trappings that came with her status.

Antony spent the winter of 41/40 BCE with Cleopatra in Alexandria, and our (*ex post facto*) Roman sources try to outdo each other in picturing his infantile and subservient infatuation with the queen, insisting that Cleopatra could get him to do anything she wished. According to Appian, 'Whatever Cleopatra ordered was done, regardless of laws, human or divine', and he recorded that, in 41 BCE, 'while her sister Arsinoë was a suppliant in the temple of Artemis at Miletus, Antony sent assassins there and put her to death'. The princess had shown herself to be an ambitious and unscrupulous enemy whom the volatile Alexandrians had once seen fit to champion as their queen – and might well do so again. Antony's decision to eliminate her does not require further explanation despite the temptation that Appian presents to see Cleopatra's hand behind the murder: the execution of the princess satisfied Antony and Cleopatra both. Arsinoë IV was buried in Ephesus in a large and splendid tomb (paid for no doubt by wealthy partisans) known as the Octagon, the design of which was based on the plinth of the Pharos Lighthouse. An examination of the remains of a female aged about twenty found there has led to the skeleton's identification as Arsinoë IV. This is certainly plausible, although far from conclusively proved; *if* the skeleton is that of Arsinoë, however, she would be the only member of the Ptolemaic dynasty whose remains have survived to the present day.

Both Antony and Cleopatra had their ulterior motives for entering into a relationship that was both personal and political. Just how much sexual chemistry there was between them is hard to say, but the queen probably looked for ways to bind Antony to her person in a permanent way, and early in 40 BCE she gave birth to Antony's twins. She named them Alexander Helios (after the Greek god of the sun) and Cleopatra Selene (named for the Greek moon goddess). The birth of the children suggests that Cleopatra attempted to reactivate with Marc Antony the political objectives she had begun with Julius Caesar, because it was the sexual bond that she had created with both Romans which helped to ensure the continued existence of the Ptolemaic dynasty and to re-establish, as far as possible, Egypt's former glory. Imperative to her plan were her children, fathered by both men.

But Cleopatra's magnetism was not entirely irresistible, for in the spring of 40 BCE Antony left Egypt for Greece and was not to see her again for four years. It was his wife, Fulvia, who drew Antony to Greece. She had become involved in a serious political quarrel with Octavian over the allocation of lands for war veterans and had fled to Athens, where, after a brief acrimonious meeting with Antony, she died. In the autumn of that year Antony made his peace with Octavian and through the Treaty of Brundisium he confirmed his friendship by marrying Octavian's beloved sister, the beautiful, intelligent and judicious Octavia, a young widow with three children from her marriage to Gaius Claudius Marcellus. With Octavia's hand in marriage came also Octavian's pledge to give over the rulership of the east of the Roman empire to Antony. And so Octavia travelled with Antony to various eastern provinces and settled to live with him in Athens. Antony enjoyed life in the culturally significant city, attending lectures (if not understanding what was said at them) and the rounds of symposia, at which he enjoyed the drinking and dancing more than the philosophical small talk. In their villa in Athens, Octavia cared for her children by Marcellus as well as Antony's two sons by Fulvia, Antyllus and Iullus, and the two daughters she bore to Antony – Antonia Major (born in 38 BCE, the future grandmother of the emperor Nero) and Antonia Minor (born in 36 BCE, the future mother of the emperor Claudius and grandmother of Caligula). Had Octavia given Antony a son at this point in his life, the scales might have tipped in favour of Octavia rather than Cleopatra– and history might have played out very differently.

Cleopatra had given him a son and a daughter, and she had at her disposal the still-impressive treasury of the Ptolemies, and so, restless still to win everlasting renown through the conquest of Parthia, Antony travelled from Athens to Antioch, leaving Octavia and the children behind, ostensibly to meet Cleopatra for summit talks. To sweeten her up before negotiations opened in earnest, Antony bestowed on Cleopatra the entire contents of the library of Pergamum in Asia Minor – some 200,000 volumes – by way of compensation for the destruction of the Alexandrian Great Library a decade before. With the precious papyri came a tranche of Roman lands in the east: the cedar-forested coast of Cilicia (the wood was ideal for shipbuilding), Phoenicia, the rich, spice-bearing lands of Arabia and Judaea (with their abundant date groves to boot), and the ancestral much-fought-over lands of Coele-Syria. Delighted with his thoughtfulness, Cleopatra forgave Antony everything and happily funded his campaign into Parthia.

It was a disaster. Within a few months Antony had lost over a third of his legionaries and close to half of his cavalry to the fierce, well-equipped Parthians. A second campaign was launched in 34 BCE in which Cleopatra accompanied the troops to the very banks of the River Euphrates; Antony was more successful this time and achieved a limited victory over the Parthians, but not enough to break their power. But it was good enough a victory to return with Cleopatra (newly delivered of another of Antony's sons, baby Ptolemy Philadelphus) to Alexandria in triumph.

On a mild autumnal afternoon in 34 BCE, when a slight sea breeze was enough to give life to the myriad colourful flags and banners that decorated Alexandria's fine public buildings, Marc Antony made a public statement that sealed Egypt's fate. The atmosphere was made deliberately festive: the Alexandrians had been promised a carnival. Therefore, every apartment block, every street corner and all the city's fountain houses were strewn with garlands of flowers, and the main thoroughfares which crisscrossed the city had been doused with perfumed water to keep the dust down when the parade passed by. It was also a failed attempt to remove the stink of the hustle and bustle of daily life, for although Alexandria enjoyed a healthy seaside climate and profited from a state-of-the-art drainage system, there were still piles of animal dung and general human waste strewn across the highways and in the back alleys. But Marc Antony had declared it to be party-time and the Alexandrians had put on their best clothes, put flowers in their hair and doused themselves in cooling scents. There was plenty to see: on day one (of the four given over to feasting and merriment) bawdy comedy shows were staged throughout the city; on the second day of the festivities the crowd was treated to a military spectacle as Marc Antony paraded the spoils of his eastern victory in front of Cleopatra, who sat, delighted, on a silver throne beneath a canopy of purple linen. She clapped along to the sound of military drums as enthusiastically as anyone in the crowd. Nobody from Rome had come to observe Antony's triumph. But in Rome, the senate thundered and railed against him. In their eyes, Antony had appropriated an unauthorized and improper Roman triumph and had staged it in Alexandria of all places – Alexandria, that hotbed of decadence!

Day three of the party took place at the harbourside with a jamboree of acrobats, and animal-trainers, and a floating pageant of decorated warships, but the highlight of the festival arrived on day four and took place at the huge gymnasium, with its vast open colonnaded courtyard, at the centre of Alexandria. So expansive was its size that it was used by Ptolemaic royalty for local investiture ceremonies, and in fact, the service which was about to occur there was modelled on the old Egyptian coronation ritual that took place at the sacred city of Memphis. The city dignitaries and representatives of towns and villages all over Egypt who had been summoned there sat on stools in the cool shaded portico, in the company of the ambassadors and dignitaries from around the Mediterranean Sea and beyond. They had each received personal invitations from the palace. A podium of silver had been erected at the centre of the courtyard and a multicoloured tapestry awning had been erected overhead, which cast long shadows on two golden thrones placed side by side beneath it. On a lower rung of the podium were four smaller thrones, also of gold.

Trumpets ripped the air and tympani drums beat out a cere-monial march as the royal family entered the courtyard in litters. Once lowered to the ground, they walked across the carpet of purple to the dais and sat upon the thrones. Cleopatra was dressed in the garb of the goddess Isis: a wrap-around gown of fine white fringed linen knotted beneath her breasts, and a wide collar of lapis lazuli, turquoise and gold that sat around her neck and shoul-ders in the old pharaonic style. On her head the queen wore an impressively large wig of black human hair, curled, ringleted and padded with sheep's wool to make it even bigger. Her eyelids were smeared in kohl in the Egyptian fashion. It is likely that her neck ached from the wig's weight, and beads of sweat gathered at the nape of her neck, for this was not her daily wardrobe – far from it. But Cleopatra liked to look the part at state occasions, and besides, she had always had a penchant for dressing-up. After all, hadn't her Aphrodite costume helped get Antony into her bed all those years ago? For his part, square-jawed Marc Antony loved to play dress-up too and when drunk (which was habitual) he enjoyed nothing more than to drag-up in Cleopatra's frocks, wigs and sashes and, with his messmates in similar attire, to conga through the dark streets of Alexandria at night. But on this day, sitting next to Cleo-patra-Isis as her equal, Antony was done up as the New Dionysus – the god of revelry and theatricality, certainly, but also the god who had, according to mythology, conquered far-off exotic India. He wore a short white tunic and a breastplate of gold, and had an impressive leopard skin hanging from his shoulders; his head was crowned with vine leaves fashioned from thin sheets of pure gold.

Caesarion sat on the throne directly below that of his mother. He was dressed as a Macedonian ruler and his costume harked back to the Ptolemies' ancestry. Next to him sat his half-siblings, the children of Cleopatra and Marc Antony. There was young Alexander, named for the illustrious Macedonian conqueror, who was given the epithet Helios, 'the Sun'; he was dressed in Persian costume, the kind of garments that had been worn in the time of Darius and Xerxes. Next there was Cleopatra Selene, 'the Moon', the only daughter of the royal house, dressed like a miniature Cleopatra (wig and all); and seated next to her was baby Ptolemy Philadelphus dressed up as a minute Armenian king. The costume was very cute, and he was attended by his wet nurse, who was there to keep him quiet and to stop him from wriggling. The royal children played a key role in this public communication of the royal family's prestige: they projected its longevity.

As Antony rose to speak, the crowd, which had been cheering wildly and had worked themselves into a frenzy, hushed in expectation. The bull-necked, broad-shouldered Roman spoke aloud, in Greek (albeit with a thick Latinized accent). He rattled off Cleopatra's many royal titles and listed the lands which came under her rule: Egypt, Cyprus, Libya and Coele-Syria. Next, he proclaimed Caesarion to be the overlord of Egypt, Cyprus, Libya and Syria, while Alexander Helios was championed as king of Armenia and Mesopotamia; young Cleopatra Selene was made ruler of Cyrenaica in North Africa. Finally, little Ptolemy Philadelphus was declared master of Phoenicia, Cilicia and Asia Minor. In other words, that afternoon Marc Antony gifted Cleopatra and her offspring the rulership of the entire eastern Roman world. Much later, Plutarch observed that Antony was at that time reviled at Rome where his actions were read as both 'hammy and arrogant'.

When he had completed his speech, Antony raised Cleopatra to her feet; then he knelt before her and, with bowed head, ennobled her with a final lofty title: Basilissa Cleopatra Thea Neotera, 'Queen Cleopatra, the New Goddess Isis'. By adopting this title, Cleopatra VII was playing a historical game in which she recast herself as her Ptolemaic ancestress, Cleopatra Thea, 'Cleopatra the Goddess', the Ptolemaic princess who had established herself as the greatest female ruler of the Seleucid realm in Syria.

Cleopatra VII was 'reborn' as Isis *and* as Cleopatra Thea simultaneously, for in claiming the name-cum-title 'Cleopatra Thea', Cleopatra VII projected her ambition to rule over foreign territories, the former Seleucid realms, just as the historical Cleopatra Thea had done in actuality. Cleopatra VII clearly knew her dynastic history; she knew all about the earlier Cleopatras – and she was determined to put her history lessons into practice.

More boldness followed. Next, Caesarion stood up and Antony, there at his side, embraced the boy by the shoulders, making it clear to all observers that he possessed the authority of a father and was Caesarion's official *kyrios* ('guardian'), at least until the boy came of age. Lifting the boy's arm high, Antony declared Caesarion to be the 'King of Kings', an ancient and much-honoured title once held by the rulers of the mighty Persian empire. The crowd went wild with pride, shouting out again and again, 'Hail King of Kings! Hail King of Kings!' But when Antony made his final pronouncement – shouting loudly above the crowd – the Alexandrians exploded with joy, for the Roman declared Cleopatra to be the 'Queen of Kings'.

Many centuries later, the celebrated Alexandrian-Greek poet Constantine Cavafy (1863–1933), in one of his best works, *Alexandrian Kings*, reflected upon the ceremonial of that day, which has been dubbed the 'Donations of Alexandria' by countless scholars. Ever alive to the feelings and impetuses of the peoples of antiquity, Cavafy speculated on what the ceremonial must have meant for the thousands of the city's resident Greeks, Egyptians and Jews who watched Antony dole out half of the Roman empire to his lover and her offspring. Cavafy conjectured:

> The Alexandrians of course understood
> that those were theatrical words.
> But the day was warm and poetic . . .
> and the Alexandrians enjoyed the ceremony,
> and got enthusiastic, and cheered . . .
> but they knew all too well what all this pomp was worth,
> what hollow words these kingships were.

The canniest of the observers of the 'Donations' ceremony must have realized that Antony's largess did not correspond with political realities. What he gave away to Cleopatra and her children was not his to give. It is true that by this time Roman generals in the east had been making and unmaking 'client kings' for decades, but this situation was different, because the 'Donations of Alexandria' laid claim to territories already under Roman administration and even to those outside of Rome's dominion. More than anything, though, the breathtaking spectacle of the Alexandrian *mise-en-scène* had been undertaken to reconfirmed Caesarion's place in the dynastic line-up of the Ptolemaic house and in the family of the Julii. The importance of the support he received from Marc Antony cannot be underestimated. After all, there is no evidence to show that Antony ever attempted to give any of his sons by Cleopatra (or the two boys born to him by his Roman wife, Fulvia) precedence over Octavian, the legal Roman heir of Julius Caesar. By 34 BCE Antony's vision of rulership was, to all intents and purposes, Cleopatra's vision. Antony, the Roman strongman in the east, had endorsed and championed the dual monarchy of Cleopatra and Caesarion and looked to a future when they, and he, would rule the world – in fact, her favourite oath became: 'As surely as I shall dispense justice on the Roman Capitol.' For Cleopatra, the events of 34 BCE were to prove climactic, for it was at this point in her already remarkable life that she truly thought she had the chance of being the queen of the world.

Probably as part of the festivities of 34 BCE, Antony and Cleopatra had their union made legal by marriage. Coins were issued in Antioch celebrating Cleopatra as the Basilissa Cleopatra Thea, and they were disseminated throughout the Levant and Asia Minor as a symbol of her desire to dominate the Roman east. Soon after the Donations ceremony, Cleopatra began the construction of a temple for Antony on the coast, close to the large harbour of Alexandria, consisting of a monumental square, a cult enclosure and a sanctuary where Antony was worshipped as Dionysus. In the middle of the square, Cleopatra erected a huge antique obelisk (it now stands in St Peter's Square in Vatican City, Rome). Very recently, near the site of the temple, archaeologists discovered a statue-base which had been dedicated to Marc Antony by one of his acolytes on 28 December 34 BCE. The dedication reads: 'To Antony, the Great, the Inimitable God and Benefactor.' A decade after Caesar's assassination, when all had looked so bleak, Cleopatra had risen phoenix-like from the ashes of Caesar's funerary pyre, with all this exciting talk of new territories, temples and divinity.

Of course, the Donations of Alexandria, the Antioch coins and the new divine temples were fantasies, mere charades, a spectacular costume drama, and nothing more. Antony and Cleopatra were playing a dangerous game, and their extravagant Alexandrian masquerade did nothing to settle the anti-Egyptian hatred that was growing exponentially in Rome and around the Mediterranean. After more than a decade of having Cleopatra in their lives, the Romans decided that they had stomached enough of Egypt's harlot-queen and her oriental ways; it was time for her to know her place, time for Rome to flex its muscle.

*

Despite Antony's snubs and adulteries, Octavia had remained his unswervingly devoted wife, but after he had spent months away from Athens, it became clear that she had been repudiated by her husband. With Antony reconciled to his Egyptian paramour in Alexandria, Octavia had no choice but to swallow her pride, close the villa in Athens, gather up all the children and take ship to Rome. As she soon as she entered the city she was met by her brother, Octavian, who insisted on making a public uproar out of Octavia's shame. He railed against Antony, whom he accused of maltreating his sister, who (he knew) was greatly loved in Rome, and garnered the support of Romans of high and low birth. In 132 BCE Antony formally divorced Octavia, thereby forcing Rome to recognize that his relationship with Cleopatra was the only one Antony considered legitimate; to emphasize the point Antony put the queen's name and image on his official Roman coinage, the silver denarii that circulated widely around the Mediterranean, thereby terminating any further pretence that his allegiance was to Rome.

Octavian now had licence to view Antony's actions not only as an insult to his dear sister but as an open declaration of war. When he learned that Antony's will, updated now and kept in Rome, was in the custodianship of the Vestal Virgins, he defied all human and divine statutes by forcing the priestesses to hand the document over to him. He read it aloud before the senate and the people, and the Romans were mortified by its contents. The will stressed that Antony acknowledged Caesarion as the son of Julius Caesar and upheld all the titles bestowed on the young pharaoh and his siblings at the Donations of Alexandria ceremony. Most damning, though, was Antony's instruction that his body was to be laid to rest in his beloved Alexandria, next to Cleopatra, even if he should die in Rome. The xenophobic hysteria whipped up in Rome because of the will can still be felt in the (mostly fictitious) propaganda penned by Virgil, Propertius and other poets, which was largely commissioned or supported by Octavian. Cleopatra was cast was a lascivious whore, a drunken nymphomaniac who even allowed her house slaves to take their pleasure on her. She acted that way because her brain was permanently 'soused in Mareotic wine', claimed Horace. From now on, the Romans were prepared to think of Cleopatra only as a 'ruinous monster' and a 'calamitous danger'. Perhaps the best example of the Roman anti-Cleopatran propaganda comes not from the elegant satiric Latin verses of the poets but in the form of a little terracotta oil lamp. Depicted on it is a caricatured diadem-wearing Cleopatra, stark naked and standing on the back of a startled-looking crocodile (the creature was Roman shorthand for 'Egypt'), clutching a date-palm frond in her left hand. Uninhibited and lustful, the queen is shown squatting down over an enormous dildo, the only thing big enough to give her any pleasure. The lamp speaks more eloquently of the Roman fantasy of Cleopatra than Virgil's verses ever could. Still, Octavian's portrayal as the *vindex libertatis*, the 'Vindicator of the Liberty of the Roman People', had been established, ready to chime with the noble ideology of the later Roman principate which he would lead as emperor.

Cleopatra, but not Antony, was declared by Octavian to be an enemy (*hostis*) of the Roman state at the end of the summer of 32 BCE. He cleverly staged-managed the people's ire and directed all their fears and hostilities against Cleopatra, who was blamed for having brought the once-noble Antony, who had been a Roman general of great standing, under her spell through the practice of the dark arts of witchcraft. The animal-headed demons she worshipped, it was said, had been evoked and propitiated to unman Antony and to make him a prisoner of Cleopatra's lust. His own addiction to soft-living (he was said by Dio to have urinated into a 'golden piss-pot, an outrage at which even Cleopatra would blench') was put down to Egyptian witchcraft too. Octavian spread the lie that Cleopatra was planning an imminent attack on Rome using all the demonic forces at her disposal, and in propagating this vision of Armageddon, he managed to transform the civil war between himself and Antony into an international conflict between Rome and the Ptolemaic kingdom.

In the spring of 31 BCE, when war broke out, Antony and Cleopatra were temporarily stationed in Greece. Cleopatra's only interest lay in defending Egypt from invasion – she had no interest in marching on Rome, as Octavian's propaganda alleged. But her influence on the war would be considerable and, in the long run, damaging, for it was she who was to blame for Antony's blunder in failing to attack Octavian on Italian soil, even though his was by far the superior military force. Cleopatra favoured instead a defensive tactic. She insisted that Egypt should be protected by a wall of ships that stretched from Cyrene in North Africa all the way to the Ionian Sea; in her mind, the war was to be entirely fought at sea. Accordingly, Antony, who possessed 500 ships and 70,000 infantrymen, made his camp on a headland in Acarnania in western Greece, at the entrance of the Gulf of Ambracia. The place was known as Actium, 'the promontory.'

Octavian sailed east with about 100 ships and landed in Dalmatia on the eastern shore of the Adriatic Sea. He mustered 24 legions, or 120,000 soldiers, and with this army he marched to the south and established a bridgehead at the Gulf of Ambracia, immediately north of the entrance to Actium. Simultaneously, Octavian's best friend, loyal right-hand man and later son-in-law, Marcus Vispanius Agrippa – a truly gifted admiral – sailed to the western Peloponnese with 300 war galleys and occupied positions along the coastline of Greece, cutting off Antony's line of communication and making it difficult for his immense army to get supplies. Next, Agrippa sailed to the north, established another important base at Patras, and finally joined Octavian at Actium. Hunger was beginning to wear out Antony's men, a fact which forced him to fight at sea. He had no choice but to break out from the Gulf of Ambracia. This was to Octavian's advantage, for unlike Agrippa, Marc Antony had no sea legs and had never shown himself to be a capable commander at sea.

During the afternoon of 2 September 31 BCE, when the northern winds, which are common on the Mediterranean Sea, gathered momentum, the decisive battle was fought. Cleopatra succeeding in breaking through Agrippa's blockade with sixty fast-moving ships. This move may have saved Cleopatra's life, but it was an unadulterated catastrophe for Antony, for it left him alone to battle Octavian and Agrippa, leading to the loss of Macedonia, Greece and Asia Minor to Octavian. Cleopatra, meanwhile, returned to Egypt and entered the harbour of Alexandria accompanied by victory songs. But she was unable to suppress the news of her defeat at Actium, nor the fact that the treasury had been almost emptied and that Egypt was practically penniless.

Fleeing Actium, Antony went to Cyrenaica to organize a counterattack against Octavian. The governor of Cyrenaica, Pinarius Scarpus, who had been installed in the office by Antony, switched sides and gave his loyalty to Octavian, and Antony was driven back out into the Mediterranean Sea. Dejected and forlorn, Antony returned to Alexandria. When he met with Cleopatra again in the royal palace, they pretended that all was well and made a great show of celebrating Caesarion's coming-of-age with banquets and royal spectacles. But things were far from normal. There was also a flurry of diplomatic activity with Octavian during which Cleopatra even offered up her own royal insignia in return for a guarantee that the throne of Egypt would remain in the hands of her children. Should that fail, Cleopatra had other ideas: she had the remains of her naval ships hauled across the eastern desert to the Red Sea, where they were made ready to carry Caesarion away to India. But before they could be used, the ships were burned by locals who hoped to find favour with Octavian.

In the spring of 30 BCE, Octavian's armies in the east and west moved against Egypt. He entered the country from Syria through Pelusium, the town which had seen so many troops coming and going over the centuries. Antony tried to repel Octavian just east of Alexandria, but when his troops deserted him for Octavian, Antony knew that he was all but finished. On 1 August 30 BCE Octavian and his forces entered Alexandria. What happened next is open to debate.

Allegedly Cleopatra took shelter in her mausoleum with her most trusted female maidservants, Charmian and Iras, although Cassius Dio maintains that that she also had a eunuch with her and that she used him to take a message to Antony, leading him to believe she had already taken her own life. Straight away, insists Dio, Antony 'asked one of the bystanders to slay him; but when the man drew his sword and slew himself, Antony wished to imitate his courage and so gave himself a wound and fell upon his face, causing the bystanders to believe that he was dead? Plutarch maintained that Antony plunged a sword into his stomach, but bungled the death blow and, learning that Cleopatra lived still, was dragged, writhing in agony, to the queen's mausoleum. He died there in her arms. He was fifty-two years old.

Centuries later, Plutarch envisaged the lovelorn Cleopatra mourning her Antony with all the passion she could muster (his account provided Shakespeare with inspiration for some of his greatest lines). Yet as tempting as it is to envisage Antony's death through the prism of a romantic tragedy, was it passionate love for Cleopatra that drove him to suicide? Although a fine story, it is unlikely. More probably, Antony's suicide was a cold pragmatic move of his own volition. He knew the shameful fate that awaited him – after all, had he not played a role in having Cicero's head and hand pinned to the speaker's podium in the city of Rome for all to witness? A public execution for his transgressions against Octavian and Rome, and a post-death humiliation, were all that awaited him. Antony's suicide was a strategic means to avoid a more disgraceful, overtly public killing.

Immediately after Octavian had entered Alexandria, he assigned one of his men, Cornelius Gallus, the task of completing and renaming Antony's temple at the harbourside; a few short weeks later, a Latin inscription on the obelisk there announced that the assignment had been carried out. The temple courtyard was now called the Forum Iulium, while the sanctuary was called in Greek the Sebasteion or, more precisely, in Latin the Caesareum. Thus was Rome's supremacy and sovereignty over Egypt stamped into the urban environment of Alexandria. The legend of Cleopatra's dominion over Antony became essential in Octavian's denigration campaign against Antony in the late 30s BCE and in the years after Actium. After all, Cleopatra had robbed Antony of his Romanness and his manliness, as Seneca was to write some decades later:

> The defeated foe made for the Nile
> On ships geared for flight – but death was near.
> Again, incestuous Egypt drank a Roman
> Leader's blood and now entombs weighty ghosts.
> Interred there was a civil war long waged with all impiety.

Octavian magnanimously permitted Cleopatra to bury Antony with royal honours and allowed her to re-enter her palace and live there, under Roman guard. He had her watched day and night, desperately wanting her to be kept alive so that she might be paraded through Rome in the triumphal procession which would certainly happen on his return to Rome. Flashbacks of the degrading spectacle of her sister Arsinoē dragged behind Julius Caesar's chariot must have haunted Cleopatra, and according to the long-lost report of her personal physician, Olympus, who was with the queen and wrote an account of her last days (they formed perhaps the basis of Plutarch's story), rather than suffer the humiliation endured by Arsinoē, she attempted to starve herself to death. Octavian threatened her with reprisals against her children and so, tentatively, Cleopatra began to eat and drink once more. It appears that it was not until all attempts at negotiating with Octavian had failed that Cleopatra was forced to find a better way to spoil Octavian's triumph.

On 10 or 12 August 30 BCE Cleopatra VII took her own life. The soldiers stationed close to her private quarters found Cleopatra dead in her bed and her two maidservants on the brink of death, one of them adjusting the crown on the queen's head – for Cleopatra had put on the robes of Isis before she died. Olympus seems to have written nothing about the manner of the queen's death, and the earliest report we have was penned by the historian Strabo, who wrote ten to forty-eight years after the event, although he was possibly in Alexandria at the time of Cleopatra's demise. He noted that her suicide tactic was uncertain: '[S]he put herself to death secretly, while in prison, by the bite of an asp or by applying a poisonous ointment', he wrote. Later, Dio commented that '[n]o one knows clearly in what way she perished, for the only marks on her body were slight pricks on the arm', but many Roman historians began to allege that she died via the bite of an asp. It was Plutarch who related the fullest version of the story, describing how Charmian and Iras brought a highly venomous Egyptian cobra to the queen by hiding it from the Roman guards in a basket of figs. But even Plutarch hedges his bets in his account, for he also implied that Cleopatra had used 'an implement' (*knestis*) – perhaps a hair-comb – to introduce the deadly toxin into her blood stream by scratching open her skin – thereby paying homage to Dio's earlier account. By far the most popular belief at the time, and for centuries afterwards, was that she allowed herself to be bitten by a snake; over time, the one asp became two as the death of Cleopatra entered into dramatic, legendary and finally mythical territory. According to Suetonius in his *Life of Augustus* (*c.* 119 CE), Octavian was enraged that Cleopatra had cheated him of a splendid victory procession by her decision to die at her own hand, and he tried to have the poison sucked from the wound by a Libyan snake charmer. The tactic was useless; the poison had already corrupted the blood and the Libyan could not bring Cleopatra back to life.

For a woman so skilled at self-promotion, death-by-cobra would certainly have been a fitting symbol for Cleopatra VII's dramatic finale, since it was the cobra – the uraeus – that had adorned the crowns worn by pharaohs and queens for millennia. The uraeus was the eye of the sun god Re, and sat there on the pharaoh's brow ready to strike at the enemies of Egypt and spit venom at those who disrupted the harmony of the cosmos. The propagandistic manner of Cleopatra's death was – as her hand-maid Charmian voiced with her own dying breath – 'one fitting for a queen descended from so many rulers'.

Octavian had Cleopatra buried with Antony in the tomb that the queen had prepared, although their graves have never been found and probably lie deep beneath the Mediterranean Sea, somewhere off the coast of Alexandria. Caesarion lived on as Ptolemy XV for a mere eighteen more days until he was butchered without compunction on the orders of Octavian, who would soon rename himself Augustus, in remembrance of the month in which he defeated Cleopatra. On 30 August 30 BCE, Octavian officially declared that Cleopatra's dynasty was finished. With the last of the Cleopatras, the final Ptolemaic queen, went the whole long and glorious world of the Hellenistic monarchs – reminding us that, as Arnold Toynbee once confirmed, 'Civilizations die from suicide, not by murder.'

The year 30 BCE was a decisive watershed in the history of the world. While Charmian's fitting epithet for Cleopatra VII encapsulated the end of the queen's dynasty, the wider significance of Cleopatra's death was expressed in more explicit and extreme terms by the Roman author Lucian, who, many decades after Cleopatra's suicide, wrote about her in an essay which explored the importance of studying the past and writing history. A good historian, Lucian argued, needs to master many subjects; any self-respecting would-be antiquarian must therefore know that 'his entire stock-in-trade is ancient history' and must have 'the capacity to call episodes to mind readily and to epitomize them with appropriate solemnity'. And what, according to Lucian, were the chronological parameters of history? What timespan would it be best for an aspiring historian to know? Lucian was clear: history began 'right from the time of Chaos and the moment when the universe was created'. And from that point on, the historian 'must know everything that happened – right down to the story of Cleopatra the Egyptian'. As far as Lucian was concerned, the death of Cleopatra VII brought history to an end. Nothing that happened after the queen's demise was worth knowing and certainly not worth writing about. History stopped in the secrecy and mystery of Cleopatra's last moments. Symbolized by her corpse, rendered unreadable by means of an unknown and invisible poison, historical narrative has failed to capture her any more than Octavian ever did.

Epilogue

'How unlike, how *very* unlike the home life of
our own dear queen . . .'

– Anonymous Englishman, on seeing
Sarah Bernhardt's performance as Cleopatra, 1895.

Constantine Cavafy was born, bred, lived and died in Alexandria
– he spent only a very short period of his life away from his home
city, first in London and Liverpool and then in Constantinople.
He was a civil servant from a good family and spoke English and
French fluently; a staunch Anglophile, he spoke his native Greek
with a British accent. In many respects, Cavafy felt like an outsider all his life. A Greek living far from Greece, a humdrum civil
servant with the soul of a great artist, he was also homosexual in a
world of heterosexual norms and laws (his poems are infused with
the perfumes of homoeroticism). He was devoted to the study
of ancient history and had an avid, obsessive eye for historical
nuance and detail. Etienne Combe, the last European director of
the Library of Alexandria in the 1930s, once recalled how Cavafy
would come to the Library almost every day and borrow many
history books; he had a great penchant for taking out heavy tomes
of inscriptions, it was observed. He loved old stones and the words
chiselled into them, so much so that ancient epigraphy enters his
poetic verses themselves. Take, for instance, the opening stanza of
his dazzling 1918 work *Caesarion*, a poem about Cleopatra VII's
ill-fated son by Julius Caesar:

Partly to throw some light on a particular period,
partly to kill an hour or so,
yesterday evening I picked up and read
a tome of inscriptions about the Ptolemies.
The exuberant praise and flattery follow a set pattern
for each of them. All are wonderful,
glorious, strong, benevolent;
everything they do is wisdom-filled.
As for the women of the house, the Berenices and the
    Cleopatras,
All of them too are awe-inspiring.

The poem shows us Cavafy the historian at work. But as a history-obsessive, Cavafy was never drawn to those moments in ancient history that others have found so compulsive – the 'Glory that was Greece', embodied in the Periclean age of Athens, or the 'Splendour that was Rome' of the Caesars. Rather, Cavafy found his inspiration in the long post-classical period of Greek history, and especially in the Ptolemaic age, which, although regarded as a period of decline by scholars, was for Cavafy a period of glory. The Ptolemaic period had witnessed the rise to prominence of Cavafy's beloved city and, as a proud Alexandrian, the era of Greek rule of Egypt spoke directly to him, very personally, like no other time in history. Cavafy felt the city's decay in modern times acutely, and his dolour was reflected in the choices he made for the settings of his history poems, each of which reflects the aftermath of ages of former brilliance or else is set in tottering times of socio-cultural turmoil, when governments collapse, kingdoms fall and cultures fade away forever. Here is the rest of *Caesarion*:

When I managed to find the date in question,
I'd have put the book away, but a passing mention
of King Caesarion, a footnote really,
suddenly caught my eye . . .
Ah, and there you stood, with that ambiguous
beauty of yours. And since history has devoted
very few lines to you, I had more liberty

to craft you in my mind's eye . . .
I made you striking, capable of deep emotion.
My imagining gave your face a handsome,
Dreamlike quality. In fact, I imagined you
so clearly last night, that when my lamp
went out (I let it go out on purpose)
I actually thought you had entered into my room;
There you were, standing before me,
just as you would have appeared in conquered Alexandria,
drained and weary, perfect in your sorrow,
still hoping for clemency from those cruel men
who kept on whispering 'too many Caesars'.

During the seventy years of his life, Cavafy witnessed a steady decline in the fortunes of once-glorious Alexandria. The lively, multiethnic mix of Egyptians, Greeks, Jews, Italians and Syrians that had been the city's calling card for centuries was dying. The fall of the Ottoman empire after the First World War only quickened its demise and Alexandria went from being a hub of imperial enlightenment to a colonial backwater. In less than half a century, Alexandria had simply lost its reputation, its identity, its panache, and this is why Cavafy clung to the image of Alexandria's Golden Age, when, under the three centuries of Ptolemaic rule, she sparkled so brilliantly.

The final century of Ptolemaic rule in Alexandria, when the Cleopatras reigned supreme, resonated very deeply and intimately with Cavafy, and his Ptolemaic-themed poems, of which there is a good crop, resonate with his favourite theme: decline and fall. They anticipate the final collapse of the last of the glorious Hellenistic monarchies and the rise to power of another, far more menacing, Mediterranean superpower – Rome. This is why, in the opening stanza of *Caesarion*, Cavafy depicts the Ptolemaic kings and queens as he does: their inscriptions insist that they were 'wonderful, glorious, strong, benevolent . . . wisdom-filled'. But history – as we now know – tells a less glorious story and in the rest of the poem, Cavafy shows that despite the bravado, the puffed-up hyperbole of self-belief, ultimately the Ptolemaic dynasty fell because it had come to be embodied by one good-looking young man, a boy born to notorious parents and considered by his enemies too dangerous to live. The end of the Hellenistic world came not with the suicide of Cleopatra, says Cavafy, but through the murder of a beautiful teenage boy, lost to history.

An unpublished poem of Cavafy's, dated November 1923, called 'The Dynasty' takes up the theme of the decline of the world of the Ptolemies and Cleopatras and highlights how that deterioration was emphasized at the time through the nicknames the Alexandrian mob so enthusiastically bestowed on their rulers (a convention we have been following in this book too):

> Who were Potbelly's kids? There was Chickpea, dishonourably
> kicked out of Alexandria, who headed to Cyprus.
> And the Son of the Cunt, heading straight from Cyprus,
> seizes Alexandria. All of this is planned by
> that Cunt herself. The Alexandrians,
> who love to ridicule, gave them the right names, no mistake.
> And it's better to call them 'Son of the Cunt',
> 'Potbelly', 'Chickpea' and 'The Cunt'
> Rather than 'Ptolemy', rather than 'Cleopatra'.

In this remarkable little poem, Cavafy brings the towering figures of history – all those god-kings and goddess-queens – crashing down from the lofty heights of their self-made pedestals; he exposes them as the flawed individuals they really were through the vulgar monikers by which they were commonly known. Understanding the haughty out-of-reach Cleopatras and Ptolemies – the Soters and Euergetes – as living human beings is the only way to understand the motivations of this truly dysfunctional ruling family, so Cavafy insists; take away their crowns and regalia and we are left with a group of very flawed and damaged individuals trying to make sense of life in a truly bizarre world.

Accordingly, in our study we have explored the fact that, as individual women and men, the Cleopatras and the Ptolemies had their separate idiosyncratic motivations, agendas and character traits which shifted course as their lives developed, their ideas morphed and their circumstances changed over the years. The Cleopatras and their menfolk were no more constant in their reactions to their life experiences than we are in ours, and if we want to understand their impulses, we must allow room for their priorities to have changed, their personalities to have developed and for emotions to have played a crucial role in their experiences of life. The Cleopatras must have felt elation, fear, uncertainty, excitement, hatred, shame, grief, and any number of other sentiments that rendered them human beings. These women lived full and dramatic lives, on a par with the plotlines of the very best Verdi operas or the most thrilling Latin American TV soaps. Perhaps this is why the Cleopatras have not fared well in scholarship: they are simply too melodramatic. In 1899, when John Pentland Mahaffy published his massive *History of Egypt under the Ptolemaic Dynasty*, he had this to say of the Cleopatras:

> These ladies show the usual features ascribed to Ptolemaic princesses – great power and wealth; mutual hatred; disregard of all ties of family and affection; their dearest object, fratricide – such pictures of depravity as make any reasonable man pause and ask whether human nature had deserted these women, and the Hyrcanian tiger of the poet taken its place.

The Cleopatras' worst crime? Being women. And worse still, being women with genuine power to wield. Mahaffy's conception of the Cleopatras as uncontrolled viragos was upheld by Edwyn Bevan in his 1902 history of the Seleucid dynasty, when he wrote of Cleopatra Thea, for example, that 'she became a politician whose heart was dead.' Elsewhere in his 1927 history of the Ptolemies, Bevan makes the Cleopatras into unfeeling monsters, insisting that 'the love of power seems to have overridden natural affection.' The historian Michael Rostovtzeff, writing in 1941, calls them 'ambitious and cruel,' while in a famous 1958 study of the Ptolemies, Hans Volkmann referred to the Cleopatras simply as 'diabolical.' The historiographic tradition, then, has attempted to make the Cleopatras either erotic sexualized fantasies (Cleopatra VII) or harridan wives and domineering mothers (the others). And yet every gender stereotype slung at them says more about the history of scholarship than about the women themselves. The mixed emotions of male commentators through time reveal perhaps more than anything else the deeply contested nature of female rulership.

That the Cleopatras lived lives of high melodrama can in part be explained by the vagaries of their own royal upbringing as they struggled to endure or survive marriage, betrayal, murder, plots, violence and loss. What, for example, did the Cleopatras *really* feel about royal incest? Disgust, desire, dignity, or duty? What was the effect on a young princess of knowing that sexual intercourse with a family relative was her lot in life? The Ptolemaic royal family was clearly a site for many sorts of feelings, and given that the domestic nexus was so closely allied to the world of politics, emotional expectations operated between these two ancillary areas. The territorial ambitions of the Hellenistic dynasties were, for rulers like Cleopatra Thea and Cleopatra VII, family matters. In their minds the two potentially separate emotional communities of home life and national and international politics naturally converged.

Cleopatra III alone makes for an interesting psychological case study. By the time of her murder at the hands of her youngest, best-loved son, Ptolemy X, Cleopatra III had conspired with her uncle/stepfather/husband to drive her mother from the marital bed and had sent three daughters into a war zone from which none escaped alive; she had made war upon one son and had plotted against the life of the other; she had sent her infant grandsons out of Egypt and they had spent their formative lives as hostages of an enemy power. This catalogue of misdemeanours might have been informed by the fact that as a teenager, Cleopatra III herself had experienced the death of her father in battle and had seen the murder of her younger brother, Ptolemy VII, who was likely killed by the man whom her widowed mother then willingly married and took to bed; she had known what hardship it was for a woman to stand alone in a patriarchal world and had needed to employ the strength of mind to create for herself a niche in which she could survive. This came via uncle Potbelly, and to ensure her existence in the dynastic system, she gave him what he most needed at the time, the only thing she had of value – her fecundity. Cleopatra III was no Lolita figure and no Lady Macbeth either; psychologically scarred and emotionally battered, she was, however, a survivor.

We have explored how Cleopatra I Syra, the brilliant, capable and astute mother of the equally remarkable Cleopatra II, provided the blueprint for what a queen was expected to do, could do in reality and was able to get away with when push came to shove. In turn, we saw that Cleopatra II's own influence undoubtedly extended to her Ptolemaic daughters and, later, to her granddaughters, all of whom were young women at the time of her death but who had resided with her at the court of Alexandria for at least a decade. The war-like Cleopatra IV, for instance, is often compared in character with her mother, Cleopatra III, but it was perhaps her grandmother Cleopatra II, who had, in her younger life, raised armies and ousted kings from their thrones, who inspired the princess to her own acts of dynastic derring-do. By acknowledging this kind of matriarchal legacy, we can begin to explore how princesses learned to be queens and how cultural and personal experiences informed decisions that affected both their family and the realm.

How far sexual allure was exercised for its own sake by the Cleopatras, and how much was exercised in pursuit of power, we will never know. Cleopatra VII was said to be a great beauty by some of her admirers (and detractors), but the surviving iconography – a far from flattering series of coin portraits in which she looks like Marc Antony in drag, and a few portrait busts ascribed with degrees of certainty to Cleopatra – suggests neither a raving beauty nor a femme fatale. If we look at the lives of the Cleopatras *en masse*, they come across as passionate, yet not, in any sense, promiscuous. These women were driven not by nymphomania but by power. They craved it and they used the men in their lives to get it. The Cleopatras were pragmatic about their personal relationships: if, after the Battle of Pharsalus in 48 BCE, Pompey had come calling victorious at Alexandria rather than Caesar, there can be little doubt that Cleopatra VII would have made a beeline for him and thrown in her lot with him instead. Stories are told that after Antony's death, with his corpse still warm, the thirty-nine-year-old Cleopatra made one last desperate pass at young Octavian, and had he reciprocated, she would have no doubt set to work on him too. As a shrewd politician, Cleopatra VII had tremendous respect for Julius Caesar's intellect and vision (his wit matched her own), whereas Marc Antony simply annoyed her. But she made the best of him and used vulgar bait – love-boats, dressing-up games and all-night binges – in order to catch a vulgar man.

Family mattered in the world of the Hellenistic dynasts. Within the Ptolemaic and Seleucid houses, we have noted how the Cleopatras were tightly interrelated as mothers, daughters, sisters, half-sisters and nieces. As a family they were hereditarily close, if not necessarily loving. To be candid, most Cleopatras were antagonistic to the other women of their bloodline – and some were out-and-out hostile, seeking to do the most harm to their closest kith and kin. Within the Ptolemaic royal house, close family members often proved to be the most dangerous enemies of all, and the labyrinthine palaces of the Ptolemies were hotbeds for nurturing political cliques, fostering plots, stirring up revolts and devising murders.

The Cleopatras inhabited a world of intricately interconnected liaisons. Some of the Cleopatras shared the same royal husband – usually a brother or an uncle or even a father – and became king-makers. Some of the Cleopatras plotted the overthrow of husbands, brothers or sons and were therefore king-breakers too. Some of the Cleopatras bullied their way to power. Some slept their way to the top. Some of the Cleopatras led armies into war and other Cleopatras commanded fleets of ships. Some of the Cleopatras murdered other Cleopatras. All the Cleopatras craved power. And all the Cleopatras, often against all odds, eventually wielded power. Most of them (but not all) turned out to be impressive rulers.

Many of the Cleopatras suffered foolish, inept or infantile male co-rulers. Cleopatra Syra had to tolerate the imbecilic decisions of her warmongering husband, Ptolemy V, although diplomatically she stood by his side and gained well-deserved divine honours as a consequence. Subsequently, at his death, she became the undisputed matriarch of the house and the dynasty's first queen-regent. Neither of Cleopatra III's co-rulers, her two sons, proved to have much flair for governance – as Cleopatra V Berenice III found out when she acquired them both as throne-partners too. In Syria, Cleopatra Thea's co-rulers included the dreadfully inept Alexander Balas and the unconscionable Demetrius II, but she had the excellent Antiochus XVII to compensate for them. Grypus and Kyzikenos brought nothing but bad luck to the successive Cleopatras who shared their beds.

Some of the Cleopatras were much better matched with their husbands in terms of vision, energy and capabilities though. Certainly, Cleopatra II benefitted from a good and productive personal and political relationship with Ptolemy VI, and Cleopatra III and Potbelly enjoyed a long working partnership even though there were, for many decades, three in their marriage. As king and queen and husband and wife, Potbelly and Cleopatra III had the advantage of mutual esteem and respect; it was a strange marriage, but somehow it worked. Even Cleopatra VI Tryphaina's marriage to her half-brother, Fluter, can be said to have been good, if undramatic.

Exploring the motivations and the psychological drives which compelled each of the Cleopatras to be the women they became is not an easy job for any historian because there is a tremendous gap in the norms of behaviour and the cultural expectations of womanhood between Hellenistic Egypt and our own time. Nonetheless, we have sought out more human portraits for our protagonists and, as a tribute to Cavafy's perceptive reading of the past, this book has attempted to make the women of the Ptolemaic royal house as human as possible. We have tried to understand what motivated them and to comprehend how they saw themselves. One thing is clear: simply by their stamina and the force of their personalities, the Cleopatras warrant their place in Egypt's noble history.

Without any doubt, sensationalism or hyperbole, the Cleopatras count among history's most significant ruling women. Each of them offers a rich biography and each, in her own way, was instrumental to the history of her time. Certainly, the Cleopatras deserve to be recognized as significant players in the politics of the Hellenistic world and, indeed, in the global history of queenship. Each Cleopatra was a bespoke creation of her own crafting – moulded, certainly, by the mores and conditions of the times in which they lived, yet unified in their abilities as women rulers and as female figureheads. For all the fascination that orbits around her, Cleopatra VII was *not* unique to the history of the Ptolemaic dynasty; in fact, she is best understood in the familial, powerfully female context that created her. Cleopatra VII comes into her own when we understood that she was one of a long line of extraordinary ruling women – that she was one of the Cleopatras.

Useful Materials

A Note on the Sources

When it comes to researching and writing histories of the world of the Cleopatras – the Hellenistic period, as it is known in scholarship – academics must face up to new realities: the source materials which are needed for the job come in a staggering variety of types and genres, and the historian needs to grapple with multiple kinds of evidence and develop the skills needed to deal with them. Historians of classical Greece traditionally hone their craft through the careful critical study of dominating historiographic texts – the writings of Herodotus, Thucydides and Xenophon – the Big Three of ancient Greek history-writing. But no such works exist for the Hellenistic period; there is not a handy historiographic collection of 'must-reads' for the era. The closest we get to the notion of a Hellenistic narrative history is the work of Polybius (200–118 BCE), whose account of the rise of Rome and the Roman interaction with the Hellenistic kingdoms appeared in the second century BCE. Although much of Polybius' text is lost and only the first five books are intact, some of the lost portions are reflected in the Latin writings of the Roman historian Livy (59 BCE– CE 17), who used Polybius as a major source for his own work. Besides which, Polybius' account of Rome's ascendency stops at 146 BCE, covering only the opening decades of the period covered by this book, so as a historian of the High Hellenistic period – as we might term the first century BCE, the age of the Cleopatras – he is of very limited use.

The most important source after Polybius is Diodorus Siculus, who wrote his world history, the *Bibliotheca Historica*, at the time of

Julius Caesar and Augustus. Apart from occasional remarks, mainly of a moralizing nature, Diodorus was normally content to reproduce his sources, keeping to one author for a long period (with here and there a cross-reference to a divergent view in a second source). Hence the value of any passage in Diodorus is limited to that of its source (if known). His dates are often inconsistent and must be treated with caution.

We know too that Trogus Pompeius, a Gaul, wrote a universal history in forty-four books entitled *Historiae Philippicae*, although this huge work survives only in the *prologi* (list of contents) and an *epitome* (summary) made by M. Junianus Justinus (Justin), who wrote at some date before or during the lifetime of St Augustine, around CE 390. The *epitome* of Trogus' expansive history is a Latin abridgement of selected quotations of the larger Greek work in which Justin permitted himself considerable freedom of digression, which, in the end, produced an idiosyncratic anthology of key events in the history of the Hellenistic world. Justin wrote for a Roman audience fixated on sensationalism, and his *epitome*, by and large, offers a lurid vision of the period: his pages are packed with the juicy, explicit and shocking exploits of Oriental kings and queens. The Cleopatras appear as vicious stereotypes in Justin's decidedly dubious work, but their presence there at all confirms that centuries after their dynasty had fallen they were still regarded as intriguing, transgressive queens.

Despite the lack of a solid surviving narrative history of the Cleopatras and their era, there is much source material we can turn to by way of compensation, for the period is defined by the wealth of archaeological, artistic and – of particular abundance – epigraphic evidence which has come down to us. The Greeks had a liking for inscriptions, a fondness which is testified through the tens of thousands of inscribed texts that survive from the cities of the Hellenistic East. They come in the shape of long (and frequently dense) civic decrees, treaties and royal proclamations, some of which (but by no means all) were inscribed on stone and set up in public, becoming civic monuments in their own right. They have a remarkable immediacy to them, for these are 'living documents', crafted for specific times and occasions, and as such they have a very different focus to any narrative histories, which are often composed much later than the events they describe. Reading an inscription allows us to come face-to-face with the participants of history as obscure cities are brought back to life.

Like inscriptions, writings found on papyri also have a sense of immediacy to them. Papyrus is a writing material made from *Cyperus papyrus*, a reed-like plant that grew in the marshes of the Nile Delta and the Fayum. It was exported from Egypt in huge quantities and has been preserved in archaeological sites throughout the ancient world, but the majority of still-existing papyrus documents have survived in Egypt, thanks to the hot dry conditions, which preserve papyrus very well. In Egypt, papyrus documents dating to the Ptolemaic period have been found in abundance in ancient rubbish dumps, in abandoned buildings and as 'cartonnage' – a kind of papier mâché made from waste papyri, used in the practice of human and animal mumification, where it was wrapped around a corpse and then covered with linen bandages. Egyptian papyri take us very close to the Cleopatras and to other individuals who inhabited their world, for we have at our disposal petitions, private letters, laundry lists, deeds, wills, marriage contracts, receipts, tax records and hundreds of assorted documents of state. However, since the damp soil around Alexandria, the Fayum and the Delta (the predominant areas of Greek settlement in Lower Egypt) has not proved conducive for the preservation of papyrus, most of the surviving examples come from the parched desert lands of Upper Egypt, where the population was predominantly Egyptian; they give us unique access to the world of the native Egyptians and were written in Demotic – an appropriately accessible language for contracts and transactions. No other part of the ancient world has provided us with such source material in such abundance; the Demotic papyri bring us into direct contact with the lives of the Greeks who settled in Egypt, and of the Egyptians among whom they settled.

There is, then, no shortage of evidence for the Hellenistic era, even though scholars acknowledge that the native voices of the occupied territories are not so readily heard as their Greek counterparts. The historian Andrew Erskine, for instance, has noted that 'the ancient historian frequently comes to the Hellenistic world with a classical training and sees Greek rule as the unifying factor. This can lead to an overemphasis on Greekness and Greek culture? But it is worth pointing out that 'Greekness' was never confined to the geography of the modern nation state of Greece. Within the new political context of the world known to the Cleopatras, Greeks were probably numerically and culturally dominant only within the major towns and big cities; by and large, local, indigenous cultures tended to dominate or hold their place in the social structures. There is evidence that while some Hellenistic monarchs promoted ideals of Hellenic superiority, others recognized the significance of the cultures with which they mixed. Although Greek and Hellenized elites did constitute the ruling classes of the Seleucid and Ptolemaic empires, many of the cities and elites had a distinct non-Greek identity, so that the world of the Cleopatras was a complex amalgamation of ethnicities, languages and literatures.

On the sources of the Hellenistic age, see especially Andrew Erskine's edited volume *A Companion to the Hellenistic World* (2005) and Peter Green's magnificent and richly entertaining *Alexander to Actium: The Hellenistic Age*, which, although published in 1990, is still very relevant. Ted Kaizer's edited *Companion to the Hellenistic and Roman Near East* (2022) is rich in source analysis, as is Rolf Strootman's *Courts and Elites in the Hellenistic Empires: The Near East after the Achaemenids, c. 330 to 30 BCE* (2016). *The Hellenistic World from Alexander to the Roman Conquest: A Selection of Ancient Sources in Translation*, edited in 2006 by Michael Austin, is an invaluable resource, as is *The Hellenistic Period: Historical Sources in Translation* (2003), edited by Roger Bagnall and Peter Derow.

The bibliography for the Ptolemies and the source materials for Ptolemaic Egypt are huge, but I recommend these books in particular: Alan Bowman and Charles Crowther, *The Epigraphy of Ptolemaic Egypt* (2020), along with their 2021 edited volume (with others) *Corpus of Ptolemaic Inscriptions, Part I: Greek, Bilingual, and Trilingual Inscriptions from Egypt, Volume 1: Alexandria and the Delta (Nos. 1–206)*. Günther Hölbl's 2001 *A History of the Ptolemaic Empire* is a masterpiece of clarity and its rich referencing steers the reader towards a host of sources. *Greeks in Ptolemaic Egypt* (2001) by Natalie Lewis is a brilliant sourcebook and analysis of Ptolemaic papyrus documentation.

Sources for the Family Trees

The main sources used for creating the family trees found throughout this book are listed below:

Justin:	Line and main marriages to Ptolemy X
	Ptolemy V
	Children of Cleopatra III
	Most diplomatic marriages of Ptolemy V, Ptolemy VI and Ptolemy VIII
	Ptolemy Apion (without name), son of Ptolemy VIII
Prol. Trogus:	Dynastic line to Cleopatra VII (fragmentary)
	Ptolemy of Cyprus
Eusebius (Porphyry):	Dynastic line to Cleopatra VII (partial)
	Daughter of Ptolemy X
St Jerome:	Dynastic line to Ptolemy VI
	Maternity of Ptolemy VIII
Strabo:	Dynastic line to Cleopatra VII (fragmentary)
	Paternity and marriages of Berenice IV
Plutarch:	Children of Cleopatra VII
Maccabees:	First two marriages of Cleopatra Thea
Josephus:	All marriages of Cleopatra Thea
	Marriages of Ptolemy V, Ptolemy VI and Ptolemy VIII
	Ithaca (Eirene), mistress of Ptolemy VIII
OGIS 162:	Ptolemy Eupator, son of Ptolemy VI and Cleopatra II

pKöln 8.350:   Ptolemy, son of Ptolemy VI and Cleopatra II

Diodorus: Ptolemy Memphites, son of Ptolemy VIII
                      and Cleopatra II

                      Eirene (Ithaka), mistress of Ptolemy VIII

Appian: Marriages of Cleopatra Selene

Livy: Name of Ptolemy Apion

Cicero: Marriage of Ptolemy XI and Cleopatra V
                      Berenice III

                      Ptolemy of Cyprus and Ptolemy XII
                      as brothers

OGIS 174:   Berenice III, daughter of Ptolemy IX

oPr Joachim 1:   Cleopatra VI, wife and 'sister' of Ptolemy XII

Dio Cassius: Families of Ptolemy XII and Cleopatra VII

                      Marriages of Berenice IV and Cleopatra VII

Principal evidence for the marriages between the Cleopatras and Ptolemies are found below:

Pharaoh	Consort	Chief Classical Source
Ptolemy V	Cleopatra I Syra	Livy 35.13
Ptolemy VI	Cleopatra II	Justin 38.8
Ptolemy VIII	Cleopatra II	Justin 38.8
	Cleopatra III	Justin 38.8
Ptolemy IX	Cleopatra IV	Justin 39.3
Ptolemy X	Cleopatra Selene	Justin 39.3
	Cleopatra V Berenice III	Justin 39.4?
		Eusebius, *Chron.* 1.65
Ptolemy XI	Cleopatra V Berenice III	Eusebius, *Chron.* 1.65
Ptolemy XII	Cleopatra VI Tryphaina	None
Berenice IV	Seleucus Kybiosaktes	Strabo 17.1.11
	Archelaus	Strabo 17.1.11

| Cleopatra VII | Julius Caesar (marriage?) | Plutarch, *Caesar* 49.3 (?) |
| | Marc Antony | Suetonius, *Augustus* 69 |

Chief Egyptian Ptolemaic Sources

<list>Inscriptions: FD III, iBucheum, iDelos, IG IX I I2, iGFayum, iGLSyr, iGPhilae, IGR IV, iLabraunda 3, ILLRP2, ISE II, LD, MAMA IX, OGIS, SIG3, Urk.

Ostraca and graffiti: gr Medinet Habu, oBodleian, odem Fs Zauzich, odem Kaplony-Heckel, odem Louvre, oMattha, odem PLBat 26, oPr. Joachim, oThebes.

Demotic papyri: pdem Ashm, pdem BM, pdem Cairo, pdem Gebel. Heid., pdem Leid., pdem Lille I, pdem Lille II, pdem Loeb, pLouvre, pdem Ox. Griffith, pdem Rylands, pdem Schreibertr, pdem Strasbourg, pdem Vaticanum, pdem Zenon, pTor. Botti, pZagreb.

Greek papyri: BGU 3, BGU 6, BGU 8, BGU 10, BGU 14, C Ord. Ptol., C. Ptol. Sklav., Chrest. Wilck., pAdler, pAmh II, pBad 2, pBon, pBouriant, pCairZen, pColl. Youtie, pColZenon 1, pColZenon 2, pDion, pEdfu 2, pEhev, pEleph, pEnt, pErasm, pFayum, pFreiburg 3, pGen 2, pGrad, pGrenf I, pGrenf II, pGurob, pHal, pHaun, pHauswaldt, pHeid 6, pHibeh 1, pHibeh 2, pJena, pKöln 2, pKöln 3, pKöln 5, pKöln 6, pKöln 8, pLille, pLondon 7, pLouvre, pOxy 1, pOxy 2, pOxy 12, pOxy 14, pOxy 17, pOxy 19, pOxy 20, pOxy 37, pOxy 55, pPetrie 3, pReceuil, pRev, pRoss.Georg., pRylands, PSI, pStrasbourg 6, pTebt 1, pTebt 3, pZenonMich, pZenPestman, SB, UPZ 1, UPZ 2.</list>

Abbreviations according to the *Oxford Classical Dictionary* and used by Ptolemaic Dynasty Background (instonebrewer.com, accessed 1 May 2023).

Principal hieroglyphic titles for the Cleopatras can be located in the following Egyptian sites:

Cleopatra I Syra: Decree – Philae, Edfu, Esna

Cleopatra II: Philae, Esna, Kom Ombo, Edfu

Cleopatra III: Dakka, Philae, El Kab, Kom Ombo, Deir el-Medineh; Luxor, Karnak

Cleopatra IV: Philae

Cleopatra V Berenice III: Kom Ombo, Philae, Edfu

Cleopatra VI Tryphaina: Edfu

Cleopatra VII: Denderah, Armant, Philae, Edfu</list>

Sources and Suggestions for Further Reading

I hope that what follows will guide enthusiastic readers to useful books and articles on the world of the Cleopatras. These are my best recommendations, but there are many other items of scholarship contained in the Bibliography, including important non-Anglophone works.

Introduction

already a legend in her lifetime: So much has been written about Cleopatra VII it would be impossible to list everything. So I limit myself here to some good studies that explore her life and legend. *Cleopatra of Egypt: From History to Myth*, a catalogue edited by Susan Walker and Peter Higgs, published to accompany a major exhibition on the queen at the British Museum in 2001, is a great starting point. Full of gorgeous illustrations, the catalogue traces the life and times of Cleopatra VII and examines her legend too. Joanne Fletcher's 2008 book *Cleopatra the Great: The Woman Behind the Legend* is a lively read, as too is Stacey Schiff's *Cleopatra: A Life*, published in 2010. In a highly recommended recent life of the queen, *Cleopatra: A Biography* (2010), Duane Roller casts Cleopatra as something of a lone wolf: 'She was the only woman in all classical antiquity to rule independently – not merely as a successor to a dead husband – and she desperately tried to salvage and keep alive a dying kingdom in the face of overwhelming

Roman pressure', he writes, adding: 'Role models for Cleopatra were limited but dynamic.' Roller posits that Cleopatra drew inspiration from the ancient Egyptian queens-regnant Hatshepsut (c. 1507–1458 BCE) and Tawosret (died c. 1189 BCE), although I suggest she could have had only very limited knowledge of these women (they had been written out of official Egyptian history millennia before Cleopatra's time). By and large, in contemporary thought, Cleopatra emerges as a woman unique to ancient history. Yet to herald Cleopatra as the 'only woman in all classical antiquity to rule independently', as Roller does, is misleading. In fact, there is a range of ancient queens who would be quick to disagree with that assessment, and many of those critical voices would emanate from the women of Cleopatra's own family.

A book I find endlessly useful and fascinating is Lucy Hughes-Hallett's *Cleopatra: Queen, Lover, Legend* (1991), which explores the lasting legacy of Cleopatra on western civilization. For more on Hollywood's Cleopatras, see my 2018 book *Designs on the Past: How Hollywood Created the Ancient World.*

her enemies, the Romans: Diana Kleiner's 2005 study *Cleopatra and Rome* does a great job of looking at Cleopatra VII from a variety of Roman gazes, including the hostile ones. If you'd like more of a background to Rome's attitudes towards the Hellenistic monarchies, see R. D. Sullivan, *Near Eastern Royalty and Rome* (1990).

recent discovery of an administrative papyrus: The papyrus, known as Berlin P 25 239, is dated to 23 February 33 BCE and is in the collection of the Ägyptisches Museum und Papyrussammlung, Berlin. It is studied and discussed in *Cleopatra Reassessed*, a scholarly volume edited by Susan Walker and Sally-Ann Ashton in 2003.

first book to bring together the lives of the seven Cleopatras: Published in 1994, John Whitehorne's *Cleopatras* is a very fine academic study, although sadly his history stops at the point Cleopatra VII ascends the throne of Egypt.

Chapter 1

On the Seleucid state, see especially Paul Kosmin, *The Land of the Elephant Kings: Space, Territory, and Ideology in the Seleucid Empire* (2014) and Eva Anagnostou-Laoutides' excellent edited volume *Culture and Ideology under the Seleukids: Unframing a Dynasty* (2021). For the role of queens and princesses in the Seleucid dynasty, consult the 2016 volume edited by Altun Coskun and Alex McAuley, *Seleukid Royal Women*. John Granger gives a very good overview of kingship in the Hellenistic world in his 2017 book *Kings and Kingship in the Hellenistic World 350–30 BC*, while his 2010 book *The Syrian Wars* is the best thing available on this complex period of history. The life of Antiochus the Great is well crafted in John Ma's *Antiochus III and the Cities of Western Asia Minor* (2000).

the most populous part of the Hellenistic world: What exactly do we mean by the term 'Hellenistic'? It actually derives from an ancient Greek verb *hellēnizō*, 'I behave like a Greek', 'I adopt Greek ways' or 'I speak Greek', and ultimately comes from the Greeks' name for themselves, *Hellēnes*. The word is first found in New Testament (*koinē*) Greek, in the Acts of the Apostles to be precise, in which the Jewish members of 'the Jesus movement' (aka the early Christian Church) are divided into two groups or types: *hellenistai* and *hebraioi*. The terms have nothing to do with ethnicity, nor with faith, and relate only to the spoken language of choice of the two groups of Christians, Greek or Hebrew. During the Early Modern period, biblical scholars thought that the Jewish *hellenistai* had used a particular Greek dialect, the *lingua hellenistica* (as they called it), and one of those scholars, Jacques Bénigne Bossuet, therefore coined the term *hellénistique*, in his 1681 *Discours sur l'histoire universelle*, to describe the language of the New Testament and the Septuagint, the 'Greek-ized' version of the Old Testament (the Hebrew bible). So, in one sense, 'Hellenistic' has a linguistic focus. Today, though, 'Hellenistic' is predominantly a scholarly convention used to define a particular historical period: 323–30 BCE. During this extended era, the

'Hellenistic world' spanned a huge tract of land and sea, running from southern Italy and the coastline of North Africa all the way through Mesopotamia and into the Hindu Kush. Yet these diverse, far-flung regions were united by the fact that they were either Greek-speaking or ruled by Greek-speaking monarchs. Therefore, historians often refer to the period 323–30 BCE as the age of the 'Hellenistic Kingdoms', although they can narrow the focus and speak of, for instance, Hellenistic Egypt or Hellenistic Judaea, Hellenistic Asia Minor or even Hellenistic India, by way of emphasizing historical and cultural connections – and the presence of the Greek language is key to this understanding – which existed in the political geography of the era.

Polybius' account of Ptolemaic overseas power reveals several matters for concern: See comments by Andrew Erskine in his article 'Polybius and Ptolemaic Sea Power' in *The Ptolemies, the Sea and the Nile*, edited by Kostas Buraselis, Mary Stefanou and Dorothy J. Thompson (2013).

Raphia Stele: See the discussion by Patrick J. O'Kernick, 'Stelae, Elephants, and Irony', published in the *Journal for the Study of Judaism in the Persian, Hellenistic, and Roman Period* (2018).

the famous Greek poetess Sappho: The bibliography on Sappho is endless, but see Jim Powell's *The Poetry of Sappho* (2019) for a great recent study.

We know it as the Rosetta Stone: Excellent studies of this iconic inscription are John Ray's *The Rosetta Stone and the Rebirth of Ancient Egypt* (2008) and Ilona Regulski's *Hieroglyphs: Unlocking Ancient Egypt* (2022). The name and titles of young King Ptolemy V are to be found on another ancient Egyptian monument in Britain. It stands in a fine country estate at Kingston Lacy, a prized property of the National Trust. The house is surrounded by an immaculately manicured lawn where a 9-metre-high obelisk casts a shadow: a monument to the adventures of William Bankes, the 'explorer' (1786–1855), heir to Kingston Lacy and its estates in Dorset and a noted traveller, antiquarian, connoisseur and art collector. Bankes had discovered the fallen obelisk in 1815, half-buried amidst the rubble of the ruins of the temple at Philae, near Aswan, and had it brought back to England and erected in his garden in 1821, the year before Champollion cracked the code of the Rosetta Stone. Until then, the hieroglyphs on the obelisk's four sides had been unreadable, but with the new-found expertise, scholars began to pour over the obelisk's inscriptions for clues to what message it contained. As it turned out, the Philae Obelisk (as it is called) recorded a complaint made by the priests of Philae, addressing the fact that visiting officials to the temple had placed too great a financial burden on them. Significantly, it was addressed to 'King Ptolemy and to Queen Cleopatra his sister and to Queen Cleopatra his wife' – this was the first time the famous name Cleopatra had been read in hieroglyphs. Having been granted the tax exemption they desired, the priests showed their gratitude by inscribing at the temple entrance a copy of their petition and the responses from Ptolemy VIII and his two Cleopatras (Cleopatra II and Cleopatra III, see Chapters 6 and 7).

the Hebrew bible's prophetic Book of Daniel: See the excellent commentary *The Book of Daniel* by André LaCocque (1979) and the 2008 commentary *Daniel* by Sharon Pace.

the preparation of the bride Pandora in Hesiod's poem *Theogony*: See interesting comments by Dora Panofsky in her study *Pandora's Box: The Changing Aspects of a Mythical Symbol* (2019).

the bride's adornment and the prenuptial bridal rituals: See my book *Aphrodite's Tortoise: The Veiled Woman of Ancient Greece* (2003) for all the rites of the Greek wedding as well as the veiling of the bride.

Chapter 2

as for all Greeks who lived beyond its borders, Egypt was a place of ancient mysteries: See David Asheri, Alan Lloyd, Aldo Corcella, Oswyn Murray and Alfonso Moreno, *A Commentary on Herodotus, Books I–IV* (2007) for the fundamental commentary resource for the early books of the Histories, including Book

2 on Egypt. Of singular importance is Alan B. Lloyd's three-volume work (1975, 1976, 1988) *Herodotus: Book II, Introduction* (I) and Commentary (II, III).

actively destroy chaos to preserve *ma'at*: See Anna Mancini, *Maat Revealed: Philosophy of Justice in Ancient Egypt* (2007). On foreigners in Egypt, see Mu-Choo Poo, *Enemies of Civilization: Attitudes toward Foreigners in Ancient Mesopotamia, Egypt, and China* (2005), and Pearce Creaseman and Richard Wilkinson's edited volume *Pharaoh's Land and Beyond: Ancient Egypt and Its Neighbours* (2017).

There had been a fixed Greek presence in Egypt ever since the late eighth century BCE: See Franco De Angelis's edited volume *A Companion to Greeks Across the Ancient World* (2020) and the excellent source collection by Nathalie Lewis, *Greeks in Ptolemaic Egypt* (2001).

Alexander the Great and his Greco-Macedonian troops had burst into Egypt: See Roberta Casagrande-Kim's edited volume *When the Greeks Ruled Egypt: From Alexander the Great to Cleopatra* (2014) for Alexander's stay in Egypt.

Ptolemy I Soter: Timothy Howe has written an excellent biography of the first Ptolemaic king, *Ptolemy I Soter: A Self-Made Man* (2018), while Ptolemy II is well covered in *Ptolemy II Philadelphus and His World* (2008), edited by Paul McKechnie and Philippe Guillaume. Ptolemy II's sister-wife is given an excellent study by Elizabeth Carney in *Arsinoe II of Egypt and Macedon: A Royal Life* (2014), and Berenice II's marriage to Ptolemy III is the focus of a 2010 article by me and Stephanie Winder: 'A Key to Berenike's Lock? The Hathoric Model of Queenship in Early Ptolemaic Egypt' in *Creating a Hellenistic World*. Branko Van Oppen de Ruiter's biography *Berenike II Euergetis* (2016), is excellent. The marriage practices of the Ptolemies are expertly analysed by Daniel Ogden in his ground-breaking 1999 book *Polygamy, Prostitutes and Death: The Hellenistic Dynasties*, which I cannot praise highly enough.

Alexandria, with its fine harbours, had come to dominate the social, cultural and economic life of Egypt: There are many fine studies of Ptolemaic Alexandria. I recommend Jean-Yves Empereur, *Alexandria Rediscovered* (1998) and *Alexandria, the Third Century BC*, edited by Christian Jacob and Francois de Polignac (1992). Judith McKenzie's 2010 study *The Archictecture of Alexandria and Egypt : 300 BC–AD 700* is wonderfully illustrated. The go-to study of the city, however, is the three-volume work by P. M. Fraser, *Ptolemaic Alexandria* (1972). On the Ptolemaic palace, see Inge Nielsen, *Hellenistic Palaces* (1999). The catalogue of a 2016 British Museum exhibition on Alexandria by F. Goddio and A. Masson-Berghoff, *Sunken Cities: Egypt's Lost Worlds*, is also well worth consulting.

celebratory procession (Greek, *pompē*): See Andrew Bell, *Spectacular Power in the Greek and Roman City* (2004). See also A. Chaniotis, 'Theatricality Beyond the Theatre. Staging Public Life in the Hellenistic World' in *Pallas* (1997).

Ptolemaic concept: *tryphē*: See James Fraser, Lloyd Llewellyn-Jones and Henry Cosmo Bishop Wright, *Luxury and Power: From Persia to Greece* (2023).

Coin portraits were the best way of creating an official image of monarchy: See A. Houghton, C. Lorber and O. D. Hoover, *Seleucid Coins: A Comprehensive Catalogue II, Seleucus IV Through Antiochus XIII* (2008); Catharine Lorber, *Coins of the Ptolemaic Empire* (2018); and Peter Thonemann's useful 2016 study *The Hellenistic World: Using Coins as Sources*.

Chapter 3

a Greek (Cretan) cavalry soldier named Dryton, a citizen of Ptolemais: His case and many others are well analysed by Nathalie Lewis in *Greeks in Ptolemaic Egypt* (2001). See also Jane Rowlandson's useful sourcebook *Women and Society in Greek and Roman Egypt* (1998).

Egyptian state religion was completely concentrated in the temples: A useful guide to Egyptian temples is Richard Wilkinson's 2000 book *The Complete Temples of Ancient Egypt*, although Ptolemaic temples are the focus of a study by Dieter Arnold, *Temples of the Last Pharaohs* (1999).

Memphis: The go-to study on Memphis is that by Dorothy Thompson, *Memphis Under the Ptolemies* (1988).

gods: On Greek royal cult in Egypt, see T. Jim, *Saviour Gods and Soteira in Ancient Greece* (2022). Richard Wilkinson's (2003) useful resource *The Complete Gods and Goddesses of Ancient Egypt* (2003) provides an excellent compendium of deities. A useful study of synchronism is R. E. Witt's classic 1971 book *Isis in the Ancient World*.

The extent of a pharaoh's divinity is much debated: See Henri Frankfort's classic 1944 study *Kingship and the Gods*. Rolf Gundlach's landmark *Der Pharao und sein Staat* (1998) is not yet available in English.

Throughout Egypt, religious cults were established where the Greek rulers were worshipped as Egyptian gods: See Paul Stanwick, *Portraits of the Ptolemies: Greek Kings as Egyptian Pharaohs* (2002) and Sally-Ann Ashton's 'Identifying the Egyptian-Style Ptolemaic Queens' in *Cleopatra of Egypt* (2001). For Greek implications, see Maria Rigoglioso, *The Cult of Divine Birth in Ancient Greece* (2009).

Chapter 4

a great rebellion: For the theme of revolt against foreign rulers, see the volume edited by J. J. Collins and J. G. Manning, *Revolt and Resistance in the Ancient Classical World and the Near East: In the Crucible of Empire* (2016). See further Timothy Howe and Lee Brice, *Insurgency and Terrorism in the Ancient Mediterranean*, an edited volume from 2006. Nathalie Lewis's *Greeks in Ptolemaic Egypt* (2001) provides excellent evidence for the unfair treatment of Egyptians by the Greek colonizers.

Oracle… apocalypse: The apocalyptic theme in Late Period literature can be found in Miriam Lichtheim's popular 1980 work *Ancient Egyptian Literature*, volume 3.

Chapter 5

So, why Hathor?: See the 2010 article by me and Stephanie Winder: 'A Key to Berenike's Lock? The Hathoric Model of Queenship in Early Ptolemaic Egypt' in *Creating a Hellenistic World*.

Temple of Edfu: See, importantly, Barbara Watterson, *The House of Horus at Edfu* (1998).

name the little one Cleopatra: One of many 'women's voices' to be found in Jane Rowlandson's *Women and Society in Greek and Roman Egypt* (1998).

Chapter 6

Nothing survives to indicate how the royal couple viewed the birth of their daughter: See Maryline Parca's fascinating 2017 article 'Children in Ptolemaic Egypt: What the Papyri Say' in *The Oxford Handbook of Childhood and Education in the Classical World*. I also recommend Walter Penrose 2018 article 'Queens and Their Children: Dynastic Dis/Loyalty in the Hellenistic Period' in *Royal Women and Dynastic Loyalty*. Of further interest is Ada Nifosi, *Becoming a Woman and Mother in Greco-Roman Egypt* (2019).

exposure was accepted as a regrettable fact of life: See Judith Evans Grubbs, 'Infant Exposure and Infanticide' in *The Oxford Handbook of Childhood and Education in the Classical World* (2017).

first-degree incest: The most important studies are those of Sheila Ager: 'Familiarity Breeds: Incest and the Ptolemaic Dynasty', *Journal of Hellenic Studies* 125 (2005) and 'The Power of Excess: Royal Incest and the Ptolemaic Dynasty' *Anthropologica* 48 (2006).

Chapter 7

Antiochus IV . . . The Sixth Syrian War was a swift and bloody affair: See John Grainger, *The Syrian Wars* (2010).

the Roman embassy to Alexandria: See Joel Allen, *The Roman Republic and the Hellenistic Mediterranean* (2020) and Richard

Sullivan's *Near Eastern Royalty and Rome* (1991). See further John Grainger, *Great Power Diplomacy in the Hellenistic World* (2017).

Jewish community of Egypt: See the excellent overview by Livia Capponi, 'Deserving the Court's Trust: Jews in Ptolemaic Egypt' in *The Hellenistic Court* (2017). Eric Gruen's edited volume *The Construct of Identity in Hellenistic Judaism: Essays on Early Jewish Literature and History* (2016) contains a collection of important essays.

Antiochus launched a vicious attack on Jerusalem: See Eric Gruen, 'Hellenism and Persecution: Antiochus IV and the Jews' in his edited volume *The Construct of Identity in Hellenistic Judaism* (2016). See further Sylvie Honigman, *Tales of High Priests and Taxes: The Books of the Maccabees and the Judean Rebellion against Antiochus IV* (2014).

Chapter 8

Demetrius' invasion of Syria in 162 BCE ... Alexander Balas: Boris Chrubasik provides an excellent study of the usurpation of the Seleucid throne throughout the Hellenistic period in his 2016 work *Kings and Usurpers in the Seleukid Empire: The Men Who Would Be King*. See also John Grainger, *The Fall of the Seleukid Empire 187–75 BC* (2015).

In a marriage of international importance, such as that between Balas and Cleopatra Thea: See Sheila Ager, 'Symbol and Ceremony: Royal Weddings in the Hellenistic Age' in *The Hellenistic Court* (2017). Monica D'Agostini is exceptionally good on Cleopatra Thea's marriages; see her article 'A Change of Husband. Cleopatra Thea, Stability and Dynamism of Hellenistic Royal Couples' in *Power Couples in Antiquity* (2019).

Chapter 9

the ritual cries of lamentation: See Maria Rosa Valdesogo, *Hair and Death in Ancient Egypt: The Mourning Rite in the Times of the Pharaohs* (2021).

most of the Ptolemies were fat: See Susan Hill, *Eating to Excess: The Meaning of Gluttony and the Fat Body in the Ancient World* (2011).

absence of information on the act of getting married: Discussed by Dominic Monstserrat in *Sex and Society in Graeco-Roman Egypt* (1996).

at Philae, a relief depicting the white-crowned Ptolemy VIII: Discussed by E. Vassilika in *Ptolemaic Philae* (1989).

Chapter 10

Antiochus VII was nicknamed 'Sidetes': See Paula Ceccarelli, 'Kings, Philosophers and Drunkards: Athenaeus' Information on the Seleucids' in *Seleucid Dissolution* (2011).

Chapter 11

the boldly aspirational Zabinas: See Boris Chrubasik, *Kings and Usurpers in the Seleukid Empire: The Men Who Would Be King* (2016). See also John Grainger, *The Fall of the Seleukid Empire 187–75 BC* (2015).

it was Grypus and not his mother who had the reputation for employing poisons and drugs: See Stephanie Winder, 'The Hands of Gods? Poison and Power in the Hellenistic Court' in *The Hellenistic Court* (2017).

Chapter 12

inviting influential Roman senators to Egypt and dazzling them with upmarket Nilotic tours: See Sally-Ann Ashton, *Roman Egyptomania* (2004).

what might today be called a 'superyacht': See Dorothy Thompson's 2013 article, 'Hellenistic Royal Barges' in *Ptolemies, the Sea and the Nile*.

he nevertheless returned to Cyprus and took cover there: See the edited volume by Katerina Carvounis and Andreas Gavrielatos, *Cyprus in Texts from Graeco-Roman Antiquity* (2023).

Cleopatra IV ... Cleopatra Tryphaina: See Walter Heckel, 'King's Daughters, Sisters, and Wives: Fonts and Conduits of Power and Legitimacy' in *Royal Women and Dynastic Loyalty* (2018). On the rivalry between the sisters, consult Maryanne L. Fisher's edited volume *The Oxford Handbook of Women and Competition* (2017) for a thorough contextualization.

The disintegration of Seleucid Syria and Rome's procurement of its rich resources made the Romans hungry for more eastern territories: See Joel Allen, *The Roman Republic and the Hellenistic Mediterranean* (2020) and Richard Sullivan's *Near Eastern Royalty and Rome* (1991). See further John Grainger, *Great Power Diplomacy in the Hellenistic World* (2017).

Chapter 13

Cleopatra III's Egyptian-style portraits: See Paul Stanwick, *Portraits of the Ptolemies: Greek Kings as Egyptian Pharaohs* (2002) and Sally-Ann Ashton's 'Identifying the Egyptian-Style Ptolemaic Queens' in *Cleopatra of Egypt* (2001). See also R. R. R. Smith, *Hellenistic Royal Portraits* (1988).

Chapter 14

Schisms and factions arose from political or personal causes as the leading Patrician families of Rome found themselves falling into cliques: See the volume edited by Nathan Rosenstein and Robert Morstein-Marx, *A Companion to the Roman Republic* (2010). See also Andrew Lintott, *Violence in Republican Rome* (1999).

Mithridates VI of Pontus: See Adrienne Mayor's highly readable *The Poison King: The Life and Legend of Mithradates, Rome's Deadliest Enemy* (2009). See also Brian McGing, *The Foreign Policy of Mithridates VI Eupator, King of Pontus* (1986).

Lucius Cornelius Sulla, the Roman proconsul and future dictator: See Arthur Keaveney, *Sulla: The Last Republican* (1982).

Chapter 15

Tryphaina was the daughter of Ptolemy X and Cleopatra V Berenice III: There is debate – see C. J. Bennett, 'Cleopatra V Tryphaena and the Genealogy of the Later Ptolemies' in *Ancient Society* 28 (1997).

in the temple of Edfu, in the passageway between the entrance pylons: See Barbara Watterson, *The House of Horus at Edfu* (1998).

launched into the Third Mithridatic War: See R. D. Sullivan, *Near Eastern Royalty and Rome* (1990) and Adrienne Mayor, *The Poison King: The Life and Legend of Mithradates, Rome's Deadliest Enemy* (2009). See also Brian McGing, *The Foreign Policy of Mithridates VI Eupator, King of Pontus* (1986).

the unscrupulous Gaius Rabirius Postumus: See Mary Siani-Davies, *Cicero: Pro Rabirio Postumo* (2001).

amici et socii populi Romani: See L. E. Matthaei, 'On the Classification of Roman Allies', *Classical Quarterly* 1 (1907). See also M. R. Cimma, *Reges socii et amici populi Romani* (1979).

Known as the Gabiniani, the Gallic and Germanic cavalrymen were to leave their mark on the city's history: See Mary Siani-Davies, 'Ptolemy XII Auletes and the Romans' in *Historia* 46 (1997).

Chapter 16

Pasherenptah, High Priest of Memphis: See Eve Reymond, *From the Records of a Priestly Family of Memphis* (1981).

he initiated the so-called Alexandrian War: See analysis by Adrian Goldsworthy in his 2003 book *In the Name of Rome: The Men Who Won the Roman Empire*.

Chapter 17

the Caesareum was an homage to Ptolemaic Egyptomania: See Judith McKenzie's 2010 book *The Archictecture of Alexandria and Egypt, 300 BC–AD 700*.

in February 44 BCE he declared himself dictator for life: See

Adrian Goldsworthy, *In the Name of Rome: The Men Who Won the Roman Empire* (2003).

it was to be known as the Cleopatrion: See Judith McKenzie's *The Archictecture of Alexandria and Egypt, 300 BC–AD 700* (2010).

Chapter 18

Arsinoë IV was buried in Ephesus in a large and splendid tomb: See Richard Oster, *A Bibliography of Ancient Ephesus* (1987) and Hilke Thür, 'Arsinoë IV, eine Schwester Kleopatras VII, Grabinhaberin des Oktogons von Ephesos? Ein Vorschlag' ['Arsinoë IV, a sister of Cleopatra VII, grave owner of the Octagon in Ephesus? A suggestion'] in *Jahreshefte des Österreichischen Archäologischen Instituts* 60 (1990).

With Octavia's hand in marriage came also Octavian's pledge to give over the rulership of the east: Richard Bauman's 1992 work *Women and Politics in Ancient Rome* remains the best overall view of the political influence of women in the late Republic and early Imperial eras and is especially good on Octavia.

vindex libertatis: On this interesting title, see Peter Stacey's 2014 article 'The Princely Republic' *Journal of Roman Studies* 104.

Octavian's best friend, loyal right-hand man and later son-in-law, Marcus Vispanius Agrippa: On this fascinating man, see the biography by Lindsay Powell, *Marcus Agrippa: Right-Hand Man of Caesar Augustus* (2015).

'[S]he put herself to death secretly, while in prison, by the bit of an asp or by applying a poisonous ointment': See Adrienne Mayor, *The Poison King: The Life and Legend of Mithradates, Rome's Deadliest Enemy* (2009) and Stephanie Winder, 'The Hands of Gods? Poison and Power in the Hellenistic Court' in *The Hellenistic Court* (2017).

Bibliography

Ager, S. 2005. 'Familiarity Breeds: Incest and the Ptolemaic Dynasty', *Journal of Hellenic Studies* 125, 1–34.

—— 2006. 'The Power of Excess: Royal Incest and the Ptolemaic Dynasty', *Anthropologica* 48, 165–86.

—— 2017. 'Symbol and Ceremony: Royal Weddings in the Hellenistic Age' in A. Erskine, L. Llewellyn-Jones and S. Wallace (eds.), *The Hellenistic Court: Monarchic Power and Elite Society from Alexander to Cleopatra*. Swansea. 165–88.

Ager, S. and Hardiman, C. 2016. 'Female Seleukid Portraits: Where Are They?' in A. Coşkun and A. McAuley (eds.), *Seleukid Royal Women*. Stuttgart. 146–72.

Allen, J. 2020. *The Roman Republic and the Hellenistic Mediterranean*. Oxford.

Anagnostou-Laoutides, E. (ed.) 2021. *Culture and Ideology under the Seleukids: Unframing a Dynasty*. Berlin.

Apter, T. 2008. *The Sister Knot: Why We Fight, Why We're Jealous, and Why We'll Love Each Other No Matter What*. London.

Arnold, D. 1999. *Temples of the Last Pharaohs*. Oxford.

Asheri, D., Lloyd, A., Corcella, A., Murray, O. and Moreno, A. (eds.) 2007. *A Commentary on Herodotus, Books I–IV*. Oxford.

Ashton, S.-A. 2001. 'Identifying the Egyptian-Style Ptolemaic Queens' in S. Walker and P. Higgs (eds.), *Cleopatra of Egypt: From History to Myth*. London. 148–71.

—— 2004. *Roman Egyptomania*. London.

Austin, M. 2006. *The Hellenistic World from Alexander to the Roman Conquest: A Selection of Ancient Sources in Translation*. Cambridge.

Bagnall, R. and Derow, P. 2003. *The Hellenistic Period: Historical Sources in Translation*. Oxford.

Bartels, J. 2016. 'The King's Daughters: Justin's Story' in A. B. Sànchez, I. Cogitore and A. Kolb (eds.), *Femmes influentes dans le monde hellénistique et à Rome*. Grenoble. 61–80.

Bartlett, B. 2016. 'The fate of Kleopatra Tryphaina, or: Poetic Justice in Justin' in A. Coşkun and A. McAuley (eds.), *Seleukid Royal Women*. Stuttgart. 135–42.

Bauman, R. 1992. *Women and Politics in Ancient Rome*. London.

Bell, A. 2004. *Spectacular Power in the Greek and Roman City*. Oxford.

Bellinger, A. 1949. 'The End of the Seleucids', *Transactions of the Connecticut Academy of Arts and Sciences* 38, 51–102.

Bennett, C. J. 1997. 'Cleopatra V Tryphaena and the Genealogy of the Later Ptolemies', *Ancient Society* 28, 39–66.

—— 2011. 'Ptolemaic Dynasty', digital genealogy. Tyndale House, Oxford. http://www.instonebrewer.com/TyndaleSites/Egypt/ptolemies/genealogy.htm

Berrey, M. 2019. *Hellenistic Science at Court*. Berlin.

Bertman, S. 2000. 'Cleopatra and Antony as Models for Dido and Aeneas', *Echos du monde classique: Classical Views* 443, 395–8.

Bevan, E. 1902. *The House of Seleucus*. London.

—— 1927. *The House of Ptolemy*. London.

Bianchi, R. S. (ed.) 1989. *Cleopatra's Egypt*. New York.

—— 2002. 'Images of Cleopatra VII Reconsidered' in S. Walker and S.-A. Ashton (eds.), *Cleopatra Reassessed*. London. 13–23.

Bielman-Sanchez, A. and Joliton, V. 2019. 'Marital Crisis or International Crisis? Two Ptolemaic Couples Under the Spotlight' in A. Bielman-Sánchez (ed.), *Power Couples in Antiquity: Transversal Perspectives*. London. 69–98.

Bilde, P. et al. (eds.) 1995. *Religion and Religious Practice in the Seleucid Kingdom*. Aarhus.

Billows, R. 1995. *Kings and Colonists: Aspects of Macedonian Imperialism*. New York.

Bouché-Leclerq, A. 1904. *Histoire des Lagides*. Paris.

—— 1913–14. *Histoire des Séleucides*. Paris.

Bowman, A. and Crowther, C. (eds.) 2020. *The Epigraphy of Ptolemaic Egypt*. Oxford.

Bowman, A., Crowther, C., Hornblower, S., Mairs, R. and Savvopoulos, K. (eds.) 2021. *Corpus of Ptolemaic Inscriptions, Part I: Greek, Bilingual, and Trilingual Inscriptions from Egypt, Volume 1: Alexandria and the Delta (Nos. 1–206)*. Oxford.

Buttrey, T. 1954. 'Thea Neotera on the coins of Antony and Cleopatra', *Museum Notes (American Numismatic Society)* 6, 95–109.

Capponi, L. 2017. 'Deserving the Court's Trust: Jews in Ptolemaic Egypt' in A. Erskine, L. Llewellyn-Jones and S. Wallace (eds.), *The Hellenistic Court: Monarchic Power and Elite Society from Alexander to Cleopatra*. Swansea. 343–57.

—— 2021. *Cleopatra*. Bari.

Carney, E. D. 2000. *Women and Monarchy in Macedonia*. Norman.

—— 2010. 'Being Royal and Being Female in the Early Hellenistic Period' in A. Erskine and L. Llewellyn-Jones (eds.), *Creating a Hellenistic World*. Swansea. 195–220.

—— 2014. *Arsinoe II of Egypt and Macedon: A Royal Life*. Oxford.

Carney, E. D. and S. Müller (eds.) 2021. *A Companion to Women and Monarchy in the Ancient Mediterranean*. London.

Carsana, C. 1996. *Le dirigenze cittadine nello stato seleucidico*. Como.

Carvounis, K. and Gavrielatos, A. 2023. *Cyprus in Texts from Graeco-Roman Antiquity*. Leiden.

Casagrande-Kim, R. (ed.) 2014. *When the Greeks Ruled Egypt: From Alexander the Great to Cleopatra*. New York.

Caßor-Pfeiffer, S. 2008. 'Zur reflexion ptolemäischer geschichte in den ägyptischen Templen unter Ptolemaios IX Philometor II Soter II und Ptolemaios X Alexander I (116–80 v.Chr.) TEIL 2: Kleopatra III und Kleopatra Berenike III in Spiegel der Tempelreliefs', *Journal of Egyptian History* 1 (2), 235–65.

Cauville, S. 1984. *Edfou*. Cairo.

Cauville, S. and Devauchelle, D. 1984. 'Le Temple d'Edfou: étapes de la construction nouvelles données historiques', *Revue d'Égyptologie* 35, 30–31.

Ceccarelli, P. 2011. 'Kings, Philosophers and Drunkards: Athenaeus'

Information on the Seleucids' in K. Erickson and G. Ramsey (eds.), *Seleucid Dissolution: The Sinking of the Anchor*. Wiesbaden. 161–80.

Chaniotis, A. 1997. 'Theatricality Beyond the Theatre. Staging Public Life in the Hellenistic World', *Pallas* 47, 219–59.

Chauveau, M. 2000. *Egypt in the Age of Cleopatra*. Cornell.

Cheshire, W. 2010/11. 'The Phantom Sister of Ptolemy X', *Enchoria* 32, 12–4.

Chrubasik, B. 2016. *Kings and Usurpers in the Seleukid Empire: The Men Who Would Be King*. Oxford.

Cimma, M. R. 1979, *Reges socii et amici populi Romani*. Milan.

Clayman, D. 2015. *Berenice II and the Golden Age of Ptolemaic Egypt*. Oxford.

Clayton, P. A. 1994. *Chronicle of the Pharaohs*. London.

Cole, S. 1981. 'Could Greek women read and write?', *Women's Studies* 8.1–2, 129–55.

Collins, J. J. and Manning, J. G. (eds.) 2016. *Revolt and Resistance in the Ancient Classical World and the Near East: In the Crucible of Empire*. Leiden.

Cooney, K. 2021. *The Good Kings*. Washington D.C.

Coskun, A. and McAuley, A. (eds.) 2016. *Seleukid Royal Women*. Stuttgart.

Creaseman, P. and Wilkinson, R. H. (eds.) 2017. *Pharaoh's Land and Beyond: Ancient Egypt and Its Neighbours*. Oxford.

D'Agostini, M. 2019. 'A Change of Husband: Cleopatra Thea, Stability and Dynamism of Hellenistic Royal Couples' in A. Bielman-Sánchez (ed.), *Power Couples in Antiquity: Transversal Perspectives*. London. 43–68.

Daly, M. and Wilson, M. 1989. *Homicide: Foundations of Human Behavior*. New York.

Davis, N. and Kraay, C. M. 1973. *The Hellenistic Kingdoms: Portrait Coins and History*. London.

De Angelis, F. (ed.) 2020. *A Companion to Greeks across the Ancient World*. Oxford.

Dodson, A. and Hilton, D. 2004. *The Complete Royal Families of Ancient Egypt*. London.

Droysen, J. G. 1833. *Geschichte Alexanders des Großen*. Berlin.

Duindam, J. 2016. *Dynasties: A Global History of Power, 1300–1800*. Cambridge.

Dumitru, A. 2016. 'Kleopatra Selene: A Look at the Moon and Her Bright Side' in A. Coşkun and A. McAuley (eds.), *Seleukid Royal Women*. Stuttgart. 253–72.

Eaton, K. 2013. *Ancient Egyptian Temple Ritual: Performance, Pattern, and Practice*. London.

Ellis, W. M. 1994. *Ptolemy of Egypt*. London.

Empereur, J-Y. 1998. *Alexandria Rediscovered*. London.

Erskine, A. (ed). 2005. *A Companion to the Hellenistic World*. Oxford.

—— 2013. 'Polybius and Ptolemaic Sea Power' in Buraselis, K., Stefanou, M. and Thompson, D. J. (eds.), *The Ptolemies, the Sea and the Nile: Studies in Waterborne Power*. Cambridge. 82–96.

Erskine, A., Llewellyn-Jones, L. and Wallace, S. (eds.) 2017. *The Hellenistic Court: Monarchic Power and Elite Society from Alexander to Cleopatra*. Swansea.

Evans Grubbs, J. 2017. 'Infant Exposure and Infanticide', in J. Evans Grubbs, T. Parkin and R. Bell (eds.), *The Oxford Handbook of Childhood and Education in the Classical World*. Oxford. 83–107.

Ferries, A-M. 2019. 'The Magistrate and the Queen: Antony and Cleopatra' in A. Bielman-Sánchez (ed.), *Power Couples in Antiquity: Transversal Perspectives*. London. 99–115.

Feyel, C. and Graslin-Thomé, L. (eds.). 2017. *Antiochus III et l'Orient*. Paris.

Fischer-Bovet, C. 2014. *Army and Society in Ptolemaic Egypt*. Cambridge.

Fisher, M. 2017. *The Oxford Handbook of Women and Competition*. Oxford.

Fleischer, R. 1996. 'Hellenistic Royal Iconography on Coins' in P. Bilde (ed.), *Aspects of Hellenistic Kingship*. Aarhus. 28–40.

Flemming, R. 2003. 'Empires of Knowledge: Medicine and Health in the Hellenistic World', in A. Erskine (ed.), *A Companion to the Hellenistic World*. Oxford 449–63.

Fletcher, J. 2008. *Cleopatra the Great: The Woman Behind the Legend*. London.

Frankfort, H. 1944. *Kingship and the Gods*. Chicago.

Fraser, J., Llewellyn-Jones, L. and Bishop Wright, H. O. 2023. *Luxury and Power: From Persia to Greece*. London.

Fraser, P. M. 1972. *Ptolemaic Alexandria*. 3 vols. Oxford.

Goddio, F. and Masson-Berghoff, A. (eds.) 2016. *Sunken Cities: Egypt's Lost Worlds*. London.

Goldsworthy, A. 2003. *In the Name of Rome: The Men Who Won the Roman Empire*. New Haven.

Grainger, J. D. 1990. *The Cities of Seleukid Syria*. Oxford.

—— 1997. *A Seleukid Prosopography and Gazeteer*. Leiden.

—— 2010. *The Syrian Wars*. Leiden.

—— 2015. *The Fall of the Seleukid Empire 187–75 BC*. Barnsley.

—— 2017. *Great Power Diplomacy in the Hellenistic World*. London.

—— 2017. *Kings and Kingship in the Hellenistic World, 350–30 BC*. Barnsley.

Green, P. 1990. *Alexander to Actium: The Hellenistic Age*. London.

Griffiths, F. T. 1979. *Theocritus at Court*. Leiden.

Gruen, E. 2016. 'Hellenism and Persecution: Antiochus IV and the Jews' in Gruen, E. (ed.), *The Construct of Identity in Hellenistic Judaism: Essays on Early Jewish Literature and History*. Berlin. 333–58.

Gundlach, R. 1998. *Der Pharao und sein Staat. Die Grundlegung der ägyptischen Königsideologie im 4. und 3. Jahrtausend*. Berlin.

Harders, A.-C. 2016. 'The Making of a Queen – Seleukos Nikator and his Wives' in A. Coşkun and A. McAuley (eds.), *Seleukid Royal Women*. Stuttgart. 25–38.

—— 2019. 'Mark Antony and the Women at His Side' in A. Bielman-Sánchez (ed.), *Power Couples in Antiquity: Transversal Perspectives*. London. 116–35.

Heckel, W. 2018. 'King's Daughters, Sisters, and Wives: Fonts and Conduits of Power and Legitimacy' in C. Dunn and E. Carney (eds.), *Royal Women and Dynastic Loyalty*. London. 19–30.

Hill, S. 2011. *Eating to Excess: The Meaning of Gluttony and Body Fat in the Ancient World*. Santa Barbara.

Hölbl, G. 2001. *A History of the Ptolemaic Empire*. London.

Honigman, S. 2014. *Tales of High Priests and Taxes: The Books of the Maccabees and the Judean Rebellion against Antiochus IV*. Berkeley.

Hoover, O. D. 2002. 'Two Seleucid Notes: II. Laodice IV on the Bronze

Coinage of Seleucus IV and Antiochus IV', *American Journal of Numismatics* 14, 81–7.

Houghton, A. 1988. 'The Double Portrait Coins of Alexander I Balas and Cleopatra Thea', *Schweizerische numismatische Rundschau* 67, 85–93.

Houghton, A., Lorber, C. and Hoover, O. D. 2008. *Seleucid Coins: A Comprehensive Catalogue II. Seleucus IV Through Antiochus XIII*. New York.

Howe, T. 2018. *Ptolemy I Soter: A Self-Made Man*. Oxford.

Howe, T. and Brice, L. L. (eds.) 2006. *Insurgency and Terrorism in the Ancient Mediterranean*. Leiden.

Hughes-Hallett, L. 1991. *Cleopatra: Queen, Lover, Legend*. London.

Hunter, R. (trans. & ed.) 1993. *Theocritus: Encomium of Ptolemy Philadelphus*. Berkeley.

Jacob, C. and de Polignac, F. (eds.) 1992. *Alexandria, the Third Century BC*. Alexandria.

Janssen, R. M. and Janssen, J. J. 1990. *Growing Up in Ancient Egypt*. London.

Jim, T. S. F. 2022. *Saviour Gods and Soteira in Ancient Greece*. Oxford.

Kaizer, T. (ed.) 2022. *A Companion to the Hellenistic and Roman Near East*. Oxford.

Keaveney, A. 1982. *Sulla: The Last Republican*. London.

Kleiner, D. E. E. 2005. *Cleopatra and Rome*. Cambridge MA.

Kosmin, P. 2014. *The Land of the Elephant Kings: Space, Territory, and Ideology in the Seleucid Empire*. Cambridge MA.

Kropp, A. J. M. 2013. *Images and Monuments of Near Eastern Dynasts, 100 BC–AD 100*. Oxford.

LaCocque, A. 1979. *The Book of Daniel*. London.

Lang, P. 2013. *Medicine and Society in Ptolemaic Egypt*. Leiden.

Leprohon, L. J. and Doxey, D. M. 2013. *The Great Name: Ancient Egyptian Royal Titulary*. Atlanta.

Lesko, B. S. 1999. *The Great Goddesses of Egypt*. Norman.

Lewis, N. 2001. *Greeks in Ptolemaic Egypt*. Oakville.

Lichtheim, M. 1980. *Ancient Egyptian Literature, Volume 3*. Berkeley.

Lintott, A. 1999. *Violence in Republican Rome*. Oxford.

Llewellyn-Jones, L. 2003. *Aphrodite's Tortoise: The Veiled Woman of Ancient Greece.* Swansea.

—— 2018. *Designs on the Past: How Hollywood Created the Ancient World.* Edinburgh.

Llewellyn-Jones, L. and McAuley, A. 2022. *Sister-Queens in the High Hellenistic Period: Kleopatra Thea and Kleopatra III.* London.

Llewellyn-Jones, L. and Winder, S. 2010. 'A Key to Berenike's Lock? The Hathoric Model of Queenship in Early Ptolemaic Egypt' in A. Erskine and L. Llewellyn-Jones (eds.), *Creating a Hellenistic World.* Swansea. 247–68.

Lloyd, A. B. (1975, 1976, 1988) *Herodotus: Book II, Introduction* (vol. I) and *Commentary* (vols. II & III). Leiden.

—— 2010. *A Companion to Ancient Egypt.* Oxford.

Lloyd, G. E. R. 1973. *Greek Science After Aristotle.* London.

Lorber, C. 2018. *Coins of the Ptolemaic Empire.* New York.

Lorber, C. and van Oppen, B. 2017. 'Clay Seal Impressions from Ptolemaic Edfu', *Quaderni ticinesi di Numismatica e Antichità Classiche* 46, 73–95.

Ma, J. 2000. *Antiochos III and the Cities of Western Asia Minor.* Oxford.

Mackie, P. 1983. *The Cleopatras, From the BBC TV Serial.* London.

Macurdy, G. 1932. *Hellenistic Queens.* Baltimore.

Mahaffy, J. P. 1895. *The Empire of the Ptolemies.* London.

—— 1899. *History of Egypt Under the Ptolemaic Dynasty.* London.

—— 1905. *The Progress of Hellenism in Alexander's Empire.* London

Mancini, A. 2007. *Maat Revealed: Philosophy of Justice in Ancient Egypt.* New York.

Manniche, L. 1987. *Sexual Life in Ancient Egypt.* London.

Matthaei, L. E. 1907. 'On the Classification of Roman Allies', *Classical Quarterly* 1, 185.

Mattusch, C. 2005. *The Villa dei Papiri at Herculaneum: Life and Afterlife of a Sculptural Collection.* Los Angeles.

Mayor, A. 2009. *The Poison King: The Life and Legend of Mithradates, Rome's Deadliest Enemy.* Princeton.

McAuley, A. 2017. 'Once a Seleucid, Always a Seleucid: Seleucid Princesses and their Nuptial Courts' in A. Erskine, L. Llewellyn-

Jones and S. Wallace (eds.), *The Hellenistic Court: Monarchic Power and Elite Society from Alexander to Cleopatra*. Swansea. 189–212.

McGing, B. 1986. *The Foreign Policy of Mithridates VI Eupator, King of Pontus*. Leiden.

McKechnie, P. and Guillaume, P. (eds.) 2008. *Ptolemy II Philadelphus and His World*. Leiden.

McKenzie, J. 2010. *The Architecture of Alexandria and Egypt, 300 BC–AD 700*. New Haven.

Mendelsohn, D. 2013. *C. P. Cavafy : Complete Poems*. London.

Miles, M. 2011. *Cleopatra: A Sphinx Revisited*. Berkeley.

Minas-Nerpel, M. 2011. 'Cleopatra II and III: the Queens of Ptolemy VIII as Guarantors of Kingship and Rivals for Power' in A. Jördens and J. F. Quack (eds.), *Ägypten zwischen innerem Zwist und äußerem Druck. Die Zeit Ptolemaios VI. Bis VIII*. Wiesbaden. 58–76.

—— 2015. 'Ptolemaic Queens in Egyptian Temple Reliefs: Intercultural Reflections of Political Authority or Religious Imperatives?' in P. Kousoulis and N. Lazaridid (eds.), *Proceedings of the Tenth International Congress of Egyptologist.. University of the Aegean, Rhodes, 22–29 May 2008*. Volume I. Leuven. 809–21.

Miron, D. 2000. 'Transmitters and Representatives of Power: Royal Women in Ancient Macedonia', *Ancient Society* 30, 35–52.

Monstserrat, D. 1996. *Sex and Society in Graeco-Roman Egypt*. London.

Mørkholm, O. 1966. *Antiochus IV of Syria*. Copenhagen.

Mysliwec, K. 2004. *Eros on the Nile*. London.

Nielsen, I. 1999. *Hellenistic Palaces*. Aarhus.

Nifosi, A. 2019. *Becoming a Woman and Mother in Greco-Roman Egypt*. London.

Noblecourt, C. D. 1991. 'Abou Simbel, Ramses, et les dames de la couronne', in R. Bleiberg and R. Freed (eds.), *Fragments of a Shattered Visage: The Proceedings of an International Symposium on Ramesses the Great*. Memphis. 127–48.

Oakley, F. 2006. *Kingship*. Oxford.

Ogden, D. 1999. *Polygamy, Prostitutes and Death: The Hellenistic Dynasties*. Swansea.

O'Kernick, P. J. 2018. 'Stelae, Elephants, and Irony', *Journal for the Study of Judaism in the Persian, Hellenistic and Roman Period* 49 (1), 49–67.

Oster, R. 1987. *A Bibliography of Ancient Ephesus. Philadelphia.*

Pace, S. 2008. *Daniel.* Macon.

Panofsky, D. 2019. *Pandora's Box: The Changing Aspects of a Mythical Symbol.* Princeton.

Parca, M. 2017. 'Children in Ptolemaic Egypt: What the Papyri Say', in J. Evans Grubbs, T. Parkin and R. Bell (eds.), *The Oxford Handbook of Childhood and Education in the Classical World.* Oxford. 465–83.

Parker, R. A., and Dubberstein, W. H. 1946. *Babylonian Chronology 626 B.C.–A.D. 45.* 2nd edition. Chicago.

Paterson, J. 2009. 'Caesar the Man', in M. Griffin (ed.), *A Companion to Julius Caesar.* Oxford. 126–40.

Peck, C. M. 2008. 'The Expulsion of Cleopatra VII: Context, Causes, and Chronology', *Ancient Society* 38, 103–35.

Penrose, W.D. Jr. 2018. 'Queens and Their Children: Dynastic Dis/ Loyalty in the Hellenistic Period', in C. Dunn and E. Carney (eds.), *Royal Women and Dynastic Loyalty.* London. 49–65.

Petrie, W. M. F. 1896. *Koptos.* London.

Petrovic, I. 2017. 'Callimachus, Theocritus and Ptolemaic Court Etiquette' in A. Erskine, L. Llewellyn-Jones and S. Wallace (eds.), *The Hellenistic Court: Monarchic Power and Elite Society from Alexander to Cleopatra.* Swansea. 143–63.

Phillipson, J. 2013. *C. P. Cavafy: Historical Poems.* Bloomington.

Pomeroy, S. 1977. *Goddesses, Whores, Wives and Slaves: Women in Classical Antiquity.* New York.

—— 1990. *Women in Hellenistic Egypt.* New York.

Poo, M.-C. (2005). *Enemies of Civilization: Attitudes toward Foreigners in Ancient Mesopotamia, Egypt, and China.* New York.

Poole, R. S. 1888. *A Catalogue of Greek Coins in the British Museum, The Ptolemies, Kings of Egypt.* London.

Powell, J. 2019. *The Poetry of Sappho.* Oxford.

Powell, L. 2015. *Marcus Agrippa: Right-Hand Man of Caesar Augustus.* Stroud.

Price, S. R. F. 1984. *Rituals and Power: The Roman Imperial Cult in Asia Minor.* Cambridge.

Quaegebeur, J. 1978. *Reines ptolémaïques et traditions égyptiennes.* Berlin

Rascovsky, A. 1995. *Filicide: The Murder, Humiliation, Mutilation, Denigration, and Abandonment of Children by Parents*. Northvale.

Ray, J. D. 1976. *The Archive of Hor*. London.

—— 2008. *The Rosetta Stone and the Rebirth of Ancient Egypt*. London.

Redford, D. B. 1986. *Pharaonic King-Lists, Annals and Day-Books: A Contribution to the Egyptian Sense of History*. Mississauga.

Regulski, I. 2022. *Hieroglyphs: Unlocking Ancient Egypt*. London.

Reymond, E. A. 1981. *From the Records of a Priestly Family of Memphis*. Stuttgart.

Rigoglioso, M. 2009. *The Cult of Divine Birth in Ancient Greece*. London.

Robins, G. 1993. *Women in Ancient Egypt*. London.

Roller, D. 2010. *Cleopatra: A Biography*. Oxford.

Rosenstein, N. and Morstein-Marx, R. (eds.) 2010. *A Companion to the Roman Republic*. Oxford.

Rosenwein, B. 2002. 'Worrying About Emotions', *The American Historical Review* 107.3, 821–45.

Rostovtzeff, M. 1941. *The Social and Economic History of the Hellenistic World*. Oxford.

Rowlandson, J. 1998. *Women and Society in Greek and Roman Egypt: A Sourcebook*. London.

Rubin, G. 1975. 'The Traffic in Women: Notes on the Political Economy of Sex', in R. R. Reiter (ed.), *Towards an Anthropology of Women*. New York. 157–210.

Rutherford, I. (ed.) 2016. *Greco-Egyptian Interactions: Literature, Translation, and Culture, 500 BCE–300 CE*. Oxford.

Samuel, A. E. 1962. *Ptolemaic Chronology*. Munich.

Sánchez, A. B. and Lenzo, G. 2015. *Inventer le pouvoir féminin : Cléopâtre I et Cléopâtre II, reines d'Egypte au IIe s.av. J.-C*. Bern.

Savalli-Lestrade, I. 2017. 'Βίος αὐλικός: The Multiple Ways of Life of Courtiers in the Hellenistic Age' in A. Erskine, L. Llewellyn-Jones and S. Wallace (eds.), *The Hellenistic Court: Monarchic Power and Elite Society from Alexander to Cleopatra*. Swansea. 101–20.

Savalli-Lestrade, I. and I. Cogitore (eds.) 2010. *Des Rois au Prince: Pratiques du pouvoir monarchique dans l'Orient hellénistique et romain*. Grenoble.

Scheidel, W. 2009. 'Sex and Empire. A Darwinian Perspective' in

I. Morris & W. Scheidel (eds.), *The Dynamics of Ancient Empires: State Power from Assyria to Byzantium*. Oxford. 255–324.

Schiff, S. 2010. *Cleopatra: A Life*. London.

Schultz, P. 2010. 'Style, Continuity, and the Hellenistic Baroque', in A. Erskine and L. Llewellyn-Jones (eds.), *Creating a Hellenistic World*. Swansea. 313–44.

Sharpe, S. 1838. *The History of Egypt Under the Ptolemies*. London.

Shaw, I. (ed.) 2000. *The Oxford History of Ancient Egypt*. Oxford.

Shipley, G. 2000. *The Greek World After Alexander, 323–30 BC*. London.

Siani-Davies, M. 1997. 'Ptolemy XII Auletes and the Romans', *Historia* 46, 306–40.

—— 2001. *Cicero: Pro Rabirio Postumo*. Oxford.

Smith, R. R. R. 1988. *Hellenistic Royal Portraits*. Oxford.

Spawforth, A. J. S. 2007. 'The Court of Alexander the Great' in A. J. S. Spawforth (ed.), *The Court and Court Society in Ancient Monarchies*. Cambridge. 82–120.

—— 2007 (ed.) *The Court and Court Society in Ancient Monarchies*. Cambridge.

Spence, K. 2007. 'Court and Palace in Ancient Egypt: The Amarna Period and the Later Eighteenth Dynasty' in A. J. S. Spawforth (ed.), *The Court and Court Society in Ancient Monarchies*. Cambridge. 267–328.

Spier, J., Potts, T. and Cole, S. E. (eds.) 2018. *Beyond the Nile: Egypt and the Classical World*. Los Angeles.

Stacey, P. 2014. 'The Princely Republic', *Journal of Roman Studies* 104, 133–54.

Stanwick, P. E. 2002. *Portraits of the Ptolemies: Greek Kings as Egyptian Pharaohs*. Austin.

Steele, C. 2009. 'Friends, Associates, Wives' in M. Griffin (ed.), *A Companion to Julius Caesar*. Oxford. 112–25.

Stephens, S. 2003. *Seeing Double: Intercultural Politics in Ptolemaic Alexandria*. Berkeley.

Stol, M. 2016. *Women in the Ancient Near East*. Berlin.

Strato, S. 2015. *L'Immagine Del Portere Nell' Egitto Tolemaico*. London.

Strootman, R. 2011. 'Hellenistic Court Society: The Seleukid Imperial Court under Antiochos the Great, 223–187 BCE' in J. Duindam,

M. Kunt, T. Artan (eds.), *Royal Courts in Dynastic States and Empires: A Global Perspective, Rulers and Elites 1*. Leiden. 63–89.

—— 2016. *Courts and Elites in the Hellenistic Empires: The Near East after the Achaemenids, c. 330 to 30 BCE*. Edinburgh.

—— 2017. 'Eunuchs, Renegades and Concubines: The 'Paradox of Power' and the Promotion of Favourites in the Hellenistic Empires' in A. Erskine, L. Llewellyn-Jones and S. Wallace (eds.), *The Hellenistic Court: Monarchic Power and Elite Society from Alexander to Cleopatra*. Swansea. 121–42.

Sullivan, R. D. 1990. *Near Eastern Royalty and Rome*. Toronto.

Tarn, W. W. 1933. 'Alexander the Great and the Unity of Mankind', *Proceedings of the British Academy* 29. London.

Tarn, W. W. and Griffith , G. T. 1952. *Hellenistic Civilisation*. 3rd edition. London.

Taylor, M. 2013. *Antiochus the Great*. Barnsley.

Thompson, D. J. 1971. *Kerkeosiris: An Egyptian Village in the Ptolemaic Period*. Cambridge.

—— 1988. *Memphis Under the Ptolemies*. Princeton.

—— 2005. 'The Ptolemies and Egypt', in A. Erskine (ed.), *A Companion to the Hellenistic World*. London, 105–21.

—— 2013. 'Hellenistic Royal Barges', in K. Buraselis, M. Stefanou and D. J. Thompson (eds.), *The Ptolemies, the Sea and the Nile: Studies in Waterborne Power*. Cambridge, 185–96.

—— 2017. 'Outside the Capital: The Ptolemaic Court and Its Courtiers', in A. Erskine, L. Llewellyn-Jones and S. Wallace (eds.), *The Hellenistic Court: Monarchic Power and Elite Society from Alexander to Cleopatra*. Swansea. 257–67.

Thonemann, P. 2016. *The Hellenistic World: Using Coins as Sources*. Cambridge.

Thür, H. 1990. 'Arsinoë IV, eine Schwester Kleopatras VII, Grabinhaberin des Oktogons von Ephesos? Ein Vorschlag', *Jahreshefte des Österreichischen Archäologischen Instituts* 60, 43–56.

Troy, L. 1986. *Patterns of Queenship in Ancient Egyptian Myth and History*. Uppsala.

—— 2008. 'The Queen as a Female Counterpart to the Pharaoh' in

C. Ziegler (ed.), *Queens of Egypt: From Hetepheres to Cleopatra*. Monaco. 154–70.

Turner, E. G. 1984. 'Ptolemaic Egypt' in F. W. Walbank et al. (eds.), *The Cambridge Ancient History* 7, Part 1. Cambridge. 118–74.

Tyldesley, J. 2001. *Ramesses, Egypt's Greatest Pharaoh*. London.

—— 2006. *Chronicle of the Queens of Egypt*. London.

Valdesogo, M. L. 2021. *Hair and Death in Ancient Egypt: The Mourning Rite in the Times of the Pharaohs*. Amsterdam.

Vandorpe, K. (ed.) 2019. *A Companion to Greco-Roman and Late Antique Egypt*. Oxford.

Van Nuffelen, P. 2004 '*Le culte royal de l'empire des séleucides: une réinterprétation*', *Historia* 43, 278–301.

Van Oppen de Ruiter, B. 2016. *Berenike II Euergetis*. New York.

Vassilika, E. 1989. *Ptolemaic Philae*. Leuven.

Vatin, C. 1970. *Recherches sur le mariage et la condition de la femme mariée à l'epoque Hellénistique*. Paris.

Vernant, J.-P. 1980. *Myth and Society in Ancient Greece*. Brighton.

Volkmann, H. 1958. *Cleopatra. A Study in Politics and Propaganda*. London.

von Hesberg, H. 1999. 'The King on Stage', *Studies in the History of Art* 56, 64–75.

Walbank, F. 1981. *The Hellenistic World*. Cambridge MA.

Walker, S. and Ashton, S.-A. (eds.) 2003. *Cleopatra Reassessed*. London.

Walker, S. and Higgs, P. (eds.) 2001. *Cleopatra of Egypt: From History to Myth*. London.

Walsh, J. and Reese, T. F. (eds.) 1996. *Alexandria and Alexandrianism*. Malibu.

Watterson, B. 1998. *The House of Horus at Edfu*. Stroud.

Wells, C. 1967. 'The Ptolemaic Jaw', *Applied Theory* 9, 768–71.

White, R. E. 1971. 'Women in Ptolemaic Egypt', *Journal of Hellenic Studies* 18, 238–66.

Whitehorne, J. 1994. *Cleopatras*. London

Wilkinson, R. H. 2000. *The Complete Temples of Ancient Egypt*. London.

—— 2003. *The Complete Gods and Goddesses of Ancient Egypt*. London.

Wilkinson, T. (ed.) 2007. *The Egyptian World*. London.

Will, É. 1966 (2003). *L'histoire politique du monde hellénistique*. Paris.

Witt, R. E. 1971. *Isis in the Ancient World*. Baltimore.

Winder, S. 2017. 'The Hands of Gods? Poison and Power in the Hellenistic Court' in A. Erskine, L. Llewellyn-Jones and S. Wallace (eds.), *The Hellenistic Court: Monarchic Power and Elite Society from Alexander to Cleopatra*. Swansea. 373–407.

Wright, N. L. 2009/10. 'Non-Greek Religious Imagery on the Coinage of Seleucid Syria', *Mediterranean Archaeology* 22/23, 193–206.

Acknowledgements

As is the always the case when it comes to publishing a new work, I am indebted to so many people. Without them this book would not have been brought to completion. In my immediate environment of Cardiff University, I have benefitted immensely from the support of colleagues and students in the School of History, Archaeology and Religion. Beyond Wales, I want to thank Alex McAuley, co-author of our previously published study of Cleopatra III and Cleopatra Thea, for allowing me to riff on our shared ideas in this current volume. I want to thank Sarah Griffith for her kind and enthusiastic assistance with picture research. The staff at Headline Books and Basic Books, especially Alex Clarke and Brian Distelberg, have been wonderfully supportive, appropriately critical, and always, *always* encouraging. Thanks goes to my agent, Adam Gauntlett, too; his keen sense of what publishers want and his clear love of history are eye-opening and inspiring. Beyond these invaluable people, I thank my family and friends for the patience and selflessness with which they have supported me in this project and beyond. I send my love and thanks to David, who kept things real and made the tea. Finally, it would be remiss of me not to mention the customer relations department of Transport for Wales.

Index

Index TK 12 Pages

Lloyd Llewellyn-Jones holds the chair in ancient history at Cardiff University. The author of *Persians*, he has published widely on ancient history and lives in Taff's Well, Wales.